SLOW CINEMA

Traditions in World Cinema

General Editors
Linda Badley (Middle Tennessee State
    University)
R. Barton Palmer (Clemson University)

Founding Editor
Steven Jay Schneider (New York
    University)

www.euppublishing.com/series/tiwc

SLOW CINEMA

Edited by Tiago de Luca and Nuno Barradas Jorge

EDINBURGH
University Press

For Trent
For Jaime and Nela

Edinburgh University Press Ltd
The Tun – Holyrood Road
12 (2f) Jackson's Entry
Edinburgh EH8 8PJ
www.euppublishing.com

Typeset in 10/12.5 pt Sabon by
Servis Filmsetting Ltd, Stockport, Cheshire
and printed and bound in Great Britain by
CPI Group (UK) Ltd, Croydon CR0 4YY

A CIP record for this book is available from the British Library

ISBN 978 0 7486 9602 4 (hardback)
ISBN 978 0 7486 9604 8 (paperback)
ISBN 978 0 7486 9603 1 (webready PDF)
ISBN 978 0 7486 9605 5 (epub)

CONTENTS

PART II. CONTEXTUALISING SLOW CINEMA

PART III. SLOW CINEMA AND LABOUR

PART IV. SLOW CINEMA AND THE NON-HUMAN

ILLUSTRATIONS

CONTRIBUTORS

Martin Brady teaches in the German and Film Studies Departments at King's College London. He has published on film (Straub-Huillet, Michael Haneke, Robert Bresson, experimental film, literary adaptation, GDR documentary and children's films, Wim Wenders, Kafka films, Brechtian cinema, *Heimat 3*, *Downfall*, Ulrich Seidl, Peter Nestler), music (Arnold Schönberg, Paul Dessau), philosophy (Theodor W. Adorno), literature (Paul Celan, Peter Handke, Elfriede Jelinek), Jewish exile architects, the visual arts (Anselm Kiefer, Joseph Beuys), the portrayal of thalidomide, and foraging. He has translated Victor Klemperer's *LTI* and Alexander Kluge's *Cinema Stories* (with Helen Hughes), and works as a freelance translator and interpreter.

William Brown is Senior Lecturer in Film at the University of Roehampton, London. He is currently working on a monograph called *Non-Cinema: Global Digital Filmmaking and the Multitude*. He is also the author of *Supercinema: Film-Philosophy for the Digital Age* (2013), and, with Dina Iordanova and Leshu Torchin, *Moving People, Moving Images: Cinema and Trafficking in the New Europe* (2010). He is the co-editor, with David Martin-Jones, of *Deleuze and Film* (Edinburgh University Press, 2012). He has also directed several zero- to low-budget films, including *En Attendant Godard* (2009), *Afterimages* (2010), *Common Ground* (2012), *China: A User's Manual (Films)* (2012), *Selfie* (2014), *Ur: The End of Civilization in 90 Tableaux* (2015) and *The New Hope* (2015).

Paul Cooke is Professor of German Cultural Studies and Director of the Centre for World Cinemas at the University of Leeds. His major publications include: *Contemporary German Cinema* (2012), *Recent Trends in German Cinema* (co-edited with Chris Homewood, 2011), *Representing East Germany: From Colonization to Nostalgia* (2005), *The Pocket Essential to German Expressionist Film* (2002).

Glyn Davis is Chancellor's Fellow and Reader in Screen Studies at the University of Edinburgh. He is the author of monographs on *Superstar: The Karen Carpenter Story* (2008) and *Far from Heaven* (Edinburgh University Press, 2011), and the co-editor, with Gary Needham, of *Queer TV: Theories, Histories, Politics* (2009) and *Warhol in Ten Takes* (2013).

Tiago de Luca is Lecturer in Film Studies at the University of Liverpool. He is the author of *Realism of the Senses in World Cinema: The Experience of Physical Reality* (2014) and the series editor (with Lúcia Nagib) of *Film Thinks: How Cinema Inspires Writers and Thinkers*. His writings on world cinemas have appeared in *Senses of Cinema, Journal of Chinese Cinemas, Cinephile, New Cinemas: Journal of Contemporary Film*, among others.

Elena Gorfinkel is Assistant Professor of Art History and Film Studies at the University of Wisconsin-Milwaukee. Her writing on marginal cinemas, women's film-making, cult and adult film, temporality, art cinema, cinephilia and embodiment have appeared in *Screen, Camera Obscura, Discourse, Framework, World Picture, Cineaste, INCITE: The Journal of Experimental Media, LOLA*, and numerous edited collections. She is co-editor, with John David Rhodes, of *Taking Place: Location and the Moving Image* (2011). Her book, *Sensational Bodies: American Sexploitation Cinema's Scenes of Looking, 1959–1972*, is forthcoming and she is co-editing the collection *World Cinemas, Global Networks*, with Tami Williams.

Michael Gott is Assistant Professor of French at the University of Cincinnati, where he teaches courses in French and Francophone literature and cinema, European Studies, and film. He recently co-edited *Open Roads, Closed Borders: the Contemporary French-Language Road Movie* (Intellect, 2013) and *East, West and Centre: Reframing European Cinema Since 1989* (Edinburgh University Press, 2014), and is completing a monograph on French-language road cinema.

Asbjørn Grønstad is Professor of Visual Culture at the University of Bergen, where he is also founding director of the Nomadikon Center for Visual Culture. His latest books are *Screening the Unwatchable: Spaces of Negation in Post-Millennial Art Cinema* (2011), *Ethics and Images of Pain*, co-edited with Henrik Gustafsson (2012) and *Cinema and Agamben: Ethics, Biopolitics and the Moving Image*, co-edited with Henrik Gustafsson (2013).

Nuno Barradas Jorge is a PhD candidate in the Department of Culture, Film and Media at the University of Nottingham. His research has appeared in the journal *Adaptation*, and the collections *Migration in Lusophone Cinema* (2014), *El Juego con los Estereotipos* (2012) and *Directory of World Cinema: Spain* (2011).

Song Hwee Lim is Associate Professor in Film Studies at the Chinese University of Hong Kong. He is the author of *Celluloid Comrades: Representations of Male Homosexuality in Contemporary Chinese Cinemas* (2007) and co-editor of *Remapping World Cinema: Identity, Culture and Politics in Film* (2006) and *The Chinese Cinema Book* (2011). Founding editor of the *Journal of Chinese Cinemas*, his monograph, *Tsai Ming-liang and a Cinema of Slowness*, was published in 2014.

Stephanie Lam is a PhD candidate in the Film and Visual Studies programme at Harvard University. Her dissertation research centres on the use of scalar concepts in recent environmental film and media. She has published in *CinéAction* and has written for A Space Gallery in Toronto. Stephanie completed her MA in Cinema Studies from the University of Toronto.

Philippa Lovatt is a Lecturer in Media and Communications at the University of Stirling and also teaches at the University of Social Sciences and Humanities, Ho Chi Minh City. She has published her research in *Screen*, *The New Soundtrack* and *SoundEffects*, and is currently writing a monograph on sound design and the ethics of listening in global cinema.

Cecília Mello is Lecturer in Film Studies in the Department of Film, Radio and Television, University of São Paulo, and FAPESP Senior Research Fellow in the Department of History of Art, Federal University of São Paulo, Brazil. She was FAPESP Postdoctoral Fellow at the University of São Paulo (2008–11), has an MA in Film and Television Production, University of Bristol (1998) and a PhD in Film Studies, Birkbeck College, University of London (2006). Her research focuses on world cinema – with an emphasis on British and Chinese cinemas – and on issues of audiovisual realism, cinema and urban spaces and intermediality. She has published several essays and co-edited with Lúcia Nagib the book *Realism and the Audiovisual Media* (2009).

Matilda Mroz is Senior Lecturer in Film and Visual Culture at the University of Greenwich, and, prior to this, was a British Academy Postdoctoral Research

Fellow at the University of Cambridge, where she also completed her PhD. She is the author of *Temporality and Film Analysis* (Edinburgh University Press, 2012), which explores duration through the films of Michelangelo Antonioni, Andrei Tarkovsky, and Krzysztof Kieslowski. She is the Associate Editor of the Routledge journal *Studies in Eastern European Cinema*.

Lúcia Nagib is Professor of Film at the University of Reading. Her single-authored books include: *World Cinema and the Ethics of Realism* (2011), *Brazil On Screen: Cinema Novo, New Cinema, Utopia* (2007) and *Born of the Ashes: The Auteur and the Individual in Oshima's Films* (Edusp, 1995). She is the editor of *Impure Cinema: Intermedial and Intercultural Approaches to Film* (with Anne Jerslev, 2013), *Theorizing World Cinema* (with Chris Perriam and Rajinder Dudrah, 2011), *Realism and the Audiovisual Media* (with Cecília Mello, 2009), among others.

Jacques Rancière is Professor Emeritus at the Université de Paris (St Denis). Among many other publications, he is the author of *The Ignorant Schoolmaster: Five Lessons in Intellectual Emancipation* (1991), *The Politics of Aesthetics: The Distribution of the Sensible* (2004), *The Future of the Image* (2007), *The Aesthetic Unconscious* (2009), *The Emancipated Spectator* (2009) and *Béla Tarr, the Time After* (2013).

Justin Remes is an assistant professor of film studies at Iowa State University. He is the author of *Motion(less) Pictures: The Cinema of Stasis* (2015), and he has published articles in *Cinema Journal*, *Screen*, the *British Journal of Aesthetics*, and *Film-Philosophy*. His research interests include experimental cinema, film theory, and aesthetics.

Julian Ross is a researcher, curator and writer based in Amsterdam. Recently completing his PhD thesis on 1960s Japanese expanded cinema at the University of Leeds, he has curated film programmes and performances for Anthology Film Archives (NYC), Eye Film Institute (Amsterdam), Rongwrong (Amsterdam), Yerba Buena Center for the Arts (SF), Gasworks (London) and Close-Up Film Centre (London). He was an assistant curator for the touring retrospective series (2011–13) on the Art Theatre Guild of Japan at the Museum of Modern Art (NYC), Pacific Film Archives (Berkeley) and British Film Institute (London). His writing has appeared in *POST*, *Aesthetica Magazine* and *Film Comment* as well as in *Impure Cinema* (2014) and *The Japanese Cinema Book* (forthcoming). He is in the short film selection committee at International Film Festival Rotterdam.

Karl Schoonover is Associate Professor of Film and Television Studies at the University of Warwick. He is the author of *Brutal Vision: the Neorealist*

Body in Postwar Italian Cinema (2012) and coeditor of *Global Art Cinema* (2010).

Patrick Brian Smith is a Frederick H. Lowy Doctoral Fellow in the Mel Hoppenheim School of Cinema at Concordia University. His research interests include avant-garde and experimental film, non-Western political and art cinemas, European antinaturalism, precarious labour and the essay film.

Rob Stone is Professor of European Film at the University of Birmingham and Director of B-Film: The Birmingham Centre for Film Studies. His major publications include: *Walk, Don't Run: The Cinema of Richard Linklater* (2012), *Screening Songs in Hispanic and Lusophone Cinema*, co-edited with Lisa Shaw (2012), *Julio Medem* (2007) and *Spanish Cinema* (2002).

Julian Stringer is Associate Professor in Film and Television Studies at the University of Nottingham. He has published widely on East Asian cinema, transnational film-making and international film festivals, and is co-editor of *New Korean Cinema* (Edinburgh University Press, 2005), *Japanese Cinema: Texts and Contexts* (2007) and *Japanese Cinema: Critical Concepts in Media and Cultural Studies* (2015). He recently organised academic conferences in Beijing (2011), Kuala Lumpur (2013) and Shanghai (2010, 2013).

C. Claire Thomson is a Senior Lecturer in Scandinavian Film at University College London. She is the author of *Thomas Vinterberg's Festen* (2013) and the editor of *Northern Constellations: New Readings in Nordic Cinema* (2006). Research for the chapter in this volume was undertaken during a period as Visiting Researcher at the Danish Film Institute, the outcome of which will be a monograph on state-sponsored short films in Denmark.

Michael Walsh is Associate Professor, University of Hartford. He has chaired cinema departments at both Binghamton University and the University of Hartford. He has published widely on film and theory. His recent articles are on Godard and Badiou (*Journal of French Philosophy*, vol. XVIII, no. 2, 2011) and on sound in installation film and video (*Oxford Handbook of New Audiovisual Aesthetics*, forthcoming).

ACKNOWLEDGEMENTS

This book would not have been possible without the unfailing support it received from Linda Badley and Barton Palmer, editors of the Traditions in World Cinema Series at Edinburgh University Press (EUP). Their unstinting help and enthusiasm led us all the way. We would also like to express our deepest gratitude to Gillian Leslie, our editor at EUP, for the impeccable efficiency with which she oversaw the book's production, and Richard Strachan for his firm guidance in the process of compiling the book. The book's initial drafts greatly benefited from readings of, or else conversations with, Sizen Yiacoup, Julian Stringer, Iain Robert Smith, Song Hwee Lim, Lúcia Nagib, Mark Gallagher and the two evaluators of the book proposal, for which we are thankful. Thanks are also due to Colin Wright and Tom Whittaker for their wise and insightful readings of this project at crucial stages, and to Maria Manuela de Castro for her assistance in the overall organisation of the book. Finally, we would like to express our gratitude to Justine O and Jia Zhangke, at Xtream Pictures, for kindly granting us permission to use a still from Jia's *Still Life* (*Sanxia Haoren*, 2006) on the cover of this book.

TRADITIONS IN WORLD CINEMA

General editors: **Linda Badley and R. Barton Palmer**
Founding editor: **Steven Jay Schneider**

Traditions in World Cinema is a series of textbooks and monographs devoted to the analysis of currently popular and previously underexamined or undervalued film movements from around the globe. Also intended for general interest readers, the textbooks in this series offer undergraduate- and graduate-level film students accessible and comprehensive introductions to diverse traditions in world cinema. The monographs open up for advanced academic study more specialised groups of films, including those that require theoretically oriented approaches. The textbooks and monographs provide thorough examinations of the industrial, cultural, and sociohistorical conditions of production and reception.

The flagship textbook for the series includes chapters by noted scholars on traditions of acknowledged importance (the French New Wave, German expressionism), recent and emergent traditions (New Iranian, post-Cinema Novo), and those whose rightful claim to recognition has yet to be established (the Israeli persecution film, global found-footage cinema). Other volumes concentrate on individual national, regional or global cinema traditions. As the introductory chapter to each volume makes clear, the films under discussion form a coherent group on the basis of substantive and relatively transparent, if not always obvious, commonalities. These commonalities may be formal, stylistic or thematic, and the groupings may, though they need not, be popularly identified as genres, cycles or movements (Japanese horror, Chinese martial arts cinema, Italian neorealism). Indeed, in cases in which a group of films is not already commonly identified as a tradition, one purpose of the volume is to establish its claim to importance and make it visible (East Central European magical realist cinema, Palestinian cinema).

Textbooks and monographs include:

- An introduction that clarifies the rationale for the grouping of films under examination
- A concise history of the regional, national, or transnational cinema in question
- A summary of previously published work on the tradition
- Contextual analysis of industrial, cultural and sociohistorical conditions of production and reception
- Textual analysis of specific and notable films, with clear and judicious application of relevant film theoretical approaches
- Bibliograph(ies)/filmograph(ies)

Monographs may additionally include:

- Discussion of the dynamics of cross-cultural exchange in the light of current research and thinking about cultural imperialism and globalisation, as well as issues of regional/national cinema or political/aesthetic movements (such as new waves, postmodernism, or identity politics)
- Interview(s) with key film-makers working within the tradition.

FOREWORD

Julian Stringer

It is always instructive to consider the extent to which film spectators speak in the tongue of slow cinema. Let us start with those at a loss for words, some of whom have warmed my movie memories with their inarticulacy. There is the colleague who tugged my sleeve at the start of *Wavelength* (1967) with the instruction to wake her up 'when the zoom reaches the other side of the room'. ('Why?', I inquired. 'Just do it', she snapped. 'I need my kip'.) Or the day in graduate school when a classmate brought his friend to *Jeanne Dielman, 23 Quai du Commerce, 1080 Bruxelles* (1976), evidently without having clued him in on what to expect. I do not know who the young visitor was, or why he came to the screening, but I do know that the daft sap sat through the entire 201 minutes – first struggling politely to hide a few yawns, then trying less successfully to stifle the hysterical giggles escaping from his mouth, and finally, approximately one shake of a duck's tail after it ended, leaping to his feet, punching the air and shouting out 'Yeeessss!', as plainly as if he had screamed his boredom and exasperation in capitalised italics. Then, too, I'll never forget the irritated individual who stormed out halfway through *Blow Job* (1964) for no discernible reason but while audibly having kittens.

The cries of the disappointed and the disgruntled compel advocates of such 'difficult' works to enunciate distinct answers to the question of what they are worth, why they matter. Cue the entrance of Tiago de Luca and Nuno Barradas Jorge and their contributors to this excellent volume, all of whom direct their questioning brains to fascinating matters of form, definition and cultural politics. Lancing the boil of incuriosity, they reveal admirable subjects for analysis. What do people expect from films? How important are viewing contexts? Can audience awareness be heightened or transformed? What are the qualities of cinematic stillness? How slow is slow?

In presenting its core findings the book journeys across space and time, tracing a continuum of 'slow-ness' in international cinema history that takes in, among others, China, Iran, Japan, Portugal, Britain and the United States, and films as diverse as *Story of the Last Chrysanthemums* (1939), *Gertrud* (1964), *Satantango* (1994), *In Vanda's Room* (2000), *What Time Is It There?* (2001), *Five: Dedicated to Ozu* (2003), *West of the Tracks* (2003), *Uncle Boonmee Who Can Recall His Past Lives* (2010). All may profitably be studied with this primer to hand.

Readers will be unable to complete this book without recognising that slow cinema is a space of and for innovation: it makes changes, offers divergence from the known. Films of slower than average pace, or longer than average duration, do not just undertake a tightrope walk between pleasure and boredom, they also tread a fine line between newness and cliché. (As various chapters acknowledge, innovation comes to the party dressed in differing guises: the political and the sociological as well as the formal and the aesthetic.) Michael Snow, Chantal Akerman, Andy Warhol, Mizoguchi Kenji, Carl Theodor Dreyer, Béla Tarr, Pedro Costa, Tsai Ming-liang, Abbas Kiarostami, Wang Bing, and Apichatpong Weerasethakul are just some of the visionary mavericks discussed in these pages. Such film-makers are to be treasured because – while working under historically diverse and specific circumstances – they have taken risks and solved problems. In anticipating needs and removing obstacles, each speaks in the tongue of creative renewal.

Slow Cinema also provides a profound insight into the nature of the medium. When an example of such work is designed and delivered with talent it can share a particular characteristic with faster cinemas of distinction – namely, intensity of experience. The art and technology of film-making transport the spectator to another world, a constructed spatial atmosphere, that may be fantastic and full of dynamic movement or else realistic and marked by everyday stasis. Either way, though, strong emotion – which encompasses both intellectual and sensual dimensions – is paramount. Alongside analysis of issues of cinematic contemplation and mental work, then, this book touches on other important qualities, such as passion, romance, seduction and sensation. As audiovisual media evolve and mutate in the twenty-first century, it will be instructive to consider the extent to which fresh approaches to these attributes are pioneered by artists as well as by critics and historians.

INTRODUCTION: FROM SLOW CINEMA TO SLOW CINEMAS

Tiago de Luca and Nuno Barradas Jorge

This is the first book to compile a collection of essays on 'slow cinema', a term that has acquired remarkable visibility in film criticism over the last decade, thus arriving attached to particular cultural phenomena and inserted within specific public debates. Before delving into an analysis of the cinematic style with which the term has become associated, a brief survey of these phenomena and debates is immediately required.

DISCOURSES

Though slowness may be identified as a constitutive temporal feature of previous films, schools and traditions, the notion has gained unprecedented critical valence in the last decade. One of the first to coin the expression 'cinema of slowness' was the French film critic Michel Ciment, in 2003, citing, as exemplary of this trend, directors such as Béla Tarr (Hungary), Tsai Ming-liang (Taiwan) and Abbas Kiarostami (Iran) (Ciment, 2003). In 2008, taking up Ciment's expression, Matthew Flanagan would expand its theoretical application in his influential article 'Towards an Aesthetic of Slow in Contemporary Cinema' which he described as based on 'the employment of (often extremely) long takes, de-centred and understated modes of storytelling, and a pronounced emphasis on quietude and the everyday' (2008). One could mention, for example, the unbroken shots in Tarr's films in which viewers simply follow characters walking aimlessly under torrential rain for more than five minutes; or the contemplative landscape imagery in the films of Carlos Reygadas

(Mexico), Lisandro Alonso (Argentina) and Lav Diaz (Philippines). Or the quotidian, narratively insignificant chores recorded in minute detail and real time in the work of these and many other film-makers who have become associated with the trend.

It was not until 2010, however, that the term slow cinema would become popularised among Anglo-Saxon film critics and cinephiles. On British shores, this was sparked chiefly by a few articles in the magazine *Sight & Sound* (see, for instance, Romney, 2010) and especially its April editorial 'Passive-Aggressive', by Nick James, who called into question the critical validity and political efficacy of 'slow films' as they demand 'great swathes of our precious time' (James, 2010). James's piece acted as the major catalyst of a heated and polarised public debate that soon encompassed other media outlets, film critics and even film scholars, such as Steven Shaviro, for whom slow cinema was aesthetically retrograde (2010).[1] Across the Atlantic, a similar debate around the worthiness of slowness would emerge a year later in the pages of the *New York Times* and beyond. Spurred on by Dan Kois, who equated the slow cinematic fare of the likes of Kelly Reichardt (United States) with unpalatable 'cultural vegetables' (Kois, 2011), film critics Manohla Dargis and A. O. Scott jumped 'In Defense of the Slow and the Boring' (Dargis and Scott, 2011) in the pages of the same newspaper. This discussion forum subsequently provided David Bordwell and Kristin Thompson the cue to historicise, in their blog Observations on Film Art, a 'polarized film culture: fast, aggressive cinema for the mass market and slow, more austere cinema for festivals and arthouses' (Bordwell and Thompson, 2011).

As these discourses demonstrate, the question of slowness in the cinema has generated controversy over its aesthetics and politics, aspects to which we will return in the course of this introduction. Let us note for now that the topic has accordingly gained momentum in academia, with studies such as Flanagan's *'Slow Cinema': Temporality and Style in Contemporary Art and Experimental Film* (2012; unpublished PhD thesis), and the publication of three books in 2014: Ira Jaffe's *Slow Movies: Countering the Cinema of Action*, Song Hwee Lim's *Tsai Ming-liang and a Cinema of Slowness* and Lutz Koepnick's *On Slowness: Toward an Aesthetic of the Contemporary*. While Flanagan historically situates a cinema of slowness within a post-war modernist and experimental tradition, Jaffe's study focuses on a wide intercultural range of contemporary films, though devoted almost exclusively to textual analysis. For his part, Lim focuses specifically on the Taiwan-based director while, nonetheless, using his films as a vehicle through which to formulate a rigorous conceptual framework for the study of slow cinema as a whole. Koepnick, finally, proposes to examine slowness not in terms of cinematic duration or a durational aesthetic but, rather, in relation to varied contemporary art practices premised upon the operation of slow-motion photography.[2]

In many ways, the present collection naturally chimes with these studies, though perhaps a bit more strongly with the first three in that many of the following chapters are concerned with the durational aesthetic more commonly associated with slow cinema. Nevertheless, as we shall see, it is also one of the aims of this book to question and expand the frameworks that have generally informed slow cinema debates up until now, thus repositioning the term in a broader theoretical space while illuminating the aforementioned film-makers, as well as several others, in the hope of mapping out contemporary and past slow cinemas across the globe. Of course, the book is by no means exhaustive, and there are important film-makers identified with the slow trend who are not covered here owing to space constraints, including Alexander Sokurov (Russia), Ben Rivers (United Kingdom), Chantal Akerman (Belgium), Albert Serra (Spain) and Nuri Bilge Ceylan (Turkey). That said, we believe that the volume's scope and coverage offer a sufficiently wide panorama of slow cinema as a global phenomenon, with individual chapters further attending to the specific contexts and traditions from which many slow films emerge – an approach which, in its depth and breadth, only a multi-authored study could undertake.

Slow cinema is, then, a rather recent phenomenon in conceptual terms, and one that furthermore shares its discursive genesis with a much larger socio-cultural movement whose aim is to rescue extended temporal structures from the accelerated tempo of late capitalism, as Lim notes in Chapter 5. Indeed, the term 'slow' has noticeably become a convenient prefix for a number of grass-roots movements such as 'slow media', 'slow travel' and 'slow food', the last famously created by Carlo Petrini in Italy in the mid 1980s. This is not to say, however, that the directors subsumed under the 'slow' banner are engaged with, or even aware of, other slow movements – which, incidentally, would sit in stark contrast to the 'accelerationist' project (see Noys, 2010). Rather, slow films would seem to share narrative and aesthetic features that lend themselves to a prevailing discourse of slowness which here finds its cinematic materialisation, even though, of course, not the same directors will crop up in the discourses mentioned earlier. This reveals the novelty of the moniker, appropriated as it is to describe a still-in-the-making and shifting canon that impresses not only in terms of its intercultural and global dimension but also because it crosses the boundaries of fiction, documentary and experimental film. Whereas there is little doubt that the usual slow-cinema contenders make fictionalised narrative films, experimental, documentary and semi-documentary film-makers, such as James Benning (Lam, in Chapter 14; Ross, in Chapter 18), Pedro Costa (Jorge, in Chapter 11), Abbas Kiarostami (Remes, in Chapter 16) and Wang Bing (Smith, in Chapter 12) among others, are equally discussed in relation to the current.

In this respect, it could be argued that the promiscuity of the 'slow' descriptor risks weakening its own methodological vigour as it is applied too indiscriminately, and the appropriateness of the term in relation to the corpus it generally describes has not gone unquestioned. Harry Tuttle, for example, vociferously rejects it as 'a mischaracterisation that induces contempt and caricature', adopting instead the more positive designation 'CCC', an acronym for 'contemporary contemplative cinema' (2010). We agree that the term 'slow' demands a judicious usage if its theoretical and critical potential is to be retained and exploited, and, indeed, one of the aims of this book is to provide more nuanced and localised understandings of cinematic slowness, including the questioning of its applicability and usefulness (see Nagib, in Chapter 1; Walsh, in Chapter 3).

That said, we believe that the ease with which the concept navigates across different cinematic modes, movements, practices and even media is, in fact, one of its strengths. It offers the opportunity to illuminate these afresh from a new angle and, in so doing, it opens up a space for theoretical reconsiderations on underexplored aspects of filmic temporality and beyond. While we concur that slowness often betrays a pejorative connotation, the sheer pervasiveness of the term, together with its wider sociocultural resonance and usage, demand that it be examined seriously in its discursive foundations and conceptual ramifications, rather than simply dismissed.

In this light, slow cinema can be seen as an unstructured film movement made up of disparate films and practices that are conceptualised as a grouping thanks to their comparable style. Yet, to borrow Bordwell's words, if we are to view cinematic style as that which mobilises 'a rich ensemble of concrete choices about camerawork and lighting, performance and cutting' (2008: 260), what choices are consistent across the body of films normally identified with a cinema of slowness and why are they considered slow?

STYLE

To examine the stylistic features mobilised by slow films is paramount if we consider that slowness, understood as a mode of temporal unfolding and as an awareness of duration, is a fundamentally subjective experience. As Matilda Mroz notes, '[w]hat for one viewer might seem too long for another might offer a moment of elongated rapture' (2013: 41). It is often the case, however, that slow time is made manifest and felt in those instances in which one is confronted with the impossibility of shaping temporal rhythms according to one's will, such as when we find ourselves stuck in a long queue or waiting for the next train. As Elizabeth Grosz, building on Henri Bergson, argues, the phenomenon of '[w]aiting is the subjective experience that perhaps best exemplifies the coexistence of a multiplicity of durations, durations both my own and outside of me' (2004: 197; see also Mroz, in Chapter 20).

As far as the cinema is concerned, one of its fundamental properties is, of course, its ability to record time and impose duration. While the new spectatorial modes evinced by portable devices are defined by an ever-greater flexibility in terms of temporal manipulation, when watched under fixed-time conditions cinema strictly enforces its own temporality. In fact, as Mary Ann Doane has shown, the 'linear, irreversible, "mechanical"' temporality of the cinematic apparatus already constituted a major source of anxiety at the time of its appearance insofar as cinema's recording of time becomes immediately 'characterized by a certain indeterminacy, an intolerable instability. The image is the imprint of a particular moment whose particularity becomes indeterminable precisely because the image does not speak its own relation to time' (2002: 163). Subsequently, cinema becomes concerned with the production and recording of 'events' whose conceptual existence is premised upon and structured around the elision of 'dead time', that is to say, 'time in which nothing happens, time which is in some sense "wasted", expended without product' (Doane, 2002: 160). It is against this background, Doane goes on, that the vertiginous emergence of narrative structures in early cinema should thus be examined: for this emergence bespeaks a desire to structure unregulated cinematic time; to make duration more tolerable, or indeed invisible, by instrumentalising it according to clearly defined and legible narrative parameters.

If slow cinema, by contrast, makes time noticeable in the image and consequently felt by the viewer, it can be argued that this is often achieved by means of a disjunction between shot duration and audiovisual content. To return to Tarr's famous walking scenes, five minutes is an unjustifiably long time to show an event seemingly devoid of narrative significance and/or momentum. As Ivone Margulies notes in her book-length study of Chantal Akerman, the definition of 'nothing happens' in the cinema is 'appended to films . . . in which the representation's substratum of content seems at variance with the duration accorded it' (1996: 21). In this respect, a popular method to evaluate and measure the slowness of a given film has been to examine its average shot length (ASL), a quantitative analysis achieved through dividing a given film's duration by its overall number of shots. This method would readily lead to the conclusion that the slow style is firmly predicated upon the application of the long take.

Yet, as Lim notes, 'how long is too long? Aside from the subjectivity of the idea and experience of time, it is striking that within film scholarship there does not seem to be a definition for how long exactly is a long take' (2014: 21). By the same token, the ASL of a given film is arguably not an entirely reliant indicator of slowness. Take for instance *Lola Montès* (1955), a film in which Max Ophuls, as Barry Salt notes, 'was continuing on his commercially dangerous course of using very long takes (ASL = 18sec.)' (1992: 312). Even if we admit that the duration of eighteen seconds amounts to a 'very long take' (it certainly does not in contemporary slow films, the ASL of which easily crosses the mark of thirty seconds), one cannot fail to notice that the long takes found in *Lola Montès* can hardly be considered 'slow'. Not only are they manufactured through a dazzling display of choreographed and sweeping camera movements, they are equally populated by hundreds of characters and extras hectically moving from one side to the other as they perform acrobatic numbers in a circus, the film's main setting. Long-take films such as Hitchcock's *Rope* (1948), Mikhail Kalatozov's *I am Cuba* (*Soy Cuba*, 1968) or Orson Welles's *A Touch of Evil* (1958), to give a few more examples, are likewise hard to be classified as slow owing to their wildly eventful *mise en scène* and/or kinetic camerawork.

At the other end of the spectrum we have directors, such as Robert Bresson and Yasujiro Ozu, who, while often invoked as precursors of cinematic slowness, made films that were entirely reliant on montage and short-length shots (see Nagib, in Chapter 1). In fact, the intriguing nature of Ozu's slowness was the subject of a 2000 lecture-turned article by Jonathan Rosenbaum, in which the film critic tentatively identifies the slowness of a film such as *Tokyo Story* (*Tokyo Monogatari*, 1953) not in its form but in its content, namely 'an elderly couple whose movements are slow, and who are seen sitting more often than standing' (2000). There is arguably far more here to Ozu's slowness, however: consider, for instance, his resolutely static camerawork, his attention to narratively insignificant incidents, and especially his focus on settings devoid of human presence, his so-called 'pillow shots'. Quantitative cutting rate, then, does not in itself explain why a film can be considered slow but needs to be analysed qualitatively in relation to other elements of film style.

In this respect, Lim has advanced a more encompassing analytical framework for a cinema of slowness that includes other stylistic parameters such as 'silence' and 'stillness' and, within the latter category, variations such as '*content of the shot*', '*camera movement*' and '*camera angle and camera distance*', among others (2014: 79–80, emphasis in original). Schoonover, in his chapter, also contributes to a more in-depth understanding of how slowness is produced in the filmic image through an analysis of non-professional performance, while Jaffe has noted the ways in which 'long shots frequently prevail over close-ups' in the slow film (2014: 3). Yet here we are also aware that this listing of devices and strategies might unwittingly reinforce the idea that slow cinema is 'formulaic and anonymous' (Smith, 2012: 72). This is a notion too often invoked in rebuttals of the slow style, which reveals the implicit assumption that it is easy to forge owing to its economical means, and the explicit one that it has become fossilised because of the immutability of its main properties.

Of course, a particular style is by no means a guarantee of quality. Yet to dismiss a group of films which adhere to comparable stylistic features seems similarly unwise. In fact, as many of the following chapters will attest, a more or less predetermined aesthetic framework often triggers the opposite result in terms of original filming approaches and creative *mise en scène* strategies. One of the objectives of this volume is to challenge essentialist ideas about the slow style through localised and close readings, moving thereby from a generic idea of 'slow cinema' to the concrete particularities of slow cinemas. In this respect, one section of the book, Part II, will be entirely devoted to 'contextualising slow cinema'. The aim here is not only to illuminate how expressions of slowness are uniquely materialised in a certain film or *oeuvre* – such as Tsai Ming-liang's aesthetics of temporal drifting (Lim, in Chapter 5) or the stills and stillness in the work of Apichatpong (Glyn, in Chapter 6) – but also how slow films are often strictly indebted to local settings and traditions – such as the specifically Philippine roots of Lav Diaz's long slow films (Brown, in Chapter 7), the American cinematic idiom and sense of place animating the work of Kelly Reichardt (Gorfinkel, in Chapter 8), and the rapidly transforming reality of China depicted in Jia Zhangke's films (Mello, in Chapter 9).

In fact, the strict adherence to realism and reality that is a trademark of slow films means that they are, quite often, naturally very distinct which leads us, in turn, to the question of the style's genealogy. That is, while slow cinema is doubtless a recent discursive phenomenon, the aesthetic models and narrative systems mobilised by the style to which such a discourse lends critical valence can arguably be traced back to previous theoretical models and filmic schools across world cinema.

LINEAGES

From the outset, the slow film immediately attests to a rehabilitation of the tenets historically associated with cinematic realism as envisioned by its most illustrious proponent, French film critic André Bazin. Starting from the premise that film has an 'ontological' relation with reality owing to its photographic basis, Bazin celebrated the fact that cinema allowed 'for the first time, the image of things [to be] likewise *the image of their duration*, change mummified' (Bazin, 2005: 15, emphasis added). Variously inspired by the philosophical currents in vogue at his time – including Merleau-Ponty's phenomenology and Bergon's notion of *durée* – Bazin cherished films that, in opposition to an aesthetics of fragmentation based on montage, preserved the continuum of reality through the use of non-professional actors, location shooting and, more remarkably, the application of depth of field and the long take, the combination of which produced what he famously conceptualised as a 'sequence shot' (2005: 35).

All of the above is by now a commonplace in film history. It is also a reductive account of Bazin's complex cinema theory. Calling the 'montage vs. sequence shot' binary 'the textbook version of Bazin', Philip Rosen (2014) has recently reminded us that such a version injects a rigid notion of cinematic specificity into Bazin's realism when the latter was, in fact, open to the fundamentally unspecific nature of cinema in its historically situated relations with other arts and the world at large, as Nagib further elaborates in her contribution to this volume. At any event, Bazin remains an important theoretical springboard for reflections on slow cinema not only because the films normally subsumed under the moniker would seem to radicalise his 'textbook version' but because a cinema of slowness is also taken to give continuity to cinematic modernism (see Flanagan, 2012; Betz, 2010) which equally finds in Bazin its conceptual genesis.

As Lúcia Nagib argues in her chapter, realism and modernism are mutually implicated categories in Bazin's thought. Yet, here, Bazin has to dismiss the modernist cinemas of the 1920s and modernism's obsession with speed as a whole in order to define his own notion of modern cinema as one largely premised on 'extended duration' and an 'accent on the everyday', both of which, as Margulies has shown, provided in the post-war period the 'traditional conjunction of modernism, realism, and politics' in film (Margulies, 1996: 22–3). Celebrating on the one hand the sequence shots of Welles, Wyler or Renoir and, on the other, neorealism's loosened narratives and empty everyday moments, the cinematic modernity championed by Bazin is predicated on ambiguous images whose indeterminate narrative import and/or temporal flow open up a space for reflection and intervention on the part of the spectator. No doubt, in hindsight, some of Bazin's favoured films may appear somewhat constrained in terms of their relatively timid temporal elongations, circumscribed as they were by dramatic and even theatrical structures (see Wollen, 2004: 252; de Luca, 2014: 18–21). For the French philosopher Gilles Deleuze, however, the films illuminated by Bazin are already the seeds of a cinema concerned with 'direct presentations of time' (Deleuze, 2005: 39).

Deleuze's hugely influential cinema books are by now well documented and duly invoked in many studies on slow cinema (and chapters in this volume) owing to his conception of the 'time-image' regime which updates Bazin's notion of modern cinema in the following terms:

> Now, from its first appearances, something different happens in what is called modern cinema ... What has happened is that the sensory-motor schema [of classical cinema, or movement-image] is no longer in operation, but at the same time it is not overtaken or overcome. It is shattered from the inside. That is, perceptions and actions ceased to be linked together, and spaces are now neither co-ordinated nor filled. Some characters, caught in certain pure optical and sound situations, find themselves condemned to wander about or go off on a trip. They are pure seers ... The relation, *sensory-motor situation* → *indirect image of time* is replaced by a non-localizable relation, *pure optical and sound situation* → *direct time image*. (Deleuze, 2005: 39, original emphasis)

Though Deleuze's pantheon is monumental in scope, his conceptualisation of the time-image thus comes to legitimise it as a by now well-known version of modernist art cinema characterised by observant and errant characters, elliptical and dedramatised narrative structures, minimalist *mise en scène*, and/or the sustained application of elongated and self-reflexive temporal devices such as the long take.[3]

Initially associated with the likes of Carl Theodor Dreyer and Michelangelo Antonioni, this aesthetic axiom would bloom in the 1960s and 1970s with the rise of art cinema European auteurs, such as Andrei Tarkovsky, Theo Angelopoulous and Jean-Marie Straub and Danièle Huillet, on the one hand, and the more radical and non-narrative experiments practised across the Atlantic by the likes of Andy Warhol, Michael Snow and Hollis Frampton, on the other, with film-makers such as Chantal Akerman further bridging these complementary tendencies in their own work. For David Campany, 'the embrace of the slow' represented by many of these film-makers 'was a sign of increasing uncertainty about the recorded image in general' and the result of a sense of disenchantment with speed and montage which, once revered for their creative and critical power in the 1920s, started 'degenerating from the promise of mass mobilization into mass destruction. The accelerated image world began to feel dehumanizing, repetitive and monotonous. In this context *slowness*, the deliberate refusal of speed, became central in vanguard art and culture' (Campany, 2008: 36, original emphasis). Peter Wollen strikes a similar chord and contends that 'the turn towards slowness which we see in the work of many avant-garde filmmakers [in the 1960s and 1970s] could best be interpreted as a reaction against the increasing speed of mainstream movies, whether it was intended or unintended' (2002: 270).

It is tempting to chart the evolution of cinematic slowness as one that finds its inaugural expressions in Bazin's pantheon, forks into modernist and experimental tendencies in the 1960s and 1970s, and arrives in the 1990s and 2000s wholly matured but now on a decidedly global scale. Yet this evolutionary approach does not come without shortcomings. For one thing, it legitimises a history of film style that is decidedly teleological and also Eurocentric. For another, it risks overlooking the aesthetic and contextual differences of individual directors and film movements by subsuming them all under the same modern and/or slow umbrella. As a result, rather than merely looking at contemporary slow cinemas as a means to examine how they rearticulate the structures and tendencies of the aforementioned films and traditions, in this book we shall also propose that these films and traditions be themselves retroactively illuminated from today's theoretical vantage point of slowness, as illustrated by Part I, devoted to 'historicising slow cinema'.

Slowness thus emerges here not only as a privileged vehicle through which to recalibrate and bring context and nuance to well-documented slow-cinema precursors, such as Dreyer (Thomson, in Chapter 2), Straub and Huillet (Brady, in Chapter 4) and 1960s durational cinema (Walsh, in Chapter 3). It also presents the historical opportunity to rethink, or even challenge and reject, traditional genealogies of film history and teleological determinism. This is what Nagib proposes in Chapter 1 in which she questions the Bazinian–Deleuzian notion of modernity as the political project of slow cinema by resorting to the case of two Japanese film-makers, Ozu and Mizoguchi, whose differing 'slow' styles cannot be accommodated by traditional world cinema chronologies and Eurocentric organisations. Julian Ross, in Chapter 18, also forges new links in film history by examining the unlikely connection between American film-maker James Benning and the 1960s collective of Japanese film-makers associated with *fūkeiron* (landscape theory) as unexpected precursors of slow cinema. More broadly, Part V of the book will attempt to move 'beyond "slow cinema"' in an attempt to expand the application of slowness in the cinema to new areas of theoretical enquiries (Mroz, in Chapter 20) and unexplored generic filmic practices, such as heritage cinema (Stone and Cooke, in Chapter 22) and the road movie (Gott, in Chapter 21).

MECHANISMS

If slowness can be, however tentatively, traced back to earlier waves in film history and attributed to different causes, the question of why it has acquired a greater visibility in our time as a global cinematic tendency nevertheless remains. That both modern life and mainstream cinema seem to have become even faster at the turn of the millennium is perhaps something to bear in mind. As Robert Hassan notes, the 'increasing rapidity at which we produce, consume and distribute commodities is now the core process, the central factor in the "economy of speed"', which 'represents an immense . . . transformation of the cultural and social forms that spin out from its epicenter' (2009: 21). Paramount among these cultural forms is, of course, cinema and, more specifically, Hollywood cinema, which, as David Bordwell (2002) tells us, now operates on the principle of an ultrafast formal aesthetics of 'intensified continuity' based on rapid editing, close framings and free-ranging camerawork. If, however, reaction to an increasingly fast world and cinema alike may provide some points of entry for ruminations on the ideological underpinnings of contemporary slow cinema, such underpinnings still fail to explain the material and institutional conditions that make such a cinema de facto possible.

Interestingly, Bordwell's own observations on the fast Hollywood model may illuminate the processes which have occasioned its alleged antithesis, for the same digital technology that enables faster shooting methods and editing patterns (2002: 22) has also contributed to the production and circulation of slowness at the turn of the millennium. As the relatively inexpensive and flexible digital equipment offers the ability to record much longer stretches of time, it enables hitherto untenable modes of production and recording based on duration and observation. As demonstrated by no fewer than eight chapters in this volume (see Jorge, Mello, Lovatt, Brown, Smith, Lim, Remes and Ross), each of which focuses on a different director, contrary to the accusation of nostalgic purism and technological backwardness that the slow film has received (see Shaviro, 2010), its proliferation around the globe is, in fact, inextricably connected to the arrival of digital technology in film production.

As far as institutional support goes, slow cinema also circulates within a specific economic and cultural sphere that has largely enabled not only its global promotion and consumption but also its production, namely: the international film festival. As Mark Betz reminds us:

> [O]ne must acknowledge the international networks of exchange within which many [of the practitioners currently identified with slow cinema] are working, in terms of not only their geographic range but also the transnational provenance of the film production (many by European finance), reception, and dissemination, frequently by major European film festivals. Increasingly, festivals are themselves commissioning and producing the work of these filmmakers, potentially binding them to a marketplace that cannot but have an effect on the stylistic choices that they make. (2010: 32)[4]

To give a privileged example, a film festival such as Rotterdam is now famous for its Hubert Bals Fund (HBF) which has financially helped many slow-cinema suspects in Latin America and Asia, such as Reygadas, Alonso, Apichatpong and Diaz.

By admitting that slow cinema circulates within, and is in turn supported by, the international film festival circuit, we are therefore not only situating slow cinema within the larger category and institution of art cinema as much as we are following Lim's call to liberate such a category 'from its economic closet to acknowledge its status as a global niche market with attendant institutions, mechanisms, and agents' (2014: 27–8). This seems especially paramount as slow cinema is often accused of catering to this particular niche market and its corresponding association with elitism and the overly aesthetic. Indeed, this accusation appears to gain in significance when we consider that the art gallery has consistently lured practitioners interested in slowness over the last decade, with directors such as Akerman, Costa, Tsai, Apichatpong and Kiarostami, among others, crossing over into the realm of the museum and making moving-image installations that often recycle and expand on their own feature films.

Through navigating within institutional realms premised upon art cinema and art practices, slow cinema is thus caught up in another debate that calls into question its cultural and political integrity. As many slow films come from Iran, Asia and Latin America, and are accordingly financed by European agents and institutions, questions hinging on power relations and national authenticity come to the fore. Miriam Ross, for example, draws attention to the 'expectations placed' on the films that are produced under the HBF scheme, including 'the desire to fit within art cinema, and the belief that they will engage with film festival audiences' (2011: 267). While Ross does not specifically address the slow style that is a recognisable trademark of many HBF films, her contention that the scheme 'restricts the access national audiences have to these works through an emphasis on film festival circulation' (267) resonates with many contemporary film-makers discussed in this book, who are often accused of turning their backs on national audiences by aestheticising their own local cultures to a privileged international elite.

There is no doubt that an examination of contemporary film and cultural production must take into account the ways in which an uneven confluence of financing sources and international institutions support and subtend such productions. And yet, can we speak of a purely 'national' or 'independent' film today? Deborah Shaw, for example, alerts us not to fall into the equally essentialist notion 'that more authentic images are presented when the funding of a film relies on purely national sources' (2013: 168). Dudley Andrew has similarly reminded us that the 'very idea of "independent cinema" has been altered by what is now a fully global network that makes *every film* quite "dependent"' (2012: ix, emphasis added). We refuse to see slow films as automatically suspicious owing to their dependence on transnational frameworks in the same way that we 'refuse to underestimate the potential of the international' (Galt and Schoonover, 2012: 10).

The scepticism, however, with which a cinema of slowness has been received goes beyond its reliance on international funding and circulation. Two other, and often interrelated, assumptions uphold the suspicion appended to the slow film, namely: that it is excessively aesthetic and that it is also retrograde in its nostalgic longing for pre-industrial temporalities and corresponding facing away from the complex multiplicity of time. As such, slow cinema ultimately raises questions related to the politics of its aesthetics, to which we shall turn by way of concluding this introduction.

POLITICS

As far as the first assumption is concerned, slow cinema's eminently aesthetic dimension, as observed in meticulously composed visual and aural compositions, would seem to sit uneasily with the subject matter of such a cinema, which Matthew Flanagan aptly summarises as follows:

The distinctive aesthetics of slow films tend to emerge from spaces that have been indirectly affected or left behind by globalisation, most notably in the films of Alonso, Bartas, Jia, Costa and Diaz . . . [M]any individual works by these filmmakers turn their attention to marginal peoples (low-paid manual labourers, poor farmers, the unemployed and dispossessed, petty criminals and drug addicts) subsisting in remote or invisible places, and depict the performance of (waged or unwaged) agricultural and manufacturing work that is increasingly obscured by the macro volatility of finance-capital's huge speculative flows. (2012: 118)

Several chapters readily attest to Flanagan's remarks, with Part III of the book specifically addressing the question of marginal labour that is at the core of many slow films. And while such a focus on the underprivileged would not constitute a problem in itself, the glaringly aesthetic, even austere, style through which these films choose to depict marginalised places and peoples brings with it the old suspicion that 'art cinema's formal surpluses' are 'semantically bankrupt, aesthetically decadent, or simply apolitical' (Schoonover and Galt, 2010: 18).[5]

Indeed, aesthetics and politics are often deemed irreconcilable in film studies, a perception in part derived from the discipline's long-standing alliance with cultural studies and its corresponding emphasis on the representational politics of popular culture. For the French philosopher Jacques Rancière, however, aesthetics and politics can be said to operate exactly on the same principle. This principle destabilises the 'consensual' social order through unexpected reframings that accordingly reconfigure modes of sensory experience by overturning the idea that only certain subjects, bodies and themes belong to the domain of the aesthetic and the sensible. Aesthetic interventions, in this sense, are not political because they have a clearly defined and didactic goal that is translated into collective action on the part of the spectators. On the contrary, aesthetics is to be deemed political because it accepts its own insufficiency as a mode of experience, one that does not give lessons and cannot predict results; one that is content with being 'configurations of experience that create new modes of sense perception' (Rancière, 2011: 9).

As Rancière elaborates in Chapter 17, which opens Part V, on the 'ethics and politics of slowness', the politics of Béla Tarr's films is not to be found in matters of plot. Rather, it resides in the rift produced by a representational focus on purely idiotic characters who are, nevertheless, 'given presence and density' through an aesthetics that is committed to 'the materiality of time' and which as such reopens 'time as the site of the possible'. Elsewhere the philosopher has also elaborated on another slow-cinema suspect, Pedro Costa, and noted how his attention 'to every beautiful form offered by the homes of the poor, and the patience with which he listens' to its inhabitants are 'inscribed in a different politics of art [that] does not seek to make viewers aware of the structures of domination and inspire them to mobilize their energies' (Rancière, 2011: 80). Rather, '[t]he politics of the filmmaker involves using the sensory riches – the power of speech or of vision – that can be extracted from the life and settings of these precarious existences' (81). While Costa knows his films will be 'immediately labelled film-festival material . . . and tendentiously pushed in the direction of museum and art lovers', he 'makes a film in the awareness that it is only a film, one which will scarcely be shown and whose effects in the theatres and outside are fairly unpredictable' (82). Cinema, Rancière concludes, thus 'must split itself off; it must agree to be the surface on which an artist tries to cipher in new figures the experience of people relegated to the margins of economic circulation and social trajectories' but it can never avoid 'the aesthetic cut that separates outcomes from intentions' (82).

Rancière's remarks can be productively extended to many practitioners under consideration in this book, who, like Tarr and Costa, are equally concerned with registering the experience and lived time of the marginalised. Directors such as Tsai, Jia, Benning, Diaz, Reygadas, Wang, for example, are all aware that a film is only a film; that it cannot transcend its status as a commodity dependent on particular institutions and networks, and that all a film can do is illuminate given realities through aesthetic interventions that may refresh the affects and perceptions of such realities. Unflinching in their minute observation of pressing local and global issues, these film-makers nonetheless refuse to offer facile, schematic or ready-made interpretations, opting instead to observe, with attention and patience, all kinds of significant as well as insignificant realities. In so doing, slowness not only interrogates and reconfigures well-established notions of aesthetic and cultural worthiness – what is worthy of being shown, for how long it is worth being shown – but also what is worthy of our attention and patience as viewers and individuals, and thus ultimately of our time and what we do with such time.

In their durational quest, however, to capture the riches of lives, realities and temporalities seemingly at odds with, or else at the margins of, dominant economic systems and networks, slow films are confronted with another accusation, that of a certain escapism as they allegedly 'turn their backs to the exigencies of the now so as to fancy the presumed pleasures of preindustrial times and lifestyles' (Koepnick, 2014: 3). Koepnick, for example, cautions that 'the wager of aesthetic slowness is not simply to find islands of respite, calm and stillness somewhere outside the cascades of contemporary speed culture' but, rather, to 'investigate what it means to experience a world of speed, acceleration, and cotemporality' (2014: 10), an operation that he locates not in durational films but, as previously mentioned, in slow-motion art practices. The political project of the slow movement as a whole has also been called under suspicion as it 'appear[s] to be about getting away, maintaining distance from the temporal and the complex multiplicity of time' (Sharma, 2014: 111).

To be sure, these accusations cannot be entirely discounted and, as Part IV shows, slow cinema's veritable emphasis on rural lifestyles and animal life should also be examined within the larger context of discourses such as 'ecocriticism' (Lam, in Chapter 14) and the 'non-human turn' (de Luca, in Chapter 15; Remes, in Chapter 16). That said, the assumption that slow cinema simply inverts speed, or else faces away from the conflicting tempo-ralities of the now, is in need of qualification. As many chapters demonstrate in this book, a durational aesthetic is more often than not appropriated as the means by which to confront, and reflect on, the 'experience of a world of speed, acceleration, and cotemporality', to use Koepnick's own words. In this respect, the fact that so many slow cinemas come from East Asia and China is noteworthy when set against the historically unprecedented pace at which modernisation has taken place in many of these regions in the last thirty years. As Mello, Lovatt and Smith explore in their chapters, directors such as Jia Zhangke (Chapter 9), Liu Jiayin (Chapter 13) and Wang Bing (Chapter 12) all deploy slowness as a strategy not to turn away from the vertiginous speed of industrialisation processes and societal changes but as a vehicle through which to confront and make sense of these processes and changes.

Similarly, slow time does not exist in a sealed-off vacuum in durational cinemas but is often resorted to as a medium to actualise and negotiate conceptually different temporalities and competing visions of time, which is to say that many cinemas under consideration here not only offer the phenom-enological experience of distended time but that they are also, epistemologi-cally, 'about' time: historical time (Rancière, in Chapter 17; Stone and Cooke, in Chapter 22), cosmological time (Brown, in Chapter 7), evolutionary human time (Mroz, in Chapter 20), non-human times (Part IV). Durational slowness, then, can be variously moulded according to a given object of attention and specific formal and narrative strategies as a means to ponder over the co-existence of multiple temporalities. This includes what it means to live in the midst of today's wildly entangled temporal configurations as well as non-human conceptions of time. More broadly, as Lim (Chapter 5), Grønstad (Chapter 19) and Schoonover (Chapter 10) respectively explore in their chapters, in a world where speed is the normative ideological paradigm underpinning late capitalism's economic labour systems, social values and the contemporary audiovisual and cultural regimes, slowness necessarily intervenes in wider political debates insofar as it speaks to this paradigm and opens up a space to look at, reassess and question these systems, values and regimes from a new sensory–perceptual prism.

As Jonathan Crary has observed, if the everyday, as a critical and aesthetic category, rests on the preservation of the 'recurring pulsings of life being lived'

(2014: 69), then the preservation of these pulsings of lived time acquires a new urgency given the current erosion of 'distinctions between work and non-work time, between public and private, between everyday life and organized institutional milieus' (Crary, 2014: 74). As the unattended temporalities and folds of everyday life become increasingly controlled, dominated and disciplined by digital networks that infiltrate every aspect of lived experience, this 'relentless capture and control of time and experience' entails an 'incapacitation of daydream or of any mode of absent-minded introspection that would otherwise occur in intervals of slow and vacant time' (Crary, 2014: 40, 88).

It is therefore in this context that the politics of slow cinema should be examined and understood, for it is not a coincidence that its emergence in the last three decades coincides with the period in which Crary rightly sees 'the assault on everyday life assum[ing] a new ferocity' (2014: 71). As the following chapters will, we hope, attest, a slow cinematic aesthetic not only restores a sense of time and experience in a world short of both, it also encourages a mode of engagement with images and sounds whereby slow time becomes a vehicle for introspection, reflection and thinking, and the world is disclosed in its complexity, richness and mystery.

Chapter Outlines

Through its wide range of contributions, the book combines an array of approaches and perspectives whose organising principle will be the developing notion of slowness as applied to cinema. Part I, 'Historicising Slow Cinema', sheds fresh light on canonical directors and movements with a view to mapping out a slow genealogy in film history. In Chapter 1, Lúcia Nagib provides a re-evaluation of the diachronic line marking out classical and modern cinemas through a comparative analysis of the differing slow styles of Kenji Mizoguchi and Yasujiro Ozu. Defying world cinema classifications based on evolutionary and Eurocentric models, Nagib instead draws on the Bazinian concept of 'impure cinema' in order to interrogate and challenge the classical–modern debate and its most recent expression as encapsulated in the fast–slow binary. C. Claire Thomson, in Chapter 2, examines Carl Th. Dreyer's film style by focusing not on the director's contemplative feature films but instead on his writings and lesser-known commissioned shorts which, she argues, offer a productive foundation upon which to revisit and bring a more nuanced perspective on the slowness commonly attributed to this film-maker. Michael Walsh, in Chapter 3, provides a historical and theoretical account on what he terms 'the first durational cinema' of the 1960s, contending that the experimental films of Andy Warhol and Michael Snow, among others, can be seen as a springboard that in some sense informs the aesthetic of contemporary slow cinema. Closing this section is Chapter 4, by Martin Brady, which retraces the slowness of a film such as Jean-Marie Straub and Danièle Huillet's *History Lessons* (*Geschichtsunterricht*, 1972) to a specifically Brechtian notion of materialism and in the light of Walter Benjamin's materialist historiography and his conception of 'dialectics at a standstill'.

Looking specifically at contemporary films and directors, Part II of the book is devoted to 'Contextualising Slow Cinema', illuminating how the slow style can be variously embedded in local roots and indebted to distinct cultural, intermedial and cinematic traditions. Chapter 5, by Song Hwee Lim, explores the distinctive crystallisation of slowness in the cinema of Taiwan-based Tsai Ming-liang as one based on the stillness of diegetic action and stationary camerawork. These features, however, are complicated by the visual trope of objects in movement which Lim conceptualises as conjuring a 'temporal aesthetics of drifting'. Like Lim, Glyn Davis, in Chapter 6, also examines cinematic stillness in Apichatpong Weerasethakul's films, though he does so in relation to the presence of photographic stills and freeze-frames in the work of the Thai director, and as an opportunity to rethink and theorise the ways in which slowness, stasis and stillness are interconnected in slow cinema. In Chapter 7, William Brown looks at Lav Diaz's *Melancholia* (2008) as a peculiarly 'long' iteration of slow cinema owing to its excessive running time, while further situating the film's aesthetic adherence to realism and real time within specifically Philippine cultural, social and rural contexts. Elena Gorfinkel, in Chapter 8, analyses the American cinematic idiom informing Kelly Reichardt's 'anti-Western' *Meek's Cutoff* (2010), and calls attention to its aesthetics of austerity and dispossession as one that conceptually resonates with the United States's current neo-liberal policies. Chapter 9, by Cecília Mello, concludes this section by exploring, through an intermedial approach, the slowness of Jia Zhangke's cinema as an aesthetic response to the speed of transformations in China as well as a quest to register the country's ephemeral cityscapes as materialised in disappearing walls.

Part III, 'Slow Cinema and Labour', focuses on the question of labour and its theoretical and political ramifications for the study of slow cinema. Karl Schoonover, in Chapter 10, harnesses the slow cinema debate as an opportunity to reconsider the conceptual stakes of labour, value and productivity as foregrounded by the category of art cinema. Focusing on the figure of the 'cinematic wastrel', Schoonover examines the ways in which this non-productive on-screen body makes visible the off-screen labour of viewing, thereby intervening in debates on the politics of spectatorship. In Chapter 11, Nuno Barradas Jorge discusses the artisanal labour and long production time that went into the making of Pedro Costa's *In Vanda's Room* (*No Quarto da Vanda*, 2000) as a consequence of the director's utilisation of digital technology, which enabled a slow film-making process based on the repetitious observation of everyday routines in a marginalised Lisbon community. Patrick Brian Smith, in Chapter 12, similarly investigates the ways in which the application of digital technology makes visible the physical human labour involved in the recording of Wang Bing's *Tie Xi Qu: West of the Tracks* (2003). As this nine-hour film documents the labour activities in a declining industrial community in China, Smith examines its style as one that foregrounds labour as a process happening simultaneously behind and in front of the camera. Another Chinese film-maker, Liu Jiayin, is the focus of Chapter 13, by Philippa Lovatt, who draws attention to the ways in which the duo *Oxhide* (*Niupi*, 2005) and *Oxhide II* (*Niupi er*, 2009), like *West of the Tracks*, foreground both the labour involved in the making of the film and that of the main protagonists as they engage in rituals of cookery. Resisting a purely visual approach, Lovatt further focuses on the ways in which sound is an essential component of the sensory experience offered by the slow film.

Part IV, 'Slow Cinema and the Non-human', addresses the emphasis on rural lifestyles and non-human environments that is a veritable hallmark of the cinematic trend. Stephanie Lam, in Chapter 14, channels Scott Mackenzie's notion of 'ecocinema' as a means to shed fresh light on film and media practices that have the environment as their object of contemplation. Bringing together the likes of Bill Viola, James Benning and online live-streaming nature cams, Lam argues that these otherwise unrelated practices are unified through the employment of an attentive gaze that elicits a renewed awareness of ecological processes. Tiago de Luca, in Chapter 15, examines the serendipitous and non-anthropomorphic quality that animates the depiction of nature and non-human living creatures in the slow cinematic aesthetic. Through a comparative analysis of two Latin American films, Carlos Reygadas's *Japón* and Lisandro Alonso's *Los muertos*, de Luca elaborates on the fascination with animal life and death that testifies to slow cinema's obsession with the contingent. Closing this section is Chapter 16, by Justin Remes, who looks at Abbas Kiarostami's *Five: Dedicated to Ozu* (2003) to examine the ways in which its non-human aesthetics, made up of lengthy shots of natural environments devoid of human presence, encourages an unorthodox mode of reception whereby the spectator is invited to sleep during the film's screening.

Part V focuses on the 'Ethics and Politics of Slowness'. Chapter 17, by Jacques Rancière, unpacks the politics inscribed in Béla Tarr's aesthetic commitment to the materiality of time, which the philosopher situates within the historical context of the end of the socialist utopia and the disenchantment of capitalism. In Chapter 18, Julian Ross expounds on the ethical implications of the landscape shot. Examining the work of the Japanese *fūkeiron* film-makers and James Benning, Ross identifies a striking similarity in their depiction of criminals in that both refuse to narrativise or judge events in the manner of news media representations, thereby leaving room for the spectator to arrive at his/her own conclusions. Asbjørn Grønstad, in Chapter 19, discusses the political potential of filmic slowness in relation to how it spatialises duration and makes visible the passing of time through diegetic inaction. This produces a contemplative aesthetics of 'presence' that provides a springboard for an ethics of seeing based on the principles of recognition, reflection and empathy.

Part VI, 'Beyond "Slow Cinema"' expands the usage and theoretical application of slowness beyond the pantheon readily associated with the term. Matilda Mroz, in Chapter 20, draws on the Bergsonian concept of evolutionary performance as a means to interrogate and elaborate on the operation of duration, and the depiction and experience of temporal unfolding, with reference to Lucile Hadžihalilović's *Innocence* (2004). Michael Gott, in Chapter 21, investigates the aesthetic and political links between the categories of slow cinema and the 'negative' road film. Looking at Abderrahmane Sissako's *Heremakono* (2002) and Marian Crişan's *Morgen* (2010), Gott examines the ways in which their pauses and delays provide political commentary on the slow journeys of immigrants to Europe and its immigration policies. Chapter 22, by Rob Stone and Paul Cooke, builds on Gilles Deleuze's notion of crystal-image to examine the 'occasion of slowness' in the genre of heritage cinema. For Stone and Cooke, these slow moments, materialised in contemplative and languid long takes, halt the forward motion of narrative and allow competing notions of time to emerge within the image.

Rethinking the critical validity of slowness at localised levels and in the present context of film as a rapidly changing technological and institutional practice, the following chapters reposition slow cinema in a broader discursive and theoretical terrain, thus developing renewed sets of understandings that will refine and redefine the stakes of slowness in the cinema.

Notes

1. For a comprehensive and perceptive account of the slow cinema debate, including its two-sided, gendered implications, see Schoonover, in Chapter 10.
2. Here it is also worth mentioning that recent books have equally explored the topic of filmic temporality broadly speaking, including Yvette Biro's *Turbulence and Flow in Film: The Rhythmic Design* (2008), Jean Ma's *Melancholy Drift: Marking Time in Chinese Cinema* (2010) and Matilda Mroz's *Temporality and Film Analysis* (2013). More remarkably, issues relating to stillness and stasis in the cinema have been the central focus of many publications, such as Laura Mulvey's *Death 24x a Second: Stillness and the Moving Image* (2006) and the anthologies *Stillness and Time: Photography and the Moving Image* (David Green and Joanna Lowry, 2005), *Still Moving: Between Cinema and Photography* (Karen Beckman and Jean Ma, 2008) and *Between Stillness and Motion: Film, Photography, Algorithms* (Elvira Røssak, 2011). As their self-explanatory titles indicate, however, these are books primarily

concerned with the relationship between cinema and photography rather than slowness per se. For an engagement with some of these publications, and their relevance to slow cinema, see Davis in Chapter 6.
3. For two recent and illuminating studies on cinematic modernism, see Kovács, 2007 and Betz, 2009. For an exemplary collection on art cinema, see Galt and Schoonover, 2010.
4. Dating from 2010, Betz's article lists practically all film-makers commonly associated with slow cinema but without making reference to the term.
5. Whether implicit or explicit, most of the aforementioned rebuttals have decried slow cinema's overly aesthetic and artistic emphasis. See in particular Kois, 2011 and James, 2010.

BIBLIOGRAPHY

Andrew, Dudley (2010), 'Foreword', in Rosalind Galt and Karl Schoonover (eds), *Global Art Cinema* (Oxford: Oxford University Press), pp. v–xi.
Bazin, André (2005), *What is Cinema?* – Volume 1, essays selected and translated by Hugh Gray (London and Berkeley: University of California Press).
Betz, Mark (2010), 'Beyond Europe: On Parametric Transcendence', in Rosalind Galt and Karl Schoonover (eds), *Global Art Cinema* (Oxford: Oxford University Press), pp. 31–47.
Bordwell, David (2002), 'Intensified Continuity: Visual Style in Contemporary American Film', in *Film Quarterly* 55:3, pp. 16–28.
Bordwell, David (2008), *Poetics of Cinema* (New York: Routledge).
Bordwell, David and Kristin Thompson (2011), 'Good and Good for You', in *Observations on Film Art* [online blog], http://www.davidbordwell.net/blog/2011/07/10/good-and-good-for-you/ [accessed 24 February 2015].
Campany, David (2008), *Photography and Cinema* (London: Reaktion).
Ciment, Michel (2003), 'The State of Cinema', address speech at the 46th San Francisco International Film Festival, available at http://web.archive.org/web/20040325130014/http://www.sfiff.org/fest03/special/state.html [accessed 24 February 2015].
Crary, Jonathan (2014), *24/7: Late Capitalism and the Ends of Sleep* (London and New York: Verso).
Dargis, Manohla and A. O. Scott (2011), 'In Defense of the Slow and the Boring', in *New York Times*, http://www.nytimes.com/2011/06/05/movies/films-in-defense-of-slow-and-boring.html?_r=1& [accessed 24 February 2015].
Doane, Mary Ann (2002), *The Emergence of Cinematic Time: Modernity, Contingency, The Archive* (London: Harvard University Press).
Deleuze, Gilles (2005), *Cinema 2: The Time-Image* (London: Continuum).
de Luca, Tiago (2014), *Realism of the Senses in World Cinema: The Experience of Physical Reality* (London and New York: I. B. Tauris).
Flanagan, Matthew (2008), 'Towards an Aesthetic of Slow in Contemporary Cinema', in *16:9*, 6:29, http://www.16-9.dk/2008-11/side11_inenglish.htm [accessed 24 February 2015].
Flanagan, Matthew (2012), *'Slow Cinema': Temporality and Style in Contemporary Art and Experimental Film*, unpublished PhD thesis. University of Exeter.
Galt, Rosalind and Karl Schoonover (2010), 'Introduction: The Impurity of Art Cinema', in Rosalind Galt and Karl Schoonover (eds), *Global Art Cinema* (Oxford: Oxford University Press), pp. 3–27.
Grosz, Elizabeth (2004), *The Nick of Time: Politics, Evolution and the Untimely* (Durham, NC and London: Duke University Press).

Hassan, Robert (2009), *Empires of Speed: Time and the Acceleration of Politics and Society* (Leiden: IDC).

Jaffe, Ira (2014), *Slow Movies: Countering the Cinema of Action* (New York: Wallflower).

James, Nick (2010), 'Passive-Aggressive', *Sight & Sound*, 20: 4, p. 5.

Jameson, Fredric (2003), 'The End of Temporality', in *Critical Inquiry*, 29: 4, pp. 695–718.

Koepnick, Lutz (2014), *On Slowness: Toward an Aesthetic of the Contemporary* (New York: Columbia University Press).

Kois, Dan (2011), 'Eating Your Cultural Vegetables', in *New York Times* http://www.nytimes.com/2011/05/01/magazine/mag-01Riff-t.html [accessed 24 February 2015].

Kovács, András Bálint (2007), *Screening Modernism: European Art Cinema, 1950–1980* (Chicago and London: Chicago University Press).

Lim, Song Hwee (2014), *Tsai Ming-liang and a Cinema of Slowness* (Honolulu: University of Hawai'i Press).

Margulies, Ivone (1996), *Nothing Happens: Chantal Akerman's Hyperrealist Everyday* (Durham, NC and London: Duke University Press).

Mroz, Matilda (2013), *Temporality and Film Analysis* (Edinburgh: Edinburgh University Press).

Rancière, Jacques (2011), *The Emancipated Spectator* (London and New York: Verso).

Romney, Jonathan (2010), 'In Search of Lost Time', in *Sight and Sound*, 20: 2, pp. 43–4.

Rosen, Philip (2014), 'From Impurity to Historicity', in Lúcia Nagib and Anne Jerslev (eds), *Impure Cinema* (London and New York: I. B. Tauris).

Ross, Miriam (2011), 'The film festival as producer: Latin American films and Rotterdam's Hubert Bals Fund', in *Screen* 52: 2, pp. 261–7.

Salt, Barry (1992 [1983]), *Film Style and Technology: History and Analysis* (London: Starword).

Sharma, Sarah (2014), *In the Meantime: Temporality and Cultural Politics* (Durham, NC and London: Duke University Press).

Shaviro, Steven (2010), 'Slow Cinema Vs Fast Films', in *The Pinocchio Theory* [online blog] http://www.shaviro.com/Blog/?p=891 [accessed 24 February 2015].

Shaw, Deborah (2013), 'Sex, Texts and Money, Funding and Latin American Queer Cinema: the Cases of Martel's *La niña santa* and Puenzo's *XXY*', in 'Latin American Cinemas Today: Reframing the National', special issue of *Transnational Cinemas*, 4: 2, pp. 65–184.

Smith, Paul Julian (2012), 'Transnational Cinemas: the Cases of Mexico, Argentina and Brazil', in Lúcia Nagib, Chris Perriam and Rajinder Dudrah (eds), *Theorizing World Cinema* (London and New York: I. B. Tauris), pp. 63–76.

Tuttle, Harry (2010), 'Slow Films, Easy Life', in *Unspoken Cinema* [online blog] http://unspokencinema.blogspot.co.uk/2010/05/slow-films-easy-life-sight.html [accessed 24 February 2015].

Wollen, Peter (2002), *Paris Hollywood: Writings on Film* (London and New York: Verso).

Wollen, Peter (2004), 'Citizen Kane', in James Naremore (ed.), *Orson Welles's Citizen Kane: A Casebook* (Oxford and New York: Oxford University Press), pp. 249–62.

PART I

HISTORICISING SLOW CINEMA

1. THE POLITICS OF SLOWNESS AND THE TRAPS OF MODERNITY

Lúcia Nagib

In this chapter, I shall re-evaluate the diachronic, evolutionist model that establishes World War II as a watershed between classical and modern cinemas, and 'modernity' as the political project of 'slow cinema'. I will start by historicising the connection between cinematic speed and modernity, going on to survey the veritable obsession with the modern that continues to beset film studies despite the vagueness and contradictions inherent in the term. I will then attempt to clarify what is really at stake within the modern-classical debate by analysing two canonical examples of Japanese cinema, drawn from the *geidomono* genre (films on the lives of theatre actors), Yasujiro Ozu's *Floating Weeds* (*Ukigusa*, 1959) and Kenji Mizoguchi's *Story of the Last Chrysanthemums* (*Zangiku monogatari*, 1939), with a view to investigating the role of the long take or, conversely, classical editing, in the production or otherwise of a supposed 'slow modernity'. Mizoguchi is notable for his lavish use of the long take and the long shot, and was accordingly hailed for his realism by Bazin's disciples in the pages of the *Cahiers du Cinéma* in the 1950s (see Rivette, 1958; Rohmer, 1957; Godard, 1968). This, however, did not suffice to secure him a place within the modern canon, as proved by Deleuze's classification of his films as 'movement image', that is, alongside the classical cinema of montage. Conversely, Deleuze placed the production of Ozu, an inveterate adept in montage throughout his *oeuvre*, under the time-image category, making it akin to modernity. Worthy of note is that Deleuze's world cinema organisation relies on a systematic disregard for chronology, despite his apparent allegiance to Bazin's diachronic model hinging on the axis of World War II. Indeed, in his assessment of Ozu and Mizoguchi, he cites randomly from their works going back to the pre-war or even to the silent period.

By resorting to Ozu and Mizoguchi in the light of this literature, I hope to demonstrate that the best narrative films in the world have always combined a 'classical' quest for perfection with the 'modern' doubt of its existence, hence the futility of classifying cinema in general according to an evolutionary and Eurocentric model based on the classical-modern binary. Rather than on a confusing politics of the modern, I will draw on another of Bazin's prophetic insights, 'impure cinema', a concept he forged in defence of literary and theatrical screen adaptations. Anticipating by more than half a century the media convergence on which the near totality of our audiovisual experience is currently based, 'impure cinema' will give me the opportunity to focus on the confluence of film and theatre in the aforementioned Mizoguchi and Ozu films as the site of a productive crisis where established genres dissolve into self-reflexive stasis, ambiguity of expression and the revelation of the reality of the film medium, all of which, I argue, are more reliable indicators of a film's political programme than historical teleology. At the end of the journey, some answers may emerge to whether the combination of the long take and the long shot is sufficient to account for a film's 'slowness' and whether 'slow' is indeed the best concept to signify resistance to the destructive pace of capitalism.

THE MODERN OBSESSION

The idea of 'slow cinema' carries within it a politics. It suggests the existence of a 'fast cinema' against which it posits itself as an advantageous alternative. At a time when commodification of speed is ruthlessly obliterating the fruition of our most basic pleasures, from eating to enjoying a beautiful landscape, it seems indeed sensible to advocate slowness as an antidote to mindless consumerism. As regards cinema, however, 'there is no uniform appreciation for slowness', as Song Hwee Lim reminds us, for what is pleasure for some might be pain for others (2014: 4). I would add that there is no consensual perception of fast and slow in the cinema, as what is an uneventful, lengthy film for certain viewers might offer a plethora of exciting incidents to others – as much as an action-packed thriller may be perceived as tediously repetitive.

To understand properly how speed is produced and experienced, it might be worth considering, in the first place, cinema's defining property of movement. Siegfried Kracauer devised two basic types of cinematic movement. The first is 'objective motion', that is, the movement of objects in front of the camera, a kind that predominated in the silent era when the camera remained mostly static. With the development of film technology, a second type came into being that Kracauer defined as 'subjective motion', which aligns the spectator's point of view with a tilting, panning or travelling camera, while bringing motionless, as well as moving, objects to his or her attention (Kracauer, 1997: 33–4). Editing, for Kracauer, also produced subjective motion insofar as 'an appropriate arrangement of shots may rush the audience through vast expanses of time and/or space so as to make it witness, almost simultaneously, events in different periods and places' (1997: 34). Film-makers of all times have relied on the variation and combination of these motions in order to fashion their styles. A director such as Ozu, for example, avoided as much as possible the movements of the camera and of the objects in front of it, relying almost exclusively on editing to impart narrative progression. Conversely, objects and camera in a typical Mizoguchi film are in perennial movement, reducing the dynamic role of editing to a minimum. This might be one of the reasons why Ozu is often seen as an early exponent of slow cinema (see, for example, Rosenbaum, 2000) whereas Mizoguchi has never been associated with it.

Theories of slowness, however, hardly ever concern movements other than Kracauer's second type of subjective motion, that is, editing, or the lack thereof, within a logic that attributes to the long take the power to delay narrative progression. The very consolidation of slow cinema as a genre in recent years is often seen as a result of digital technology insofar as it allows for the 'hyperbolic application of the long take', as Tiago de Luca has aptly put it (2011: 83). The fact, however, remains that the reliance on the long take does not necessarily elicit the experience of slowness by the spectator, for its use attains radically different results, say, in a contemplative film, such as *Liverpool* (Lisandro Alonso, 2008), and in a sci-fi action feature, such as *Children of Men* (Alfonso Cuarón, 2006). Moreover, thanks also to digital technology, a shot can now be so short, and the shots so many, that they tend to become indistinguishable from one another in a flux that paradoxically resembles a never-ending single take rather than clearly identifiable sets of images, as is typical of current CGI-saturated commercial cinema.

These examples demonstrate the insufficiency of the long take to determine, on its own, the speed of a film as experienced by the spectator, suggesting a wider agenda behind the scholarly focus on it. In fact, the quarrel between montage and time-space continuity goes back a long way and involves the question of realism. It was first launched by André Bazin in his famous article 'The Evolution of the Language of Cinema' where he separated between 'those directors who put their faith in the image and those who put their faith in reality' (1967: 24). Directors of that kind, such as Jean Renoir and Orson Welles, were hailed by Bazin for their reliance on depth of field (or the long shot) and the sequence shot (or the long take) which reflected their 'respect for the continuity of dramatic space and, of course, of its duration' (1967: 34). Bazin went as far as imagining 'a film by Stroheim composed of a single shot as long-lasting and as close-up as you like' (1967: 27) and of dreaming with Zavattini of the ultimate realist film, consisting of 'ninety minutes of the life of a man to whom nothing ever happens' (1967: 37).

Not that slowness ever featured on his agenda and, in fact, he was wary of the possible disruptive effects entailed by the excessive duration of a shot. An example is *The Earth Trembles* (*La terra trema*, Luchino Visconti, 1948) which he lauds for its long takes that allow us to see 'the whole operation; it will not be reduced to its dramatic or symbolic meaning, as is usual with montage' (2005: 43). But he goes on to blame Visconti for running counter to 'some filmic principles' and refusing 'to sacrifice anything to drama'; as a result, he says, *The Earth Trembles* 'bores the public' (45). Rather than speed, Bazin's realist politics concerned doubt, or, in his words, 'ambiguity of expression' as enabled by the surplus of time and space contained in the long-take/long-shot combination, in contrast to the 'unity of meaning' imposed by montage. Allowing the eye to wander in depth of field and linger on the events through their duration, 'ambiguity of expression' invited 'both a more active mental attitude on the part of the spectator and a more positive contribution on his part to the action in progress' (1967: 36) – an idea that closely resonates with Brecht's defence of active spectatorship and advanced by at least a decade the self-reflexive political cinema that would flourish in the 1960s on the basis of spectatorial agency and participation.

More problematically, however, Bazin chose to give this democratic and inclusive aesthetics the name of 'modern cinema'. It was undoubtedly a coherent choice insofar as it represented the culmination of his evolutionist approach, according to which the best films ever made could not but be located in his own time, that is, in the immediate aftermath of World War II. 'Modern cinema' thus starts with Italian neorealism in the late 1940s, excluding from its ranks not only what Bazin calls the 'classical' Hollywood cinema but pre-war modernist cinema itself, as represented by Eisenstein and Soviet cinema, German expressionism and the European avant-gardes in general, owing to their allegiance to montage. Though circumstantial and transient at origin, this model has prevailed in film studies ever since, having been lavishly applied to signify almost any narrative films produced outside the Hollywood system from World War II onwards and obscuring the prophetic quality of Bazin's realist programme and political agenda. Beyond the questionable opposition between modernity and modernism, this model is further flawed by the fact that many realist film-makers of Bazin's pantheon, starting with Jean Renoir, were active much before the war and already resorting to the techniques he deemed both realist and modern. Conversely, most neorealist film-makers never actually made use of the long-take/long-shot combination, if you just think of Rossellini's quick-fire montage in *Germany Year Zero* (*Germania anno zero*, 1947) which is more akin to the urban velocity featured in a modernist film such as *Berlin: Symphony of a Great City* (*Berlin: die Synfonie der Grosstadt*, Walter Ruttmann, 1927) than to any idea of contemplative slowness – and, in fact, in both films, urban speed culminates in suicide.

These contradictions have, however, not stopped Bazin's diachronic division from continuing to be widely adopted in film scholarship, not least thanks to the endorsement it received from the most influential film philosopher of all time, Gilles Deleuze, who translated the classical-modern binary into 'movement-image' versus 'time-image'. And so it happens that the political trumps of contemporary slow cinema are retroactively explained, yet again, in terms of its modernity, as Matthew Flanagan in his excellent study of slow cinema reiterates:

> Contemporary slow cinema is an eventual descendant of the international modern cinema that emerged in the late 1940s, one that attempted to restore belief in 'the tatters of this world' by creating an aesthetic regime that reflected the post-war struggle to (re)connect with a new reality (Deleuze 2005: 166). This impulse began with post-war Italian neorealism and continued most forcefully in European modernist film of the 1950s and 1960s, and the high modernist, structural and materialist cinema of the 1960s and 1970s. The notion of slowness, in this context, comprises one of the most potent signifiers of the Modern in post-war cinema, and the forms that it has assumed have been diverse and changeable. (2012: 4)

The first question arising from this modern lineage is how it could have sprung to life after a single historical event and continued to evolve through time and space forever invulnerable to the threats from its various adversaries. And how could it reject any links with preceding modernisms, while still calling itself 'modernist', as in the quote above, rather than simply 'modern', as Bazin would have had it? For suffice it to remember city films such as *Nothing but Time* (*Rien que les heures*, Alberto Cavalcanti, 1926), *Metropolis* (Fritz Lang, 1926) or even, ten years later, Chaplin's *Modern Times* (1936), all littered with clocks and other time-related motifs, to realise that the preoccupation with time was not at all a privilege of post-war modernity. The feverish editing together of a fragmented real, as carried out in the urban films of Dziga Vertov and other modernist film-makers, was wholly reflective (and critical) of the vertiginous velocity of an all-engulfing industrialism. More significantly, if technological advancement allowed these film-makers to play at will at the editing table with materials harvested fresh from the city life, this was done in response to preceding traditions relying on time and space uncut, as exemplified by the extraordinary long takes in depth of field found in Yevgenij Bauer's films of the 1910s. Miriam Hansen, in her famous piece 'The Mass Production of the Senses: Classical Cinema as Vernacular Modernism' (2000), alerts us to 'how Russian cinema got from the Old to the New within a rather short span of time; how the sophisticated *mise en scène* cinema of the Czarist era, epitomized by the work of Yevgenij Bauer, was displaced by Soviet montage aesthetics' (2000: 333) – but she then goes on to claim modernity, not to post-war modernism but to the classical Hollywood cinema, given the influence of the latter on the Soviet-era productions!

As well as exemplifying the inflationary and mutually exclusive claims to modernity from competing parties, including from classicism itself (more of which below), Hansen's statement also exposes the major contradiction in visions of post-World War II cinematic modernism, namely that the attachment to phenomenological time and space, as represented by the long-take/long-shot combination, did not wait for the trauma of World War II to be widely practised – and, I should add, it had never been a privilege of European cinema. Mizoguchi is a striking example of someone who, already in 1939, after experimenting with montage of all sorts, decided, from *The Story of the Last Chrysanthemums* onwards, to apply his skills and technical know-how to the procedure he called 'one-scene-one-cut' which would wait more than a decade to be christened by Bazin as *'plan-séquence'* ('sequence-shot', or the long take). His purpose, in that particular film, as explained by his faithful scriptwriter, Yoshikata Yoda, was 'to shoot long takes in depth of field and wide angle in order to bring to life the theatrical space and allow Shotaro Hanayagi [in the protagonist role] to act naturally' (Yoda, 1997: 63). Granted, this procedure had little to do with documenting reality as it happens before the camera, its intention being rather to allow film actors to perform in a continual mode as in theatre, within the walls of a studio, and for this reason might be considered unfitting to models hinging on the neorealist combination of location shooting, non-professional acting and independent production. But then Bazin's view of realism was elastic enough to accommodate theatre and literature, as expressed in his concept of 'impure cinema', which welcomed as 'realistic' films that were not at all subservient to the unpredictable real but, instead, faithful to their theatrical or literary origins.

One could hence conclude that Mizoguchi was practising Bazinian realism long before World War II, and not being the first at that, given the aforementioned example of Yevgenij Bauer. Could it be that montage and the long-take/long-shot combination are both responding to the same phenomena, and are consequently not at all antagonistic but part of a single, overarching, critical assessment of industrial modernity? And could it even be that the preoccupation with time is not a privilege of modern cinema but of cinema in general, cinema itself being a modern medium? I am certainly not the first to formulate these questions which threaten to ruin many a well-constructed fortress in defence of post-World War II cinematic modernity. Tom Gunning, for example, had already raised the alarm in the following terms:

> Is it true that modernity can be related to anything . . . to attractions and narrative, to shocks and flows, to continuity and discontinuity? And isn't this sort of universal reference therefore meaningless? Am I not simply supplying another, only more dangerous, form of the obvious statement that cinema developed in modern times and therefore can be related to modernity – dangerous, because the statement can be applied to any sort of formal device? (Gunning, 2006: 312)

Diagnosing with precision the difficulty, and possible uselessness, of the modern banner, Gunning, nonetheless, defines his own theory of 'cinema of attraction', with regard to early cinema, as a 'claim about modernity', albeit one that will not reduce 'film history and modernity to a night in which all cows appear black' (2006: 312). I believe, however, that the time has come to find a more productive and politically meaningful alternative to such a vague appellation.

Beyond the Eurocentric Modern

As I have stated elsewhere (Nagib, 2014), Bazin's defence of modern realism against what he deemed to be the antirealist modernists was politically motivated. In lieu of an elitist art adept in cinema's pure qualities of speed and montage, Bazin defended an impure cinema able to translate the sophistication of literature and theatre into a language accessible to a wider public, cinema being the mass medium par excellence (Bazin, 1967: 75). A key point thus emerges from this discussion, which is the view of film as the meeting point of all other arts and media. In this, Bazin was in line with the most politicised thinkers of modernity, including Adorno, who predicted that 'film's most promising potential lies in its interaction with other media, themselves merging into film' (1981–2: 201). It was also Adorno who, as Hansen puts it, attributed to cinema a leading role in modern art but only insofar as it rebelled against its own status as art (Hansen, 2012: 218). This sends us back to modernity being an innate attribute of cinema, this time, however, a self-reflexive and self-destructive one, given its technological base. As we know, Benjamin saw with apprehension the fact that cinema was a mechanically reproducible art form that lacked an original, hence the aura of authenticity, because 'its social significance, particularly in its most positive form, is inconceivable without its destructive, cathartic aspect, that is, the liquidation of the traditional value of the cultural heritage' (1999: 215). Adorno, however, saw a way out for cinema's artistic potential by differentiating technology from technique, the latter opening up for individual creativity and driving film away from its medium specificity:

> The most plausible theory of film technique, that which focuses on the movement of objects, is both provocatively denied and yet preserved, in negative form, in the static character of films like Antonioni's *La Notte*. Whatever is 'uncinematic' in this film gives it the power to express, as if with hollow eyes, the emptiness of time. Irrespective of the technological origins of the cinema, the aesthetics of film will do better to base itself on a subjective mode of experience which film resembles and which constitutes its artistic character. (Adorno, 1981–2: 201)

Following the cue of Kracauer's view of movement as the defining element of cinema, Adorno posits 'technique' as the contribution of an individual artist, but one which expresses itself as resistance to the self-destructive speed of modern technology.

Nonetheless, it is still the term 'modern' that continues to be repeatedly resorted to in film scholarship to signify the kind of self-reflexive stasis or 'uncinematic empty time' which Adorno refers to, and is comparable in many ways to Bazin's defence of realism based on time and space uncut and of impure cinema. And it so happens that the world new waves from the 1960s and 1970s, as well as the more recent 'slow cinema', are all usually defined as 'modern' or 'neo-modern' (Orr, 2000) thanks to their recourse to self-reflexive stasis and Brechtian-style anticinematic devices, as epitomised by Godard's use of conflicting media in his films. This raises the question I want to explore further of whether politics could reside not in cinema's ineffable modernity but in modes of resistance to its fundamental property of movement that brings it closer to other arts and media, that is, to non-cinema.

But before I delve into this question through the analysis of two Japanese canonical examples, another issue must be clarified: if modern cinema is the one that rebels, albeit in vain, against the self-destructive modern speed, what would then be classical cinema? How would the conservative adherence to medium specificity in Hollywood classical cinema compare, for example, with the medium-specific adherence to montage on the part of Eisenstein and the historical avant-gardes? Clearly classicism cannot equate with modernity, and yet critics of the highest standards have been twisting and turning their phrases to identify 'modernism' whenever they need to find laudable traits in their favourite classical films. Miriam Hansen highlights the self-reflexive potential of old Hollywood classics – for example, the excessive physicality of the slapstick comedy (2000: 342–3) – to explain how such films could have sparked what she calls 'vernacular modernisms' elsewhere in the world, including the case of Soviet cinema. More recently, Laura Mulvey formulated a similar argument, drawing on the self-reflexive effect of the rear-projection device, which 'smuggles something of modernism' into the 'classical' narrative, as seen in some Hitchcock films (2011: 208).

In her excellent book about the Japanese post-war golden age, Catherine Russell was quick to adopt Hansen's vernacular-modernism theory to justify what she herself defines as the contradictory appellation of 'modern classicism' (2011: xiii), with reference to this canonical output. My question is simply: would there not be a more suitable and accurate conceptual model to address the artistic contribution made by such films? My view is that the application to other cinemas of a model drawn from European history, which is controversial in its own ground, inevitably distorts the history of these cinemas. In the Japanese case, 'modernity' is believed to have been first introduced in the country, coming from the West, during the Meiji Restoration, starting in 1868, a belief embraced, for example, by the acclaimed historian Eric Cazdyn, who states: 'Unlike the West, where capitalism proper is about two hundred years old and the history of film is only half that long, in Japan the two histories share about the same span of time – one hundred years (2002: 2). This argument of the belated entrance of Japan into modernity is a favourite among writers to explain the aesthetic features of Japanese cinema as a whole. However, the view that Japan had no experience of capitalism prior to the Meiji era is a gross exaggeration, as it is to believe that it had remained immune to modernity until then. Not only did Japan have in its history economic structures based on accumulation of wealth that then led to an easy adaptation to fully fledged capitalism, but it is also common knowledge that many so-called modern procedures in art were first developed there or in neighbouring Asian countries. It is no novelty that Brecht's concepts of alienation effects were drawn from Japanese and Chinese theatre techniques. Brecht used the famous expression *Verfremdungseffekt* for the first time with reference to the Chinese actor Mei Lan-fang and his theatre company when they performed in Moscow in 1935 (Willett in Brecht 1964: 99n). In his article 'Alienation Effects in Chinese Acting', Brecht lists a series of devices he deems 'antiillusionistic' in the Chinese theatre, all of which he would later employ in his own epic theatre, including the rejection of realistic mimesis, the use of symbols, the actors' emotional control, the absence of a fourth wall and the construction of the sets before the eyes of the audience (Brecht, 1964: 91 ff.).

All these devices can be identified in the two cases I will analyse below to demonstrate that the best 'classical films', even when they adhered to generic formulas, were in constant dialogue with 'uncinematic' intermedial devices aimed at producing stoppages in time, self-reflexivity and medium awareness, all of which, since the Frankfurt School, Bazin and Deleuze, have been considered the quintessence of modern cinema. It is for no other reason that filmmaker Yoshishige Yoshida referred to Ozu's work as 'anti-cinema' in the very title of his book on the film-maker (2003) as, in his view, Ozu contravened not Hollywood's conventional grammar but all medium-specific dramatic rules. I hold the view that the best films ever made in the world are 'uncinematic' in one way or another, and more often than not they are so through the use of intermedial devices, as Bazin had brilliantly intuited in his Impure Cinema article. There is no better proof of this than in Japanese canonical cinema, where intermediality is widespread, and I will start precisely with Ozu to illustrate my point.

IMPURE CINEMA AS POLITICAL CINEMA

Floating Weeds (1959), a film that Ozu exceptionally shot at Daiei rather than at his home studio, Shochiku, is a remake of an earlier film, *A Story of Floating Weeds* (1934), both belonging to the genre *geidomono*. As Tadao Sato explains, '*geidomono* are films where the protagonist, male or female, is a practitioner of one of the traditional Japanese arts such as kabuki, puppet theatre (*bunraku*), or traditional dance' (2008: 77). It was particularly resorted to in the late 1930s as an alternative to governmental demands for propaganda films. The 1959 film is self-reflexive already from the fact that it is self-citation but all the rest also seems to be in compliance with Brecht's precepts of alienation effects. Needless to say, Ozu was not the least worried about Brecht but simply following his own kind of 'classical modernism' which included any number of 'uncinematic' devices. For example, what Kracauer considered the basic subjective movement in cinema is consistently disregarded in that the camera, as typical in Ozu, remains mostly static. Rather than a backward attachment to silent-film procedures, this represents an *evolution* in Ozu's career in that camera movements were relatively common in his silent films, becoming increasingly rare and almost non-existent in his latter films (Richie, 1974: 105 ff.). In contrast to silent-cinema practices, however, objects placed in front of the camera, causing what Kracauer called objective motion, also remain mostly static in the form of characters seated and conversing with each other in frozen attitudes, in the famous Ozu-style framing of parallel figures and shot/reverse-shot montage. The second source of subjective movement, in Kracauer's definition, is the only one permanently at work, namely editing, enabling the film to take the viewer across different places and times. Through the negation of two key cinematic movements, the sense of stasis is thus conveyed, despite the numerous incidents in the film – and without the slightest recourse to the long take.

This is compounded by disruptive devices which are constantly at work to bring any action back to a standstill, including actors with an outspoken wooden performance, such as the heart-throb Hiroshi Kawaguchi, in the role of Kiyoshi, whose casting Richie attributes to his being 'the son of one of the most important writer-producers at Daiei' (2004) but there is no denying

Ozu's own delight in this particular feature. There is, however, the odd movement, mostly to do with theatrical performances which, as in a musical, disrupt the narrative thread to draw the viewer's attention to the artificiality of the story and the reality of the medium. By embracing theatre as its subject matter, the film strays away from medium specificity but it also derides theatre itself by focusing on a kind of popular and lower form of kabuki, a travelling theatre called *taishu engeki* (Russell, 2011: 29). This in turn, through Ozu's lens, contravenes kabuki's most treasured tradition of the *onnagata,* as well as Japanese cinema's female star system, by showing at a certain point Japan's legendary actress Machiko Kyo, in the role of actress Sumiko, impersonating a male warrior.

All too often I have read that Ozu's 'curtain shots' or 'pillow shots' are randomly chosen images aimed at producing ellipses of time and space. For Deleuze (2005: 13 ff.), for example, they are pure optical and sound images. Such assessments, however, overlook their crucial narrative role which often includes self-commentary and reflexivity. Suffice it to look at the staging of a second theatrical scene in *Floating Weeds,* a dance piece by the younger

Figure 1.1 Transitional shots in *Floating Weeds* (1959) are in tune with Brecht's recommendations that lighting and other theatre equipment should remain visible to the audiences.

actress, Kayo, played by the dazzling Ayako Wakao, accompanied by a child apprentice. Kabuki is rife with children's roles, as 'it is in these that the actor of the future first tests his mettle' (Scott, 1999: 166). Children also proliferate in Ozu's films, where they add a comic note, and the child actor in this scene is no exception. The series of transitional shots, or curtain shots, that precede the dance scene is carefully chosen in order to radically inflect the narrative, as they show empty spaces and then the makeshift lighting of the venue, indicating the general poverty of the theatre and the calamitous low attendance at the show (Figure 1.1). These shots are entirely in tune with Brecht's recommendations for his own epic theatre that lighting and other theatre equipment should remain visible to the audiences, thus causing the effect of double reflexivity: for the audience within and outside the film. The dance then presented is all about breaking the fourth wall and poking fun at the performance itself, with the child actor, expected to mime perfectly the moves of the main dancer, constantly interrupting his performance, even jumping down the stage to collect small money packs thrown at them by the audience, then bowing reverentially in gratitude, and calling the spectators' attention to the reality of the actor in the play within the story (Figure 1.2).

Figure 1.2   In *Floating Weeds*, the child performer calls the spectators' attention to the reality of the actor in the play within the film.

Another disruptive procedure relates to the reversal of the voyeuristic position. Sumiko becomes suspicious of Komajuro, her lover as well as her boss, who had brought his troupe to the small seaside village with the secret intention of visiting his old lover, Oyoshi (played by Ozu's favourite Haruko Sugimura) and son, Kiyoshi. Sumiko then asks her actor colleagues to help her identify Oyoshi, resulting in a collective spying on the audience by the actors from the backstage through the cracks of the curtain, turning the theatre audience into spectacle, and making the film spectators aware of their own voyeurism, a role now usurped by the objects of their gaze (Figure 1.3). In addition, while we are given abundant insight into the actors preparing for the stage, there is precious little in terms of their actual acting, least of all from Komajuro, the big star, whose acting is only once hinted at through the off-screen sound of his recitation (Figure 1.4). The film is, moreover, replete with devices meant to highlight duration and the passing of time, despite the regular cuts, as the theatre troupe idles in utter boredom and on empty stomachs in the small village only to please the troupe's leader.

It is the goings-on on the backstage and surroundings of the theatre venue, endlessly delaying, and finally denying, the culmination of their preparations, which account for the actual spectacle taking place in ordinary life. Despite his endearing attachment to his past lover and son, Komajuro's leadership over his troupe is enforced through choleric outbursts and spanking of his actresses when they act against his will, with unusual physicality for an Ozu film. These actions are all the more realistic for stemming from a *mise en scène* entirely

Figure 1.3 In *Floating Weeds*, collective spying on the audience by the actors from backstage through the cracks of the curtain turns the theatre audience into spectacle.

Figure 1.4   In *Floating Weeds*, the lead actor, Komajuro, is shown at length as he prepares for the stage but we never see his actual performance.

aware of its artifice and for this reason all the more effective in the criticism they level against the hierarchical system within both theatrical and familial traditions in Japan. Whether such a film should be called 'slow' or 'modern' is, in my view, irrelevant, as its politics relies much more on the relentless querying of the spectator's role within and outside the film through the revelation of the reality of both the theatre and the film mediums, creating Bazin's much cherished space for ambiguity of expression and spectatorial participation.

Now look at this other example, extracted from another *geidomono*, *The Story of the Last Chrysanthemums* (1939), a theatre-themed story chosen by Mizoguchi to eschew the pressure he was under of making propaganda films in an increasingly militarised Japan. In stylistic and technical terms, this film stands in direct opposition to Ozu's *Floating Weeds*, as it is a dazzling display of the long take and the long shot that none of Bazin's favourite realist film-makers had ever achieved, with perhaps the exception of Orson Welles. Integrity of time and space, the two preconditions for the Bazinian modern realism, is the rule in a film which is normally considered the quintessence of Japanese classicism. The film also offers fertile ground for the discussion of technique versus technology, between the old and the new, through an entirely self-reflexive questioning of styles of performance for film, for theatre and for both combined. More importantly, its political impact derives entirely from the suspicion brought upon medium specificity, along the lines of Bazin's insight into impure cinema as the locale of a productive crisis where established genres dissolve into self-reflexivity, ambiguity of expression and the revelation of the reality of the medium, all of which, I argue, are more reliable indicators of a film's political programme than modernity or historical teleology.

The Story of the Last Chrysanthemums is the adaptation of the novel of the same title, a fictionalised biopic of Onoe Kikunosuke II, the actor and stepson of one of kabuki's most famous actors in his time, Onoe Kikugoro V, situating the film within the *geidomono* genre and offering Mizoguchi an opportunity to exercise his in-depth knowledge of Japanese traditional arts. He even contemplated the possibility of casting the legendary actor Kikugoro VI, the legitimate son of Kikugoro V, to play the role of his father in the film, which, in the end, never happened. In an interview, Mizoguchi relates an interesting story about a meeting with Kikugoro VI:

> I went to the kabuki . . . and I met him [Kikugoro] in the backstage. 'Today I will perform in a cinematic way, pay close attention', he told me. Seen from the audience, his performance appeared indeed different from usual, it was, so to say, more realistic, with very natural and essential movements. (cited in Aprà, Magrelli and Pistagnesi, 1980: 143)

Mizoguchi goes on to say that he was not entirely convinced by the actor's delivery on that day owing to the contrast it produced with the rest of the cast who continued to act in the traditional kabuki fashion. This episode is certainly the inspiration for the astonishing opening of *The Story of the Last Chrysanthemums*, showing precisely a moment of 'bad acting' by the young Kikunosuke and performed by the famous *shinpa* and film actor Shotaro Hanayagi. The play in question is *Ghost Story of Yotsuya*, a piece full of special effects, including the trick called *toitagaeshi*, through which actors insert their faces into holes on dummies, in this case, the ghosts of the murdered lovers Oiwa and Kohei (Kirihara, 1992: 151). The ghosts are uncovered by the great kabuki star, Kikugoro V, in the role of a samurai, who then confronts his stepson, Kikunosuke, onstage, in an exquisitely choreographed fight. Sato reminds us that when Mizoguchi started in the silent film era, using *shinpa* actors in the Nikatsu Mukojima Film Studio, they were still using the *onnagata*, or female impersonators; however, no close-up shots could be taken because, for example, their Adam's apples would show up (2008: 21). In this scene, however, Hanayagi does deserve some of the rare medium close-ups of the film, as if Mizoguchi wanted to make two statements: 1. this is cinema; 2. this is good film acting but bad acting for traditional kabuki (Figure 1.5). As

Figure 1.5   Kikunosuke's first theatrical apparition in *The Story of the Last Chrysanthemums* (1939): good film acting but bad acting for traditional kabuki.

a result, we, the spectators, feel that the actor's performance is excellent and are puzzled to see it repeatedly condemned within the plot, first by his irate stepfather, then by everybody else, as inadequate. Ambiguity of expression and consequently spectatorial participation are thus enabled, positing the film spectator as the unlikely authority to judge an actor's performance in two different mediums.

Kikunosuke is no less puzzled about the quality of his acting than the film spectator, as a network of secrecy and pretence surrounds his presence. This is conveyed through an abundant recourse to kabuki props, including platforms, fences, sliding doors and screens. One or more of those props are always placed between Kikunosuke and those who are secretly slighting his acting, in a way that closely resembles the workings of the *odogu* (props) in kabuki. The interesting effect of *odogu*, as described by Scott, is that it interferes not only with space construction but also with time: '*Kido* [a particular arrangement of *odogu*] allows the audience to watch the actions of different people and even the workings of their minds simultaneously. It overcomes time and dimension and enables he onlooker to see through walls' (199: pp. 153–4).

This device is used by Mizoguchi to introduce a kind of cinematic movement Kracauer had not predicted, consisting of space-time compression within the shot and, in so doing, obtaining one of the most accomplished theatrical *mise en scène* ever applied to film – while also shattering the premise that the long take necessarily slows down the narrative pace. Here is an example. After noticing the disguised mockery behind his back on the part of his theatre colleagues and adulating geishas, Kikunosuke returns home in the small hours to find his little brother's wet nurse, Otoko, on the pavement trying to get the baby back to sleep. A long take of five minutes starts by focusing on Otoku on the pavement as Kikunosuke appears and promptly dismisses his rickshaw to walk along with her the rest of the way. As they walk, Otoku tells Kikunosuke for the first time with all honesty that his acting is bad, her daringness making room for a slow kind of ballet in which the two characters swap places ahead of each other as they walk, Kikunosuke occasionally lowering his head in painful realisation of the truth about his acting, and Otoku bowing politely but unrepentantly. Rarely has the fair division of power as the basis for genuine love been so elegantly and powerfully displayed as in this scene where the lack of cuts allows the female and male actors alternately to lead the camera forward in a smooth tracking shot. During their walk, a series of unlikely events takes place, such as the passing of a pedlar selling wind chimes, one of which Kikunosuke buys to distract the baby. As Otoku has remarked on it being two in the morning, one wonders how a pedlar could be passing by, and he is not the only unlikely creature around: shouts and clapping noises, apparently stemming from other street vendors, are heard, and another street seller rushes past the couple with his trolley, amid occasional women of the night. This unusual nocturnal crowd serves as information to the viewer of the general demographics in the area at all times but one which can be conveyed only through disregard of chronology and spatial coherence within the shot.

Thinking along the lines of kabuki, however, clarifies this condensation as analogous to the workings of the *odogu*, and also the principle of the sound design. There is hardly any extradiegetic music in this film but there is a constant diegetic soundscape, constructed with hidden sources, aimed at creating the atmosphere of street noises according to the kabuki convention, including the sound of the *hyoshigi*, consisting of two quadrangular sticks of hardwood clapped together. In this particular scene, we can hear the *hyoshigi*, combined with the shouts of the vendors and other noises which are essential in kabuki plays to convey the atmosphere of the city (Scott, 1993: pp. 73 ff.). Most crucially, kabuki explains the camera position below the pavement which fails to identify with any plausible point of view of an observer within the scene but would make perfect sense as the point of view of a kabuki play spectator, sitting below the stage. Estrangement is thus elicited at every level to bring home to the film viewer the specificities of both the film and the theatre media, as they produce clash and creative crisis at the crossroads of tradition and technology.

Figures 1.6 and 1.7   In *The Story of the Last Chrysanthemums*, there is a profusion of *odogu*-style props, including barred doors and screens.

As a result of his romance with Otoku, which is forbidden because of the class and hierarchical gulfs between them, Kikunosuke is expelled from his stepfather's house. He leaves for Osaka and leads a life of utter poverty as a lowly actor, alongside a consumptive Otoku. Towards the end of the film, however, Kikunosuke makes a triumphant return to the kabuki house in Tokyo, having become an accomplished actor. The film then gives us a long kabuki scene, showing him in the famous female role of Sumizome through a series of long- and middle-range shots, allowing the viewer scant access to the actor's facial features and actual performance, thanks to the profuse use of *odogu* props, including screens, barred banisters and other obstacles (Figures 1.6 and 1.7). In fact, in this most edited section of the film, there seems to be a frantic competition for vantage points to observe the actor's performance on the part of Kikunosuke's family members and helpers from various points in the backstage and, more crucially, of Otoku who, at a certain point, is crouching in a corner of the backstage but entirely visible behind her performing lover (Figure 1.8). Despite this hide-and-seek play with the camera, the sense of a real kabuki theatre is imparted in quasi-documentary

Figure 1.8   There is a frantic competition for vantage points to observe Kikunosuke's performance in the role of Sumizome, in *The Story of the Last Chrysanthemums*. Otoku is seen crouching in a corner of the backstage behind her performing lover.

Figure 1.9 In *The Story of the Last Chrisanthemums*, theatre is placed within its social context, that is, its audience, without which it cannot exist.

long shots of the packed auditorium. Once justified, kabuki's artificial acting becomes cinema but only by also becoming uncinematic. At the same time, cinema's ability to produce scale reversal and the close-up, the main pillar of the star system, is rejected, denying the actor the privilege of individual fame while placing theatre within its social context, that is, its audience, without which it cannot exist (Figure 1.9). In becoming theatre, that is, non-cinema, film becomes political and exuberantly alive amid a cheering audience within which the actor submerges, echoing that public Bazin so cherished and found inseparable from any understanding of the film medium.

Would a film such as this qualify as classical or modern, fast or slow? Its beauty, and political power, lie precisely in highlighting the futility of all these categories, together with cinema's (and theatre's) unattainable pursuit of the perfect performance.

Concluding Remarks

German film-maker and philosopher Alexander Kluge asserts that 'cinema has existed for over ten thousand years in the minds of human beings' in the form of 'associative currents, daydreams, sensual experiences and streams of consciousness. The technical discovery only made it reproducible' (1975: 208). I would like to conclude by suggesting, along these lines, that chronological classicism and evolutionary modernity, if they may apply to the technology of late capitalism, are entirely inadequate to explain the creative power lying in the human mind across history and geography. Neither can the quarrel between slow and fast cinema, as the most recent expression of the classical-modern debate, adequately account for cinema's aesthetic and political values. These lie much more in an open understanding of cinema which includes its own negation through the recourse to other arts and media, entailing self-reflexive stasis, ambiguity of expression and the revelation of the reality of the film medium which is no other than that of life itself.

BIBLIOGRAPHY

Adorno, Theodor W. (1981–2), 'Transparencies on Film', in *New German Critique*, n. 24/25, autumn–winter, pp. 199–205.
Aprà, Adriano, Enrico Magrelli and Patrizia Pistagnesi (1980), *Il cinema di Kenji Mizoguchi* (La Biennalle, Mostra internazionale del cinema, Venice: Edizioni RAI).
Bazin, André (1967), 'In Defense of Mixed Cinema', in *What Is Cinema?*, vol. 1, edited and translated by Hugh Gray (Berkeley, Los Angeles and London: University of California Press), pp. 53–75.
Bazin, André (1967), 'The Evolution of the Language of Cinema', in *What Is Cinema?*, vol. 1, edited and translated by Hugh Gray (Berkeley, Los Angeles and London: University of California Press), pp. 23–40.
Bazin, André (2005), 'La Terra Trema', in *What Is Cinema?*, vol. 2, essays selected and translated by Hugh Gray (Berkeley, Los Angeles and London: University of California Press), pp. 41–6.
Benjamin, Walter (1999), *Illuminations*, edited and with an Introduction by Hannah Arendt, translated by Harry Zorn (London: Pimlico).
Brecht, Bertolt (1964), *Brecht on Theatre: The Development of an Aesthetic*, edited and translated by John Willett (London: Methuen).
Cazdyn, Eric (2002), *The Flash of Capital: Film and Geopolitics in Japan* (Durham, NC and London: Duke University Press).
Deleuze, Gilles (2005), *Cinema 2: Time-Image* (New York and London: Continuum).
de Luca, Tiago (2011), 'Realism of the Senses: A Tendency in Contemporary World Cinema', in Lúcia Nagib, Chris Perriam and Rajinder Dudrah (eds), *Theorizing World Cinema* (London and New York: I. B. Tauris), pp. 183–206.
Flanagan, Matthew (2012), *'Slow Cinema': Temporality and Style in Contemporary Art and Experimental Film*, unpublished PhD thesis.
Godard, Jean-Luc (1968), 'Mizoguchi fut le plus grand cinéaste japonais. La Cinemathèque lui rend hommage après sa mort', in *Jean-Luc Godard par Jean Luc Godard* (Paris: Cahiers du Cinéma/Belfond).
Gunning, Tom (2006), 'Modernity and Cinema: A Culture of Shocks and Flows', in Murray Pomerance (ed.), *Cinema and Modernity* (New Brunswick, NJ and London: Rutgers University Press), pp. 297–315.
Hansen, Miriam B. (2000), 'The mass production of senses: classical cinema as vernacular modernism', in Christine Gledhill and Linda Williams (eds), *Reinventing Film Studies* (London: Arnold), pp. 332–50.

Hansen, Miriam Bratu (2012), *Cinema and Experience: Siegfried Kracauer, Walter Benjamin, and Theodor W. Adorno* (Berkeley, Los Angeles and London: University of California Press).

Kirihara, Donald (1992), *Patterns of Time: Mizoguchi and the 1930s* (Madison, WI: University of Wisconsin Press).

Kluge, Alexander (1975), 'Kommentare zum antagonistischen Realismusbegriff', in *Gelegenheitsarbeit einer Sklavin: Zur realistischen Methode* (Frankfurt am Main: Surhkamp).

Kracauer, Siegfried (1997), *Theory of Film: The Redemption of Physical Reality* (Princeton, NJ: Princeton University Press).

Lim, Song Hwee (2014), *Tsai Ming-Liang and a Cinema of Slowness* (Honolulu, HI: University of Hawai'i Press).

Mulvey, Laura (2011), 'Rear-Projection and the Paradoxes of Hollywood Realism', in Lúcia Nagib, Chris Perriam and Rajinder Dudrah (eds), *Theorizing World Cinema* (London and New York: I. B. Tauris), pp. 207–19.

Nagib, Lúcia (2014), 'The Politics of Impurity', in Lúcia Nagib and Anne Jerslev (eds), *Impure Cinema: Intermedial and Intercultural Approaches to Film* (London and New York: I. B. Tauris), pp. 21–40.

Orr, John (2000), 'Introduction', in John Orr and Olga Taxidou (eds), *Post-war Cinema and Modernity: A Film Reader* (Edinburgh: Edinburgh University Press).

Richie, Donald (1974), *Ozu* (Berkeley, Los Angeles and London: University of California Press).

Richie, Donald (2004), 'Stories of Floating Weeds', article in the brochure accompanying the DVD set of *A Story of Floating Weeds* and *Floating Weeds*, The Criterion Collection.

Rivette, Jacques (1958), 'Mizoguchi vu d'ici', *Cahiers du Cinéma*, 81, March 1958.

Rohmer, Eric (1957), 'Universalité du génie', *Cahiers du Cinéma*, 73, July 1957.

Rosenbaum, Jonathan (2000), 'Is Ozu Slow?', *Senses of Cinema*, 4, http://sensesofcinema.com/2000/feature-articles/ozu-2/ [accessed 23 January 2015].

Russell, Catherine (2011), *Classical Japanese Cinema Revisited* (New York and London: Continuum).

Sato, Tadao (2008), *Kenji Mizoguchi and the Art of Japanese Cinema*, edited by Aruna Vasudev and Latika Padgaonkar, translated by Brij Tankha (Oxford and New York: Berg).

Scott, A. C., *The Kabuki Theatre of Japan* (Mineola, NY: Dover Publications).

Yoda, Yoshikata (1997), *Souvenirs de Kenji Mizoguchi* (Paris : Cahiers du Cinéma).

Yoshida, Yoshishige (2003), *Ozu's Anti-cinema*, tranlated by Daisuke Miyao and Kyoko Hirano (Ann Arbor, MI: University of Michigan Press).

2. THE SLOW PULSE OF THE ERA: CARL TH. DREYER'S FILM STYLE

C. Claire Thomson

INTRODUCTION

The very last shot of Carl Th. Dreyer's very last film, *Gertrud* (1964), devotes forty-five seconds to the contemplation of a panelled door behind which the eponymous heroine has retreated with a wave to her erstwhile lover. The camera creeps backwards to establish Dreyer's valedictory tableau on which it lingers, immobile, for almost thirty seconds: the door and a small wooden stool beside it. The composition is of such inert, grey geometry that, in its closing moments, this film resembles nothing so much as a Vilhelm Hammershøi painting, investing empty domestic space with the presences that have passed through its doors and hallways. If, in this shot, the cinematic image fleetingly achieves the condition of painting, it is the culmination of a directorial career predicated on the productive tension between movement and stillness, sound and silence, rhythm and slowness.

At the end of *Gertrud*, where the image itself slows into calm equilibrium, we witness the end point of an entropic career. As Dreyer's film style slowed, so, too, did his rate of production. The intervals between his last four major films – the productions that write Dreyer into slow cinema's prehistory – are measured in decades, not years: *Vampyr* (1932), *Vredens Dag* (*Day of Wrath*, 1943), *Ordet* (*The Word*, 1955), *Gertrud* (1964).[1] Studios were reluctant to engage a director who made such difficult films so inefficiently or, rather, made such slow films so slowly. The fallow periods between feature films, however, obliged Dreyer to undertake other kinds of work. In addition to journalism, he took on commissions to make public information films sponsored by the Danish Government Film Committee (Ministeriernes Filmudvalg).[2] As a result, this period in Dreyer's career furnishes us not only with written accounts of the motivations and strategies underlying the style of his later films but also with a handful of short films in which he was able to experiment with key elements of his style.

This chapter centres on Dreyer's writings and short-film output of the 1940s in an attempt to pry his better-known works away from the ossified premises upon which they tend to be 'offhandedly' appropriated as a 'convenient point of reference' for slow cinema (Flanagan, 2012: 6). In what follows, a selective overview of extant critical approaches to Dreyer's style sketches out how posterity has canonised his *oeuvre* as one of singular slowness, and how these readings chime with more recent attempts to map slow cinema as a concept. The chapter then engages in more detail with Dreyer's own defence of what he prefers to call the 'rhythm' of his films. The chapter concludes with a reading of one of Dreyer's most popular films in its day, the public information short, *De naaede Færgen* (*They Caught the Ferry*, 1948). This commission required Dreyer to put his grasp of cinematic rhythm to work in the service of depicting terrifying speed, compressed into the space of just eleven minutes. The shortness of Dreyer's short film about speeding invites a more nuanced perspective on the slowness of his slow cinema.

Dreyer's Slowness

Solely on the basis of his reputation for the long take, Carl Th. Dreyer is assured a place in what is still a 'makeshift canon' of slow cinema (Flanagan, 2012: 6). At a modest forty-five seconds, the final shot of *Gertrud* is a mere half of the average shot length (ASL) of that film, and, indeed, shorter than the one-minute ASL of its predecessor, *Ordet* (Bordwell, 1981: 64). Bordwell argues that in *Ordet*, Dreyer's long take has a metafilmic function: 'to foreground the shot itself as a component of cinematic perception' (151). Though ASL can be rather a blunt tool (Flanagan, 2012: 10), it can be useful in quantitatively corroborating an instinctive impression that a given Dreyer film is 'slower' than the historically or culturally specific norms of editing against which it is measured. Beyond the long take, however, a number of recurring themes in older Dreyer scholarship are echoed by recent critical discussions on slow cinema. In what follows, selected classic and newer work on Dreyer is brought into conversation with commentary on slow cinema, organised around three of the broad traits which Flanagan (2012: 4, 100) sees as predicated on slow cinema's 'undramaticness': dedramatised narrative form; duration; and everydayness.

Slow cinema's innovations in narrative form are not confined to the length of takes and the speed of editing. For Flanagan (2012: 6, 99 ff.), narrative in slow cinema is 'undramatic' or even absent. Tiago de Luca discusses the historical reception and politics of the 'dedramatization' of narrative, concluding that, in contemporary slow cinemas, 'the sequence shot tends to undermine dramatic momentum through a sustained focus on meticulously composed images evacuated of narrative information, which enhances, and aestheticizes, the materiality of the cinematic event' (de Luca, 2014: 21). In resisting conventions of narrative chronology, such films also disrupt causality, ultimately unsettling the very notion of the 'event'. A comparable disruption of the relations between narrative form and event in Dreyer's case is central to David Bordwell's seminal 1981 work, *The Films of Carl-Theodor Dreyer*. From *Vredens Dag* onwards, Bordwell identifies a shift from the temporal and spatial *'discontinuity'* of *La Passion de Jeanne d'Arc* (1928) and *Vampyr* towards a *'very slow continuity'* (Bordwell, 1981: 143, emphasis in original) that extends the duration of events and the intervals between them (140–3). A decade later, in *Ordet,* the cumulative effect of *mise en scène*, actor movements, and the long take would etiolate the distinction between narrative and non-narrative elements (150–64). Movement thus becomes as important as event; this chimes with Dreyer's defence of the rhythms of his films, as we shall discover. Bordwell sees in *Gertrud* the intensification and culmination of this elevation of form over dramatic content: '[n]arrative events – dialogue, gesture, character confrontations – become swallowed up in cinematic structures, like pennies tossed into a canyon' (176).

That canyon is time, be it the classical unity of *Ordet* or *Gertrud*'s quiet endurance of lived time. An interest in duration is another point of convergence of Dreyer and slow cinema, where duration is one means to 'fill the void' left by an etiolation of drama (Flanagan, 2012: 100). Dreyer does explore duration through contemplative, static, long takes, as in *Gertrud*'s final shot. But a more distinctively Dreyerian strategy is to articulate duration by effacing space: panning slowly over a group of faces or around a room, for example, or substituting slow, gliding pans for the more conventional shot–reverse shot. One prominent reading of the complexity of space–time and duration in Dreyer comes from Gilles Deleuze. Dreyer's presence in Deleuze's work spans both *Cinema 1* and *Cinema 2*; Deleuze's discussion of Dreyer seeds the time–image in the first volume, and vice versa. Of the oft-remarked lack of depth and perspective in Dreyer's compositions, Deleuze comments that his medium and full shots function analogously to close-ups by subsuming space in time:

> By suppressing 'atmospheric' perspective Dreyer produces the triumph of a properly temporal or even spiritual perspective. Flattening the third dimension, he puts two-dimensional space into immediate relation with the affect, with a fourth and fifth dimension, Time and Spirit. (Deleuze, 1986: 107)

Dreyer thus anticipates the post-war regime of the time–image. A recurring and rich temporal trope in this respect is the moment of death as durational. The moment of death is torturously extended through cross-cutting in *Joan of Arc*; a slow-dawning revelation as in *Mikäel* (1924); a reversible transition between stillness and movement as in *Ordet*; inevitable, imminent but indefinitely suspended for Anne at the end of *Vredens Dag*; or anticipated by Gertrud, quietly thinking of her headstone, behind her closed door.

While Deleuze's primary fascination is time, his insistence on 'Spirit' echoes a persistent strand of Dreyer criticism: the metaphysical dimension of his films. If contemporary slow films by directors such as Tsai Ming-liang, Apichatpong Weerasethakul or Lisandro Alonso,[3] fill the narrative void with everyday practices such as eating, sleeping, washing, or even masturbating, such images would be anathema to critics and fans swooning over the spiritual endeavours of Dreyer's Joan of Arc or Johannes Borgen. Critics' emphasis on the transcendent has often played down Dreyer's attentiveness to the fleshliness of his filmic bodies, though Deleuze is not guilty here: his concept of the 'affection–image' is grounded in Dreyer's treatment of faces in *Jeanne d'Arc* (Deleuze, 1986: 106–8). An influential voice regarding Dreyer's 'transcendental style' is Paul Schrader who sees *Ordet* as Dreyer's most thoroughgoing example of the transcendental film-making more consistently practised by Bresson and Ozu (Schrader, 1988: 10, 132). Transcendental style shows a tendency towards stasis, reducing film narrative to repeatable ritual devoid of human 'culture or personality' (11). For Schrader, however, Dreyer always fails to achieve stasis, ultimately asserting the social and material reality of the body and the cultural context (134–6). For example, when Inger is raised from the dead at the end of *Ordet*, the viewer expects the transcendent but, instead, is presented with the immanent (137). Or, as de Luca writes, Dreyer 'foreground[s] the flesh as the vehicle for a spiritual dimension' (2014: 46). As we shall see later, bodies are crucial in the construction of Dreyer's filmic rhythm: walking and talking are quotidian acts, regarded by critics in Dreyer's day as banal and tedious.

Another dimension of everydayness in Dreyer's films is set design. His holistic approach to psychological realism is well documented: sets were furnished with authentic fittings sourced from the appropriate locus. He would remove the non-essential, leaving the actors to inhabit a space invested with the essence of an authentic environment. Mark Sandberg has studied Dreyer's occasional use of the found set, seeing this as the logical culmination of a consistent approach to set design which is more about 'mise-en-milieu' than *mise en scène*:

> The best way to characterise Dreyer's use of the film set is to call it an ongoing ontological experiment, the goal of which was to explore the question of performative attachment: under what conditions might an

actor be said to truly inhabit a space? What qualities of location, prop, and set design lead to that result? (Sandberg, 2006: 24)

Such attention to set design seems paradoxical in the light of Dreyer's flattening of three-dimensional space. The film set is for inhabitation by the actors, however, not apprehension by the audience. This strategy results in two affinities between Dreyer's filmic milieux and the everydayness with which slow cinema fills its dramatic voids. First, while Dreyer's long takes may not have the primary goal of lingering in a quasi-documentary fashion on realistic environmental details, what they capture is the actor subsisting in authentically lived, quotidian space. Second, the careful sourcing of authentic artefacts for Dreyer's sets implies a charged relationship between actors and the objects around them. Occasionally, artefacts transcend their status as props through tactile appropriation by actors. For example, the candlesticks, carried back and forth to the windowsill by Inger and Johannes in *Ordet*, are everyday objects essential to the creation of an empty moment – albeit one laden with religious symbolism – where nothing happens except slow transportation of candles across a room. Carney (1989: 235–8) connects the cinematography here to Inger's maternal, corporeal grace as she moves the candlesticks, makes coffee, provides solace. Granted, this is not the sense of banal everydayness produced in slow cinema by, say, excessive focus on bodily functions, or close examination of household paraphernalia. Nevertheless, Dreyer's commitment to authenticity in his *mise en milieu* invests his work with the 'materialist impetus' which de Luca (2014: 12) sees as fundamental to slow cinema's renegotiation of realism.

There are dangers inherent in identifying affinities between Dreyer and contemporary slow cinema. One is the attribution of direct influence where none may exist, though this concern is pre-empted by Carlos Reygadas's flagrant claim of filiation in the form of his reappropriation of *Ordet*'s miracle in *Stellet Licht* (*Silent Light*, 2007). Another danger is the post hoc assimilation of the strangeness of the older films judged by modern standards of the radical. Conversely, we can lose sight of the innovativeness of new works by trying to pin down their canonical inspirations. Bordwell makes the important point that Dreyer's late films seem less radical in their slowness to post-1960s audiences. *Vredens Dag*, for example, though 'readily watchable' today, was widely regarded in the 1940s as 'intolerable' in its slowness (Bordwell, 1981: 140); *Ordet*'s long takes were 'extraordinary stylistic devices' even in the 1950s (151). If the trajectory of Dreyer's artistic development is narrated here by Bordwell as entropic, his inscription into the historiography of the art film is teleological: Dreyer's late films are constructed as ahead of their time, 'presag[ing] the tempo of the 1960s "art film"' (140). Conversely, in 1943, *Vredens Dag* was slated as a relic of the cinematographic past, prompting Dreyer to pen a defence of his style, to which we now turn.

DREYER'S RHYTHM

Contemporary Danish critics concurred that *Vredens Dag* was an unsuccessful gamble. Dreyer had not made a feature since *Vampyr* in 1932, and this new film did not, as anticipated, reinvigorate Danish cinema. One reviewer described the film as lifeless, monotonous and exhausting, the actors smothered by the tendency to dedramatise even the violent events (Kragh-Jacobsen, 1943). For another, Dreyer's genius patently belonged to an earlier era; the film's clumsy, unrealistic dialogue and slow rhythms would lead future generations to date the film to the transition period between silent and sound film (Gtz, 1943). Unwittingly, Gtz's account of the film's rhythmic anachronisms dissects how Dreyer's style foreshadows that of today's slow cinema generation: 'But the film mostly consists of long pauses, panning over details, background noise and the ticking of clocks. Close-ups of corn and tree-tops, doors opening and closing, and everyone constantly wishing each other goodnight' (Gtz, 1943).

Within a fortnight of the premiere, Dreyer had prepared a response to the critique that his film was not of its time. He delivered a speech at the Copenhagen Students' Union on 1 December and the text was printed in the newspaper *Politiken*, the next day with the title 'Lidt om Filmstil' ('A Little on Film Style'). This substantial piece was later published in the anthology of Dreyer's writings on film, *Om Filmen*, and it constitutes one of the most comprehensive accounts of Dreyer's cinematic strategies in his own words.[4] The essay justifies, to borrow slow cinema terminology, the film's undramaticness and everydayness in terms of psychological realism: 'And isn't it true that the great dramas play out quietly? People hide their feelings and avoid showing on their faces the storms raging inside them' (Dreyer, 1959: 65).

A crucial passage in 'A Little on Film Style' explicitly tackles the issue of slowness, responding to criticism that the 'rhythm' of *Vredens Dag* was 'too heavy, too slow'. Fast rhythm can work well if justified by the action, concedes Dreyer. But rhythm for rhythm's sake often conceals an emptiness, a throwback to the silent era, when actors and images 'flew' across the screen (64). He thus conceives of rhythm as obtaining both within and between shots but expands the notion to bodies on screen. Dreyer explains that the popular (as opposed to critical) success of Swedish films of the 1920s was partly due to their 'natural, living rhythm', with human bodies moving as in real life. He insists on an interdependence (*samspil*) between story, atmosphere and rhythm in a film, and observes that this interplay affects the viewer's state of mind (*sindsstemning*) and thus his/her ability to absorb the film (Dreyer, 1959: 64). He discusses how soft, rhythmic, horizontally flowing camera movements are apprehended (*opfanget*) by the eye while vertical forms break this spell, creating drama (63). Applying this principle of complex rhythmic interplay to *Vredens Dag*, he writes:

It is the plot and the milieu in *Vredens Dag* that determines its broad, peaceful rhythm, but this serves two other goals as well: on the one hand, it expresses the slow pulse of the era – and on the other it emphasises and supports that monumentality which the playwright achieved in his text, and which I have tried to transfer to the film. (Dreyer, 1959: 65)

This passage is the site of a little curiosum of Dreyer scholarship. Justifying his ponderous rhythm, Dreyer uses the suggestive metaphor 'at udtrykke epokens langsomme pulsslag', which translates literally as 'to express the slow pulse of the era'. In the published English translation, the phrase is rendered thus: 'to underline the slow pulse of the ear' (Dreyer, 1973: 134). This is no mistranslation; the Danish word *'epoke'* (epoch or era) can hardly be mistaken for *'øre'* (ear). This is a printer's productive solecism, the typographical equivalent of a Freudian slip. The misplacement of the 'r' transforms Dreyer's expressed concern with capturing the seventeenth-century workaday rhythms into an ambition to mimic the rhythm of blood pumping through the human body. At first glance, though, the misprint 'the slow pulse of the ear' seems credible because it sustains the notion of corporeality in the wake of the discussion of bodily movement in Swedish films. It chimes, too, with his calibration of filmic rhythm with plot and with the viewing eye, and the co-creation of rhythm among these elements.

'The slow pulse of the ear' also highlights another aspect of Dreyer's theory of rhythm: how sound affects rhythm in the 'talkies'. In *Vredens Dag* he was inspired by recent unspecified American and French 'psychological' films which developed a new filmic rhythm appropriate to the sound film, rediscovering the importance of facial expression and gesture (66). Such films have 'a calmness [ro] in the rhythm, which enables the viewer to rest [hvile] in the images and listen to the words' (Dreyer, 1959: 63).

'A Little on Film Style', then, consistently resorts to the notion of 'rhythm' as the end to which all aspects of style are the means. But rhythm is itself the means to another end: conjuring a historical environment. Authentic rhythm need not be slow, only justified.

DREYER'S SHORTS

The twelve years between *Vredens Dag* and *Ordet* must not be understood as a hiatus in Dreyer's 'real' career. In fact, his work on commissioned informational shorts was arguably a condition of possibility of both these feature films. Dreyer's first short film project, *Mødrehjælpen* (*Good Mothers*, 1943) was conceived by his admirers in the Danish Government Film Committee as an informal test of Dreyer's ability to stick to a budget and schedule. The accounts from *Mødrehjælpen* were made available to Palladium Film by the head of the committee to persuade the company to produce what would become *Vredens Dag* (Kimergård, 1992: 16, 49).

Neither can Dreyer's shorts and features be disentangled stylistically. Granted, it is disingenuous to describe his shorts as masterpieces; several have a gentle air of tedium about them ('en let pust af kedsomhed over sig'), as Lars Bo Kimergård puts it (1992: 49). Nevertheless, there are moments in Dreyer's short films where the kernel of a later iconic image, camera movement or editing technique seems to crystallise, re-emerging in one of his late features. This chimes with the committee's policy: directors were given artistic control and free hands to interpret their brief, ensuring that the resulting films were of high quality. This was particularly important in the case of films about Danish culture for overseas distribution, and crucial for any project allocated to Dreyer whose fame would ensure interest at film festivals abroad (Kimergård, 1992: 49). So we see, for example, anticipated in *Mødrehjælpen* the motif of shadows of swaying leaves used in *Vredens Dag*; or *Ordet*'s cinematography informed by the slow arc-and-pan camera movement, and lighting used to illuminate sculptures in *Thorvaldsen* (1949) (Bordwell, 1981: 156). Counter-intuitively, the long take is not impossible in the short film: the thirteen-minute *Den danske Landsbykirke* (*The Danish Village Church*, 1947) contains two shots of around thirty seconds each.

DREYER'S SPEED

By any measure, *De naaede Færgen* was the most successful and popular of Dreyer's shorts and, indeed, ranks among the most enduringly successful of the short film productions overseen by Danish state agencies in the post-war period. Commissioned by the Government Film Committee for a road safety campaign, the film was an adaptation of a 1925 novella by Johannes V. Jensen (1873–1950), a Dane awarded the Nobel Prize for Literature in 1944. Jensen was a chronicler of modernity, a motorbiking enthusiast who wrote equally compellingly of the pleasures of technology and of humankind's earliest history. Jensen's tachomania was referred to in his Nobel citation: 'The faster the pace, the greater his enchantment' (Hallström, 1944). The adaptation of Jensen's text hardly seems the ideal brief for the master of slow cinema. And yet Dreyer fulfilled the remit to widespread approval: during the short film's theatrical run, along with *The Bandit of Sherwood Forest* (dir. Harry Levin and George Sherman, 1946), it was seen by 270,000 cinemagoers in Denmark, and schools and clubs continued to hire 16 mm copies with alacrity for more than a decade.[5] A still also featured on a commemorative stamp in 1989.

De naaede Færgen depicts the motorcycle ride of a young couple, Sophus and Elvira, across a Danish island. We meet them as they arrive on a ferry; for unspecified reasons, they must catch the next sailing from the far side of the island. The time available to cover the ground is unfeasibly short, as revealed in an opening conversation with a ferryman: forty-five minutes to cover 70 kilometres (44 miles). An agonising ninety seconds pass between this exchange and the moment when their motorbike leaves the ferry: a series of cross cuts between the agitated couple, the approaching harbour entrance, and the gangway slowly being lowered construct a standing start that intensifies the impact of the frenzied ride that follows.

For seven-and-a-half minutes, the film alternates between shots of the bikers' perspective on the road or the vehicles they pass, often at a canted angle; mid shots and close-ups on the bikers responding to their escapades and to the speedometer; long shots of the bike passing across the landscape; and an aerial perspective on the bike's front and back wheels, showing the changing road surfaces as they progress across the terrain.[6] The shot list specifies 117 shots altogether in eleven minutes, more than the 114 racked up in *Ordet*'s two hours (Bordwell, 1981: 146). In the terms of 'A Little on Film Style', images and bodies are flying across the screen. In Deleuzean terms, the scenario is almost a literal manifestation of the spatio-temporal relations we would expect from classical cinema or the movement–image regime, in which 'perception is organised in obstacles and distances to be crossed, while action invents the means to cross and surmount them' (Deleuze, 1989: 40). Cumulatively, however, this middle section is much more concerned with constructing a sensory experience of space–time than it is with cause–effect relations or spatio-temporal continuity. It is a 'purely optical and sound situation' (Deleuze, 1989: 3): the bikers observe and inhabit the road and landscape, are windswept, sway subject to

Figure 2.1   Close-ups of the bike's speedometer match the engine's pulse in *De naaede Færgen* (*They Caught the Ferry*, 1948).

G force. This is a film almost entirely devoid of dialogue: the only exchanges are between Sophus and the sceptical ferryman and, later, a petrol station attendant. Thus, the auditory environment is dominated by the engine noise, its pitch changing with variations in speed. The shot list specifies four times (shots 23, 31, 44 and 84) that the 'rhythm' of the engine's 'explosions' must match the speedometer. The journey's space–time is parcelled out in the milliseconds of the engine's thrum. Shots, bodies, camerawork, engine noise, all work together in a purposeful interplay that leaves the contemporary 'rhythm for rhythm's sake' that Dreyer so disdained in the dust.

Dreyer's research materials for *De naaede Færgen* included a 1944 newsletter published by the Danish motorcycle manufacturer Nimbus whose motorbike (along with the company's test driver and his wife) appear in the film. The newsletter reprints a 1917 essay by Johannes V. Jensen on the pleasures and perils of motorbiking in which he compellingly recounts the novelty of experiencing space at speed:

> Yes, we see in a different way, to a different tempo, flashes of things close-by, the trees lining the road, the ditches, vehicles, impressions which immediately imprint themselves in the memory just as clearly as everything else we see, perhaps even sharper. What is new is how the more distant views and horizon are visible; the foreground rushes past, but the background, the land itself, begins to live in a peculiar way, moves in rhythmic lengths, one horizon opens out onto another, the relief of the landscape unfolds, not in fixed planes, but in movement [. . .] we experience the land more as a whole, how it is sculpted. (Jensen, 1944: 10)

Jensen goes on to say that contours unnoticed by the walker are visible when compressed into the shorter time taken by the motorbike to cover the same ground. Thus, Jensen makes something else apparent in Dreyer's film: neither contemplation of the material environment nor apprehension of duration are predicated on slowness. The pulse of this era – the 1940s – is not the slow ticking of seventeenth-century clocks which bored the reviewers of *Vredens Dag*. Modernity has its own pulse – the engine's hum, the undulations of the landscape seen at twentieth-century speed – and the pulse of the ear is the fast-beating heart of the exhilarated (or terrified) rider. Dreyer adjusts his filmic rhythms to the rhythm of the combustion engine and its effect on vision: shot 24, for example, specifies that the roadside trees are filmed as the motorcyclists see them, as 'flickering lines'.

As the title suggests, the couple catches a ferry in the end – but it is Charon's barge across the River Styx. As in *Ordet*, the film performs an act of ontological gymnastics at its conclusion: a mythological or religious force erupts through the veil of reality, here in the form of a demonic driver who forces the couple off the road. The final double exposure layers a departing ferry over a misty Charon punting downstream with two coffins, to the sound of bells tolling.

Conclusion

With this abrupt deceleration into an achronic afterlife, there remains a temporal paradox. If Dreyer's vindication of *Vredens Dag*'s slowness rests on the desire to enact 'the slow pulse of the era', this can also justify the rhythmic calibration with modernity's velocity in *De naaede Færgen*. It is less obviously helpful, however, in respect of the increasingly radical slowness of *Ordet* and *Gertrud*, both of which evoke twentieth-century milieux with the historical exactitude to which Dreyer was devoted. The knowingly technophile tempo of *De naaede Færgen* reveals Dreyer's defiance of the rhythms of modernity in *Ordet* and *Gertrud* to be deliberate. In his valedictory long take on Gertrud's closed door, Dreyer obliges us to take the time we need to grasp the impulse that unites him with today's directors of 'slow': to render palpable, in stillness, the human pulse of time.

Notes

1. This list does not include Dreyer's Swedish feature, *Två Människor* (*Two People*, 1945), 'repudiated' by Dreyer and usually quietly excised from his *oeuvre* (Carney, 1989: 4n1).
2. For a more detailed account of Dreyer's state-commissioned film-making, see Thomson (forthcoming) and Kimergård, 1992. All Dreyer's shorts can be viewed at http://english.carlthdreyer.dk/Films/Kortfilm.aspx
3. See, respectively, chapters by Lim, Davis and de Luca in this volume.
4. An English translation is printed in Skoller's anthology (Dreyer, 1973). All English translations in this chapter are my own, however.
5. My calculations based on annual reports in the archive of the distribution agency, Statens Filmcentral (held by the Danish Film Institute), indicate that *De naaede Færgen* was hired 3,077 times between 1950 and 1963, each hire accounting for an unknown number of screenings in schools, clubs etc. to audiences of unrecorded size. This places the film consistently in the top ten most hired films annually in the same period.
6. The shot list is available at http://english.carlthdreyer.dk/Films/De-naaede-faergen.aspx

Bibliography

Bordwell, David (1981), *The Films of Carl-Theodor Dreyer* (Berkeley, Los Angeles and London: University of California Press).
Carney, Raymond (1989), *Speaking the Language of Desire: The Films of Carl Dreyer* (Cambridge: Cambridge University Press).
Deleuze, Gilles (1986), *Cinema 1: The Movement-Image* (Minneapolis, MN: University of Minnesota Press).
Deleuze, Gilles (1989), *Cinema 2: The Time-Image* (Minneapolis, MN: University of Minnesota Press).

de Luca, Tiago (2014), *Realism of the Senses in World Cinema: The Experience of Physical Reality* (London: I. B. Tauris).

Dreyer, Carl Th. [1943] (1959), 'Lidt om Filmstil', in Carl Th. Dreyer, *OM FILMEN. Artikler og interviews* (Copenhagen: Nyt Nordisk Forlag Arnold Busck), pp. 62–9.

Dreyer, Carl Th. (1973), 'A Little on Film Style', in Donald Skoller (ed.), *Dreyer in Double Reflection. Carl Dreyer's Writings on Film* (Cambridge, MA: Da Capo Press), pp. 127–34.

Flanagan, Matthew (2012), *'Slow Cinema': Temporality and Style in Contemporary Art and Experimental Film*, unpublished PhD dissertation, University of Exeter.

Gtz [pseudonymous reviewer] (1943), '"Vredens Dag" savnede Tempo og Nerve', *Politiken*, 14 November, 1943.

Hallström, Per (1944), 'Presentation: The Nobel Prize in Literature 1944', www.nobelprize.org/nobel_prizes/literature/laureates/1944/presentation.html [accessed 23 April 2014].

Jensen, Johannes V. [1917] (1944), 'Paa Motorcykel', *Nimbus Nyt*, nos 15–16, pp. 9–12. (Danish Film Institute, Dreyer Archive, D I, C: De nåede færgen, 1).

Kimergård, Lars Bo (1992), *Carl Th. Dreyers kortfilmengagement i perioden 1942–1952*, unpublished cand. phil. dissertation, University of Copenhagen.

Kragh-Jacobsen, Svend (1943), 'Tempoet tog Livet af "Vredens Dag"', *Berlingske Tidende*, 14 November 1943.

Sandberg, Mark B. (2006), 'Mastering the House: Performative Inhabitation in Carl Th. Dreyer's *The Parson's Widow*', in C. Claire Thomson (ed.), *Northern Constellations: New Readings in Nordic Cinema* (Norwich: Norvik Press), pp. 23–42.

Schrader, Paul [1972] (1988), *Transcendental Style in Film. Ozu, Bresson, Dreyer* [Da Capo Press (no place indicated)].

Thomson, C. Claire (forthcoming), '"Education, Enlightenment, and General Propaganda": Dansk Kulturfilm and Carl Th. Dreyer's Short Films', in Mette Hjort and Ursula Lindqvist (eds), *Companion to Nordic Cinema* (London: Blackwell).

3. THE FIRST DURATIONAL CINEMA AND THE REAL OF TIME

Michael Walsh

Duration is one characteristic of the film avant-garde of the 1960s that is not shared with the historical avant-garde of the 1920s. Of course, there were long films during the silent era – Griffith's *Intolerance* (1916), Abel Gance's *Napoleon* (1927) – but these were narrative, naturalistic and epic; the classics of the historical avant-garde are either short (the Dada and surrealist films) or feature length (the Soviet films) and, as David Campany (2008: 36) has noted, tend to be preoccupied with motion rather than stillness, speed rather than stasis. Properly durational films, by which I mean films that radically subtract dramatic incident and interest, offer an unprecedented challenge to expectations of running time, and foreground time as a formal element of cinema, are not seen until the era of Andy Warhol's *Sleep* (1963) and *Empire* (1964), Ken Jacobs's *Star Spangled to Death* (1956–60, 2002–4), and Michael Snow's *Wavelength* (1967) and *La Région Centrale* (1971).

Warhol and Jacobs are the founding figures of this first durational cinema, and so I shall look in some depth and detail at one film by each, *Sleep* and *Star Spangled to Death*. These two films establish a dialogue between a subtractive or minimalist aesthetic which has been clearly dominant in durational film-making, and connects most plainly with the idea of slow cinema, and a more encompassing, encyclopedic kind of durational film, less familiar but nonetheless historically insistent. Some of the important figures from the beginning of durational cinema in fact made both kinds of film. Ken Jacobs has to his name not only the sprawling *Star Spangled to Death* but also the more rigorous *Tom, Tom, The Piper's Son* (1969), and Michael Snow made not only the ultraminimalist *La Région Centrale* but also the comically exten-sive catalogue of sound/image relationships which is *Rameau's Nephew By Diderot (Thanx to Dennis Young) by Wilma Schoen* (1974), a film whose very title is durational. Later, in European art cinema, the same dialogue between austerity and grandiosity recurs in the contrast between Claude Lanzmann's *Shoah* (1985) and Hans-Jurgen Syberberg's *Hitler: A Film From Germany* (1977). Later still, in the current cycle of durational work in galleries and museums, we can see this same contrast in the restraint and repetition of David Claerbout's fourteen-hour *Bordeaux Piece* (2004) versus the exuber-ance and inclusiveness of Christian Marclay's twenty-four-hour *The Clock* (2010).

So durational films have been typically, even predominantly, slow but there are enough landmark exceptions to constitute a counter-tradition, and this is one reason to understand durational cinema as cognate with, rather than identical to, slow cinema. Other significant differences are historical (dura-tional film-making long precedes slow cinema) and sociohistorical – what I am calling the first durational cinema emerges from the lofts and alternative screening spaces of the tightly knit New York avant-garde of the early 1960s (Warhol and Jacobs shared performers; Jacobs and Snow shared equipment) while slow cinema is usually associated with a larger and looser group of inter-national directors of fiction features who made their reputations at globalised film festivals beginning in the 1990s.

The rethinking of cinematic time undertaken by the first durational cinema might be understood in Deleuzean terms; the distinction between the 1920s and 1960s avant-gardes maps readily enough on to that between movement–image and time–image. I shall instead take some theoretical cues from Alain Badiou, however, and will associate the two kinds of durational film with his ideas of the void (minimal, austere) and the multiple (encyclopedic, encom-passing). Badiou is a Lacanian; I shall argue that these ideas of the void and the multiple can themselves be associated with the concepts of the Lacanian Real and reality respectively, and that this philosophical/psychoanalytic input will give us an understanding we would not otherwise have of what is at stake in durational cinema's foregrounding of time.

To borrow another term from Badiou, the durational turn is an exemplary artistic 'event', whose consequences reverberate to this day not just in avant-garde film but in art cinema (Chantal Akerman, Béla Tarr, Lav Diaz), in docu-mentary (Wang Bing), and in gallery installation (Douglas Gordon, Tacita Dean). This variety of names and projects is intended to suggest that a good part of the interest of durational cinema is that it crosses some established critical boundaries. Yet the aesthetic, cultural and commercial differences between avant-garde film, art cinema, documentary, and gallery art can not be just wished away. So let us instead try to understand the history of durational cinema as a series of 'knight's moves', that is, a story of enthusiasms and abandonments, eclipses and rediscoveries, erasures and reinscriptions.

HISTORICAL, CRITICAL AND THEORETICAL PERSPECTIVES

For a first example, consider the argument of P. Adams Sitney that the 'structural cinema' of the later 1960s and early 1970s, despite being 'spiritually at the opposite pole' from Warhol, was nonetheless inconceivable without his example:

> To the filmmakers who first encountered these films in the mid-sixties (. . .), these latent mechanisms must have suggested other conscious and deliberate extensions: that is, Warhol must have inspired, by opening up and leaving unclaimed so much ontological territory, a cinema actively engaged in generating metaphors for the viewing, or rather the perceiving, experience. (1974: 373)

Similarly, the 'second new wave' in French cinema (especially films such as Chantal Akerman's *News From Home* [1976] and Straub/Huillet's *Fortini/Cani* [1976]) would surely never have included so many rigorous long takes and remedially simple camera movements without the example of the New York avant-garde, yet that is not to say that the two movements are easy to reconcile. Warhol aside, the New Yorkers tended to slight the significance of anyone who made features intended for any kind of theatrical release, believing that the running time of a film should be determined by its concept, not by the established habits of conventional cinemas. For their part, the Europeans were animated by a leftist and/or feminist politics perhaps personally congenial to some of the New Yorkers but left at best implicit in their films. This was the situation memorably described by Peter Wollen in 1975:

> Film history has developed unevenly, so that in Europe today there are two distinct avant-gardes. The first can be identified loosely with the Co-op movement. The second would include film-makers such as Godard, Straub and Huillet, Hanoun, Jancso. Naturally there are points of contact between these two groups (. . .) but they also differ quite sharply in (. . .) aesthetic assumptions, institutional framework, type of financial support, type of critical backing, historical and cultural origin. (1975: 171)

When we say that durational cinema radically subtracts conventional dramatic interest and foregrounds time as a formal element of cinema, the historical dominance of minimalism should be kept in mind. This point is perhaps best exemplified by the only apparently paradoxical case of the durational short – Warhol's *Screen Tests* (1964 on) are three-minute rolls, some of the Fluxus films made with the ultra-slow-motion camera, such as Joe Jones's *Smoking* (1966), are just a few minutes long, and Larry Gottheim's *Fog Line* (1970) is eleven minutes. As these examples suggest, there is considerable overlap between what I am calling the first durational cinema and what Sitney calls 'structural film'. The terms are not synonymous, however. Durational films are not necessarily structural (for example, *Star Spangled to Death*) while structural films are not necessarily durational (for example, *Arnulf Rainer*, Peter Kubelka, 1960; *The Flicker*, Tony Conrad, 1966; and *Piece Mandala/ End War*, Paul Sharits, 1966). *Arnulf Rainer* and *The Flicker* are completely abstract whereas what I am calling the first durational cinema is necessarily representational; for a thoroughgoing subtraction of conventional dramatic interest to have its effect, the image presented must be one that could, in principle, begin a conventional dramatic sequence.

So what happens when narrative is not just slowed but voided in films that run for many hours? The first, classically minimalist, answer comes from some 1964 programme notes on *Sleep* by Henry Geldzhaler (a curator who was himself the subject of a ninety-minute fixed-take Warhol film): 'The slightest variation becomes an event . . . As less and less happens on the screen, we become satisfied with almost nothing and find the slightest shift in the body of the sleeper or the least movement of the camera interesting enough' (1964: 300). Later, Paul Arthur understood Warhol's films as cueing formal and theoretical questions normally unasked even in the domain of the avant-garde:

> What is a shot, a sequence, a dramatic action? How are we to fix the boundaries between fiction and documentary effects, between narrative and non-narrative, architectonics and randomness? What is the seat of authorship and the extent of its agency; does it reside in cinematography, direction, acting, writing, the social contexts of image consumption? (1989: 148)

We might supplement this with some questions of our own (What is a figure? What is an event? What is the cinematic signifier?) but the basic point should be clear: the first durational cinema both prompts such questions and gives us unprecedented amounts of time to consider them.

Note, however, that quite different kinds of consideration can equally well occupy that time. Connecting ontology and perception, Sitney's remarks on Warhol suggest phenomenology, while Arthur's account of Warhol as destabilising film language, genre, authorship, and spectatorship suggests post-structuralism. For my own part, as mentioned, it is to Alain Badiou that I shall turn for some theoretical perspectives which resonate with durational cinema.

As many by now will know, Badiou's *Being and Event* (1988) seeks to refound ontology on axiomatic set theory, and takes philosophically seriously the idea that all mathematics is constructible from the empty set, the set that has no members but is itself included in every set. With this in mind, we can understand the reorientation of cinematic time undertaken by the 1960s avant-garde as an indication that postmodern duration is founded on the void, on the zero, on what Badiou calls the 'presentation of presentation'. We can't take this idea too literally; *Sleep, Empire,* and *Wavelength* are not films of nothing, though it seems fair enough to construe them as a kind of approach to the cinematic zero. Among Badiou's own exemplary artists is Malevich whose painting *White on White* he describes as the staging of a minimal but decisive difference between the real and the semblance or appearance: 'What takes place barely differs from the place where it takes place. It is in this "barely", in this immanent exception, that all the affect lies' (2005: 98).

In *Deleuze: The Clamor of Being* (1997), Badiou describes Deleuze as following Spinoza in an idea that nothing is missing from being. In his *Pocket Pantheon* (2008), Badiou counterposes to this a whole tradition of French thinkers (Sartre, Althusser, Lacan, Derrida) who, despite their sometimes violent critiques of each other, all seem to share an idea that things revolve around a nothingness, a lack in being, a *mise en abyme*. With his talk of the void as the proper name of being, Badiou seems to belong with them. Yet, though he is a Lacanian, Badiou is not nearly as tragic a thinker as Lacan; for him, the void is not a hole in being around which reality is organised but something more like the formal premise of being. For Badiou, the uniqueness of the void ensures the multiplicity of being; it is just because everything is founded on the void that being is infinite. What ancient philosophy disputed as the one and the many is by Badiou reframed as the none and the many. With this in mind, we can not only associate the minimal kind of durational film with the void and the encompassing kind with the multiple but also suggest a kind of existential bond between the two.

The first volume of *Being and Event*, which develops the ontological idea of an inconsistent multiplicity founded on the void, can be broadly aligned with what Lacan calls the Real. The second volume, which tries to reconcile this ontology with a logical world of objects and appearances, can be broadly aligned with what Lacan calls reality. The distinction between reality and the Real is counter-intuitive, elusive, and always vulnerable to critical backsliding; scholars commonly use the phrase 'the real' to refer to things that Lacan would almost certainly have assigned to reality. So, to review: the Lacanian Real is whatever is resistant to symbolisation; it is all those things with which we can never come to terms; it is whatever cannot be integrated into our infinite universe of signifiers and objects. To relate this directly to the topic of durational cinema, we might say that time belongs to the Lacanian Real while all symbolisations of time belong to reality. Time is Real in that we can never grasp it; clocks and watches and calendars that count time in seconds, minutes, hours, days, and years are all symbolic systems that retrieve a reality from the Real of time. Thus, the first durational cinema distends into Real time the clock-measured, exactly repeatable running time that has been a formal quality of cinema at least since the introduction of synchronous sound. Badiou writes: 'the event extracts from one time the possibility of another time' (2009a: 348). The way that the representational realities of these films pitch us into an encounter with the Real of time is one reason that they work not to fulfil the neorealist prescriptions of Cesare Zavattini but, instead, to rejoin the experimental tradition of making emphatic the formal conditions of the medium. Ivone Margulies puts this well: Zavattini's idea of an ultimate neorealist film about a man to whom nothing happens for ninety minutes is 'iterative', humanist, treating the man in question as a representative of all men, while Warhol's durational epics are literal, hyperreal, allowing 'no space for the heroic' (1993: 37).

Founding Films

Two of the most famous of the first durational films, *Sleep* and *Wavelength*, are also among the most misdescribed of all experimental films, and the mis-description is the same in both cases; the radical conceptual simplicity of the films, however authentic, is exaggerated. Thus, *Wavelength* is described as a forty-five-minute zoom across a loft and, while strictly this is true, it hardly does justice to an image-track alive with abrupt cuts and lighting changes, switches from day to night, fogged frames, light flares, superimpositions, and dissolves. The film's literal exclusion, however, from the frame of the poten-tially narrative elements it introduces in the first twenty minutes still stands as an allegory of the relationship of durational cinema with conventional ideas of story. The zoom moves impassively, inexorably, on towards its appointment with the yellow chair and the photographs pinned to the wall between the windows, and the things that we might have construed as characters and story events are simply left behind.

For its part, and despite the emergence of a whole cadre of more careful scholars – Callie Angell (1994), Branden Joseph (2005), J. J. Murphy (2012) – *Sleep* is still sometimes described as eight hours of a static shot of a man sleep-ing. It is true that there is no shot in the film that shows anything other than a man asleep, that the great majority of shots in the film are taken from static camera positions, and that, when we do see camera movements, they are no more than shakes or slight reframings. Even the handheld shots at the end of the film are held very steadily as though to de-emphasise camera movement. The film is in fact five hours and twenty minutes long, however, and contains some twenty-two separate shots. None of these lasts more than four minutes, and some are just a few seconds long. So the glassy stasis of *Sleep* derives not from 'one static shot' but, instead, from two other factors. The first, which on its own accounts for one third of the running time, is that material captured at twenty-four frames per second is displayed at sixteen frames per second, so-called 'silent speed', pointing us once again to the dialectic in durational film between a repeatable running time and an intimation of eternity.

The second factor, as Branden Joseph (2005) has emphasised, is repetition. Heavily reliant on loop printing, *Sleep* repeats individual shots, short sequences based on simple assemble editing, and complete 100-foot rolls. After forty-six minutes of the film, we have seen a total of only five minutes of original footage. After 185 minutes, we have seen twenty. In the ultraminimal third and fourth reels, two three-minute camera rolls, repeated sixteen and twenty times respectively, yield no less than 173 minutes of running time, more than half the whole film. The entire 320 minutes of *Sleep* seems to derive from only a little more than thirty minutes of footage. Joseph (2005) connects the repetitions of *Sleep* to Warhol's paintings of the period, the gridded and serial treatments of the Mona Lisa, Jacqueline Kennedy, and news photos of disasters. The point is well taken and might be extended; if the first six shots in *Sleep* could be somehow rendered simultaneously, their six different angles on the same sleeping body might prove reminiscent of analytical cubism. Yet subsequent is not the same as simultaneous. Many a viewer who has no problem with *Eight Elvises* or *Ethel Scull 36 Times* (both Warhol paintings of 1963) will struggle with the twenty cycles of the same 100-foot roll which begins after 185 minutes of *Sleep* and continues for the next eighty-six minutes.

There are sequences in *Sleep* in which the viewer may not realise that she/he is watching looped footage, but, in this fourth reel, the light gradient between the beginning and the end of the roll is steep enough that the rebeginnings are hard to miss. Such changes in brightness (sometimes sudden, sometimes gradual), along with small movements of the lips and throat, and the eyeball flutters beneath closed lids that are associated with REM sleep, are typical of events in *Sleep*. More dramatic developments are a movement of the shoulders that hoists an armpit up into the lower part of the frame and, in the final reel, an adjustment of sleeping position that lifts the arm over the head.

In *The Black Hole of the Camera* (2012), J. J. Murphy makes a case that *Sleep* is not erotic. Few commentators have anything like his film-maker's understanding of film stocks, exposure, grain, lighting, and the work of the lab. But *Sleep* is a film by a gay man of his handsome partner sleeping naked. If not erotic in the sense that it is likely to arouse the spectator, *Sleep* must nonetheless be understood as proximate to sexuality; it is hard to watch without wondering whether any of these particular sleeps are post-coital. Skirting the edge of what was showable in 1963, the film's second shot has the hair on

Giorno's lower belly out of focus in the foreground. The eighth, ninth, and tenth shots make up a sequence frankly centred on his backside. The ninth is a medium long shot of the sleeper on his side with his back to the camera, centred on his buttocks on both the vertical and horizontal axes. If this remedially simple framing is not already enough to make us think that Giorno's body is being appraised sexually, the tenth shot is a close-up of the fan of hair at the base of his spine and the dark cleft between his buttocks.

Sleep is the kind of durational film that readers are most likely to know but, before concluding, I want to say something about the historically first example of the other kind, that great shaggy dog of a film, Ken Jacobs's *Star Spangled to Death* which includes an intertitle summarising itself as 'six hours forty-five minutes of obscure found-films combined with 1950s New York street theater and misery and humiliation in the time of Bush'. It is essential here to understand that we are talking about found films rather than found footage. One reason that the film is so long and, for some viewers, so difficult is that it quotes a whole series of found films (an African safari documentary, promotional pieces for Franklin D. Roosevelt and Nelson Rockefeller, Richard Nixon's Checkers speech, amateurish nude dancers, a television documentary about mother love among chimpanzees, a cartoon version of *Uncle Tom's Cabin*) more or less in their entirety. The quoted films do not run to feature length but some are as long as thirty minutes and the many interpolations make them seem much longer. Note also that 'the time of Bush' is represented on the image-track by just a couple of sequences, a Manhattan street protest against the Iraq War and Rudolph Guiliani testifying to the 9/11 Commission. So the 'misery and humiliation' is mostly found in the dozens of intertitles and the hundreds of single-frame flash-texts, the latter legible only on a DVD with remote in hand. This surfeit of written material changes the temporality of the text in some basic ways. It makes an already very long film considerably longer; it means that the film so viewed has no exactly repeatable running time; and it tries to find a resolution for the contradictions of a project which was begun in the 1950s, shelved for decades, and then completed on video between 2002 and 2004.

Star Spangled to Death is emphatically a sound film whose earliest date, 10 August 1920, is that of the first recording of African American vernacular music, Mamie Smith's 'Crazy Blues'. Its latest date, 30 May 2005, is that of the George W. Bush sound bite that plays on the DVD home screen. Neither the dozens of found films nor the similar number of sound samples are evenly distributed across these eighty-five years, however. Instead, they cluster strongly around the moment of the film-maker's birth in the early 1930s, though the next thirty years are also well represented. After that, that is to say the end of the first phase of principal photography, we get only a few stray segments representing the 1960s and 1970s and not much of anything for the 1980s and 1990s. So the bulk of the film is focalised around the first thirty years of Jacobs's life, from Depression and New Deal through war and McCarthyism to the New Frontier and escalation in Vietnam. As this language suggests, *Star Spangled to Death* is very much an American film, though its preoccupation with anti-Semitism is strongly informed by European Jewish experiences.

The Dada troupe that performs in a basement courtyard numbers ten but it has two principals, Jack Smith and Jerry Sims, who preside respectively over the first and second halves of the film. Smith is increasingly acknowledged as one of the founders of American performance art; Sims would quite likely be forgotten if not for his place in Jacobs's work. Smith is tall, blonde, good-looking, Gentile and, if not exactly happy, certainly madcap. Sims is stunted, dark, unappetising, Jewish and miserable. These polarisations are actively thematised by the film, with Smith playing 'The Spirit Not of Life but of Living' and Sims as 'Suffering'. Smith dances and prances, delighting in the variously startled, amused and annoyed reactions of New Yorkers when he comes leaping past wearing a paper bag on his head and garlanded with netting. Sims sits down in the gutter, stretches his arms like a crucified Christ across the wheel arch of a parked car, and cries. The *mise en scène* of the courtyard

Figure 3.1   Jack Smith and bystanders in *Star Spangled to Death* (1956–60, 2002–4).

sequences relies on a set festooned with curtains and hangings, a large bank of ready-made props (watering cans, spectacles, mirrors, dolls, advertising signs, bicycle wheels, stepladders, umbrellas, bowler hats), simultaneous movement on two or three different planes of depth, and clowning and mugging from the performers. The effect is variously reminiscent of the Dada and surrealist films, of von Sternberg, and of Welles.

Sitney's *Visionary Film* distinguishes between a mythopoetic or psychodramatic kind of film-making and a structural or conceptual kind. In the case of durational cinema, I am suggesting, the original dialectic is between Warhol and Jacobs, the first representing a cinema of distancing and subtraction, the second a cinema of sensory overload and social disgust. Despite appearances, Warhol is punctual; duration is one tactic among the others in his work that can be associated with an aesthetic break or event. Jacobs is singularly unpunctual; for him, duration is metonymic of almost half a century of returning to and reworking the same film, with disorienting results for the standard conceptions of temporality, priority, sequence and order. There is a straightforward view of this which is that Jacobs was simply unable to finish, had fallen out with many of the members of the original troupe, and as one of his own intertitles suggests, was worried that his depiction of Jerry Sims was complicit with an oppressive idea of the Jew as eternal victim. Yet this practical/biographical account misses something interesting not just about *Star Spangled To Death* but about Jacobs's work as a whole. As Tom Gunning was the first to recognise, much of Jacobs's work is premised on the 'actual pastness of the film image, its existence as the trace of things past, the ghost-like embers of events long ended and figures now dispersed' (1982: 53). In other words, Jacobs seems to have decided that the intrinsically temporal nature of film makes it legitimate both to move on from and, at the same time, continue to work with previous aesthetic values; elsewhere in his filmography, *The Winter Footage* is dated 1964/1984, and the Nervous System performance piece *Coupling* is listed 'Lumière Brothers 1896/Ken Jacobs 1996'. At the time of writing, Jacobs's most recent screening included a restoration to its original running time of his first film, *Orchard Street*, dated '1955/2014'. So for this film-maker, a nearly obsessional relationship with the Real of time includes editing intervals of almost sixty years.

CONCLUSION

What is the relationship between what I have been calling the first durational cinema and the slow or contemplative cinema identified by a number of commentators in recent years? There is a number of possible answers. We could propose that the first durational cinema is a wellspring that must in some sense inform all subsequent slow cinemas; despite all the difficulties with the distribution of films and of commentaries on films (language barriers, censorship barriers, economic barriers, barriers of mixed and uneven development) the transnational nature of contemporary film culture makes it implausible that slow cinema directors, such as Hou Hsiao-Hsien and Pedro Costa, would, as beginners, have known nothing of earlier minimal cinemas. On the other hand, we could distinguish quite sharply between durational film-making and slow cinema. By general agreement, slow cinema refers to fiction features with characters and stories, however nominal or minimal, and its critics (Yvette Biro, Ira Jaffe) tend to construct genealogies that either don't go back much further than the 1980s or consist of art-house directors such as Dreyer, Ozu, and Bresson. Nor can it be critically helpful just to mash together everything slow, everything durational, everything contemplative. If the concept of 'slow cinema' is to keep any forensic value and avoid the fate of terms such as 'postmodernism', which ended up rather vacuously trying to subsume the very high modernism against which it was initially defined, then it must designate something that can be both related to and distinguished from forerunning and cognate tendencies. It is mostly for this reason that I have argued that the history of durational cinema is best understood diagonally, as a series of knight's moves, in which concepts can cut across categories but categories do not thereby disappear.

One key pivot-point, however, lies in what we might call the second durational cinema which emerges in Paris in the late 1960s, with Jacques Rivette and Jean Eustache, and hits its stride in the 1970s with Jean-Marie Straub and Danielle Huillet, Chantal Akerman, and Marguerite Duras. The year 1975, with *Moses und Aaron*, *Jeanne Dielman*, and *India Song* all shown at Cannes was a high-water mark. In this sequence, Rivette and Eustache stand for the more encompassing tendency while Straub/Huillet, Akerman, and Duras are all, in their different ways, minimalists. This second durational cinema, as focalised around a particular time and place as the first, but as we have seen, distinguished from it both by its political modernism and by consisting of fictions with named characters, points more directly to twenty-first-century slow cinema but will have to be the subject of a future study.

BIBLIOGRAPHY

Angell, Callie (1994), *The Films of Andy Warhol: Part II* (New York: Whitney Museum of American Art).

Arthur, Paul (1989), 'Flesh of Absence: Resighting the Warhol Catechism', in M. O'Pray (ed.), *Andy Warhol Film Factory* (London: British Film Institute), pp. 146–53.

Badiou, Alain ([1997] 2000), *Deleuze: The Clamor of Being*, translated by Louise Burchill (Minneapolis, MN: University of Minnesota Press).

Badiou, Alain (2005), *Le Siècle*, my translation (Paris: Seuil).

Badiou, Alain ([1988] 2007), *Being and Event*, translated by Oliver Feltham (London: Continuum).

Badiou, Alain ([2006] 2009a), *Logics of Worlds. Being and Event II*, translated by Alberto Toscano (London: Continuum).

Badiou, Alain ([2008] 2009b), *Pocket Pantheon: Figures of Postwar Philosophy*, translated by David Macey (London: Verso).

Biro, Yvette. (2006). 'The Fullness of Minimalism', *Rouge* 9, http://www.rouge.com.au/9/minimalism.html [accessed 9 June 2014].

Geldzahler, H. ([1964] 1970), 'Some Notes on *Sleep*', in P. Adams Sitney (ed.), *Film Culture Reader* (New York: Praeger), pp. 300–2.

Gunning, Tom (1982), 'Looking Backward: Ken Jacobs Presents the Past', in *10 Years of Living Cinema* (New York: Collective for Living Cinema), pp. 53–6.

Jaffe, Ira. (2014), *Slow Movies: Countering the Cinema of Action* (Chichester: Wallflower Books).

Joseph, Branden (2005), 'The Play of Repetition: Andy Warhol's *Sleep*', *Grey Room* 19, pp. 22–53.

Margulies, Ivone (1993), *Nothing Happens: Chantal Akerman's Hyperrealist Everyday* (Durham, NC: Duke University Press).

Murphy, J. J. (2012), *The Black Hole of the Camera: The Films of Andy Warhol* (Berkeley, CA: California University Press).

Sitney, P. Adam (1974), *Visionary Film: The American Avant-Garde* (Oxford: Oxford University Press).

Wollen, Peter (1975), 'The Two Avant-Gardes', *Studio International* vol. 190 no. 978, pp. 171–5.

4. 'THE ATTITUDE OF SMOKING AND OBSERVING': SLOW FILM AND POLITICS IN THE CINEMA OF JEAN-MARIE STRAUB AND DANIÈLE HUILLET

Martin Brady

Recently, as this volume amply demonstrates both in its essays and the scholarship with which they engage, film studies has been gripped by a fascination with 'slow cinema'. A substantial body of theoretical writing has defined and expanded, both geographically and historically, the corpus of films admitted to the pantheon which now encompasses a diverse range of films from early cinema through to myriad contemporary works from the mainstream to the experimental. It is not the intention of this chapter to rehearse these debates or redefine the cannon.[1] Instead the aim is simply to look at one film, in its time paradigmatic for an entirely different kind of cinema, Brechtian materialism, as an essay in the political potential of slowness, or at least the attention to detail that it may attempt to encourage.

BERTOLT BRECHT'S 'ATTITUDE OF SMOKING AND OBSERVING'

Brecht is not a playwright, poet, essayist, or film-maker whom one would generally associate with slowness though many of the film-makers purported to be influenced by him clearly are, among them Jean-Marie-Straub and Danièle Huillet, and Jean-Luc Godard (at least in his most experimental works for large and small screen from 1967 to 1978). In defining the ideal mode of spectatorship to encourage intellectual reflection alongside emotional engagement, however – it is a persistent misconception that he disapproved of the latter – Brecht coined a neat phrase: 'the attitude of smoking and observing'. Given the time taken to smoke an average cigarette, Brecht's dictum certainly suggests a leisurely mode of reception. Significantly, Brecht suggested that this relaxed attitude be adopted when reading – specifically the projections planned for the staging of *The Threepenny Opera* (*Die Dreigroschenoper*): 'On reading the projections on screen the audience adopts the attitude of smoking and observing' (Brecht, 1988–98: 24, 59).

Brecht's plays of the period would, on the face of it, appear to encourage the very opposite. The music theatre pieces and Learning Plays of the late 1920s are often frenetic, verging on manic. At least one piece of this period, however, the much neglected *Baden-Baden Learning Play on Acquiescence* (*Das Badener Lehrstück vom Einverständnis*, 1929) suggests that Brecht was, after all, attempting to find performative equivalents for the mode of reception he wanted to foster.

INSTRUCTIONS ON SPEED

The play, Brecht's most experimental completed work, is a compendium of different media and linguistic registers: loosely based on the story of the failed attempt in 1927 of Charles Nungesser to fly across the Atlantic, this 'cantata' (originally with a score by Paul Hindemith, later withdrawn) includes verse, prose, commentary, slapstick comedy, and quasi-liturgical responses, and – at least in its original version – incorporated dance, photographic projections and a film interlude starring Valeska Gert. It is symptomatic that this reflection on technology, altruism, and progress is populated, unlike its euphoric predecessor – *The Lindbergh Flight* (*Der Lindberghflug*, 1929), a celebration of the triumph of its eponymous hero – by Crashed Airmen for whom movement is a thing of the past:

> Fly no longer.
> Now no more do you have need of swiftness. [. . .]
> Lie there still and be
> Content.
> Not high above our heads
> Not far from us
> And no more in motion
> But immobile
> Tell us who you are. (Brecht, 1997: 24)

Only once they have crashed to earth and ceased to move forward can the Airmen begin to understand their failures, both technological and ideological. As the Crashed Airman replies to the Leader of the Chorus who uttered the lines just quoted:

And all my thoughts were of machines and the
Attainment of ever greater speed.
I forgot in my exertions
My own name and identity
And in the urgency of my searching
Forgot the final goal I sought. (Brecht, 1997: 24)

Slowness, Brecht appears to be suggesting, can allow the goal – defined in the final scene as altering oneself to alter the world, constantly revolutionising the revolution – to be reached more swiftly. In a remarkable scene entitled 'Instruction' the Speaker reads from a book of 'Commentaries' which are a strange mixture of Christian parables and Buddhist teaching. Instructed to strip themselves naked literally and metaphorically to start again from scratch, the Airmen gradually achieve insight:

Now I learn to see that a man
Must lie prostrate and not strive
For heights, nor depths, nor yet velocity.
THE SPEAKER *reading*:
2. When the thinking man was overtaken by a great storm, he was seated in a large carriage, taking up much room. The first thing that he did was to descend from his carriage. The second was to take off his cloak. The third thing was that he laid himself down on the ground. Thus he con-quered the storm in his smallest dimension. (Brecht, 1997: 34)

Though many of its scenes are terse and abrupt, the play also experiments with methods of retardation and repetition. Most famously, a sequence of photographs of mutilated corpses from World War I, which apparently caused outrage at the play's premiere in Baden-Baden in 1929, not only interrupts the action but is also repeated to facilitate spectatorial reflection:

Ten photographs of dead bodies are shown. The Speaker then says: 'Second contemplation of the dead', *and the photographs are shown again.* (Brecht, 1997: 32–3)

WALTER BENJAMIN AND 'DIALECTICS AT A STANDSTILL'

A philosophical underpinning to this seemingly contradictory notion of achiev-ing insight more swiftly through slowing down or, indeed, stopping entirely can be found in the writings of Brecht's friend and admirer, Walter Benjamin. Benjamin's materialist historiography, most succinctly defined in his late essay 'On the Concept of History' (*Über den Begriff der Geschichte*, 1940), calls for the remorseless forward motion of history to be arrested to facilitate change: 'The historical materialist cannot do without the concept of a present which is not a transition but in which time is avowed and has also come to a standstill' (Benjamin 1977: 259). What is significant here is that the arresting of the relentless movement of the chronicle requires brute force. The historical materialist has to be 'man enough, to explode the continuum of history'; as Benjamin concludes in the final section of the essay, in a much-quoted formulation, 'thinking involves not only the movement of thoughts but also their arrest (*Stillstellung*)' (Benjamin, 1977: 260). In his unfinished *Arcades Project* (*Das Passagen-Werk*, 1927–40) Benjamin defined the objective of the historian as 'dialectics at a standstill' (Benjamin, 1983: 577) and offered two strategies for its attainment: montage and a commentary structure. Both of these are present in Brecht's *Baden-Baden Learning Play* and in the film to which I now wish to turn, itself an adaptation of a Brecht text, Jean-Marie Straub and Danièle Huillet's *History Lessons* (*Geschichtsunterricht*, 1972).

Straub–Huillet's Passages of Film: 'a film that one shoots is always about the present' (Rosenbaum, 1982b: 6)

The title of the film has led some commentators to suggest that *History Lessons* is an experiment in translating Benjamin's concept of history into filmic practice. It certainly attempts what Brecht, in his 'sociological experiment', *The Threepenny Trial* (*Der Dreigroschenprozeß: Ein Soziologisches Experiment*, 1931), refers to as a 'refunctioning of film' (Brecht, 1978–98: 21, 449). In Straub–Huillet's case, the most conspicuous tool for this 'refunctioning' is radical slowness.

History Lessons is based on Brecht's fragmentary novel, *The Business Affairs of Mr Julius Caesar* (*Die Geschäfte des Herrn Julius Caesar*), written between 1937 and 1940. According to Straub, he and Huillet 'only used sections from the novel which were a discussion on economics [. . .] I judge the texts we did select as amongst the strongest I know' (Engel, 1975: 20). The passages chosen are from Books 1 and 3: 'the rest of the novel wouldn't have interested me. There are a lot of things like anecdotes', Straub claimed (Engel, 1975: 20). These sections of Brecht's novel are completely devoid of action and almost entirely static, consisting of protracted dialogues between a young historian (in modern clothes in the film) and various figures who knew 'the untouchable model for all dictators' personally (in historical costume) (Brecht 1978–98: 17, 171).

Straub–Huillet have acknowledged that their materialist, Brechtian method of adaptation, which has encompassed writers as diverse as Heinrich Böll, Cesare Pavese, Marguerite Duras, Franz Kafka, Friedrich Hölderlin, and Elio Vittorini, amounts to an 'appropriation of the classical heritage' and also claimed that *History Lessons* is 'all Marx, but it's not from Marx' (Witte, 1976: 211; Engel, 1975: 26).

SLOW WALKS

History Lessons begins with very brief shots of three Fascist maps of the declining Roman Empire, and a statue to Caesar erected by Mussolini. This precipitous prologue lasting a mere fifteen seconds in total is followed by the first of three extended car drives – *Spaziergänge* or strolls, according to Straub – through the narrow streets of working-class Rome. Each consists of a single, uninterrupted shot of nine or ten minutes duration. The abrupt shift from public, monumental, imperial history, alluded to at breakneck speed, to its byways is reminiscent of the extraordinary opening of Brecht and Slatan Dudow's film *Kuhle Wampe* (*Kuhle Wampe oder: Wem gehört die Welt?*, 1932), in which the classical columns of the Brandenburg Gate dissolve after a mere four seconds into the factory towers of working-class Berlin. Moreover, the three car journeys and the shots of running water which separate the young man's interviews (with a banker, peasant, lawyer, and writer) constitute the main body of the film and serve a similar function to the documentary inserts of trees, water, and factories that punctuate *Kuhle Wampe*. It is these slow drives that will be the main focus of this chapter. First, however, it is necessary to contextualise them within the film's political methodology.

As the many commentators on this canonical Brechtian film were quick to point out, *History Lessons* is as Brechtian in its style as it is in its source material: 'this is not simply a Brecht adaptation but a cinematic reading of certain parts of the novel chosen for political reasons' (Witte 1976: 194). Martin Walsh is not the only commentator to claim 'it is a pity [Brecht] never lived to see *History Lessons*' (1981: 61).

FILM AS DOCUMENTATION AND DURATION

Maureen Turim has pointed out that the film employs all the tools of the (materialist) historian, 'maps, monuments, memoirs, financial accounts, interviews' (1986: 231), and, in his illuminating essay on the film, Gilberto Perez concludes that: 'Every film by Straub/Huillet may be described as a document of documents, a juxtaposition of traces from different times in the past, concrete pieces of evidence to be compared with one another in the present' (1982: 12).

The present, Theodor W. Adorno's *hic et nunc* and Benjamin's 'now-time' (*Jetztzeit*), incorporates the past. Inevitably most commentators, including Martin Walsh and Barton Byg in two particularly stimulating commentaries on the film, are drawn to comparisons both with Benjamin and the serial music of Schoenberg, not least given that *History Lessons* was followed by the first two Straub–Huillet films on the composer.[2] Such interpretations, however, are only part of the story. Interestingly, both Walsh and Byg seem to sense that something is missing in their scholarly exegeses and feel compelled to acknowledge, at least in passing, the film's beauty. This beauty is, I would suggest, inseparable from the film's slowness. I will return to this question in what follows.

BRECHT AND THE *JOUISSANCE* OF SLOWNESS

Having concluded that the audience has to work rather hard in the film and 'co-produce, rather than consume', Walsh changes tack and proclaims that *History Lessons* is 'a text of "*jouissance*"' rather than mere *plaisir*: 'Just as Brecht liberates us from the normative image of Caesar, so Straub/Huillet free us from the visual–aural chains of cinematic illusionism' (1981: 61, 77). Once again, it is through slowness, exemplified by the three car journeys, that this freedom is attained.

It is not simply the ensnarement of illusionism and narrative that the spectator is freed from but also the ensnarement of speed. Byg, having noted the compulsion to construct meaning, identifies in the film a 'sense of play in the filmmaker's art and the joy implicit in the discovery of the free interplay between aesthetic beauty and harmony and "meaning"' (Byg, 1995: 135). This free interplay demands time, and it is this that the film offers the audience in abundance, not only in the car drives but also in the leisurely pace of the dialogues they disrupt. Paradigmatically, one of these conversations, with the banker (shot 16), takes place during an unhurried stroll along a hillside road (behind the Roman Villa Aldobrandini), and is symptomatic of the film's measured tempo.

SLOWNESS AS THE LESSON OF HISTORY

Both Walsh and Byg identify a liberating moment in *History Lessons*. According to Byg, it is a form of release that is lacking in Brecht's unfinished novel in which the narrator is not afforded insight and does not undergo any discernible transformation. Like others before him, Byg sees Brecht's own crisis as an exiled artist commenting on Hitler reflected in this irresolution. In the film, however, he finds 'a liberating effect both on the narrator and the viewer' (1995: 135).

Commentators have spent many happy pages deconstructing the extraordinary montage and framing of the interviews in *History Lessons*. While Walsh sees both the young man and banker as equally trapped by the camera and their roles, Byg asserts that, while 'the banker is a captive of both the shot and the text; the young man is free' (Byg, 1995: 134). Certainly, we have been encouraged by the film to identify with the young man. He is the driver of the car which roams through the alleyways of Rome for almost exactly a third of the film's duration; he is the detective piecing together the evidence. In the manner of a narrator in a Learning Play he is the interrogator of the witnesses, sometimes probing, sometimes silent. As Straub–Huillet point out, he is also the one character in contemporary dress and he is frequently positioned as the audience's representative within the *mise en scène*. His gradual disappearance from the frame and escape from the formal straitjacket of the film's structure – underscored by his increasing taciturnity and physical distance from the banker – suggest that he is, in Byg's words, capable of 'using the tools of perception to become less susceptible to the manipulative power of either historical stories or analyses and to make use of them while leaving them behind' (Byg, 1995: 138). In doing so, he demonstrates that he has learnt the lessons of history, chief among them being the 'Discovery of Slowness', as the title of Sten Nadolny's famous novel (*Die Entdeckung der Langsamkeit*, 1983) would have it. It is this discovery that the film passes on to the audience in an unexpectedly visceral, some would say provocative, manner in the 'interminable' car drives.

BRECHT AND SLOW BEAUTY: A REVOLUTIONARY ERUPTION

What commentators – but not the film-makers themselves – have tended to overlook in their comments on the film is, as alluded to above, its remarkable beauty: its measured pace, its language, framing, and structure. Little has also been made of the important part played by nature – the trees, the flowers which act as an almost surreally beautiful backdrop to the final interview with the banker, the images of a stream, mountains and the sea, all of which point to an enduring natural, diurnal rhythm.

The final image of the film is of a fountain in the Via Giulia in Rome in the shape of a woman's head spewing water. Like the mountain stream flowing across the shots which frame the interview with the peasant and the car driving through the thoroughfares of Rome, this image shows a passage through and out of the frame. Straub has noted that the woman is not only a counterpoint to the patriarchy that monopolises the film for the first fifty-five of its fifty-six shots but is also vomiting at the banker's final remark: 'My confidence in him had proved well-founded. Our small bank was no small bank any more' (Brecht, 1978–98: 17, 319). The water is literally and metaphorically an *Ausbruch*, an eruption of rage by the people. The point is underscored by the snatch of Bach's *St Matthew Passion* which accompanies this final shot: 'Open your fiery pit, o Hell / Wreck, ruin, engulf, shatter / With sudden force / The false betrayer, the murderous blood!' (Huillet, 1976: 76)

But the outburst at the end of the film is not only devoid of movement, the flowing water aside, but also quite protracted. Not only does the final shot last one minute and fourteen seconds (with its sound continuing over the closing credits) but also, conceptually at least, is extended much further given that the same shot opens Straub–Huillet's next film, *Introduction to Arnold Schoenberg's Accompaniment to a Cinematographic Scene* (*Einleitung zu Arnold Schoenbergs Begleitmusik zu einer Lichtspielscene*, 1972), a gesture which suggests – metaphorically at least – a cinema of extreme duration. In extending the shot across two films Straub and Huillet establish a protracted hiatus to imply that the eruption of revolutionary rage persists. Revolution is, and, indeed, should be, a long drawn-out process.

STALLING AND OVERTAKING

Perez, in the essay quoted above, has noted that the three car journeys through Rome are complexly framed:

> Without any cuts or pans, or even the slightest wavering, the city is pho-tographed from the fixed vantage point inside the moving car, through a kind of grid constituted by the two side windows on the left and right of the screen, the windshield at the center, and an open sun roof at the top. [. . .]
>
> We are denied the illusion of reality without being allowed to forget the fact of its photographic reproduction – the fact that this is a picture taken of reality, not a firsthand experience of the streets of Rome but not a self-contained design apart from life either. [. . .]
>
> Straub and Huillet materialize the commerce between the image and reality peculiar to a medium which is both pictorial and documentary. The camera is identified with that other machine carrying it around, the car, as equally subject to the constraints of being in the world, with limited access to a concrete historical situation. (Perez, 1982: 10)

Of course, the city life we see from the car is not itself going any faster or slower than would normally be the case. The disjunctive, disturbing experience for the spectator arises from the fact that we are expected to watch it in three long unbroken shots: first for nine minutes and twenty-nine seconds (shot 5), second for ten minutes and seven seconds (shot 38), and third for ten minutes and eighteen seconds (shot 45).[3]

What is significant about the young man's driving, moreover, is that it is exasperatingly slow, not simply for the spectator, for whom the real issue is probably the duration of the three episodes rather than the speed of what is shown, but especially for the other road users. Horns are repeatedly sounded by cars and motorbikes and, on a number of occasions, both are seen to over-take the young man at pace as he crawls along the byways of Rome. In one

Figure 4.1 *History Lessons*, 1972.

instance, during the third sequence, the frustration of a fellow road user almost results in a collision. The audience is left wondering whether the young man's pace is occasioned by innate tentativeness (the psychological interpretation), a lack of acquaintance with the area he is driving through (the narrative explanation), a desire to find something en route (the political interpretation), or is to allow us to find things (the pedagogical interpretation). One is ultimately left unsure as to whether the decision to drive so slowly is his or that of the directors and/or the cinematographer and sound technician occupying the rear seats. The fact that the actor/driver, Benjamin Zulauf, is credited as an 'assistant' in the opening production credits suggests that he is both within and without the film's diegesis.

What is certain is that the young man's measured pace – which, on at least one occasion, even results in the car stalling – does encourage one to concentrate on the busy streets with their crumbling buildings, passers-by, cyclists, and people seated outside bars and restaurants. One might notice, for example, the preponderance of women, the relatively large number of children, and, in the third automotive stroll, an increasing number of posters bearing a hammer and sickle on the walls of the buildings. Indeed, it would be fair to suggest that the last are the pay-off for attentive scrutiny of the cityscape, the political reward, so to speak.

Perez describes the young man's charting of the city as 'conducting a scrutiny', 'exploratory' and 'interrogative' (1982: 12). Karsten Witte claims that the audience follows the drives with the same rapt attention that they bestow on the accounts of Caesar's nefarious business dealings – the young man/driver thus functions as a representative for the audience within the diegesis and serves not simply as a witness but as a teacher (1976a: 194). As in Brecht's *Baden-Baden Learning Play* we encounter the notion that slowness is instructive and enlightening, or at least a means to enlightenment. Not, of course, in any transcendental, ambient or spiritual way, rather in a materialist sense. As the dramatist Mark Ravenhill has put it, reviewing an eight-hour durational performance by Krystian Lupa (*Factory 2*, 2008), 'I was truly being treated as an adult, someone who didn't need to be constantly diverted, who had chosen to be here and was being given space for my own responses' (Ravenhill, 2009). Jonathan Rosenbaum recalls an instructive discussion regarding enlightenment through protracted observation following the screening of *History Lessons* at the Edinburgh Festival:

> Asked at the Edinburgh Film festival why the long sequences inside a car being driven through Rome in *History Lessons* were included, Straub replied (I quote from memory), in order to empty the theatre, because people who are not able to look at the street will never be able to understand class struggle. (He added that being able to look at the street was not necessarily easy, that it had taken him some time to learn himself.) (Rosenbaum, 1982a: 2)

If this is the case, then, in its making and viewing, *History Lessons* is a 'Learning Film'. Moreover, given the audience's (almost) inevitable discomfort at the protracted drives, their visceral involvement makes them part of the action – almost more so than the conspicuously calm and unflappable driver of the car – as was envisaged in Brecht's Learning Plays which, in their earliest, most radical manifestations, were intended to do away with the (passive) audience entirely and collapse the distinction between production and reception. I would suggest that this is obliquely figured in the framing of the automotive strolls: along with the four views out of the car windows discussed by Perez and others, there is also a fifth 'frame', that of the rear-view mirror in which we see the face of the young man driving, reflected back to us as an 'image within an image'. This framing of the act of looking self-reflexively highlights the common ground between the driver and the audience, not least given that attentive looking is, obviously, essential to both car-driving and cinema-going (at least insofar as it is not mere distraction).

In Straub–Huillet's film irritation is a key tool in the learning process. It is also perhaps the most consistent feature of their works from their debut, *Machorka-Muff* (1962), through to *Itinerary of Jean Bricard* (*Itinéraire de Jean Bricard*, 2008), completed after Huillet's death in 2006.

SLOWNESS AS ESTRANGEMENT (*VERFREMDUNG*)

History Lessons is neither the first nor the last time that Straub–Huillet use the passage of a car through a cityscape as a metaphor for the process of enlightenment. In *Not Reconciled or, Only Violence Helps Where Violence Rules* (*Nicht versöhnt oder Es hilft nur Gewalt wo Gewalt herrscht*, 1965) a post-war returnee confronts his former tormentor in a car travelling through Cologne; *The Bridegroom, the Comedienne and the Pimp* (*Der Bräutigam, die Komödiantin und der Zuhälter*, 1968) opens with a four-minute nine-second travelling shot from the side window of a car along the main road of Munich's red-light district, the Landsbergerstrasse. Here the revealing insight into the shadier side of the economic miracle is underscored by an accompanying extract from J. S. Bach's *Resurrection Oratorio*. In the documentary *Too Early Too Late* (*Trop tôt, trop tard*, 1980/81) we go round and round a roundabout in Paris for five minutes and twenty seconds. *Too Early Too Late* in fact contains more durational shots than any other film of Straub–Huillet, alluding to one of cinema's first observational films – the Lumière Brothers' *Workers Leaving the Lumière Factory* (*La Sortie des usines Lumière à Lyon*, 1895) – in a static, unbroken shot of ten minutes and sixteen seconds showing workers leaving a Cairo factory. What the film tells us, paradigmatically and in accord with *History Lessons*, is that change demands attention to detail, attention to detail demands time, time demands slowness. In discussion with Jonathan Rosenbaum, Straub claimed he was inspired here by 'the use of suspensions and slow tempos' in the late quartets of Beethoven (Rosenbaum, 1983: 197).

Straub–Huillet's first travelling shot from a car, along the Landsbergerstrasse in Munich, has become iconic, partly because of the directors' generosity – they provided Rainer Werner Fassbinder with a substantial out-take for his first feature *Love is Colder than Death* (*Liebe ist kälter als der Tod*, 1969) – but also because it was imitated by other admirers and disciples, most notably Wim Wenders, who quoted it in his last student short, *3 American LPs* (*3 amerikanische LPs*, 1969), in which a similarly slow drive ends up, rather more explicitly, in a drive-in cinema, and also in his first feature film, *Summer in the City – Dedicated to the Kinks* (1970), where it is accompanied by the Kinks' song 'Too Much on My Mind'. This example is illuminating because it demonstrates how simply the topos of the automotive stroll can be reconfigured (and depoliticised) to become paradigmatic for a very different kind of slow cinema, one that is meditative, moody, and subjective.

'ONE MAY FIND THE EXPERIENCE UNBEARABLE; THAT SOMETIMES HAPPENS'
(DANEY, 1982: 19)

Critics have noted that *History Lessons* initially elicited negative responses from its audiences (and some critics). Anecdotal evidence would suggest this is still the case.[4] Perhaps the incomplete nature of the car drives is key here. They possess the fragmentary quality Brecht characterised as a key feature of Epic Theatre: all start *in medias res* and they end with the car still in motion; on the most basic level this means that the audience has no way of knowing when they will end as they fail to provide a structural or narrative 'pay-off' or cadence. This open-ended quality is, of course, metonymic of the film itself and, indeed, of Straub–Huillet's *oeuvre* as a whole; one might even add of Brechtian political modernism more widely. *Itinerary of Jean Bricard* virtually reiterates the automotive strolls of *History Lessons* though, this time, the view is from a boat on the Loire: the film opens with a travelling shot of the banks of the river lasting thirteen minutes and forty-eight seconds (with a single cut at three minutes and thirty-eight) and ends with a second of four minutes forty-four. Again the audience is left to interpret what passes by and, should they so wish, construct a narrative or rationale to explain the seemingly disproportionate amount of attention being afforded to it. Between the two river sequences a story of resistance to National Socialism is related. This provides a means to (re)interpret the river in the framing sequences. It is a film which, to appropriate a phrase from Ravenhill, doesn't 'stop to worry that I might get bored' (Ravenhill, 2009). This is also the case with the drives in *History Lessons*, and it is this that justifies its designation as *Unterricht*: the scenes between the drives, the dialogues, reveal the machinations of Roman (proto-) capitalism and, with this 'evidence', the audience is encouraged to view the narrow streets of present-day (now again historical) Rome in a different light, be it as a product of a long history of class struggle or whatever. Just as Brecht intended his virtually action-free novel to shed light on the business dealings of National Socialism (as the liberal use of anachronistic Nazi turns of phrase in the utterances of his Roman protagonists highlights), so Brecht's dialogues illuminate the present; for them to do so we need time to learn the lessons and collect the evidence. In the cinema and, paradigmatically, in *History Lessons*, the 'refunctioning' of spectatorship and the resulting attainment of political insight are possible only through the *dispositif* of Brechtian slow cinema.

NOTES

1. Of the works most frequently cited in this field, only Matthew Flanagan deals at any length with Straub–Huillet, though he relegates their Marxism to a footnote, suggesting that it is 'not [. . .] necessarily important to note' (2012: 125). Tiago de Luca has only a passing reference to Straub–Huillet (2014: 23), further suggesting

that their work has hitherto been marginal to discussions of slow cinema, despite its centrality to the writings of Deleuze and others.
2. The serial method of composition allowed Schoenberg to escape from the brevity of his totally chromatic works: dodecaphony directly encouraged more expansive, less fleeting musical structures. In the 1950s it was to facilitate the development of 'slow music' (minimalism), when La Monte Young extended the durations in his early, Webern-inspired *Trio for Strings* (1958).
3. All shot durations given in this chapter are taken from the Straub–Huillet Éditions Montparnasse DVDs to enable like-for-like comparisons.
4. At a screening of the film at the Brecht-Haus in Berlin in February 2014 the audience became increasingly restless across the three car journeys.

BIBLIOGRAPHY

Benjamin, Walter (1977), *Illuminationen* (Frankfurt am Main: Suhrkamp).
Benjamin, Walter (1983), *Das Passagen-Werk*, edited by R. Tiedemann, 2 vols (Frankfurt am Main: Suhrkamp).
Brecht, Bertolt (1988–98), *Werke*, edited by W. Hecht, J. Knopf, W. Mittenzwei and K.-D. Müller, 30 vols (Berlin and Frankfurt am Main: Aufbau Verlag/Suhrkamp Verlag).
Brecht, Bertolt (1997), *The Baden-Baden Lesson on Consent*, in *Collected Plays: Three* (London: Methuen).
Byg, Barton (1995), *Landscapes of Resistance: The German Films of Danièle Huillet and Jean-Marie Straub* (Berkeley, Los Angeles and London: University of California Press).
Daney, Serge (1982), 'Cinemeterorology', translated by Jonathan Rosenbaum, in J. Rosenbaum (ed.), *The Cinema of Jean-Marie Straub and Daniele Huillet* [*sic*] (New York: The Public Theatre), p. 19.
de Luca, Tiago (2014), *Realism of the Senses in World Cinema: The Experience of Physical Reality* (London and New York: I. B. Tauris).
Engel, Andi (1972), 'Andi Engel talks to Jean-Marie Straub, and Danièle Huillet is there too', *Enthusiasm*, 1 (1975), pp. 1–25.
Flanagan, Matthew (2012), *'Slow Cinema': Temporality and Style in Contemporary Art and Experimental Film*, unpublished PhD dissertation, University of Exeter.
Huillet, Danièle and Jean-Marie Straub (1976), 'History Lessons – Scenario', *Screen*, 17: 1, pp. 54–76.
Perez, Gilberto (1982), 'The Modernist Cinema: The History Lessons of Straub and Huillet', in Jonathan Rosenbaum (ed.), *The Cinema of Jean-Marie Straub and Daniele Huillet* [*sic*] (New York: The Public Theatre), pp. 9–14.
Ravenhill, Mark (2009), 'The Joy of Slow Theatre', *The Guardian*, 20 April 2009, http://www.theguardian.com/stage/2009/apr/20/mark-ravenhill-slow-theatre [accessed 1 August 2014].
Rosenbaum, Jonathan (1982a), 'Introduction: Once it was Fire . . .', in Jonathan Rosenbaum (ed.), *The Cinema of Jean-Marie Straub and Daniele Huillet* [*sic*] (New York: The Public Theatre), pp. 2–4.
Rosenbaum, Jonathan (1982b), 'Straub and Huillet on Filmmakers They Like and Related Matters', in J. Rosenbaum (ed.), *The Cinema of Jean-Marie Straub and Daniele Huillet* [*sic*] (New York: The Public Theatre), pp. 5–8.
Rosenbaum, Jonathan (1983), *The Front Line: 1983* (Denver, CO: Arden Press).
Turim, Maureen (1986), 'Textuality and theatricality in Brecht and Straub/Huillet: *History Lessons* (1972)', in E. Rentschler (ed.), *German Film and Literature: Adaptations and Transformations* (New York and London: Methuen), pp. 231–45.

Walsh, Martin (1981), *The Brechtian Aspect of Radical Cinema: Essays by Martin Walsh* (London: BFI Publishing).

Witte, Karsten (1976a), 'Kommentierte Filmographie', in U. Gregor, R. Hohlweg, P. W. Jansen, H. H. Prinzler, W. Schütte, K. Wetzel and K. Witte (eds), *Herzog / Kluge / Straub* (Munich and Vienna: Carl Hanser Verlag), pp. 179–204.

Witte, Karsten (1976b), 'Interview', in U. Gregor, R. Hohlweg, P. W. Jansen, H. H. Prinzler, W. Schütte, K. Wetzel, K. Witte (eds), *Herzog / Kluge / Straub* (Munich and Vienna: Carl Hanser Verlag), pp. 205–18.

PART II

CONTEXTUALISING SLOW CINEMA

5. TEMPORAL AESTHETICS OF DRIFTING: TSAI MING-LIANG AND A CINEMA OF SLOWNESS

Song Hwee Lim[1]

In a Calabrian village in southern Italy, an elderly goatherd tends to his flock by day and copes with his cough by night, workmen meticulously build a mound-like kiln to turn wood into charcoal, and an enormous tree is felled and trimmed before being erected in the centre of the village for a celebratory ritual. Seasons come and go, the goatherd dies, and a lamb is born. Michelangelo Frammartino's *Le Quattro Volte* (2010) bears the trademark of what has been called a cinema of slowness, and exemplifies a resurgence, within contemporary world cinema, of a commitment to the use of non-professional actors, location shooting, natural lighting and the long take. In this chapter, I shall delineate the context in which this cinema of slowness emerges, explicate the concept of cinematic slowness, and provide an illustration of this slow cinema by drawing on examples from the films of Tsai Ming-liang. I shall argue that Tsai's cinema of slowness challenges us to rethink the relationship between stillness and movement through a temporal aesthetics of drifting.

Fittingly, *Le Quattro Volte* comes from a nation that christened cinematic neorealism over sixty years ago. Not coincidentally, this country also gave birth to the Slow Food movement in 1989 when McDonald's plan to open a branch at the foot of the Spanish Steps in Rome triggered demonstrations at the proposed site and a movement that was founded in Paris in December that year (Kummer, 2002: 20–2). Taking a cue from the Slow Food movement, many organisations and enterprises promoting the concept of slow living have since flourished. As Carl Honoré states in his bestselling book, *In Praise of Slow: How a Worldwide Movement is Challenging the Cult of Speed*, this movement inevitably 'overlaps with the anti-globalisation crusade', and a 'genuinely Slow world implies nothing less than a lifestyle revolution' (2004: 16, 17).

Within this discourse on slowness, globalisation is seen to be having a particularly homogenising effect on culture, leading to 'the McDonaldization of society' (Ritzer, 1993) in which both food and people have become supersized. By contrast, the Slow movement advocates downsizing to the level of the local, and places emphases on organic origins, artisanal processes and ethical products. These values are anathema to speed which is seen as the arch-enemy of slowness. Though there has not been a corresponding Speed movement over the same period, it can be argued that speed is so ubiquitous in modern life that it passes as natural; hence its ideological force, like the naturalising ones in relation to gender and sexuality, for example, must be unveiled and challenged precisely because of its seeming transparency.

In *The Speed Handbook: Velocity, Pleasure, Modernism*, Enda Duffy pinpoints the emergence of the cult of speed to the turn of the twentieth century when the invention of the motor car was 'repackaged as a sensation and a pleasure to be put at the disposal of the individual consumer', a 'modernist mobile architecture' which offered 'a new pleasure to the masses' (2009: 5, 6). A century later, the ideology of speed, like the inescapable car advertisements on our multimedia screens, has become the mainstay of modern consciousness, to the extent that any celebration of slowness is immediately cast, in Duffy's terms, as either 'reacting to' or 'reactionary in relation to' speed, and 'out-of-date' (2009: 50). It is against this background that we can begin to address a question posed by Milan Kundera: 'Why has the pleasure of slowness disappeared?' (1995: 3) – a question that, I would suggest, can be approached only through historicisation. For there is no uniform appreciation for slowness (pleasure for some, pain for others) nor is there a singular explanation for its supposed disappearance. Indeed, the first question to ask is not so much why slowness has seemingly disappeared but rather where and when an ideology of slowness reigns supreme, and where and when it has lost its currency. Only by identifying exact moments in which and precise locations wherein slowness manifests in specific configurations of knowledge and power can we begin to understand why it has been regarded as pain or pleasure, and why it has appeared or disappeared.

While 'conspicuous consumption' was the hallmark of the leisure class in the United States at the beginning of the twentieth century (Veblen, 2007), a hundred years later 'sustainability' has become the buzzword for the intelligentsia, activists, and middle-class consumers, marking a paradigm shift from quantity to quality, from waste to taste, and from speed to slowness. It is no accident that both a cinema of slowness and a Slow movement appeared at the turn of the twenty-first century. While they may not feed off each other in a conscious manner, their coeval emergence bespeaks a desire, albeit expressed in distinct social spheres and in disparate ways, to formulate a different relationship with time and space. More specifically, the Slow movement can be seen as an attempt not only to counter the compression of time and space brought about by technological and other changes but also to bridge the widening gap between the global and the local under the intense speed of globalisation. In tandem with the rise of ecocriticism, the environmental movement, and the antiglobalisation brigade, the Slow movement signals a political turn in public consciousness that now sees the local as imbricated within the global. This consciousness is reflected in slogans such as 'Think Globally, Act Locally', and in the popularity of books such as Naomi Klein's *No Logo* (2000) and Eric Schlosser's *Fast Food Nation* (2002).

At the same time, a cinema of slowness has appeared in many parts of the world to address both the speeding up of modern life in the social sphere and the treatment of time in narrative films. While, throughout the history of cinema, there have been films that can be regarded as slow (however problematic or subjective the qualifications may be), the discourse on slowness in cinema is fairly new. Within this discourse, the names of some usual suspects make regular appearances (Béla Tarr, Alexander Sokurov, Lisandro Alonso, Theo Angelopoulos, Pedro Costa, Hou Hsiao-hsien, Abbas Kiarostami) while others from an earlier era are routinely cited as precursors of this tendency (Ozu, Antonioni, Tarkovsky, Akerman), with artists and movements associated with avant-garde film-making and video art also invoked as kindred spirits (Andy Warhol, Michael Snow, structural film).

The concept of slowness poses a challenging theoretical question for film studies not only because it is predicated upon the profound and complex notion of time, a subject of much scientific and philosophical inquiry over the ages, but also because time (or slowness) is, to a great extent, a matter of perception and experience, and it can never merely be an objective temporal (or rhythmic) measurement. Any engagement with time – even in the form of watching a film – is invariably contingent upon constantly changing factors (both individuated and circumstantial), from a person's disposition, his or her physical and psychical state at the time, the immediate and larger environment, to other historical, social, and cultural specificities. Cinematic time is, thus, both ontological and phenomenological. One person's idea and experience of slowness could well be that of another person's speed.

It is somewhat surprising that, given the centrality of time in film, and despite a recent surge in publications on the very topic, very little has been written on the specific subject of cinematic rhythm and pacing, and even less on the concept of slowness and its various (cinematic and extra-cinematic) functions.[2] I propose narratorial subject and duration as two aspects that are central to the concept of cinematic slowness. If the films of Chantal Akerman can be summed up as, suggests the title of the book devoted to their study, *Nothing Happens*

(Margulies, 1996), this phrase should not be taken merely as a descriptor of the property of supposedly slow films. Rather, it should lead us to pose a more fundamental question about what qualifies as a legitimate subject in film – the very notion of 'thing,' and what counts as 'nothing' within a film's narrative. At the same time, the duration accorded to filming a narratorial subject deemed as 'nothing happening' features prominently in the debate on slow cinema, raising the corresponding question about the justification not just for representing so-called 'nothingness' but, perhaps more crucially and controversially, for representing it over a long (and for some, longer than 'necessary') duration.

In addition, I suggest that these two aspects manifest themselves in the following concrete cinematic forms: narratively, a trope of waiting that may, for some spectators, become a source of boredom; durationally, the use of long takes that has been identified as a hallmark of a cinema of slowness. Within film scholarship, Gilles Deleuze's distinction between movement–image and time–image is key to a rethinking of what might constitute a legitimate 'thing' or 'happening' in film narratives, and the duration accorded to its representation. For Deleuze, it is the direct time–image, 'a little time in the pure state' that 'rises up to the surface of the screen' in post-war modern cinema (2005: xi–xii). The implication of Deleuze's concept of the time–image is to open up a space – both cinematic and discursive – in which time itself can become a new subject of representation. Tellingly, Tsai Ming-liang's view on cinematic temporality is illustrated via an example on waiting. Asked in an interview about his notion of time, Tsai explained that he often felt, when he saw other people's films, that 'the time in them isn't real enough, it's either too short or too long' (Rivière and Tsai, 1999: 105). He also talked about the ways in which his films differ in their relation to time:

> So, for instance, in some films, to show that the hero has been waiting for quite a time you'll be shown five cigarette stubs in the ashtray. Normally, for a scene like that I will film the character for as long as it takes him to smoke five cigarettes. That's real time, but it's very difficult to handle because the audience will get bored. But I think I do this deliberately because I want them to feel that the hero is in a state of anxiety, waiting for something that may not happen, etc. I don't just want them to know logically that the hero has been waiting for a long time; no, I also want them to feel this real waiting time. (Rivière and Tsai, 1999: 107)

With film-makers such as Tsai taking a literal approach to temporal realism using single long takes, the audacity or scandal, depending on one's view, of a cinema of slowness lies precisely in its representation of 'content [that] seems at variance with the duration accorded it' (Margulies, 1996: 21): it is not simply that nothing happens in these films but that it takes too long for nothing to happen. But how long is too long? And does duration necessarily correlate to boredom?

It must be noted that boredom does not occur only when a film is 'too slow' because 'fast films can also bore' (Misek, 2012: 137) and, like the experience of time (and slowness) itself, boredom is highly subjective. In *A Philosophy of Boredom*, Lars Svendsen notes instances of 'situative boredom' (here drawing on Heidegger) in which it is 'not time itself or the things themselves, but the situation in which they are placed that can give rise to boredom' (2005: 119). Thus, in his essay, 'Dead Time: Cinema, Heidegger, and Boredom', Richard Misek suggests that cinema is a privileged site of situative boredom because 'it imposes duration' (2012: 134). According to Karl Schoonover, art cinema 'exploits its spectator's boredom', and the debate about film spectatorship has been restaged today as an 'opposition of time wasted versus time labored' (2012: 66, 67). The terms of this debate betray modernity's investment in temporality because the notion of waste is deemed unacceptable under the logic of Taylorist efficiency and productivity even though capitalism itself is based upon wasteful material consumption to secure its prosperity. Indeed, today we live in a so-called 'cash-rich, time-poor society' in which money and goods can be squandered but not time. This is because time is not just money; rather, it is more valuable than money.

It is in this context that we can appreciate the paradoxical notion of waste within capitalist modernity: at once material necessity and temporal luxury. Under the logic of capitalism, there can be no greater luxury than the luxury of time or, rather, the crime of boredom. For to be bored is not to have made full use of time, to be inefficient, to waste time. If mainstream cinema's aim is to provide 'escapism' from boredom by utilising 'various forms of speed (activity-filled narratives, rapid camera movement, fast cuts, up-tempo soundtracks, and so on) to keep us entertained' (Misek, 2012: 135, 137), the slow art film, on the other hand, invites us to reconsider the value of waste even as this notion of waste challenges conventional ideas about utility, productivity, and labour.

Why does an aesthetics of cinematic slowness matter? In *The Politics of Aesthetics*, Jacques Rancière emphasises that the term aesthetics 'does not refer to a theory of sensibility, taste, and pleasure for art amateurs' (2006: 22). Rather, he sees aesthetic acts as 'configurations of experience that create new modes of sense perception and induce novel forms of political subjectivity' (Rancière, 2006: 9). In this light, a cinema of slowness is much more than a temporal aesthetics that appeals to a certain class of audience with a particular taste for art cinema. By formulating a different relationship between film images and the audience through the use of long takes, extended duration, and the trope of waiting, this cinema comprises aesthetics acts that promote new modes of temporal experience, new ways of seeing, and new subjectivities that are politically committed to an ethos of slowness.

Unlike Deleuze's two books on cinema, which take post-war Europe as the dividing line and draw mainly from films made in Europe and the United States as examples, the body of films routinely cited as belonging to a cinema of slowness originates from a wider geography across the world. Given that we are looking at an anglophone discourse that has emerged largely out of consumption of such films at international film festivals and art-house cinemas in Europe, North America, and Australia, it might be tempting to see a cinema of slowness as, in part, a form of Western consumption of postcolonial visuality, with its attendant politics of othering and exoticisation. While such a mode of consumption cannot be totally discounted, however, Europe's strong representation among the usual suspects of slow cinema film-makers problematises this reading whereas the conspicuous absence of directors from the United States (with the exception of Gus Van Sant, perhaps) reinforces the association of Hollywood cinema with speed.

It would be impossible to generalise why slow films have appeared quite independently of, yet somehow resonating with, one another across these geographical locales over the past two decades or so. As I mentioned earlier, the coeval emergence of a cinema of slowness and the slow movement at the turn of the twenty-first century bespeaks a desire to bridge the gap between the local and the global under a new mantra of sustainability. A European aesthetics of slowness, in both everyday life and film, is arguably borne out of material comfort because the societies that underpin such ideological investment can, quite literally, afford to do so in their late capitalist stage of economic development; slowness, for Europe, is at once temporal and material luxury to which it can aspire and attain. On the other hand, a turn to slowness in rapidly developing regions, such as East Asia, may arise from an anxiety towards wholesale modernisation and industrialisation, and thus a desire to hold on to a less hectic pace associated with an agricultural past.

Yet we know that, within each country and each region, there exist huge income inequalities and urban/rural divides that complicate a simple dichotomy along the line of so-called First World versus Third World economies. Argentinian director Lisandro Alonso's film, *Freedom* (*La Libertad*, 2001) derives its temporality, like the Welsh film *Sleep Furiously* (Gideon Koppel, 2008) and Hungarian director Béla Tarr's film *The Turin Horse* (*A Torinói ló*, 2011), from the daily routines of peasant life. The condition of ennui may also transcend urban/rural as well as cultural divides so that boredom experienced by the youth can be translated into similarly glacial temporality in Jia Zhangke's *Unknown Pleasures* (*Ren xiaoyao*, 2002) and Bruno Dumont's *The Life of Jesus* (*La vie de Jésus*, 1997). Furthermore, a spiritual or poetic dimension often finds its expression in a more considered pace or in the form of cyclical temporality, as the films of Apichatpong Weerasethakul and Theo Angelopoulos demonstrate.

To illustrate one property of slow cinema, I shall now move on to discuss the visual trope of drifting objects or organisms that runs across three Tsai Ming-liang films. Towards the end of his 2001 film *What Time Is It There?* (*Ni nabian jidian*), a suitcase belonging to the sleeping female protagonist (Chen Shiang-chyi) drifts on the pool in Le Jardin des Tuileries in Paris, only to be fished out by the male protagonist's (Lee Kang-sheng) dead father (Miao Tien) with the handle of his umbrella. This visual trope is picked up in *I Don't Want to Sleep Alone* (*Heiyanquan*, 2006), which closes with a floating mattress on which the three central characters (Chen, Lee, and Norman Atun) are asleep, this time on the pool in a construction site in Kuala Lumpur. In *Visage* (*Lian*, 2009), a naked man (Atun) lays afloat on a metal structure in a musical number set in the underground water tunnel of the Louvre; the film closes with the appearance of Tsai and Lee Kang-sheng, along with a drifting stag, by the same pool in Le Jardin des Tuileries.

These instances foreground a stillness of diegetic action as the characters are mostly asleep and the camera also remains largely static (except for the shot in the water tunnel). The drifting objects, however, problematise the relationship between stillness and movement because they simultaneously embody both: they are still objects in motion. Death is, in a sense, the ultimate form of stillness. Sleep, on the other hand, is the state closest to death in its stillness and to drift in hovering between consciousness and unconsciousness, stillness and movement. It is no coincidence that, in all three drifting moments in Tsai's films, either the protagonist is asleep or else the drifting objects are also sleeping objects. These sleeping moments are an extreme form of diegetic (in)action, during which the audience is effectively abandoned by the characters, thrown into an empty time and space in which stillness and slowness prevail. In other words, the audience is left to drift in these empty moments of stillness.

In these empty moments, the boundary between the time of the living and the time of the dead, as well as that between the space of the living and the space of the dead, is constantly crossed because drifting accepts no limits and respects no boundaries. In *What Time Is It There?*, this crossing of the boundary between the dead and the living is represented through Buddhist–Taoist symbolisms in the film's ending. Shiang-chyi's drifting suitcase in the pool stands in for a floating lotus lantern which, in Buddhist–Taoist folk practice, is released on water to help the deceased cross from the realm of the living to the realm of the dead. This symbol is accompanied by the reflection of a Ferris wheel in the pool, recalling the concept of reincarnation (in Chinese, *lunhui*, literally, rotating of the wheel). Sure enough, in the next shot the dead father makes an appearance – for the first time since the film's enigmatic opening shot but this time in Paris – to fish out the suitcase while Shiang-chyi remains asleep in the foreground.

Figure 5.1 Delivering the dead: drifting suitcase as floating lotus lantern in *What Time Is It There?* Copyright: Homegreen Films/Arena Films, 2001.

For Leo Charney, the work of Marcel Proust articulates modern drift 'as a state of consciousness collapsed into a mode of re-presentation' so that drift is not so much an ontological experience but an epistemological process: an 'oblique approach' towards experiences of drift, 'a strategy of knowing the thing rather than the thing itself' (1998: 9, 10). Drift, in Charney's reading, is form, not content. Tsai's cinema, I would contend, structures drift both as epistemology and ontology, form and content. I mentioned earlier that the audience is left to drift in Tsai's empty moments of stillness. Rather than making a conscious attempt to make sense of them, a mental state of drifting may, in fact, be most suited to the experience of the inexplicable enigma and ambiguity in these moments. Drifting, here, becomes a way of knowing.

On the other hand, drift is also deliberately incorporated into Tsai's empty moments as a representational trope. This is most clearly demonstrated in the way in which the duration of Tsai's static long takes allows living organisms to drift contingently into the frame. In the shot with the floating suitcase in *What Time Is It There?*, the take is held for more than ten seconds after the suitcase has drifted out of the frame – a long empty moment that serves no narrative function – only to see a pigeon walk into the frame from the right, as if on cue, along the edge of the pool to exit at the other end of the frame. This serendipitous moment epitomises drift as both form and content, epistemology and ontology. It features a drifting suitcase by design but extends the duration of the shot to allow a pigeon to drift into the frame by chance. Insofar as it is a representation of drift and (for the audience) an experience of drifting, it is also, in itself, a mode of drifting. The drifting of the pigeon into the frame may not be the (melo)dramatic event typical of mainstream narrative cinema but it cannot simply be dismissed as 'nothing happening'.

More importantly, the serendipity of this shot is achieved through what I shall call a temporal aesthetics of drifting which allows time itself to drift within the shot. The 'life form' that best embodies drifting in terms of a disregard for physical and temporal boundaries is, perhaps, the ghost. In *Visage*, the mother's ghost is exorcised when it is shown leaving the Taipei home so that Lee Kang-sheng, who plays a director who had been making a film in Paris until he received news of his mother's death, could return to Paris to finish shooting. The first shot following the departure of the mother's ghost from the Taipei flat is set in an underground water tunnel in the Louvre. Lee, immersed in water to his waist, treads gingerly while clutching a bunch of incense sticks in his right hand, indicating that the never-ending business of mourning for the dead continues halfway across the globe.

This time, Tsai's camera moves, or rather, drifts. The take begins with a 'floating' shot following Lee from the back towards a light source. As the camera slowly catches up with and closes in on him, Lee stands still by the wall of the tunnel, allowing the camera to overtake him, casting its shadow on the wall ahead of him. This silent long take of nearly a minute ends with a cut to a Chinese musical number lip-synched by the supermodel turned actress, Laetitia Casta (lavishly dressed in costume designed by Christian Lacroix), that is set in the same tunnel, with Norman Atun floating naked on a metal structure, first asleep, then with eyes open but remaining largely motionless.

The appearance of the shadow of a camera in this shot surpasses all self-consciously metacinematic moments in Tsai's *oeuvre*. More crucially, this camera is one that 'tracks' on water, catching – indeed, filming – its own shadow as it drifts. This staged drifting is a form of 'structured wandering' (Charney, 1998: 10). It negotiates the dialectical relationship between stillness and movement, casting (in both senses of the word) drift both as epistemology and ontology, form and content: the camera drifts in order to reveal its own drifting. Rather than use one camera to film another camera in the shot, here the presence of any camera is denied. Instead, by using a single camera to capture its own shadow, this shot turns the cinematic camera into a metafilmic, self-conscious subject staging an inward gaze upon itself, as if looking into a mirror in search of its own image – here cast as a spectral shadow whose materiality remains elusive, out of sight, unfathomable.

Tsai's metafilmic moments unveil cinema as carefully staged, an illusion whose materiality always lies somewhere beyond or outside its representation and whose concealment of the camera creates, precisely, the illusion of reality. In interviews Tsai repeatedly invoked the Buddhist–Taoist idea of *jinghua shuiyue* (flowers in the mirror, moon in the water) to explain what he had tried

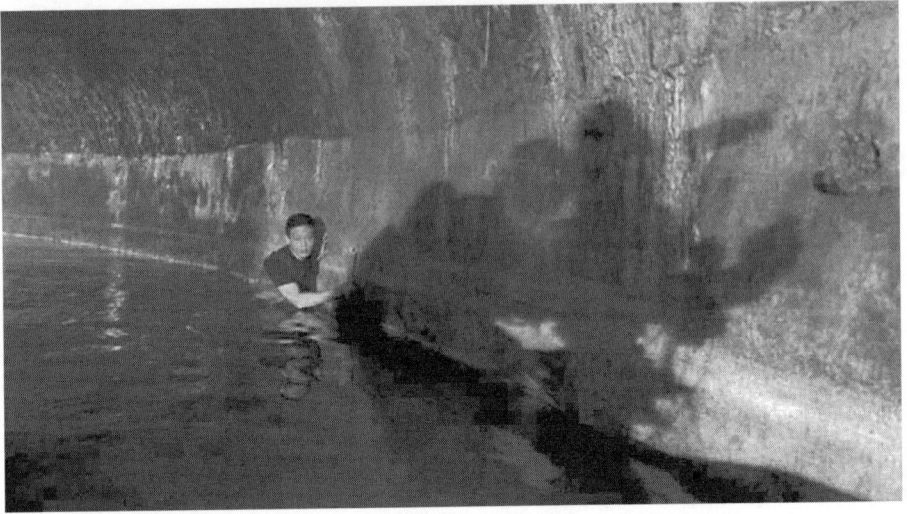

Figure 5.2 Drifting camerawork: 'floating' camera casts its own shadow on the wall of the water tunnel in *Visage*. Copyright: Homegreen Films/JBA Production/Le Musée du Louvre/Circe Films/Arte France Cinéma/Tarantula, 2009.

to express in *Visage*, a concept that sees the world as an ungraspable illusion, like the reflection of flowers in the mirror or of the moon in the water.[3] In an essay in which she argues against the investment of 'an anthropomorphic realism' on images by identity politics, Rey Chow contends that accepting images as artifice would 'liberate us from the constraints of literal, bodily identification'. She suggests that we have yet 'to come to terms with the radical implications of cinema's interruption of the human as such – indeed, with its conjuring of human beings as phantom objects' (2001: 1392–3). Tsai's meta-cinematic moments and images of reflection in pools and mirrors are a step towards this undoing of anthropomorphic realism which partly explains why his representations (of queer sexuality, for example) are not always amenable to identity politics (see Lim, 2006, Chapter 5).

These empty moments in Tsai's films highlight, instead, a temporal aesthetics of drifting that complicates the relationship between stillness and movement. The drifting subjects and objects in the endings of these films trespass various boundaries – that between the realm of the living and the realm of the dead with the spectral presence of the father; between the straitjacket identificatory definitions of homosexuality and heterosexuality with the formation of a threesome; and between the human world and the animal world with the interaction between Tsai, Lee and the stag. What these moments also share is a sense of slowness, achieved through the stillness of the camera, the stillness of diegetic action, and a temporal aesthetics of drifting. Tsai's cinema of slowness urges us to contemplate the subject of stillness through its stillness, and on drifting as a temporal site for the mediation between stillness and movement.

NOTES

1. I thank the University of Hawai'i Press for granting permission to use material from my book *Tsai Ming-liang and a Cinema of Slowness* (2014) in this chapter.
2. Yvette Bíro's book (2008) stands as a rare example of dedicated exploration on the subject, though her discussions tend to be of a summary nature, providing sketches of plot and other elements rather than delving deeply into close analysis of film sequences. I have not had the opportunity to consult Ira Jeffe's book (2014) on 'slow movies' because it has just appeared at the time of the final preparation of this chapter.
3. See, for example, Wang and Lin (2010: 172–3) and the making-of documentary of the film, *Flowers in the Mirror, Moon in the Water* (*Fleurs dans le miroir, lune dans l'eau*; François Lunel, 2009).

BIBLIOGRAPHY

Bíro, Yvette (2008), *Turbulence and Flow in Film: The Rhythmic Design*, translated by Paul Salamon (Bloomington and Indianapolis, IN: Indiana University Press).

Charney, Leo (1998), *Empty Moments: Cinema, Modernity, and Drift* (Durham, NC and London: Duke University Press).

Chow, Rey (2001), 'A Phantom Discipline', *PMLA*, 116: 5, pp. 1386–95.

Deleuze, Gilles (2005), *Cinema 2: The Time-Image*, translated by Hugh Tomlinson and Robert Galeta (London and New York: Continuum).

Duffy, Enda (2009), *The Speed Handbook: Velocity, Pleasure, Modernism* (Durham, NC and London: Duke University Press).

Honoré, Carl (2004), *In Praise of Slow: How a Worldwide Movement Is Challenging the Cult of Speed* (London: Orion).

Jeffe, Ira (2014), *Slow Movies: Countering the Cinema of Action* (New York: Wallflower Press).

Klein, Naomi (2000), *No Logo* (London: Flamingo).

Kummer, Corby (2002), *The Pleasures of Slow Food: Celebrating Authentic Traditions, Flavors, and Recipes* (San Francisco, CA: Chronicle Books).

Kundera, Milan (1995), *Slowness*, translated by Linda Asher (New York: Harper Collins).

Lim, Song Hwee (2006), *Celluloid Comrades: Representations of Male Homosexuality in Contemporary Chinese Cinemas* (Honolulu, HI: University of Hawai'i Press).

Margulies, Ivone (1996), *Nothing Happens: Chantal Akerman's Hyperrealist Everyday* (Durham, NC and London: Duke University Press).

Misek, Richard (2012), 'Dead Time: Cinema, Heidegger, and Boredom', in Julia Vassilieva and Constantine Verevis (eds), *After Taste: Cultural Value and the Moving Image* (London and New York: Routledge), pp. 133–41.

Rancière, Jacques (2006), *The Politics of Aesthetics: The Distribution of the Sensible*, translated and with an introduction by Gabriel Rockhill (London and New York: Continuum).

Ritzer, George (1993), *The McDonaldization of Society* (Thousand Oaks, CA: Pine Forge Press).

Rivière, Danièle, and Tsai Ming-liang (1999), 'Scouting', translated by Andrew

Rothwell, in Jean-Pierre Rehm, Olivier Joyard and Danièle Rivière, *Tsai Ming-liang* (Paris: Dis Voir), pp. 79–118.

Schlosser, Eric (2002), *Fast Food Nation: What the All-American Meal is Doing to the World* (London: Penguin Books).

Schoonover, Karl (2012), 'Wastrels of Time: Slow Cinema's Laboring Body, the Political Spectator, and the Queer', *Framework* 53: 1, pp. 65–78, reprinted in this volume (Chapter 10).

Svendsen, Lars (2005), *A Philosophy of Boredom*, translated by John Irons (London: Reaktion Books).

Veblen, Thorstein [1899] (2007), *The Theory of the Leisure Class*, edited and with an introduction and notes by Martha Banta (Oxford: Oxford University Press).

Wang, Yu-yen, and Lin Wen-chi (2010), 'Yongjin quanbu liqi, jiang dianying tuixiang jizhi de ziyou: *Lian* daoyan Cai Mingliang' (Use all the energy to push cinema to an extreme freedom: *Face* director Tsai Ming-liang), in Lin Wen-chi and Wang Yu-yen (eds), *Taiwan dianying de shengyin* (The voice of Taiwan cinema) (Taipei: Shulin, pp. 163–76).

6. STILLS AND STILLNESS IN APICHATPONG WEERASETHAKUL'S CINEMA

Glyn Davis

About an hour and twenty minutes into Apichatpong Weerasethakul's Palme d'Or-winning *Uncle Boonmee Who Can Recall His Past Lives* (*Loong Boonmee raleuk chat*, 2010, hereafter *Uncle Boonmee*), the titular character lies in a cave, close to death, being looked after by members of his family. Boonmee (Thanapat Saisaymar) describes a dream that he had the previous night, of having arrived in the future by a time machine:

> The future city was ruled by an authority able to make anybody disappear. When they found 'past people', they shone a light on them. That light projected images of them onto the screen. From the past, until their arrival in the future. One of those images appeared, these 'past people' disappeared.

As Boonmee recalls his dream, the audience of Apichatpong's film is presented with a series of ten still images, each held on screen for contemplation. These static images include: seven of soldiers, three of which also include someone dressed in a gorilla costume; two of young men in T-shirts and jeans, throwing objects and taking photos by the side of a river; and a final image of circular marks on a dirt road.

This sequence is preceded by shots in which little movement occurs (clouds drifting across the moon, a pair of red glowing eyes shifting in the cave's darkness), and is followed by a return to moving images of Boonmee dying, his body approaching the stillness of death. The 'photographic' interlude in *Uncle*

Boonmee is influenced by Chris Marker's *La Jetée* (1962), echoing the latter film's science-fiction, time-travel tale, narrative concern with figures of authority who hold the power to erase undesirables, and formal and conceptual interest in the permeable boundaries between memories, photographs and cinema. I shall return to the relationship between these two films later in this chapter. This brief, three-minute sequence in *Uncle Boonmee*, however, provokes questions in its own right. At a diegetic level, what is the relationship between the dream that Boonmee recalls and the stilled images that we see? How do these stilled images relate to other moments of calm, pause or stasis within *Uncle Boonmee*? Indeed, what are the roles of the photographic image and of stillness within the distinctive temporality of Apichatpong's cinema, a treatment of time which is, as James Quandt notes, 'malleable, flowing rather than fixed and linear, subject to the abeyances of wonder, memory, desire' (2009a: 26)?

In this chapter, I want to use this sequence as a starting point for thinking through the place of stills and stillness in Apichatpong's cinema – and, more broadly, in slow cinema as a whole. Born in 1970, Apichatpong studied architecture in Thailand and fine art in Chicago. A notably prolific film-maker, he has made six feature films so far: *Mysterious Object at Noon* (*Dokfa nai meuman*, 2000, hereafter *Mysterious Object*), *Blissfully Yours* (*Sud sanaeha*, 2002), *The Adventures of Iron Pussy* (*Hua jai tor ra nong*, 2003), *Tropical Malady* (*Sud pralad*, 2004), *Syndromes and a Century* (*Sang sattawat*, 2006, hereafter *Syndromes*), and *Uncle Boonmee*. Interspersed among these cinema-released titles, he has created a significant volume of shorter works – some for film festivals, many intended as gallery installations, a number toying with ideas that then find their way into his longer features. Though he does not feature in all critical and theoretical considerations of slow cinema, Apichatpong is identified as a significant contributor to the corpus by Flanagan (2008, 2012) and Romney (2010), as well as in Shaviro's now well-known critique (2010).[1] Anderson (2009), Ingawanij (2013) and others have demonstrated the importance of positioning Apichatpong's films within the context of South-east Asian cinema, politics and history. As James Quandt (2009a: 27–30) identifies, however, the director's work also requires situating in relation to a range of international frameworks: directors, movements, themes, philosophies. Though this chapter makes use of some writings about Asian cinema, it draws more heavily on texts that explore the interrelations between film, photography and speed (not that these two topics are mutually exclusive, of course).

Song Hwee Lim argues in his book *Tsai Ming-liang and a Cinema of Slowness* that a common feature of slow cinema is stillness. Lim's conception of cinematic stillness incorporates a style of filming (a static, fixed camera recording long takes), as well as particular forms of content (sparse, pared-down diegetic action). These 'strategies . . . allow ample time to instil a sense of slowness and to create moments of nothing happening, during which our minds can contemplate as well as drift' (Lim, 2014: 81).[2] A similar argument, linking formal stillness to the psychological drift of the audience, is made by Ira Jaffe. In his book *Slow Movies*, Jaffe devotes a chapter entitled 'Stillness' to discussions of Gus Van Sant's *Elephant* (2003) and Aleksandr Sokurov's *Mother and Son* (*Mat i syn*, 1997). As he writes, 'Both Van Sant and Sokurov create films that encourage the spectator to drift off, yet also to think about and fill in aspects of plot, space, time and character deliberately left unclear by the filmmaker' (Jaffe, 2014: 46). Lim and Jaffe, then, both imply that cinematic stillness may occasion a spectator's psychological 'stepping outside', a mental journey away from the film on screen – to a removed vantage from which the film can be contemplated as a textual object or, indeed, fleetingly forgotten, the mind focused on alternative topics.

Of course, stillness is not merely a concern for slow cinema directors. As Laura Mulvey notes, 'cinema has always found ways to reflect on its central paradox: the co-presence of movement and stillness, continuity and discontinuity' (Mulvey, 2006: 12). Over the last two decades, accompanying the rise of digital technologies for making, distributing, and viewing films and photographs, reflections on this paradox by practitioners and theorists have proliferated. A library of texts devoted to examining the relationships between photography and cinema, including the dynamics of stillness and movement each can embody and express, has appeared (including Stewart, 2000; Green and Lowry, 2006; Mulvey, 2006; Beckman and Ma, 2008; Campany, 2008; Røssaak, 2011). These writings consider a broad array of interrelated concerns. To what extent does the appearance and spread of digital photography and cinema undermine long-held understandings regarding the identities of these cultural forms, and of medium specificity? How, for instance, are the arguments of Roland Barthes or André Bazin, regarding the ontology of photographic imagery, unsettled or undone? Has Barthes's notion of the distinct temporal rhetorics that photography and film separately employ – the 'having been there' past tense of the photograph, the 'being there' present-ness of film – become outmoded (Barthes, 1977: 45)? Through all of these discussions, the still and stilled image – the photograph, the film still, the individual film frame or photogram, the freeze-frame, stillness as a particular dynamic of cinema and photography – recurs.

One topic which repeatedly surfaces is whether stillness and stasis can have political force. Mulvey, for instance, discusses the value of what she terms 'delayed cinema' as a counterpoint to the lively realm of contemporary experience. As she writes,

At a time when new technologies seem to hurry ideas and their representations at full tilt towards the future, to stop and to reflect on the cinema and its history also offers the opportunity to think about how time might be understood within wider, contested, patterns of history and mythology. Out of this pause, a delayed cinema gains a political dimension, potentially able to challenge patterns of time that are neatly ordered around the end of an era, its 'before' and its 'after'. The delayed cinema gains further significance as outside events hasten the disappearance of the past and strengthen the political appropriation of time. (Mulvey 2006: 22–3)

For Mulvey, as for other theorists, stasis, slowness and delay are useful counterpoints to the hectic pace of contemporary life. These temporalities challenge dominant notions of progress and goal-oriented activity, introducing the prospect of taking the time to think differently, and of thinking time differently. And for these authors, cinema provides one key location for manifesting, and thus thinking through and engaging with, such stillness.

Taking up the challenge posed by these writers, this chapter makes three interrelated arguments. First, as a correlative to Lim's analysis of Tsai Mingliang's cinema, I shall highlight the extent to which stillness is a central dynamic in the films of Apichatpong Weerasethakul. Second, I shall argue that the stillness in Apichatpong's output is concerned both with exploring the complex relationships between still photographs, film frames, and moving images, and with interrogating stillness as a dynamic that has specifically cinematic manifestations. Third, I shall propose that the moments of stillness in Apichatpong's cinema are often where his most overtly political statements are expressed. The remainder of this chapter is structured through examinations of two specific forms of stillness in Apichatpong's films: the deployment of photographs or photo-like images, for which Chris Marker's work serves as an influence; and a more Warholian form of stillness which incorporates (among other elements) an architectural gaze and durational long takes. That is, this chapter will first discuss photographs and freeze-frames, and their relationship to slowness (a topic that Lim and Jaffe do not explore in detail), then move to an interrogation of cinematic stillness and stasis, linking Lim's observations to Apichatpong and other instances of slow cinema.

Marker, Photographs and Stilled Images

As I have already highlighted, one of the ways in which Apichatpong's films engage with the notion of stillness is through their deployment of photographs and stilled images. Though photos appear in his gallery work – *0116643225059* (1994), for instance, features an image of Apichatpong's mother intercut with footage of an apartment in Chicago – the interrogation of their potency is more sustained in his feature films. Across the chronological run of *Mysterious Object*, *Tropical Malady*, *Syndromes*, and *Uncle Boonmee*, photographs – or photo-like images – appear as part of each film's content. *In Mysterious Object*, the nurse Dogfahr (Somsri Pinyopol) shows photographs of the outside world to a disabled boy in her care. Though this activity is depicted, the audience is not presented with examples of the pictures: we do not see what he sees. In contrast, just before the midway interval in *Tropical Malady*, when the shift into the 'tiger' narrative occurs, Keng (Banlop Lomnoi) sits on a bed and looks at photographs of Tong (Sakda Kaewbuadee), his object of desire. A medium close-up shows the photographs being slowly leafed through. In both these instances, the photographs serve as referents of the absent, distant or lost, resemblances of elements of the real and/or diegetic world located beyond the currently depicted scene.

In his later features, Apichatpong's deployment of still images becomes more complex. In *Syndromes*, Dr Nohng (Jaruchai Iamaram) inspects a number of photographs shown to him by his girlfriend while they discuss a new work location to which she wishes to move. As he flips through the photographs, the viewer is presented with seven static images, each held for several seconds: one of a truck shot through the curtained window of another vehicle; one taken inside a company's computer room; the others showing exteriors of industrial buildings (see Figure 6.1). It is unclear whether this string of images is supposed to have been recorded at the same organisation or location. The images of industry, combined with the pace of Apichatpong's cinema, may remind some viewers of Antonioni's slow cinema precursor *Red Desert* (*Il Deserto Rosso*, 1964). At the same time, the scene arguably exemplifies what

Figure 6.1 Still used in *Syndromes and a Century* (*Sang sattawat*, 2006).

Jonathan L. Owen identifies as one of Apichatpong's main political themes: the depiction and exploration of 'specific realities of globalized capitalism – and its working conditions' (Owen, 2013: 243). While it is unclear whether the seven images we are shown in this sequence in *Syndromes* are the same as those seen by Dr Nohng, they make narrative sense in relation to the synchronous voice-over. And yet the appearance of these 'photographs' seems somehow jarring, dissonant: with each image, the visual channel of the slow film has temporarily stopped or jammed.

Making sense of the ten images and accompanying dream-recounting voice-over in *Uncle Boonmee* with which this chapter's discussion began requires setting the sequence in a Thai context. *Uncle Boonmee* grew out of Apichatpong's multi-screen installation *Primitive* (2009). The ten photographs are a record of a participatory art project that Apichatpong conducted with local youths in the village of Nabua, in north-east Thailand, as part of *Primitive*. Nabua has historical significance: it was the site of first skirmishes between communists and state forces in the mid 1960s. As May Adadol Ingawanij points out, '[k]nowing this extra-textual information transforms the photomontage into what looks like stilled gestures of reenactment' (2013: 106): the youths in the images could be the children of those who fought on behalf of the communist cause or the state. Ingawanij highlights the extent to which discussions of Thailand's violent past were repressed by those in power but also notes that photographic records of brutality have been crucial in unlocking that history. Set against this particular extratextual context and the 'reenactment' photographs, Boonmee's dream of a future in which those in power subjugate individuals by draining their memories sounds equally like a recollection of Thailand's turbulent history. This sequence, then, is one of Apichatpong's most pointedly political; it also serves as a rupture in the film's unfolding, the frozen form of the photographs interrupting its gentle but perceptible flow.

Why do these photographic sequences in *Syndromes* and *Uncle Boonmee* have such an unsettling force? Raymond Bellour, in his essay 'The Film Stilled', engages with Deleuze's *Cinema I* and *Cinema II* and the place of the still image in Deleuze's articulation of the distinctions between 'the movement–image' and 'the time–image'. Bellour asks 'what happens to film when the snapshot becomes both the pose and the pause of film?' (1990: 105). That is, what effects might the appearance of photographs within a film's diegesis and textual content have? Given the repeated appearances of photographers and photographs in examples of slow cinema – including Van Sant's *Elephant*, Hou Hsiao-hsien's *Three Times* (*Zui hao de shi guang*, 2005), and Lav Diaz's *Century of Birthing* (*Siglo ng pagluluwal*, 2011) – this query is of significance for the movement as a whole. Discussing Rossellini's *The Machine That Kills Bad People* (*La macchina ammazzacattivi*, 1952), Bellour writes that rephotographing a photograph stops the movement of the shot. [. . .] The paradox is that this effect does 'stop' the film and even brings to mind the physical gesture of stopping the film on an editing table. But it can't be captured by bringing the film to a standstill, because it vanishes. One has the feeling that something impossible is trying to be articulated. (107)

Garrett Stewart, expanding on Bellour's arguments, notes that 'the cinematic insert of the refilmed still print is often visibly "recessed" from the screen plane' (Stewart, 2000: 41). Such moments are not especially troubling. More disruptive, providing 'decisive irruption of the illusionistic system', are 'the encompassing (often elegiac) stasis of either a full-screen photograph or a multiplied single photogram [that is, a freeze-frame]' (41). The photographic sequences in *Syndromes* and *Uncle Boonmee* both fill the frame, presented not as (or not merely as) objects malleable to human touch but as constituent components of cinematic flow – albeit static ones. Stewart identifies why such a presentation of stilled images by cinema serves as a 'decisive irruption': 'A photograph appears to contain its image . . ., whereas a film seems to constrain what it places on view' (41). The visual fields of film and photography, then, operate through distinct tensions. Inserting photographic stills into cinema's temporal unfolding can reveal these (often hidden) dynamics, bringing them to the awareness of audiences, rupturing the unfurling of the diegesis, and potentially unsettling the viewer's immersion in the text.

James Quandt identifies the photography sequence in *Syndromes* as 'one of [the director's] *La Jetée* moments' (Quandt, 2009a: 93). Apichatpong has admitted that the stills sequence and accompanying time travel tale in *Uncle Boonmee* 'is very clichéd – it's like Chris Marker!' (quoted in Hasted, 2010). In theoretical accounts of the relationships between photography and cinema, Marker's *La Jetée* (1962) is often identified as a touchstone text. This black-and-white film, under thirty minutes in length, is composed almost entirely of still photographs, except for one brief moment in which a woman's eyes blink repeatedly. Throughout his film-making, Marker often combined still and moving images: *Letter from Siberia* (*Lettre de Sibérie*, 1957), for example, incorporates still photographs, location footage, archival stock and animation, while *The Sixth Side of the Pentagon* (*La sixième face du pentagone*, 1968) opens and closes with sequences of black-and-white photographs. As Sarah Cooper argues, Marker's repeated use of photographs in his films is one aspect of a wider engagement with stasis and stillness which itself is 'part of a broader rethinking of temporality, beyond a mechanical or technological description of cinema' (Cooper, 2008: 4–5). This characterisation of Marker's work seems to resonate with the wider slow cinema movement and the aims, intentions and styles of many of its key practitioners. Indeed, Cooper's perspective on Marker suggests that a future sustained exploration of the director's influence on slow cinema, and a reading of his work as slow, could be extremely valuable.

La Jetée remains Marker's best-known work. It is not the only film that has been made by primarily, or entirely, assembling photographs. Noël Carroll names a number of others – including Nagisa Ôshima's *Band of Ninja* (*Ninja bugei-chô*, 1967) and Hollis Frampton's *Poetic Justice* (1972) – in an essay devoted to identifying the ontology of cinema. For Carroll, films composed of photographs are distinct from slide shows:

> as long as you know that what you are watching is a film, even a film of what appears to be a photograph, it is always justifiable to entertain the possibility that the image *might* move. On the other hand, if you know that you are looking at a slide, then it is categorically impossible that the image might move. (Carroll 2006: 125, emphasis in original)

With Apichatpong's sequences of photographs in *Syndromes* and *Boonmee*, the viewer may anticipate the return of moving images – or, indeed, *pace La Jetée*, expect one of the photographs to move, however incrementally. Alternatively, given that these sequences arrive late in each film, at a point when the viewer will have become accustomed to the director's favoured slow storytelling rhythms, their impact may be more unsettling, drawing attention to the fragile distinction between stillness and movement.

Certainly, for some theorists, this is the key to *La Jetée*'s power and impact. As Catherine Lupton notes, the film's photographs are assembled cinematically, using film grammar including cuts, fades, and dissolves, 'with establishing shots, eyeline matches, shot–countershot, close-ups and so forth, all working to create a sense of narrative coherence and momentum' (Lupton, 2004: 91). If still photographs can be arranged in such a way, does cinema actually need to move? For Uriel Orlow, Marker's film 'proposes a middle ground, an undecidability between photography and cinema' (Orlow, 2007: 181); therein lies its radical charge. As Orlow writes, *La Jetée* 'proposes a powerful critique of an essentialist medium-specificity of photography and cinema which relies on the opposition of movement and stillness' (181). The photographic sequences in Apichatpong's films are brief, fleeting, and therefore do not operate as a sustained and comprehensive thesis on movement and stillness, in the manner of *La Jetée*. These scenes, however, interject the still or stilled image into films whose dominant temporality is a sedate or slow one, thus inviting audiences to consider when, and how, a slow film becomes a still one, and the ways in which slowness, stasis and stillness are interrelated. What happens when a slow film becomes even slower – that is, when it seems to stop? Does all slow cinema threaten to grind to a halt – and if so, what would be the repercussions and ramifications of such a collapse?

WARHOL, DURATION AND THE EVERYDAY

James Quandt highlights three 'formative figures' who influenced Apichatpong while he was studying at the Art Institute of Chicago: Bruce Baillie, Marcel Duchamp, and Andy Warhol. Compared to Baillie and Duchamp, Quandt writes, the 'importance of Warhol seems both more profound and more elusive' (2009a: 15); he proposes a number of possible ways in which Warhol's influence on Apichatpong can be detected. Here, I want to stress the pivotal position that Andy Warhol occupies in the history of cinema's interrogations of stillness. Warhol's experiments with duration and stasis include *Kiss* (1963), *Sleep* (1963), *Eat* (1964), *Empire* (1964) and *Henry Geldzahler* (1964), as well as the hundreds of *Screen Tests* made between 1964 and 1966. In part, like Chris Marker, Warhol explored stillness through a questioning of the relationships between cinema and photography: as Callie Angell notes, the *Screen Tests* 'were conceptualized and shot as direct approximations or imitations of still photography' (2006: 13). But Warhol also deployed other tactics to examine stasis: extreme running times; slowed down projection speeds; a focus on everyday activities that are normally ignored or marginalised by narrative cinema. In the final section of this chapter, I want to identify some of the ways in which the stillness of Apichatpong's cinema is both indebted to, and distinct from, that of Warhol.

Apichatpong has noted his admiration for *Empire*, saying that 'this film reminds us of the simple beauty of the film material itself – the patience, the act of watching film, lights being turned on in the building' (quoted in Quandt, 2009b: 252). It is possible that Apichatpong's background studying architecture enhances the appeal of this particular Warhol work for him. Certainly, he conceptualises cinema and architecture as operating in related ways: 'Architecture has its own stories, it is just another way to tell stories. It is characterised by how a person experiences art by using space and time. It is walking from one point to another, which is very similar to cinema' (quoted in Pansittivorakul 2006). Can the specific stillness of *Empire* – its unflinching durational gaze at a historically resonant building – be detected in Apichatpong's own output? Though *Syndromes* is most often identified as a film about Apichatpong's parents, it could also be read as an architectural portrait focused on two hospitals, one rural and one urban – and, indeed, as a sustained commentary on these distinct spaces. From this perspective, the sequence towards the end of the film, in which the camera slowly tracks through corridors, past brief incidental glimpses of staff and around the basement, can be configured as a durational portrait of a building – though one with more varied content and camera mobility than Warhol's *Empire*. In fact, Apichatpong has made one film focused solely on a piece of architecture: his single-screen installation *Emerald* (*Morakot*, 2007) which combines footage of a derelict hotel in Bangkok with a soundtrack of several voices recounting dreams, memories and poems. Where *Empire* may provoke consideration of the connections between architecture, political power and (post)colonial reach, *Emerald* invites reflection on the aesthetics of ruined buildings, the ethics, effects and affects of abandonment.[3]

For James Quandt, one of Warhol's influences on Apichatpong can be detected in the latter's 'use of locked shots and extended duration' (2009a: 15). Quandt connects the upturned, sun-dappled face of Roong (Kanokporn Tongaram) at the end of *Blissfully Yours* and Keng's playful interactions with the camera while *Tropical Malady*'s introductory credits roll with the ambivalent gaze of the hustler in Warhol's *Blow Job* (1964). He might equally have compared these two scenes with Warhol's *Screen Tests* series, and its registration of the myriad ways in which individuals perform and behave when a camera's unflinching gaze is trained on them. Beyond Quandt's examples, long, static takes appear with regularity throughout Apichatpong's films, as they do across the field of slow cinema as a whole. *Syndromes* opens with a sustained shot of wind gently shaking trees; a few minutes later, as the film's credits start, the camera sits still and captures a breeze scuffing the surface of a field. The final static shot of *Mekong Hotel* (2012), which lasts for several minutes, depicts leisure boats skipping up and down a river, filmed from a distance at which they can only just be seen.

Jihoon Kim also notes Apichatpong's use of 'shots with extended duration that exceed narrative economy' (Kim, 2010: 128). 'This dilation of time', he suggests, 'allows viewers to become engrossed in the spatial properties of the individual shots and consciously aware of screen time' (128). In contrast to Quandt, Kim relates these long takes to the director's movement between the realms of video-based gallery works and cinema: 'Video is associated with excessive duration in a way that film is not. Apichatpong carries this technical affinity of video into the visionary and tactile long-takes of his feature films' (131). Apichatpong, of course, is not the only director associated with slow cinema to move between producing screen works for galleries and theatrical exhibition: to name several others, Wang Bing, Michelangelo Frammartino, Nicolas Pereda, and Ben Rivers also operate comfortably in both realms. If the long takes in Apichatpong's feature films are indebted to his facility with video art, then it is worth asking to what extent a similar influence recurs, more broadly, across slow cinema as a whole. The stillness and slowness of screen works by many of the movement's directors, I would argue, facilitate a collapsing of the gallery into the cinema, and the cinema into the gallery.

Of course, long takes are only one component of the articulation of cinematic stillness. As Song Hwee Lim identifies, stillness and slowness are also related to the amount of content in the shot, performance and *mise en scène*, camera movement and framing, and pacing. He stresses the concentration, in much slow cinema, on undramatic and quotidian 'events', noting that 'cinematic stillness can be achieved even when there is bodily movement within the static shot because the movement is primarily of an everyday nature, contributing not so much to the drive of the narrative force as to a sense of nothing happening' (93). 'Everydayness', as depicted in slow cinema, can take the form of necessary tasks (eating, drinking, sleeping), of carrying out manual labour, or of idly passing the time.[4] The stillness of some of Warhol's films is produced by an atrophied, drawn-out depiction of mundane activities: Robert Indiana eats a mushroom very slowly, nibbling; John Giorno sleeps, and the only movement on screen is that of his chest gently rising and falling.

While Apichatpong does not challenge his viewers by toying with such extremes, elements of the everyday take up considerable amounts of screen time in his feature films. As Brett Farmer notes of *Blissfully Yours*, for instance, the first forty minutes of the film depict 'the prosaic minutiae of the characters' daily lives, observed with exacting detail in a sequence of durational vignettes: visiting the doctor, shopping at the market, driving in the car, working in a factory'. This produces a 'condition of routinised anomie and numbing constraint' (Farmer, 2006) which the characters escape from by heading into the countryside in the film's second half. And yet the rural venture also features quietly mundane activities: a picnic, snoozing in the sun. Similarly, in *Uncle Boonmee*, characters spend considerable amounts of time sharing an evening meal or watching television together; in one sedate sequence, Boonmee and his sister Jen (Jenjira Pongpas) tend tamarinds and bees in his orchard grounds. The sense of stillness in these scenes is attained, in significant part, from their sustained depiction of the mundane.

Stephen Koch (1973) linked Warhol's fascination with stillness to the artist's preoccupation with death. Song Hwee Lim also notes that '[d]eath is, in a sense, the ultimate form of stillness', 'stillness embodied' (2014: 105). The connections between death and still photographs have been made by a number of theorists, including Roland Barthes (1981), photos capturing something that is instantly lost, serving as mementos of that which has been. It is thus appropriate that the death of Uncle Boonmee is matched, formally, with a series of photographs, his last moments accompanied by still images. And yet Boonmee is likely to be reincarnated, reanimated. The stillness of his form will give way to new movement. Indeed, Apichatpong's depiction of Boonmee's passing serves as emblematic of slow cinema's stillness. The character is slow, slowing, still, but on the cusp of potential new motion; the frame is stilled, static, to the extent that cinema's affiliation with movement is unsettled; the diegesis is charged with semantic gaps and lacunae that invite interpretation. Back in the cave, red-eyed figures watch from the darkness as Boonmee's life drains away. They do not blink.

NOTES

1. Please see the introduction to this volume.
2. See also Lim's chapter in this volume which is based on material from his book on Tsai.
3. In 2010 Apichatpong also made a film called *Empire*, an eighty-second trailer for that year's Viennale. An underwater pod, possibly a camera, bubbles along in the depths; we see footage shot inside caves; in a similar space, a hand sifts through dust and shrapnel, lifting a shell towards the camera, the final few seconds of footage illuminated by a stroboscope. Though Apichatpong's *Empire* is distinct in form and content from Warhol's film of the same name – the Viennale film is brief, in colour, shot underground, and accompanied by an eerie soundtrack – the use of the title seems to be an intentional echo.
4. For a more sustained exploration of slow cinema's 'everydayness', see Flanagan, 2012: 99–105.

BIBLIOGRAPHY

Anderson, Benedict (2009), 'The Strange Story of a Strange Beast: Receptions in Thailand of Apichatpong Weerasethakul's *Sat Pralaat*', in James Quandt (ed.), *Apichatpong Weerasethakul* (Vienna: FilmMuseumSynemaPublikationen), pp.158–77.
Angell, Callie (2006), *Andy Warhol Screen Tests: The Films of Andy Warhol Catalogue Raisonné* (New York: Harry N. Abrams/Whitney Museum).
Barthes, Roland (1977), 'The Rhetoric of the Image', in Barthes, *Image, Music, Text*, translated by Stephen Heath (New York: Hill and Wang), pp. 32–51.
Barthes, Roland (1981), *Camera Lucida: Reflections on Photography* (New York: Hill and Wang).
Beckman, Karen and Jean Ma (eds) (2008), *Still Moving: Between Cinema and Photography* (Durham, NC and London: Duke University Press).
Bellour, Raymond (1990), 'The Film Stilled', *Camera Obscura*, 24 (September), pp.99–124.
Campany, David (2008), *Photography and Cinema* (London: Reaktion).
Carroll, Noël (2006), 'Defining the Moving Image', in Noël Carroll and Jinhee Choi (eds), *Philosophy of Film and Motion Pictures: An Anthology* (Malden, MA: Blackwell), pp. 113–34.
Cooper, Sarah (2008), *Chris Marker* (Manchester: Manchester University Press).
Farmer, Brett (2006), 'Apichatpong Weerasethakul, Transnational Poet of the New Thai Cinema: Blissfully Yours', *Senses of Cinema* 38 (January–March), archived online at http://www.sensesofcinema.com/contents/cteq/06/38/blissfully_yours.html [accessed 19 July 2014].
Flanagan, Matthew (2008), 'Towards an Aesthetic of Slow in Contemporary Cinema', *16:9* 29, archived online at http://www.16-9.dk/2008-11/side11_inenglish.htm [accessed 19 July 2014].
Flanagan, Matthew (2012), *'Slow Cinema': Temporality and Style in Contemporary Art and Experimental Film*, unpublished PhD thesis.
Green, David and Joanna Lowry (eds) (2006), *Stillness and Time: Photography and the Moving Image* (Brighton: Photoworks/Photoforum).
Hasted, Nick (2010), 'Apichatpong Weerasethakul', *Little White Lies*, 24 November, archived online at http://www.littlewhitelies.co.uk/features/articles/apichatpong weerasethakul-13035 [accessed 19 July 2014].
Ingawanij, May Adadol (2013), 'Animism and the Performative Realist Cinema of Apichatpong Weerasethakul', in Anat Pick and Guinevere Narraway (eds),

Screening Nature: Cinema Beyond the Human (Oxford and New York: Berghahn), pp. 91–109.

Jaffe, Ira (2014), *Slow Movies: Countering the Cinema of Action* (New York: Columbia University Press).

Kim, Jihoon (2010), 'Between Auditorium and Gallery: Perception in Apichatpong Weerasethakul's Films and Installations', in Rosalind Galt and Karl Schoonover (eds), *Global Art Cinema: New Theories and Histories* (Oxford: Oxford University Press), pp. 125–41.

Koch, Stephen (1973), *Stargazer: The Life, World and Films of Andy Warhol* (New York: Praeger).

Lim, Song Hwee (2014), *Tsai Ming-liang and a Cinema of Slowness* (Honolulu, HI: University of Hawai'i Press).

Lupton, Catherine (2004), *Chris Marker: Memories of the Future* (London: Reaktion).

Mulvey, Laura (2006), *Death 24x a Second: Stillness and the Moving Image* (London: Reaktion).

Orlow, Uriel (2007), 'The Dialectical Image: *La Jetée* and Photography-as-Cinema', in David Campany (ed.), *The Cinematic* (London: Whitechapel Gallery), pp. 177–84.

Owen, Jonathan L. (2013), 'The Migrations of Factory Style: Work, Play and Work-as-Play in Andy Warhol, Chantal Akerman, and Apichatpong Weerasethakul', in Ewa Mazierska (ed.), *Work in Cinema: Labour and the Human Condition* (New York: Palgrave Macmillan), pp. 227–47.

Pansittivorakul, Thunsk (2006), 'A Conversation with Apichatpong Weerasethakul', *Criticine: Evaluating Discourse on Southeast Asian Cinema*, 30 April, archived online at http://www.criticine.com/interview_article.php?id=24 [accessed 19 July 2014].

Quandt, James (2009a), 'Resistant to Bliss: Describing Apichatpong', in Quandt, ed., *Apichatpong Weerasethakul* (Vienna: FilmMuseumSynemaPublikationen), pp. 13–100.

Quandt, James (ed.) (2009b), *Apichatpong Weerasethakul* (Vienna: FilmMuseumSynemaPublikationen).

Romney, Jonathan (2010), 'In Search of Lost Time', *Sight and Sound*, vol. 20, no. 2, pp. 43–4.

Røssaak, Eivind (ed.) (2011), *Between Stillness and Motion: Film, Photography, Algorithms* (Amsterdam: Amsterdam University Press).

Shaviro, Steven (2010), 'Slow Cinema Vs Fast Films', *The Pinocchio Theory*, 12 May, archived online at http://www.shaviro.com/Blog/?p=891 [accessed 19 July 2014].

Stewart, Garrett (2000), *Between Film and Screen: Modernism's Photo Synthesis* (Chicago, IL: University of Chicago Press).

7. *MELANCHOLIA*: THE LONG, SLOW CINEMA OF LAV DIAZ

William Brown

Lav Diaz does not make short films. Or rather, while we should acknowledge that Diaz has made relatively short, feature-length films – *Elegy to the Visitor from the Revolution* (*Elehiya sa dumalaw mula sa himagsikan*, 2011) is only eighty minutes long – and while we should make clear that Diaz has even made short films 'proper' (*Purgatorio*, 2009, is a mere sixteen minutes), he is best known as a maker of long films. Most famous among these are *West Side Avenue* (*Batang West Side*, 2001, 315 minutes), *Evolution of a Filipino Family* (*Ebolusyon ng isang pamilyang Pilipino*, 2004, 660 minutes), *Heremias* (*Heremias – Unang aklat: Ang alamat ng prinsesang bayawak*, 2006, 540 minutes), *Death in the Land of Encantos* (*Kagadanan sa banwaan ning mga engkanto*, 2007, 540 minutes), *Century of Birthing* (*Siglo ng pagluluwal*, 2011, 360 minutes), *North, the End of History* (*Norte, hangganan ng kasaysayan*, 2013, 250 minutes), the recent *From What is Before* (*Mula sa kung ano ang noon*, 2014, 338 minutes), and, the focus of this chapter, *Melancholia* (2008, 450 minutes). In addition to making long films, however, Diaz also makes slow films, as I shall explain presently.

To say that long films are not necessarily the same as slow films might seem counter-intuitive. Nonetheless, there is clear evidence that the two do not always correlate: Tsai Ming-liang's *What Time is it There?* (*Ni na bian ji dian*, 2001) is, for Song Hwee Lim, a paradigmatic slow film (Lim, 2014: esp. 104–15) which lasts 116 minutes. *The Lord of the Rings: The Return of the King* (Peter Jackson, 2003) is, conversely, 201 minutes in length but is rarely considered to be a slow film. Indeed, given the rise of 'quality television' and the way in which many audiences invest tens of hours of their time in watching a show such as *Breaking Bad* (Vince Gilligan, 2008–13), duration is not necessarily the issue when we compare slow cinema, including the slow cinema of Lav Diaz, to other, 'faster' audiovisual products. For a film to be slow, it need not be long but it must, on the whole, reject many of the tropes of conventional mainstream cinema – both that from Hollywood and the rest of the world. If mainstream cinema is, in the language of David Bordwell (2006: 117–89), characterised by an 'intensified continuity' in which there is a relatively rapid cutting rate (an average shot length of about four seconds), constant action on screen, a permanently moving camera, and extreme variation in shot sizes (from long shots to close-ups), as well as loud sound in the form of dialogue, music, explosions and more, then slow films convey 'physical stillness, emptiness and silence', as well as 'minimalism' in relation to cinematic techniques: a slow cutting rate, less camera movement, and a general tendency towards long(er) shots over close-ups (Jaffe, 2014: 4). As Manohla Dargis summarises, 'one [mainstream cinema] fosters distraction while the other [slow cinema] encourages contemplation' (Dargis, 2008; quoted in Jaffe, 2014: 4).

While many of his films are long, then, Lav Diaz's films are also slow, as I shall demonstrate in relation to *Melancholia,* which won Best Film in the Orizzonti section of the 2008 Venice Film Festival, and which has been described by one reviewer as 'madly uncommercial' (Scheib, 2008). Allowing for some human error, *Melancholia* is composed of 149 shots during its 450-minute duration, meaning that it has an average shot length of 181 seconds, or just over three minutes. This is significantly longer than the four-second average shot length of a mainstream film. What is more, a few jump cuts aside, there is no within-scene editing in *Melancholia*, meaning that nearly every scene is filmed in a single take. The film does feature several pans and handheld sequences in which the camera moves but the majority of *Melancholia* is also composed of events filmed in long shot and from a fixed position. The lack of close-ups, in particular, means that our attention is shifted away from an emotional engagement with the characters and more towards the contemplative relationship with events that Dargis describes above in relation to the work of Jia Zhangke. Towards the end of *Melancholia*, there are combat scenes with various gunshots being fired. But, on the whole, the film is also very quiet, with protracted scenes featuring little on the soundtrack beyond the rustling of wind in the trees and the regular sound of rainfall, and little on the image track except characters smoking, walking, thinking (often huddled) and, perhaps, waiting. While long, therefore, Diaz's films are also slow cinema in accordance with the definition(s) of slow cinema given by Jaffe, Lim and others.

The question now becomes: why does Diaz adopt the techniques associated with slow cinema and what does he achieve in making long and slow films such as *Melancholia*? In part, and as per the subtitle of Jaffe's book, Diaz is 'countering the cinema of action' that is the mainstream. As a member of the Philippine New Wave, which also includes the likes of Adolfo Alix Jr, Jeffrey Jeturian, Raya Martin, Brillante Mendoza, Auraeus Solito and Khavn de la Cruz, Diaz is not simply countering the mainstream cinema of Hollywood but also Philippine mainstream cinema, with many Philippine 'new wave' films being censored, banned and generally struggling to find mainstream audiences at home (see Trice, 2009). That said, with the exception of some of Martin's work (*Now Showing*, 2008, is 280 minutes long), Diaz is the only Philippine new-wave film-maker who makes such long films and who is as committed to the aesthetics of slow cinema. In Khavn's documentary, *Philippine New Wave: This is Not a Film Movement* (Philippines, 2012), Diaz talks about the 'fascism' of mainstream cinema that is made simply for entertainment purposes, the implication being that he sets out not uniquely to entertain but also to achieve something else.

I shall discuss the possible nature of this 'something else' shortly. But first, I shall suggest that another reason why Diaz is a slow film-maker is because of his being technologically enabled by digital film-making equipment. As he himself avows in *Philippine New Wave*, digital technology has 'liberated my cinema' in that he can go further, shoot for longer and generally adopt the long and slow aesthetic that was much harder to achieve with analogue technology (see also Caruncho, 2008; Baumgärtel, 2012). Given that he makes digitally enabled long and slow films so consistently, Diaz is almost unique, not just among Filipino film-makers but also in world cinema today. That said, within the Philippine context, Diaz also differs greatly from his fellow new wave members because the majority of events in his films take place outside of Manila. Others make films that often take place in the country's capital, as is made clear by titles such as *Manila* (Adolfo Alix Jr and Raya Martin, 2009), *Manila in the Fangs of Darkness* (*Maynila sa mga pangil ng dilim*, Khavn de la Cruz, 2008) and *Mondomanila, or: How I Fixed My Hair After a Rather Long Journey* (Khavn de la Cruz, 2009). Diaz's films, meanwhile, regularly feature small towns and the Philippine jungle. To be clear: Diaz is not the only film-maker to set his films in small towns and/or in the Philippine jungle, as happens in *Melancholia*. Raya Martin's *Independencia* (2009) is also set in the jungle – even if it was, in fact, shot on a sound stage and lasts 'only' seventy-seven minutes while also featuring numerous cuts and being made to look like a classical, silent film. Furthermore, Brillante Mendoza's *Captive* (2012) is similarly set largely in the jungle but is a film told in a much more (if not fully) conventional, intensified continuity style. Diaz, then, is the only film-maker to shoot outside Manila and/or in the jungle so consistently and certainly the only film-maker to combine this rejection of the city with extreme durations and slow cinema aesthetics. By looking specifically at *Melancholia*, we can investigate more closely why the regional and/

or jungle setting leads Diaz to become a proponent of a specifically Philippine, long and slow cinema.

Melancholia opens in the leafy and wet municipality of Sagada, about 270 kilometres (168 miles) north of Manila. A prostitute, Jenine (Angeli Bayani), walks around, occasionally encountering a pimp, Danny (Perry Dizon), who tries to convince her to work for him, and a nun, Sister Carmella (Malaya Cruz), who is collecting alms for the poor. Jenine, Carmella and Danny are not real people, however, but characters performed by Julian Tomas (Danny) and two women who carry out these performances as some sort of therapy: Alberta (Jenine) lost her revolutionary husband, Renato, ten years previously, and Julian rescued Rina (Carmella) from suicide. Back in (a distinctly quiet) Manila, Alberta and Julian meet and deconstruct their experiences in Sagada. Julian talks to a writer (Bodgie Pascua) about a novel that he has written called *The True History of Philippine Cinema*. And Alberta finds, rescues from prostitution and, with the help of her own mother (Carme Sanchez), tries to look after Hannah (Yanyan Taa), the teenage daughter of two members of the Bayan (an alliance of leftist organisations in the Philippines) who were 'disappeared' in 1997. Alberta and Julian travel south to see the discovery of the bodies of two revolutionaries, Manuel Tirano and Gigi Fernandez, before attending Rina's funeral following her suicide. Alberta finds a book called *Melancholia*, which is written by Julian.

The film then switches to an extended flashback of Renato (Roeder Camanag) and two other unnamed revolutionaries (presumably Tirano and Fernandez, played by Dante Perez and Raul Arellano), hiding from, and being hunted by, the military. Renato discards various letters that he writes to Alberta as one of his companions goes insane and appeals to the enemy to find and kill him. This summarily takes place as Tirano and Fernandez are shot by unseen military assailants. Renato, however, escapes, only to be carried, bleeding, on a horse and then buried by locals who carry out a traditional dance. Back in the film's present, Alberta finds Julian by a river and tells him that Patricia is long since dead. Julian denies his own identity and, while the film ends without us necessarily knowing who Patricia is, the credits list Patricia as being played by the same actor as a *kundiman* singer (Cooky Chua) whom Julian at one point films in a dream/memory sequence, implying she is his dead wife.

Pedro Henrique Trindade Kalil Auad says that 'almost nothing happens' in *Melancholia* (Auad, 2013: 339, my translation). The above (incomplete) synopsis perhaps makes clear that this is not the case; much happens in the film. And yet Auad may be correct in a way that he does not make clear. If the film involves dream sequences that are not really marked as such (for example, moments when Julian interacts with a punk band in his living room), as well as jumps in time that equally are not signalled in any clear fashion (in particular flashbacks), then the veracity of any event that we see is slowly called into question. When we combine this with the idea that Alberta and Julian have various personas in the film, then which is the real and which is the fake character becomes hard to tell. Are Jenine and Danny acting Alberta and Julian, or vice versa? When Alberta's wheelchair-bound and former revolutionary colleague Ramon (Soliman Cruz) refuses to corroborate her and Renato's revolutionary past, as happens after the Sagada episode, then similarly what is true/real becomes not fixed but malleable, as does the seeming fact that Renato's body is never discovered, unlike those of his two colleagues. Finally, because the film that we are watching bears the same title, *Melancholia*, as the book that Julian writes in the film, then how are we to know that we are not seeing simply a filmed version of Julian's book, rather than a 'true' story? That Julian is even proposed at one point as being God suggests that he perhaps has engineered the entire story, again creating doubt about the reality of anything in the film. While more happens than Auad lets on, then, in some senses nothing may happen in the film, in that it is all Julian/Danny's fictive creation.

I shall return shortly to the lack of clarity regarding the truth status of much of what we see in the film. Auad's brief remark about *Melancholia*, however, also belies perhaps how, as a Brazilian writing about the film, he is not aware of the way in which the film also says much about the Philippines. As Just Another Film Buff says on their blog, *The Seventh Art*,

> [t]here is another specific problem in screening Diaz's films worldwide. That he is a very 'Filipino' filmmaker. All his works are deeply rooted in the country's history and politics. Any attempt to view the films in a decontextualized manner is only futile. That makes Diaz one of the most uncompromising of directors working today. (Just Another Film Buff, 2010)

Diaz affirms as much when he says that his long, slow cinema is only partially a response to the fast-paced films of Hollywood; much more they are his way of representing 'my culture. That is what I want to share as a Filipino' (Baumgärtel, 2012: 175). So much so, it would seem, that Diaz 'can't compromise it! Length is not really the issue, commitment [to representing his culture] is' (Nepales, 2007). And that culture is a culture in which slowness is a common experience: 'we Filipinos . . . are not governed by the concept of time. We are governed by the concept of space. We don't believe in time . . . If we were governed by time, we would be very progressive and productive' (Baumgärtel, 2012: 174; see also Tolentino, 2012: 135).

Given that various scholars relate slow cinema precisely to Gilles Deleuze's (2005) concept of the time–image, in that an absence of cutting allows events to unfold at their own pace, rather than at the pace determined by the movement both of the characters on-screen and of the editing (see, for example, Lim, 2014:

18–19; Jaffe, 2014: 68–9), it seems contradictory for Diaz to emphasise not time but space here. This characteristically Philippine emphasis on space over time, however, relies for Diaz on an understanding of time as 'progress' and 'production'. That is, time is the mechanised, clockwork time that, for Deleuze, is characterized more by movement – or the subjection of time to the machinations of modernity. When Rolando B. Tolentino suggests that Diaz's cinema involves 'the transcendence of space over time, space controlling time that anchors the time of the present as a juncture for social realities' (2012: 135), he is, in fact, describing something similar to Deleuze's time–image; Diaz's emphasis on space is also an emphasis on events unfolding in, precisely, their own time, rather than at a pace demanded by 'progress' (*Melancholia* also evokes the time–image through its confusion of fact and fiction; as the experience of time as lived is not chronometrical but malleable – time stands still, time flies – so, too, is the mental/experienced hard to separate from the objective).

If Deleuze's concept of the time–image can – at least broadly speaking and contrary to Diaz's disavowal of time as the focus of his work – be applied to Diaz's cinema, how is it uniquely Philippine? It is uniquely Philippine because of Diaz's *mise en scène* and location shooting: we see Sagada and its own, slow pace of life, with trucks, jeepneys and cars – as signifiers of modernity – only rarely bursting forth down its winding roads; even in the urban sections, most shots are full not of the bustle of urban life but stillness and quietude as, even during a rock concert, we see Alberta next to the slow progress of a river; and we see the southern jungle, its trees and other plants impassive to the events that unfold between them. What is more, in telling a story of former Bayan members, *Melancholia* is clearly rooted in a specifically Philippine history (even if the history of the Philippines is one that is a complex intertwining of cultures as a result of historical occupations by both the Spanish and Americans). Intrastate violence has taken on three forms in recent Philippine history: military action against the existing regime (as happened during the popular uprising against the Ferdinand Marcos regime between 1986 and 1990); Moro, or Muslim nationalists, seeking a state independent from the Philippines (as depicted in Mendoza's *Captive*); and communist insurgents, typically from Bayan parties who, like the Moro nationalists, remain active to this day. Lauro (Emman dela Cruz), who bumps into Alberta in Sagada and who tries to expose her performance as Jenine, sums up the aims of the Bayan thus: 'It's a belief that everybody's equal. That a society is really free if there are no rich and poor.' While both the communist insurgents (and Moro nationalists) have been guilty of perpetrating violence towards civilians, the group has also suffered numerous extrajudicial killings and enforced disappearances, resulting in many *desaparecidos*, occasionally discovered in mass graves, as happens in *Melancholia* with Renato, Tirano and Fernandez. Diaz himself attests:

[t]he political situation in my country has been the same since the Marcos years: there have been many killings, and this new government is very cruel in the way it deals with activists. In the last three years alone, almost a thousand activists have been tortured or murdered, or have gone missing. Almost three hundred journalists have been killed in this period too, so it's still the same. That lady president [Gloria Macapagal-Arroyo, 2001–10] is one of the most corrupt presidents that we've ever had. (Ingwanij et al., 2009)

For this reason, Alexis A. Tioseco (though not talking about *Melancholia*) suggests that '[y]ou can feel the weight of history, of the past, in every frame of a Lav Diaz film. It's written in the worn wrinkles on the faces of his characters, in their stammered speech, their furrowed brow; their moments of silence' (Tioseco, 2006).

Diaz himself says that propaganda has no place in art (Ingwanij et al., 2009). If *Melancholia* is about the fate of Bayan insurgents, however, is there not the risk that Diaz's claim is disingenuous, and that his films reflect a communist ideology, one that is reflected in Diaz's seeming ambition 'to change the Filipinos' (and rest of the world's) perspective of their country and culture' (Just Another Film Buff, 2010) – this ambition being the 'something else' that Diaz wants to achieve in his film-making above and beyond entertainment? As Diaz himself says: educating people with cinema is 'a long slow struggle. Re-education isn't an easy process. You have to recondition their [viewers'] minds that cinema is broader than just fast cuts and colour and a lot of adornment' (Caruncho, 2008). The fast cuts, colour and adornment that Diaz evokes here bring to mind the spectacular nature of mainstream (or 'fast') cinema or, as Jonathan Beller terms it in relation to Philippine visual culture, the way in which the society of the spectacle 'coordinates the production of consciousness with the production of commodities, and, therefore, with the production of capital' (2006: 5). In other words, mainstream cinema is a cinema of education or, put more forcefully, propaganda in that it encourages viewers to adopt the capitalist logic of the society of the spectacle. In rejecting the techniques of spectacle and in moving towards a cinema that, in its long takes, long shots and emphasis on space, adopts many of the tropes associated with cinematic realism, Diaz in *Melancholia* is moving precisely away from cinema as propaganda – and the 're-education' that he is seeking to induce is an uneducation, a deprogramming away from capitalism.

In moving away from capitalism, perhaps it is only natural that Diaz takes us away from the capital, Manila, in *Melancholia*, as well as in his other films. Beller also notes that 'abstract art indexes the becoming-abstract of the world as the becoming-abstract of the visual' (Beller, 2006: 3). This 'becoming-abstract' of the world is the move away from realism that is mainstream cinema – and the rendering spectacular of the world that is capitalism. Put differently, when humans do not see what is in front of them for what it is (in all of its strangeness and difference) but, instead, see clichés or easy-to-comprehend and easy-to-consume images (spectacles), then abstraction is taking place: reality is replaced by symbols, and I need not pay much attention to what is in front of me, because I 'read' and/or 'understand' what I am seeing 'already'. In his study of Philippine visuality, Beller argues that various Philippine artists and film-makers, especially Hector R. Ocampo, have at times appropriated abstraction in order to create politically charged artworks that speak of a desire for independence in face of the Philippines' colonial history and contemporary globalisation. Applied to films, the process of abstraction can be understood the moment a viewer expresses unhappiness about the length of a film 'because they got the film already' (and didn't see the need for the film to go on as long as it does – surely a common response to *Melancholia*).

In making a film that is hard to understand, in that *Melancholia* is heavily elliptical, we do not know how much time has passed between sequences nor necessarily in which direction (flashback, flashforward) and, because the whole film may, indeed, be a dream or Julian's fiction, Diaz somehow negates this capitalist process of abstraction. But if Diaz puts forward less a capitalist and more a 'communist' vision of the world (whatever that is or might be), *Melancholia* is not 'propaganda' because of its realism. The long takes, the locations used for shooting and the general effect of real time (the time it takes for Jenine to smoke a cigarette on her balcony in Sagada is the time it takes for actress Angeli Bayani to smoke a cigarette) combine to suggest that the emphasis on space in *Melancholia,* which, in turn, suggests a time–image film, helps to create a film that gets away from abstraction but which returns towards realism – even if *Melancholia*, in being black-and-white and involving framed images that have a specific duration, cannot be called entirely realistic. That said, the film also does not shy from demonstrating that it is a work of art with self-consciousness, via reflexivity, made clear as Julian has written *Melancholia*, the very film we may be watching. In other words, *Melancholia* not only lets much pro-filmic reality into it via its slow pace, its Philippine locations and its long duration (it is realistic) but it also does not shy away from demarcating itself clearly as a film (rather than pretending to be real).

Beller also argues that capital relies upon what he terms 'heliotropism' (Beller 2006: 2). From the Greek word ἥλιος, meaning sun, heliotropism is tied to capital because, for abstraction to take place and for spectacles to be created, vision is required which, in turn, requires light. Cinema is often thought of as the combination of movement and photography, or the process of writing with light. That is, cinema is inherently heliotropic, as Beller would term it. Or at least, cinema is *typically* heliotropic in that it brings to light/makes visible various aspects of the world, be that as part of a fiction or a documentary film.

In reality, however, there is not just light but also darkness, even if darkness is considered uncinematic because, literally, if one films darkness, one cannot see anything – except perhaps for darkness itself. Towards the end of the Sagada sequence, Jenine and Danny discuss darkness. 'All gold, diamonds, humans beings come from the dark', says Danny. Even saints, he insists, come from the darkness that is the woman's womb. Jenine says that she is afraid of the dark while Danny insists that darkness is the greatest equaliser and that anything is possible in the dark. Jenine says that she works in the dark (as a 'prostitute') and that this means that people do not look at her as a human being. Danny insists that he does see Jenine as a human being, to which Jenine retorts that this is because of his business interests as a pimp. Woman, says Danny, is the biggest business in the world, before both recount how they grew up, Jenine as an abused orphan, Danny begging near cinemas in Manila. In this exchange, we have a sense of Danny, at least in theory (because Danny is seemingly Julian's creation and thus not 'real'), endorsing the absence of light and, in part, rejecting heliotropism, perhaps even cinema itself (perhaps it is no coincidence that it is a novel entitled *Melancholia* that Julian writes – as opposed to making a film). While Jenine says that she is afraid of the dark, the making spectacle of woman – which makes of woman the world's biggest industry – is also part of the heliotropic process of cinema and thus of capital. That is, in the dark, we may have no identity and cannot be known but we are perhaps also without prejudice, with prejudice being akin to abstraction and the a priori reading of meaning into the visual (we see what we want to, 'getting' a film before it has even finished). *Melancholia* is not only in black-and-white, with parts of the frame regularly black, but it also features many night-time sequences that are dimly lit, as well as sections of black leader between certain scenes/sequences. Diaz creates a film that, paradoxically, is somehow anticinematic – not only as a result of its digital construction (this is a film made without material film), nor simply as a result of its uncommercial length and slow style. It is also anticinematic because that same style arguably involves not bringing something from the darkness to light – as per the discovery of Tirano and Fernandez's skeletons – but trying to show us darkness itself. We do not know what has happened to Renato. The 'darkness' that is his story is what we see instead.

Like darkness, time is often considered to be invisible. One cannot 'see' time and, being invisible, time is, like darkness, hard to understand. *Melancholia*'s slowness again emerges here as important: in showing us long, long takes in which 'nothing' happens, we begin to see that other invisible component of the world, time. Time, like darkness, is indifferent towards the prejudices and hierarchies of humans; it equalises everything in that everything falls into decay and ruin. The equality of everything is, of course, the goal of communism. *Melancholia* thus uses techniques associated with realism (long takes, locations) to demonstrate the 'communism' of darkness, of time, and thus, perhaps, of the universe itself (not least because our sun will die and eventually we shall all be plunged into darkness, even if new stars and life forms emerge in other parts of the universe). This means that *Melancholia* paradoxically encourages us to see the world not in an abstract fashion but for what it is once again. This is paradoxical because, as a film, *Melancholia* involves an abstraction of its own – this is a film and not the real world that I am seeing. Nonetheless, by relativising our vision, making us conscious of how abstraction is perhaps part of vision, and in trying to bring into our awareness a darkness, a time, and an invisibility that defies the very nature of vision (and the taking advantage of vision that is heliotropic, capitalist and spectacular cinema), then *Melancholia* is a film that tries to 're-educate' audiences, while not being propaganda. *Melancholia* is the work of an artist asking us to engage differently with the world, not that of a film-maker trying to convince us of a particular world view.

Nadin Mai reads *Melancholia* as being about 'death time' and the reflection of a 'concentrationary universe'. That is, *Melancholia* features, in particular, Renato and colleagues in the jungle waiting to die, an excruciating, consistent deferral of death that is hard to take (hence Renato's colleague literally appealing to be killed). This, in turn, reflects the way in which the contemporary world is constructed increasingly like a concentration camp in which death similarly comes slowly (Mai, 2014). While I find Mai's reading partially compelling, I think that, in some senses, it overlooks the sheer life of *Melancholia*. By this, I mean that, as I watch the jungle sequence with Renato and colleagues, my sense of time and my desire for 'action' begin to change and soon I find myself marvelling at how raindrops make quiver a branch and leaves that extend from off-screen and into the foreground of one of the section's various images. That is, I suddenly find joy in the minutiae of the film because everything is seemingly alive. That all must pass is no doubt a source of melancholy but that melancholy is all the more bittersweet (and, thus, precisely melancholic, rather than, say, sad) because of the beauty that is derived from the smallest of things – as I begin to see time, darkness, *Melancholia* the film and perhaps the rest of the world itself without prejudice, as equal. *Melancholia* is a specifically Philippine iteration of slow cinema; but, as we become overwhelmed by the images (feeling worried that one simply cannot take in all of the massive, minute detail of each and every shot: how many drops of rain and quivering branches did I miss in this world that is brimming with life?), the film takes us into a philosophical realm that is also universal.

ACKNOWLEDGEMENT

The author would like to thank Matthew Flanagan for bootlegging a set of DVDs of *Melancholia* for him.

BIBLIOGRAPHY

Auad, Pedro Henrique Trindade Kalil (2013), 'The Air-Condition Nightmare: 21st Century Cinema,' *Animus: Revista Interamericana de Comunicação Midiática*, 12: 23, pp. 330–47.

Baumgärtel, Tilman (2012), '"Digital is liberation theology": Interview with Lav Diaz', in Tilman Baumgärtel (ed.), *Southeast Asian Independent Cinema* (Hong Kong: Hong University Press), pp. 171–8.

Beller, Jonathan (2006), *Acquiring Eyes: Philippine Visuality, Nationalist Struggle, and the World-Media System* (Manila: Ateneo de Manila University Press).

Bordwell, David (2006), *The Way Hollywood Tells It: Story and Style in Modern Movies* (Berkeley, CA: University of California Press).

Caruncho, Eric S. (2008), 'To Hell and Back with Lav Diaz', *Sunday Inquirer Magazine/ Philippine Daily Inquirer*, 12 October, http://showbizandstyle.inquirer.net/sim/ sim/view/20081012-165978/To-Hell-and-Back-with-Lav-Diaz [accessed 31 October 2014].

Dargis, Manohla (2008), 'Cannes Journal: Box-Office Beasties', *New York Times*, 19 May, http://www.nytimes.com/2008/05/19/movies/19cann.html?_r=0 [accessed 31 October 2014].

Deleuze, Gilles (2005) *Cinema 2: The Time–Image*, translated by Hugh Tomlinson and Robert Galeta (London: Continuum).

Ingwanij, May Adadol, Graiwoot Chulphongsathorn, Wiwat Lertwiwatongsa and Alexis Tioseco (2009), 'Lav Diaz in Conversation', *Lumen*, September, http://lumen journal.org/issues/issue-i/diaz [accessed 1 November 2014].

Jaffe, Ira (2014), *Slow Movies: Countering the Cinema of Action* (London: Wallflower).

Just Another Film Buff (2010), 'The Films of Lav Diaz', *The Seventh Art*, 16 May, http:// theseventhart.info/2010/05/16/the-films-of-lav-diaz/ [accessed 31 October 2014].

Lim, Song Hwee (2014), *Tsai Ming-liang and a Cinema of Slowness*, Honolulu, HI: University of Hawai'i Press.

Mai, Nadin (2014), 'The concentrationary university in the films of Lav Diaz (paper)', *The Art(s) of Slow Cinema*, 8 September, http://theartsofslowcinema.com/2014/09/08/ the-concentrationary-universe-in-the-films-of-lav-diaz-paper/ [accessed 2 November 2014].

Nepales, Ruben V. (2007), 'Interview with Lav Diaz', *Global Nation: Celebrating the Filipino Spirit Worldwide*, 6 September, http://globalnation.inquirer.net/diaspora/ diaspora/view/20070906-87037/Interview_with_Lav_Diaz [accessed 31 October 2014].

Scheib, Ronnie (2008), 'Review: "Melancholia"', *Variety*, 29 September, http://variety. com/2008/film/reviews/melancholia-3-1200470200/ [accessed 31 October 2014].

Tioseco, Alexis A. (2006), 'A Conversation with Lav Diaz', *Criticine*, 30 January, http:// criticine.com/interview_article.php?id=21 [accessed 1 November 2014].

Tolentino, Rolando B. (2012), 'Marcos, Brocka, Bernal, City Films, and the Contestation for Imagery of Nation', *Kritika Kultura*, 19, pp. 115–38.

Trice, Jasmine Nadua (2009), *Transnational Cinema, Transcultural Capital: Cinema Distribution and Exhibition in Metro-Manila, Philippines, 2006–2009*, unpublished PhD thesis, Indiana University.

8. EXHAUSTED DRIFT: AUSTERITY, DISPOSSESSION AND THE POLITICS OF SLOW IN KELLY REICHARDT'S *MEEK'S CUTOFF*

Elena Gorfinkel

Occupying a unique place in American independent film-making, Kelly Reichardt's cinema sits at the cusp of experimental and classical film traditions. Reichardt's autonomous creative practice and relatively low budgets have linked her style with international art cinema, both historical (neorealism) and contemporary (slow cinema). Reichardt often works with the tropes of a specifically American idiom – the road film – and her films *Old Joy* (2006), *Wendy and Lucy* (2008) and *Meek's Cutoff* (2010), and the recent *Night Moves* (2013) all notably employ the beckoning horizon of wide-open north-western landscapes and their tarnished promises of freedom, autonomy, and self-reliance. Deploying austerity as an aesthetic, Reichardt's films frequently perambulate and get lost with the wanderers, mountain men, drifters and the socially displaced and marginalised at their centre. Her films trace the trajectory of these precarious travellers circuitous or arrested journeys, as well as the affective slackness of their suspended agency, their 'stuckness,' non-productivity, and inability to progress within the harsh demands of an exhausting, social, material world. Landscape and physical detail work in her films to index or to unravel the already frayed bonds that draw people together and apart, in impoverishment and in rituals of the everyday, in relations of dependency and debt.

REICHARDT'S SLOWNESS

Reichardt's slow style across these works bears qualities of austerity, drift and a fascination with affects of exhaustion and processes of embodied labour.

Her films are frequently described with adjectives such as minimalist, austere, restrained, reticent, observational, spare, oblique, reserved, undecorated. This chapter examines the political and theoretical implications of the aesthetics of austerity in Reichardt's 'anti-Western' *Meek's Cutoff* (hereafter *Meek's*). *Meek's* is emblematic of the scope of Reichardt's contribution to the slow tendency emergent in contemporary world cinema, whose primary features include temporal dilation, liberal use of distant framings and the long take, and a focus on a phenomenological realism (Flanagan, 2008). Tiago de Luca emphasises slow cinema's preoccupation with physicality and corporeal realism, a 'fascinat[ion with] the physicality of animate and inanimate matter, bodies and landscapes . . . [the] deflat[ion of] narrative progression . . . through which the perceptual and material qualities of the image are enhanced' (de Luca, 2011: 42; de Luca, 2014). Song Hwee Lim, examining Tsai Ming-liang's cinema of slowness, further articulates slow cinema's formal elements, linked to both narrative subject matter, which privileges scenes of empty time and waiting, and a durational aesthetic embedded in the use of extended long takes (Lim, 2014: 11–42). Additionally, slow films evacuate eventfulness, in the pursuit of dedramatised scenarios in which incident replaces event, and sheer profilmic happening challenges structures of legible or discrete causality.

Reichardt's works focus on the observation of everyday and laborious processes; her use of muted and sparse dialogue and ambient sound, her preference for stripped, evacuated landscapes, solitary characters or situations of estrangement, and for reticent performance styles from actors position her within the above continuum of tendencies seen in global slow films. Yet Reichardt approaches these minor temporalities and quotidian textures from specifically American cinematic idioms and through a persistent utilisation of an American sense of place. Her artisanal, small-scale mode of production – *Meek's* was her first film made on 35 mm and her first with a seven-figure budget – materially inscribes the aesthetic possibilities of the films in terms of a discourse of austerity. Austerity, a loaded term, resonates with a twenty-first century economic order and the neoliberal imperatives and policies of the George W. Bush and post-Bush era that insist that citizens do less with less, policies of resource attrition that have led to the dispossession of the already marginalised. In that sense, Reichardt's austere slowness is an aesthetic responsive to the harsh economic and ideological realities of the United States's political contemporaneity. I thus use austerity here to signpost a formal drive within the film-maker's work but one that is conceptually inseparable from these socio-economic, materialist underpinnings.

While Reichardt consistently relies on long takes and a durational, observational style, her intervention in a global slow cinema aesthetic comes less in the use of literal extended duration but, more prominently, in the linkage of quotidian activity and forms of arduous, painful labour with temporalities of exhaustion and dispossession for subjects on the margins of American life. Slowness for Reichardt operates as a vitally allegorical, as much as a formal, material. In this sense her work is both *distinct from* and *coextensive with* her slow cinema contemporaries globally. *Distinct* in that it often evokes or conforms closely to certain elements of classical film form and shot structure, and bears a stronger attachment to character subjectivity. Geoff King, in his reading of *Meek's* as representative of the persistence of a low-budget mode of indie production thought to have waned in a post-Miramax era, calls this the film-maker's 'relatively slow style' as measured against her more 'radical' contemporaries on the one hand and a Hollywood norm on the other (King, 2013: 22). Indeed, compared to the extremes of extended takes in the work of film-makers such as Béla Tarr or Tsai Ming-liang, Reichardt's shot durations (her long takes average ten to thirty seconds) fall short. Lim notes that film studies as a field has largely been unable to settle on a definitive length for what counts as a proper long take. The very subjective nature of temporal experience will always militate to make a 'metrics' of slow a futile task, one that would run counter to the *criticality* of the concept of slowness (Lim, 2014: 21–2).

Thus, if we detach slowness from a purist metric of duration, Reichardt's work is exceedingly *coextensive* with the aims and aesthetics of slow cinema in that her very shooting, editing and framing strategies propound slowness as a thematic, allegorical and political condition as much as a purely formal one, or one of sheer or mere duration. Recently, Lutz Koepnick has critiqued a definition of slowness as a style or strategy that should attend merely to temporal and literal duration, suggesting instead that

> aesthetic slowness registers and reflects on the coexistence of multiple streams of time in our expanded present . . . the wager of aesthetic slowness is not simply to find inlands of respite, calm and stillness somewhere outside the cascades of contemporary speed culture. It is to investigate what it means to experience a world of speed, acceleration and cotemporality. (Koepnick, 2014: 10)

This dialectical nature of slowness can position Reichardt more forcefully within an expanded field of slow aesthetic practices.

That sensory impression of slowness in Reichardt's style doubtless played a role in *Meek's* prominence in a widely read critical dispute in the *New York Times*. Dan Kois's essay 'Eating Your Cultural Vegetables' (see the Introduction for further discussion) polemically confessed that the author had reached a point of 'cultural fatigue' from having to dutifully watch slow art films. *Meek's Cutoff* served as Kois's prime example, which he described as a 'quiet arduous chronicle of a long journey . . . seemingly portrayed in real time . . . by the [film's] end, I could sympathize with the settlers' exhaustion;

I felt as if I'd been through a similarly grueling experience' (Kois, 2011). It is hardly surprising that fatigue is the central affect, especially with regard to a film so concerned with weariness as a physical and existential condition of gruelling transit. As I argue elsewhere, slow art cinema's legacy of archiving both profilmic weariness in performing bodies and in producing extrafilmic fatigue in the spectator is simultaneously vast and relatively unexamined (Gorfinkel, 2012/2013). Despite wide critical acclaim for *Meek's*, this unpleasurable response to the austere temporality of the film was also in other quarters positioned as part of Reichardt's rigorous, feminist, 'materialist' but 'unsensual' aesthetic (Denby, 2011).

Unending Days, Monotonous Drift

Meek's Cutoff's slowness derives in large part from its lack of explicit narrative exposition or contextualisation and its observational accumulation of passages and processes. The film script – written by Reichardt's frequent collaborator, novelist Jon Raymond – reconstructs the events of an actual, arduous expedition led by the hired mountain man, Stephen Meek, to take emigrants across the mountains and Oregon desert trail in 1845 in search of a place to settle in the state's Willamette Valley. Lost from the outset, their ostensible goal, arrival at their intended destination, is converted to basic survival, a pursuit of water and its liquid sustenance. Reducing the scale of the actual expedition of hundreds to a fictionalised group of three families, the film presents their parched, punishing quest as a Beckett-inflected scenario of absurdity, bound by waiting, opacity and non-knowledge. Character backstory, the details and reasons for travel are elided or only obliquely given. The group's trust in Meek (Bruce Greenwood), a raconteur guide prone to tall tales, braggadocio and irascibility, becomes a tenuous act of faith, desperation, or reckless abandon. The settlers quietly wonder after his intentions and the possibility of foul play. This precarious trust frays further with the arrival of a lone Cayuse Indian (Rod Rondeaux). The frightened settlers hold the Native American captive, unable to communicate with him. He becomes a source of suspicion, hostility, anxious wonder and uncertainty – a pure site of difference, an empty sign of unfathomable alterity. His language and words, presented unsubtitled, are as incomprehensible to the settlers as theirs are to him. In their unending monotonous transit through windy salt flats, rocky desert hills and wiry sagebrush, they suffer numerous setbacks and losses. After a stand-off between Emily Tetherow (Michelle Williams), the film's anchoring character, and wife of Soloman (Will Patton), and Meek, their failing guide, the group entrust in the tribesman their hope that he will guide them to water. In multiple registers, of narrative, theme, and form, goal orientation and telos are confounded and derided, and the expedition's transit seems like a maddening loop, without a capacity to progress.

The ambiguous ending reinforces the film's emphasis on movement without advancement. A faint flicker of promise remains in their discovery of a lone tree that appears, as if an apparition, bearing some greenness – a harbinger of water? – below dead, gnarled top branches. Meek announces that he is at the Indian's and, by extension, Emily's command proclaiming that 'we're all just playing our parts now. This was written long before we got here.'

Meek's grounds its detached gaze in the perspective of the wives in the travelling party who, during moments of crisis and decision-making, are often framed together spatially, and apart from the men. Sound further exacerbates this distance as Reichardt makes dialogue low or inaudible, highlighting the women's straining to hear and, instead, deploying ambient elemental noises. The film emphasises the women's muted observation and suspended agency, constructing out of their partial views, limited knowledge, and enforced distance from the men's actions, the anchoring perceptual frame of the film. Invested in the women's marginality to the central action, and decentring and displacing a privileged sense of narrative action altogether, *Meek's* presents us instead with elliptical segments of the dread, monotonous time of their travel and brute encounter with the Oregon Trail, the desert an impediment and silent adversary.

The film's opening emblematises Reichardt's slow style as an instantiation of austerity and narratological and pictorial restraint. It also establishes the minor rhythms that will organise its sparse narrative. The first six or so minutes of the film consist of thirteen shots taken from a detached observational distance, and in long takes. The first image shows the migrants traversing the girth of a rushing river. Slowly, in long shot, first one, then a second, then a third woman, cautiously wades through the water, waist deep, moving from screen left to screen right. One carries a basket and one a birdcage on her head. The camera tracks slightly leftwards to readjust, as we spy them from river level. The low position of the camera limits the expansiveness of the shot, emphasising the verisimilitude of the experience of fording the water's depth.

A subsequent shot, in long take, shows male travellers standing at the opposite bank, attempting to manoeuvre their Conestoga wagons into the water, and the camera slowly pans left to follow their movement. We see two oxen, faces mutely waiting in the hill's horizon. Dialogue is absent, as the forceful sound of the river swells, and the murmurs of animal and elemental life flood over the images. These distant framings deliberately give way to closer, medium shots of more specific tasks of labouring: a pregnant woman drying out wet clothing amid yellow thistles (Shirley Henderson); the filling of a water bucket from the rocks by a male traveller (Patton); and of one of the caravan's wives (Williams) scrubbing a wooden bowl on the rocks, her bonnet concealing her face. A woman's face shrouded in her bonnet (Zoe Kazan) is seen in medium close-up as she gingerly pours some water into her yellow canary's cage. A donkey is readied for travel, chewing impassively as a grizzled man (Greenwood), in ostentatious red shirt, loads the saddle on the animal, his back to the camera.

Overlaid with this image a subtle sound bridge grows progressively louder, a scraping which mirrors and reinscribes the rustling, abrasive auditory landscape that has given this very austere space its brooding, verisimilar texture. The scratching is revealed in the subsequent shot. A young emigrant (Paul Dano) carves the word 'LOST' into the dry carcass of a toppled tree, its smooth surface whittled by wind and time. The first words, spoken or read, that we encounter in this film, this communiqué is a proclamation of a diegetic place, a location in narrative time, and perhaps an existential state. An expressive act addressed ostensibly to no one, lostness, a common trope in Reichardt's cinema, here signals an asynchronous time. The SOS is a conversation, like a time capsule, with a future temporality that has yet to arrive, as well as a material inscription of a wearisome present. The voyagers appear to us in the film's beginning already estranged, in a nowhere place, the irony of which the rest of the film will elucidate.

AUSTERE FRAMES, RESTRICTED MOVEMENTS

As evident in this opening and throughout the film, Reichardt's interest in omission, restriction, and limited, rigorously structured perspectives can be seen in the construction of these scenes in medium and long shots, and primarily stationary, contemplative camera set-ups. This element of restriction is also pronounced in her use of a 1.33:1 (4:3) aspect ratio, instead of the customary 1.85:1. To the extent that her aesthetic is organised by scarcity, difficulty, obstruction and impediment across her films, the boxier shape of the frame of 1.33:1 and the avoidance of widescreen delimits the visual field. Reichardt has commented that the square frame was also an instrument of manipulating narrative time, in that 'you wouldn't see tomorrow or yesterday in the shot' as you could in the wider expanse of the desert horizon (Longworth, 2011). Such framing also dispenses with a romantic orientation to landscape and the representation of westward expansion as a magisterial exercise in a mastery of, and a triumphalist claim to, space. While the genres of Western and road film are strongly associated with the monumentality of scale and beautified vision, Reichardt seeks 'de-romanticization' (Dietrich, 2011; Klinger, 1997). Reichardt has also linked the square frame and the restricted visual field of the space to the social and visual constraints signified by the women's bonnets. The headwear provides a figurative sight line and framing point of view (POV) which serve as blinkers that eliminate peripheral vision but also control an experience of space and time (Longworth, 2011; Dietrich, 2011). All these choices highlight what cannot be known, prognosticated or understood.

Sound and light are also key elements deployed by Reichardt in pursuit of a formal austerity. In addition to the general inaudibility of dialogue, when the men speak and the women look on, dialogue, albeit minimal and clipped, is often reserved for night-time or moments of halted transit. Silences, stalled conversations, and elliptical speech also prevail, as the film's ambient sound returns strikingly to recurrent tropes and motifs – the creaking wagon wheel – a rhythm that marks this monotonous time – the sound of the animals hooves, wind, the rustling of brush, footsteps and the jostling of objects in wagons. In addition, the transitions between the punishing sunlight of daytime and the pitch dark of night-time provide stark, unexpected contrasts. Night scenes strain and challenge the spectator's vision, as low lamplight and firelight barely illuminate actors' faces. These aesthetic strategies of extreme naturalism underscore the opacity and non-knowledge so central to the temporality of this uncertain journey.

Barbara Klinger suggests that the road film, like the Western, participates in an 'atavistic romanticism' of the nation through its figuration of landscape. Discussing *Easy Rider* (1969), she claims that the film's pictorial, cinematographic radiance – for example, in the use of lens flares and 360-degree pans in Monument Valley – reinscribes, despite a countercultural pedigree, a nationalist ideology through a beautified or majestic landscape aesthetic (Klinger, 1997: 189). In contrast, Reichardt's road saga, while examining the mythos of the west, shoots landscape as a sphere of danger and suspicion, threat and contingency (Dietrich, 2011). Wide picturesque vistas that emphasise ease or mastery of movement are avoided and, while long shots are prominent, Reichardt usually connects the impact of environment on bodies through the registration of affects of fatigue, weariness, in the residues of dirt and dust on hands, faces and garments, through arrested movements, and stalling gestures. The material environment is unforgiving. It exacts its toll on bodies, psyches and things, tracing an intractable time and a depletion of energy and resources.

The Oregon desert's very tactile textures – rockiness, brambles and shrubs, dust and wind, cracked earth, as well as a monochromatic tone of tan dryness – provide a haptic inhospitability and a sense of alien threat. Such images of barrenness gain an apocalyptic charge, summoning an ecological imaginary of blight and ruin, a time outside time. This aesthetic approach also produces some of its more hallucinatory, 'uncanny' aesthetic features: the yellow canary in this landscape (an indulgent piece of property that signals both naive idealism and sentiment); the women's floral pastel dresses in hues of yellow, green and pink against the dusty dry earth; or the scene of Glory White running back across the cracked salt flats to recover a lost scarf.

Reichardt studiously avoids presenting her landscapes as fulsome or sublime. For example, a later scene uses the cinematographic bounty of the 'magic hour' between dusk and nightfall to shoot the setting sun and the tawny orange hues of the sky against the darkening silhouettes of the moving caravan of vehicles, animals and human bodies. The time of day, in the darkness of the figures, produces an effect of foreboding. Lens flares bestow on the image a peculiar cruelty. The last shot in this scene reveals the canary's cage swinging from the frame of the Gatelys' wagon, mordantly empty, a small death elided. The encroaching fall of night is thus made sinister and mournful as their movement grinds futilely on.

'A Trance of Walking'

> I wanted to give a different view of the west from the usual series of masculine encounters and battles of strength, and to present this idea of going west as just a trance of walking. (Reichardt, in Gilbey, 2011)

The shooting of the film mirrored and recreated, in minor key, the restricted resources, duress and arduousness of the actual historical journey. Cast and a bare-bones crew spent a difficult time in the Oregon desert, setting up camp in the Horseshoe Motel in Burns, Oregon, a town with a population of three thousand, a two-hour drive from the desert locations. Operating without the frills of a bigger-budgeted shoot, Reichardt recalled the challenging production environment, calling the desert 'the great equalizer' (Longworth, 2011). The film-maker also remarked that 'Paul [Dano] and Zoe [Kazan] were saying that the strangest thing for them was after walking across that desert for a month, to get in a plane and fly across that area in a minute' (Adams, 2011). The arduousness of the emigrants' travel, on foot and via caravan, and the obstinacy of space as a medium of tracing time are no doubt here rendered in the calling forth of images of transit that challenge the ethos of freedom, velocity and speed, as well as the luxury of meandering drift or time luxuriated usually associated with modernist *flânerie* and its senses of drift. In the road film's quest structure and in the spatial conquest narratives that underwrite the Western, travel and transit are bestowed with the quality of autonomy and individuation. *Yet Meek's* associates physical movement with struggle, difficulty, blockage, impediment and endurance rather than with freedom.

The romance of drift, as contingent process and route to sovereignty, is converted thus into a space of considerable risk. Matthew Flanagan has described how slow cinema, at least from one of its originary sites in Michelangelo Antonioni's modernism, is often situated as a 'cinema of walking' (Flanagan, 2008). Wandering is a primary feature of the modern art cinema more broadly, linked with urban modernity and the preponderance of the *flâneur* and '*flâneuse*' in post-war cinema (Betz, 2009). Walking has a central place in contemporary global instantiations of slow style, especially in the form of the extended following shot that moves with the characters perambulations.

Walking in *Meek's* is stripped of this capacity for virtuosity in the mirroring of camera movement or individuation with the walkers. Camera movement is thus always subtle, and never ostentatiously materialised in the baroque tracking shot, in contrast, for example, with the cinema of Tarr or Carlos Reygadas. In *Meek's* the protagonist's walks often highlight the temporality of blocked advancement, the futility of progress, and the sheer endurance of its process. A series of shots articulates the temporal weariness of the walk through the desert, the exhaustion of drift. Emily and Millie are seen in long shot hobbling slowly with stiffening gaits against the wind but remaining in the same place within the composition for the duration of the take, their faces worn, their features slackened (See Figure 8.1).

This sense of time, as both embedded in minutiae *and* trance-like in its temporal shifts, is tied to accounts of the historical reality Reichardt aimed to reconstruct. In interviews, Reichardt has remarked on the journal entries she studied of actual emigrants, particularly the women, on the Meek expedition in 1845. She noted the settlers' attenuated sense of time, and how radically alien their temporal and spatial experience of travel might seem to a twenty-first-century sensibility (Quart, 2011: 41). The final shots which comprise the opening sequence emblematise the unexpectedly conjoined elements of movement,

Figure 8.1 The punishing walk on the salt flats, *Meek's Cutoff* (2010).

slowness and hypnagogic trance. A forty-second take presents the three wagons and the entire travelling party traversing the frame from background to foreground. They walk leading their wagons, curving towards the camera and then out of frame, as we see and hear the din of the river's water flowing behind them. All the emigrants pass out of frame, leaving the 'empty' image of the riverbank. An image superimposition slowly appears. One distant hillscape transforms into another and we see a moving caravan of wagons silhouetted, from a further, iconic distance, traversing the hilly edge of an even further horizon. The river appears slowly to dry out in the process of the image's transition from shot to shot, the water replaced by a more arid, tawny vista.

This slowly rendered lap dissolve, over the course of two takes and close to two minutes, creates an eerie spatio-temporal effect of time passing, in the condensation and ellipsis of narrative events, as well as the droning circularity and state of waiting such travel has induced. The monotony of a day edges indistinctly into the next, temporal difference eviscerated. The image of the settlers, who have just left the image on screen left, materialises their return as specks on the horizon on screen right. It articulates a sense of time marked by exhaustion that incorporates the hallucinatory and evocative as much as the realist. Both a clarion of the iconicity of the Western, and an instance of 'hyperreal' minimalism, this sequence speaks to the contradictory and distinct nature of Reichardt's formal manipulation of time and her use of slowness as an allegorical material, as much as, or in excess of, sheer durational material. The superimposed shot extends the fundamental strangeness of the settlers' presence in and to this landscape, their basic alienness converted into an arresting temporal abstraction within the image.

LABOURING BODIES

Labour and the effort of endurance are central to *Meek's Cutoff*'s production of slow time. Noting the transformation in the original settlers' diary entries, Reichardt indicates how exhaustion winnowed the real emigrants' capacity for descriptive detail, 'the diaries . . . begin with big ideas and grand dreams when they start out, but as they go on, the trip turns into a stripped-down, bare-bones list of chores (e.g., pitching a tent). I thought of *Nanook of the North* while making it' (Quart 2011: 41). Robert Flaherty's landmark ethnographic film (1922) is, indeed, a crucial point of contrast for *Meek's*, as Reichardt clearly borrows the temporality of the observation of discrete labour processes (in *Nanook*, for example, the seal hunt, the building of the igloo). *Meek's* likewise takes pains to show us extensively the fixing of wagon wheels, the setting up of camp, collecting kindling, starting fires, knitting, mending clothes, laundry, looking after the cattle, the grinding of wheat, the cooking. But we rarely see an action proceed from ostensible beginning to end, as in *Nanook*, except for key dramatic episodes such as the lowering of the wagons into the steep ravine or the widely discussed scene of Emily loading and firing the shotgun when she first spies the Cayuse (Lattimer, 2013: 40). The film's more quotidian actions are mere facts that must be attended to for the grinding time of survival.

While based in historical reality, the gendered division of labour is striking in the ways it produces spaces of solitariness amid presumed collectivity. It also highlights the spatial organisation of knowledge, as the men deliberate, making decisions, while the women are responsible for social reproduction and the care of the expedition. After they have come upon an inhospitable alkaline lake, an extended sequence shot from the women's waiting perspective frames an image of the men, standing in a line with their backs to women and camera, inaudibly discussing what to do. As they speak, the body of water seems to taunt the group as if a cruel mirage. The film's form apprises us that knowledge and access to information are like water, among many scarce resources.

Gender, exhaustion and labour systematically adjoin questions of race, a relationship complexly negotiated within the film. Starting the breakfast fire in the darkness of morning, Emily Tetherow (Williams) states begrudgingly, barely visible in lamplight, 'working like niggers once again'. The shot reveals two more lanterns and fires slowly starting in the background as the two other wives, Glory White (Henderson) and Millie Gately (Kazan) perform their morning chores. This contradictory association of their labour with a racial horizon of a pre-civil war slavery economy, and the women's positioning with other forms of chattel, resonates strikingly with the racial and gender politics that thread throughout the rest of the film.

Emily Tetherow seems the most progressive force in the film, in contrast to Meek's fear-mongering and racism; she is the character who shows the most (proto-liberal) empathy for the Cayuse captive. Her politics are ambivalent, however, reinscribing her racial and economic privilege and patrimony, her sense of white Eurocentric pride. The scene of her mending the Indian's moccasin expresses the stakes of dependency, as Emily rationalises to Millie her offer of seeming care in sewing his shoe, 'I want him to owe me something'. Establishing a capitalist logic of debt as the essential social bond or condition of their relationality, Emily further speaks to the native as he looks on and she sews, explaining that the needle is a 'pin for sewing . . .' and launches into a 'civilising' lesson: 'you can't even imagine what we've done, the cities we've built'. The rawness and tension of the act are highlighted by one of the scarcer close-ups of the film, on the Indian's bare, soiled foot, resting on the sienna earth. Another ironic inscription of capitalist exchange value is also resident in Gately's naive offering of blankets to the Cayuse in exchange for his knowledge about where water might be – which invokes the history of the spread of smallpox among Native American tribes through contaminated blankets given to them by British settlers in the eighteenth and nineteenth centuries.

Despite these moments of coloniser hubris towards the Cayuse, the larger narrative arc destabilises the notion of property which underwrites the logics of self-possession that motivates Manifest Destiny, conceived as central to the American 'character'. In the most 'climactic' scene in which the Tetherows lose their wagon and their remaining water during their arduous descent into a deep valley, property, material wealth and capital are jettisoned, questioned, made cruelly irrelevant. Even earlier, the Tetherows are forced to lighten the load of their wagon to ease the weight pulled by their animals. Soloman Tetherow's mother's clock is the first, highly symbolic, object to be shuttled, along with a rocking chair, another palliative bourgeois object to soothe the passing rhythms of time. Later, during a delay due to the fixing of a wagon-wheel axle, Jimmy White's discovery of gold presents another absurd confrontation with their exhausting journey's revaluation of value, as Tetherow remarks that 'you can't drink gold' and that they must keep moving in order to make good time before sunset. They leave a marker of the gold's location, like Gately's lost sign, again for a future time that has yet to materialise.

DISPOSSESSION, INDETERMINATE ENDS

The hauntingly ambiguous conclusion of the film – itself a reflexive outcome of resource restriction, as Reichardt's budget ran out before they could shoot the last scripted scene – offers the discovery of the tree and Meek's abdication of his power, in effect to the woman and the Native American. Whether a renunciation of leadership, the emergence of an alternative episteme, or a recalibration of collective will, the equivocal ending presents another mode of dispossession, a 'giving in' and 'giving up' – seen in very different form elsewhere in Reichardt's cinema (Gorfinkel, 2012/2013: 342). The Cayuse may still lead them to water or into the hands of fellow tribesmen or to death. The film ends, emblematically, on a long shot of the Cayuse walking alone across the desert plain. As such, dispossession operates throughout *Meek's* as an inevitable, determined effect of movement itself, one dynamised by the 'alchemy' of ideology, racial rights, land rights and the drive of colonisation and settlement itself. To be able to imagine the claim on land as property, on persons as property and on the self as property in one breath, in the developing ethos of American possessive individualism in this represented historical moment, is also to be caught in the winds of its unfathomable violence and its drive to the abstraction of the human subject (Athanasiou and Butler, 2013).

Reichardt's cinema asks us to confront the couplet of austerity and dispossession through the experience of a grinding time of movement without seeming end, one that stresses and wears, and one that the travellers can only endure. Reichardt's slowness thus configures time not as a vehicle of progress or heroic telos but as a sphere of blockage, delay, arrest and duress. In the refrain of the settlers' plaintive question of 'how much longer/farther?', we can indeed ask how much more can be endured, and *for how long*, before something is found? Reichardt's constitutive aesthetic mode is an exercise in slowness as a politics of the difficulty of survival and endurance, from the perspective of a 'late liberal' geopolitical moment (Povinelli, 2011) and the subjects at its utmost margins. In the solitary, exhausted drift of the film's final image, Reichardt's austere aesthetic seems to ask, what can one truly *have* without possession *but* attachment to the materiality of time?

Bibliography

Athanasiou, Athena and Judith Butler (2013), *Dispossession: The Performative in the Political* (Cambridge and Malden, MA: Polity Press).

Adams, Sam (2011), 'Kelly Reichardt and Jon Raymond' (Interview), *The Onion AV Club*, 26 April, http://www.avclub.com/article/kelly-reichardt-and-jon-raymond-55095 n.p. [accessed 15 December 2014].

Betz, Mark (2009), *Beyond the Subtitle: Remapping European Art Cinema* (Minneapolis, MN: University of Minnesota Press).

de Luca, Tiago (2011), 'Gus Van Sant's *Gerry* and Visionary Realism', *Cinephile: The University of British Columbia's Film Journal*, 7. 2, autumn, pp. 43–50.

de Luca, Tiago (2014), *Realism of the Senses in World Cinema: The Experience of Physical Reality* (New York and London: I. B. Tauris).

Denby, David (2011), 'Strange Trips', *The New Yorker*, 11 April, http://www.newyorker.com/magazine/2011/04/11/strange-trips [accessed 1 December 2014].

Dietrich, Joy (2011), 'O Pioneers! Kelly Reichardt's Anti-Western', *The New York Times*, 7 April, http://tmagazine.blogs.nytimes.com/2011/04/07/o-pioneers-kelly-reichardts-anti-western/ [accessed 15 December 2014].

Flanagan, Matthew (2008), 'Toward an Aesthetic of Slow in Contemporary Cinema', *16:9*, no. 29 (November), http://www.16-9.dk/2008-11/side11_inenglish.htm [accessed 15 December 2014].

Gilbey, Ryan (2011), 'Kelly Reichardt: How I Trekked Across Oregon for Meek's Cutoff then Returned to Teaching', *The Guardian*, 8 April, http://www.theguardian.com/film/2011/apr/09/kelly-reichardt-meeks-cutoff [accessed 15 December 2014].

Gorfinkel, Elena (2012/2013), 'Weariness, Waiting: Endurance and Art Cinema's Tired Bodies', *Discourse*, 34: 2–3, spring–autumn, pp. 311–47.

King, Geoff (2013), 'Indie's Continuities: The Persistence of American Independent Tradition in Kelly Reichardt's *Meek's Cutoff*', *Revue Française de'Etudes Américaines*, no. 136, pp. 15–27.

Klinger, Barbara (1997), 'The Road to Dystopia: Landscaping the Nation in *Easy Rider*', in Steven Cohan and Ina Rae Hark (eds), *The Road Movie Book* (New York: Routledge), pp. 179–203.

Koepnick, Lutz (2014), *On Slowness: Toward an Aesthetic of the Contemporary* (New York: Columbia University Press).

Kois, Dan (2011), 'Eating Your Cultural Vegetables', *New York Times Magazine*, 29 April, http://www.nytimes.com/2011/05/01/magazine/mag-01Riff-t.html [accessed 15 December 2014].

Lattimer, James (2011), 'Beyond Neo-neorealism: Kelly Reichardt's *Meeks Cutoff*', *Cinephile: The University of British Columbia's Film Journal*, 7.2, autumn, pp. 37–42.

Lim, Song Hwee (2014), *Tsai Ming Liang and the Cinema of Slowness* (Honolulu, HI: University of Hawai'i Press).

Longworth, Karina (2011) 'Going the Distance with *Meek's Cutoff* Director Kelly Reichardt', *Village Voice*, 7 April http://www.villagevoice.com/2011-04-06/film/ going-the-distance-with-meek-s-cutoff-director-kelly-reichardt/ [accessed 15 December 2014].

Povinelli, Elizabeth (2011), *Economies of Abandonment: Social Belonging and Endurance in Late Liberalism* (Durham, NC: Duke University Press).

Quart, Leonard (2011), 'The Way West: A Feminist Perspective: An Interview with Kelly Reichardt', *Cineaste*, 36: 2, spring, pp. 40–2.

9. IF THESE WALLS COULD SPEAK: FROM SLOWNESS TO STILLNESS IN THE CINEMA OF JIA ZHANGKE

Cecília Mello

China today exports in six hours as much as it did in the whole of 1978. During the first half of the 2000s, it climbed from the seventh to the third place on the list of the world's largest economies, and by the end of the decade it had surpassed Japan to become the world's second largest. Since the late 1970s, the country went from 20 per cent urbanisation to today's 54 per cent, with urban population growing by more than 500 million. Six thousand miles of track were built only in the past eight years, and the country has already invested in over one thousand high-speed trains. The expressway network of China is the longest in the world, and the biggest hydroelectric power plant is also Chinese. And, as it is worth mentioning, all this and a lot more happened in just over three decades.[1]

It might seem incongruent to open a chapter on *slow cinema* with a list of the fastest economic and social changes ever observed in history. Yet any discussion of Jia Zhangke's cinema and its relationship with time, be it fast or slow, cannot but start with the reality of contemporary China, a country that has been on the fast track since the transition from a planned economy to a socialist market economy, starting from Deng Xiaoping's Era of Reforms (*Gaige Kaifang*, 1978–92). And this is because his films have, since the mid 1990s, been both reflecting and reflecting *on* the new Chinese historical and social conjuncture of intense transformation. In fact, one could argue that the originality of his aesthetic contribution seems to corroborate the idea that cinema's greatest innovators tend to thrive in periods of cultural and historical transition when a new conjuncture calls for the articulation of a new language – or new languages – better suited to address and respond to a new reality (Mello, 2006).

The articulation of an original aesthetics in Jia Zhangke's *oeuvre* springs first and foremost from a desire to film disappearance, to register and to preserve – through cinema's unique recording ability – an ephemeral cityscape. As the director has acknowledged in several interviews in the past decade (see, for instance, Berry, 2009; Fiant, 2009; Jia, 2009; Mello, 2014c), he is conscious of how memory is a spatial as much as a temporal phenomenon, and of how a disappearing space brings with it the loss of memory. From this Jia derives an urgency to film these spaces and these memories, as well as a seemingly contradictory slowness in observation that is one of the marks of his style. To begin with, this slowness has to be understood as an act of resistance in the face of the speed of transformations which the director regards as a 'form of violence' imbued with a 'destructive nature' (Mello, 2014c). In this sense, it might seem coherent to place it within the current trend of cultural movements in favour of slowness which appear as a form of reaction or resistance to capitalism and its obsession with productive time (and the lack of it). China's embracing of a socialist market economy, or state capitalism as opposed to market capitalism, has brought with it an accelerated form of economic expansion that also translates into an accelerated politics of time. Slowing down cinema through greater shot lengths, the use of the long take and by embracing a delayed narrative style (Mulvey, 2006), one that would disrupt Communism's grand narrative of progress of social realist Chinese films, would function, on one level, as an aesthetic response to the violence of speediness.

This dialectics of fastness and slowness which lies at the core of Jia's cinema, however, should not be understood as a contradiction. Quite the opposite, it derives precisely from the intimate relationship that it nurtures with the real, for the experience of being in China today means to be confronted with the everyday coexistence of contraries. Its urban spaces, for instance, are an exaggeration of a dynamic definition of space as proposed by contemporary geography (Massey, 2005), founded on the notion of an 'unequal accumulation of times', in the words of Milton Santos (2004: 9). In cities such as Beijing and Shanghai, old and/or historical buildings still persist next to the immense skyscrapers that erupted in the past decade or so, and, with them, a way of life that seems to exist out of step with the twenty-first century. This superimposition of temporalities which defines contemporary China can also be understood as a cultural trace, related to both its written and its spoken language, in which the frequent use of popular sayings, literary references and stereotypes suggests a lingering past, one that is made present through speech. This also confers a collective weight to a discourse in the first person singular (Portugal and Xiao, 2013). This coexistence of past and present, slowness and fastness, subsists despite the radical ruptures seen in China in the twentieth century, a country that, from the Proclamation of the Republic in 1911 to the Communist Revolution of 1949 and from the Cultural Revolution (1966–76) to the Era of Reforms (1978–92), has repeatedly tried to wipe away the past and reset the counter of history.

As well as relating to China's reality of fast transformations as a form of resistance, Jia's slow cinematic style is equally achieved through his use of aesthetic resources related to cinematic realism, typically employed in post-war European cinema (especially Italian neorealism), as well as in more recent trends that both recuperate and update a preoccupation with duration and an extended notion of time. As Giuliana Bruno explains,

> Unlike early modernism, which was more interested in speed, velocity, and acceleration, the late modernism that emerged in the postwar period conceived of modernity as inhabiting different, extended temporal zones, and it set out to explore this new shape of modern times. Broadening, expanding, fragmenting, layering, exploring, rethinking time marked a new international filmic movement. (Bruno, 2007: 199)

During the post-war period, the transition from the 'movement–image' to the 'time–image' as identified by Gilles Deleuze, following André Bazin's conception of modern cinema, gained shape through the use of long takes, a slow acting style[2] and a focus on the time of non-action, which delayed the efficient narrative of cause and effect crafted and perfected by more commercial cinematic practices. In this sense, Jia Zhangke's cinema is part of a lineage of realist cinema starting from neorealist directors, such as De Sica and Rossellini, continuing through to Antonioni, Bresson, Hou Hsiao-hsien, all of whom are frequently cited by Jia as great influences on his work. More recently, it also engages with the idea of a 'return of the real' in contemporary world cinema, in tandem with a renewed interest in the notion of realism in academic studies of film and audiovisual theory (Nagib and Mello, 2009). Jia's use of the long take and the slowing down of narrative observed, albeit in different degrees, in all of his films to date, from his short *Xiao Shan Going Home* (小山回家 *Xiao Shan Hui Jia*, 1995) to his most recent *A Touch of Sin* (天注定 *Tian Zhu Ding*, 2013), can thus be regarded as part of an international trend of cinematic realism, alongside the work of Tsai Ming-liang, Carlos Reygadas, Gus Van Sant, Apichatpong Weerasethakul and Béla Tarr, all champions of the long take so cherished by Bazin (de Luca, 2014).[3]

While taking these aspects of his *oeuvre* into account, I propose to consider slowness not as the 'other' of a more efficient narrative of cause and effect that characterises American Hollywood cinema but in connection with the interbreeding of cinema and architecture. The idea here is to avoid measuring slowness in terms of the length of shots or the rhythm of bodies and camera movements, and to shift the focus from time towards space, from slowness towards stillness. But it is not a question of the stillness of the moving image's twenty-four frames but rather the stillness of walls in the country of walls that is China. In Jia's cinema, these walls are first and foremost real structures, made of concrete or bricks, some still standing after hundreds of years, others already in ruins. In some cases, such as in *Platform* (站台 *Zhantai*, 2000), the splendid city walls of Ping Yao suggest not only immobility and entrapment but also the past and the weight of history which is the necessary 'slow' or 'still' counterpart to the fastness of the present. These city walls once again reappear in some of the most significant moments of *A Touch of Sin* which looks at the present state of violence in China and its new landscape of globalisation but never fails to invite the past into it, in the most material way possible.[4] In this chapter, though, I chose to focus on architectural structures that function as signifiers of the passage of time and as containers of individual and collective memory against the backdrop of an unstable real. As I will suggest, in *Xiao Wu* (小武 *Xiao Wu*, 1997), *The World* (世界 *Shi Jie*, 2004) and *Still Life* (三峡好人 *San Xia Hao Ren*, 2006), various walls, from the vernacular courtyard residences of northern China to the half-green walls of the public buildings and the ruins of Feng Jie in the Three Gorges, Jia promotes slow architectural journeys through mnemonic walls, marked by inscriptions and made of layers of superimposed temporalities. These walls carry the marks of the subjective memory of those who lived within them – from the traces carved by Xiao Wu and Xiao Yong to measure their heights in *Xiao Wu*, to Erguniang's deathbed note transferred to the hospital's wall in *The World*, and to the multitude of half-destroyed walls adorned with fading posters and written words in Feng Jie, still carrying the memory of a whole city. This series of inscriptions finds its counterpoint in the character 'chai' (拆 demolition), written in various buildings in Fenyang and in Feng Jie as a sign (an index) of their imminent destruction. This leads to a reflection on the archeological (Bruno, 2007) and geological (Andrew, 2013) aspects of his cinema which, while being firmly rooted in the soil of contemporary China, are nevertheless 'soaked' in elements of the past, working as a lament for, and as a source of resistance, to the loss of slowness and memory. Therefore, by focusing on the interbreeding of cinema and architecture, this analysis stresses the hybrid nature of the cinemato-graphic art as well as the multiple temporal layers that make up Jia Zhangke's cinema, capable of containing both the China of globalisation and reform and the China of millennial traditions. It also highlights the mnemonic and affec-tive value of the indexical trace in cinema (Rosen, 2001; Wollen, [1969] 1998), whose temporal politics is imbricated in cinema's materiality and its ability to articulate the eternal and the ephemeral.

Touching the Past with your Fingers

Jia Zhangke's first feature film, made in 1997, is titled after its main character, Xiao Wu, played by Jia's film schoolmate Wang Hongwei. Shot in 16 mm in Fenyang, Shanxi Province, the film was born out of the director's wish to capture the urban space and its transformations which so impressed him upon returning home after a long period of absence. Little Wu from the title is a charmingly gauche pickpocket who, during the course of the film, is rejected by his friends and family, being finally arrested by the police. Entirely filmed on location, the camera follows Xiao Wu as he walks through the city, criss-crossing various derelict constructions and old buildings. One such place is the house of his old friend Xiao Yong (Hao Hongjian), previously a fellow pick-pocket, now a semi-successful businessman. His forthcoming wedding is the talk of the town, and attracts the attention of the local television broadcaster. Xiao Wu finds out about the grand occasion but soon realises that he is not invited to the party. This betrayal will be the first disappointment faced by the increasingly marginalised character, and the failure of their friendship finds a parallel in the spatial instability of the city, undergoing a process of intense transformation that brings about a loss of reference. The Chinese character 拆 (chai) – which means 'demolish' – can be seen painted on various buildings and walls of the city, and an eviction warning at the start of the film reveals how Xiao Wu's cousin's shop will soon be knocked down, along with all the buildings in the street.

But if the character 'chai' can be seen in the walls of Fenyang as an index of spatial destruction, instability and ephemerality, so typical of China's contemporary era of fast transformations, the memory of Xiao Wu and Xiao Yong's friendship is also inscribed in the brick wall of Xiao Yong's house, pointing towards the permanence of a past which still insists on emerging against the speediness of change. These traces appear for the first time in a scene that shows Xiao Yong, just outside the gate to his courtyard house in front of a brick wall, speaking on his mobile phone. At the end of the conversation he stops to observe a few marks on the wall which are the marks of his height and of Xiao Wu's height through the years. For a brief moment, he pauses, touches the wall and then walks out of frame. A few moments later, a long take, which shifts from a point of view shot to one that follows Xiao Wu from behind, shows him on his way to his old friend's house. He walks by the same place then backtracks, noticing the same marks. He stops and touches the wall in a parallel gesture.

The traces on the wall function as a bond between Xiao Yong and Xiao Wu, comparable to the tattoo that both have on their arms. These are the sort of marks that resist the passage of time, either carved on the wall or engrained on the skin. Xiao Yong has tried to reinvent himself as a businessman but he carries the past on his arm, as Xiao Wu points out to him by lifting his sleeve and showing him his tattoo. In the same vein, the character 'chai' may signal disappearance but the walls of Xiao Yong's house seem to tell a different story. Through the two separate sequences described above, Jia Zhangke thus unites Xiao Yong and Xiao Wu through a shared memory. It could be said that, by doing so, he emphasises the present nature of this past memory against the background of a transient and amnesiac urban space. Here, it is worth recalling how Bertrand Russell, in *The Analysis of Mind*, describes how the memory of a past event is in fact contained, or has a causal connection, with the present:

> Everything constituting a memory-belief is happening *now*, not in that past time to which the belief is said to refer. It is not logically necessary to the existence of a memory-belief that the event remembered should have occurred, or even that the past should have existed at all ... Hence the occurrences which are *called* knowledge of the past are logically independent of the past. (Russell, 1924: 159–60, original emphasis)

Memory, seen here by Russell as contained in the present, independent of the existence of the past, emerges in *Xiao Wu* in the form of indexical traces left on the walls of Xiao Yong's residence, bearing an existential link between the objects (the two friends) and their representation (the traces that signal their height). In the present tense, memory's spatial dimension is thus highlighted for, as Edward Casey suggests, the embodiment as a necessary condition of remembering points towards a place: 'As embodied existence opens onto place, indeed *takes place in place* and nowhere else, so our memory of what we experience in place is likewise place-specific' (Casey, 2000: 182, original emphasis). Memory is thus a point of connection between the event remembered, the person remembering it and the place of the remembered.

This understanding of memory as an event which belongs in the present rather than in the past, and which exists in space rather than in time, can be extended, as Giuliana Bruno points out, to its relationship with architecture:

> Let us recall that the art of memory was itself a matter of mapping space and was traditionally an architectural affair. In the first century AD, more than a hundred years after Cicero's version, Quintilian formulated his architectural understanding of the way memory works, which became a cultural landmark. To remember the different parts of a discourse, one would imagine a building and implant the discourse in site as well as in sequence: that is, one would walk around the building and populate each part of the space with an image. Then one would mentally retraverse the

building, moving around and through the space, revisiting in turn all the rooms that had been decorated with imaging. Conceived in this way, memories are motion pictures. (Bruno, 2007: 20)

Still according to Bruno, the difference between Quintilian's art of memory and, for instance, Plato's wax tablet or Freud's 'Mystic Writing Pad' is that the kind of inner writing related to the mnemonic activity in Quintilian is architectural: 'Places are used as wax. They bear the layers of a writing that can be effaced and yet written over again in a constant redrafting. Places are the site of a mnemonic palimpsest' (Bruno, 2007: 21, original emphasis).

In *Xiao Wu*, this spatial dynamics of memory, which is akin to cinema's own spatial dynamics, frequently appears through the use of the long take associated with a handheld camera, employed to traverse the meandering corridors, side streets and patios that make up the web of courtyard residences still standing in the heart of Fenyang. Here, yet another dimension of this memory emerges, for the wall that carries the subjective memory of Xiao Wu and Xiao Yong belongs to a traditional courtyard cave dwelling, known as *guyao* (箍窑). These architectural structures, traversed like a labyrinth by Jia Zhangke in *Xiao Wu*, are today quickly disappearing, alongside the other typical Chinese vernacular dwelling called *siheyuan* (四合院), the famous courtyard houses of Beijing and the northern provinces. In Fenyang, most of the courtyard houses, be them *guyao* or *siheyuan*, have been destroyed, along with the ancient city walls. Therefore, by inscribing the traces of the characters' memories and of their old friendship on the wall of a *guyao*, Jia is able to bring together the individual and the collective, the house and the city, past and present, all within the same indexical trace, carved into the wall and into the film strip. Here, I use Peter Wollen's semiotic translation of Bazin's ontology of the photographic image, by which ontology was identified with the indexical sign, in Charles S. Peirce's terms, for stressing 'the existential bond between sign and object' (Wollen, [1969] 1998: 86).

Following this line of thought, the 16 mm celluloid could be seen as a modern wax tablet, able to produce indexical images in its surface through the photochemical reaction provoked by the incidence of light through the camera lens. And the indexical nature of the traces on the wall, charged with memory, is related with the indexical nature of the cinematographic image, equally charged with a pastness and at once a container and a producer of memories (Bruno, 2007).

This coexistence of different temporal layers, which define the city of Fenyang, is made even more evident through the gesture adopted by Xiao Wu and Xiao Yong when faced with their past. Both walk by the wall, slow down, stop, walk back, look at the traces and touch the wall, before moving forward again. The gesture – as well as the brief pause – unite them and seem to give this memory a shape, to make it present, spatial, palpable: a memory at hand's reach.

GREEN WALLS AND DIGITAL EFFECTS

If, in *Xiao Wu*, the indexical and mnemonic trace is the image of the past brought to the present through architecture and cinema, in *The World* the inscription on the wall could at first glance be seen as more prosaic whereas, in fact, it is as charged with a pastness and the weight of history as the traces on the brick wall. Shot entirely in digital by Jia Zhangke's long-time collaborator Yu Lik-wai, *The World* is concerned with the lives of a group of friends who work and live in Beijing's World Park, mainly Zhao Tao (Zhao Tao), her boyfriend Chen Taisheng (Chen Taisheng) and his home-town friends Sanlai (Wang Hongwei) and Chen Zhijung, nicknamed Erguniang (Little Sister), who travel from Fenyang to Beijing to look for work. In the film, Sanlai and Erguniang are examples of China's post-1978, so-called 'floating generation', formed by millions of internal migrants who travel within the country in search of work opportunities.

Typically, the two friends from Shanxi find a job in construction; not long after, Erguniang has a serious work accident and has to be taken to hospital. Taisheng, who works in the World Park, is notified and rushes to see him. On his deathbed, Erguniang gives him a piece of paper which turns out to be a handwritten note. Next we see Taisheng leaving the room and meeting Sanlai in the corridor, both devastated by the tragedy. He hands him Erguniang's note, and the camera slowly starts to pan towards the hospital's half-green wall which will take over the whole frame. The long take ends with the contents of the note slowly appearing, through the use of a digital effect, on to the sturdy green wall, a screen made of concrete, only to disappear soon after. The note consists of a list of very small debts owed by Erguniang.

Through this brief sequence, it is possible to observe how Jia Zhangke has once again employed an architectural structure as a vehicle and a container of a character's subjectivity. In *The World*, however, it is not the case of an indexical trace because the inscription on the wall appears through a digital effect. Would this be a commentary on the crisis of indexicality brought about by digital technology which allows for the creation of images with no referent in the real world? This thought derives from the fact that, while choosing to inscribe Erguniang's note on the wall making it public and somehow more permanent, Jia is equally quick to erase it. This digital inscription is therefore ephemeral, a bit like the character himself, who dies with no further explanation, and not unlike so many others of the floating generation workers in China today. But it might not be wise, as Philip Rosen advises in *Change Mummified: Cinema, Historicity, Theory* (2001), to think of the digital as the 'other' of analogical technology. In fact, *The World*, despite being shot in digital, and regardless of its use of flash animation, electronic music and the location itself – the park where everything is simulacra – does not support the idea of a division between 'real' and 'artifice' – something that could favour a simplistic reading of the film as a critique of the latter. Rather, it seems to point towards a confusion between both, corroborating the point made earlier in this chapter about the coexistence of contraries, so typical of the reality of China's cities.

The half-green wall of the hospital harks back to the Communist era and appears frequently in Jia Zhangke's films, in public offices, schools, waiting rooms in railway stations, cinemas, theatres, factories and hospitals. The emphasis on green, which even takes over the whole chromatic tonality of his film *24 City* (二十四城记 *Er shi si cheng ji*, 2008), is related to the director's own childhood memories of looking at green walls and connecting them with the idea of 'the system' (Mello, 2014c). Thus, the green wall, like the wall of the courtyard house before it, is at once a personal memory and a collective memory. It unites the whole country under the same pattern of green but cannot carry the digital trace of Erguniang's note for more than a few seconds. This might also be because this memory is somewhat dislocated, given that it belongs to an internal migrant, out of place in Beijing, floating, uprooted, far from his native province and from the brick walls of his home town, Fenyang, which, contrary to the green wall of the hospital, carry for years the traces of Xiao Wu and Xiao Yong.

And it is not by chance that the same green wall reappears in Jia's next feature film, *Still Life*, in a scene that quotes Hou Hsiao Hsien's *The Boys from Fengkuei* (風櫃來的人, 1983). Here, in Jia's 'slowest' film to date, also shot in digital and in which the long takes and slow camera and acting movements abound against the backdrop of a cityscape on the brink of disappearance, the half-green wall itself is almost completely destroyed. Floating on air, barely sustained by a derelict building, this wall is defined by a hole that opens towards the cityscape. It is, like most of the walls seen in *Still Life*, a broken wall, fractured, precarious, soon to disappear completely like the building that is seen collapsing in the distance thanks to the use of computer-generated imagery (CGI). Yet, however ephemeral the walls of Feng Jie might be, they still carry the traces of individual memories in the form of writings, graffiti, posters, calendars and photographs, resisting the force of 'chai' 拆. As Jia Zhangke puts it,

> Once I walked into someone's room by accident and saw dust-covered articles on the desk. Suddenly it seemed the secrets of still life fell upon me. The old furniture, the stationery on the desk, the bottles on the window sills and the decorations on the walls all took on an air of

poetic sorrow. Still life presents a reality that has been overlooked by us. Although time has left deep marks on it, it still remains silent and holds the secrets of life. (Jia, 2006: 2)

And it is as if searching for the 'secrets of life' that Jia sets out on an archeological exploration of these silences, these 'still lives' that hide behind the chaos of demolition, for they make up the memory of a whole city of over two thousand years which refuses to be forgotten.

Figure 9.1   Indexical memories on the brick wall. *Xiao Wu* (1997).

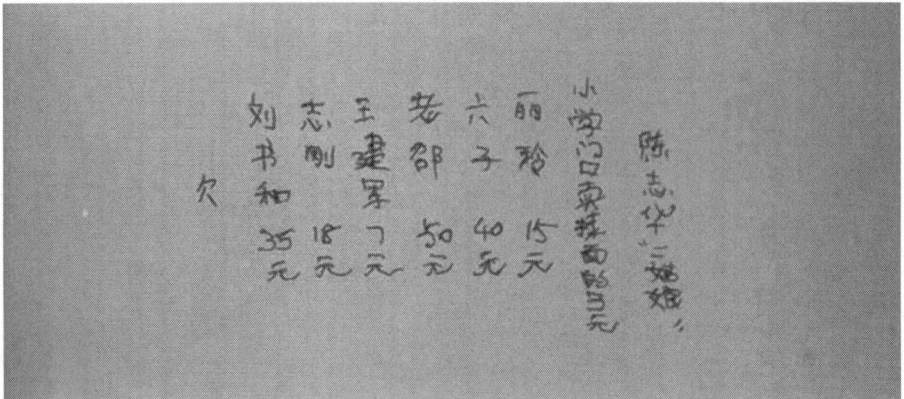

Figure 9.2   Digital memories on the green wall. *The World* (2004).

Figure 9.3   The intangible wall. *Still Life* (2006).

CONCLUSION

Jia's cinema's praise of slowness and stillness as a response to the intensity of spatial transformation and the loss of memory is not an isolated voice within China's contemporary artistic and cultural manifestations. As Sheldon H. Lu explains, 'chai [tearing down] is indeed the theme of much of contemporary Chinese visual culture. It points not only to the physical demolition of the old cityscape but also, more profoundly, to the symbolic and psychological destruction of the social fabric of families and neighborhoods' (Lu, 2007: 137–8). Along the same lines, Jean Ma observes that 'this obsession with memory itself paradoxically points to a sense of profound loss as it contemplates a past always on the verge of slipping away' (Ma, 2010: 11). Thus, it would be fair to say that this search for the many temporal and spatial layers shrouded behind China's globalisation process is related to the crisis of memory that affects the country of amazing economic and social indicators. In the examples discussed above, Jia Zhangke excavates these layers by allowing his cinema to interbreed with the architectural structure of walls, be they from ancient courtyard dwellings or those from the Communist era. I believe that here lies the most revealing and political aspects of his cinema of slowness, a slowness that is as spatial as it is temporal, a slowness that becomes an unstable stillness, and a slowness that ultimately transforms the search for memory – this extraordinary amalgamation of subjectivity and history – into a filmic archeological, architectural and emotional exploration.

Notes

1. Source: *The Economist*, 2014a; 2014b.
2. Jia's cousin Han Sanming, who appears in many of his films, has a distinctively slow manner of talking, reacting, walking and moving that contributes to the slowing down of the narrative. A prolific parallel could be drawn between Sanming and Xiao Kang, Tsai Ming-liang's alter ego and the epitome of 'slow acting' in cinema.
3. At the same time, if Jia's slow cinematic style has a transnational quality, it also partially derives from his cinema's interbreeding with Chinese landscape painting and the notion of 'empty space'. See Mello, Cecília, 'Space and Intermediality in Jia Zhang-ke's *Still Life*', *Aniki: Portuguese Journal of the Moving Image*, no. 2, June 2014b).
4. I discuss the importance of walls in Jia Zhangke's cinema in my forthcoming monograph *Intermediality, Aesthetics and Politics in the Cinema of Jia Zhangke*.

Bibliography

Andrew, Dudley (2013), 'Além e abaixo do mapa do cinema mundial', in Stephanie Dennison (ed.), *World Cinema: as novas cartografias do cinema mundial* (Campinas: Papirus), pp. 35–50.
Bazin, André (2002), *Qu'est-ce que le cinéma?* (Paris: Les Éditions du Cerf).
Berry, Michael (2009), *Jia Zhangke's 'Hometown Trilogy'* (London: BFI).
Bruno, Giuliana (2007), *Public Intimacy: Architecture and the Visual Arts* (Cambridge, MA and London: MIT Press).
Casey, Edward (2000), *Remembering: A Phenomenological Study* (Bloomington, IN: Indiana University Press).
de Luca, Tiago (2014), *Realism of the Senses in World Cinema: The Experience of Physical Reality* (London: I. B. Tauris).
Fiant, Antony (2009), *Le cinéma de Jia Zhang-ke: no future (made) in China* (Rennes: Presses Universitaires de Rennes).
Jia, Zhangke (2006), *Still Life*, DVD booklet (London: BFI).
Jia, Zhangke (2009), *Jiaxiang* 1996–2008 (Pequim: Peking University Press).
Lu, Sheldon H. (2007), 'Tear Down the City: Reconstructing Urban Space in Contemporary Chinese Popular Cinema and Avant-Garde Art', in Zhang, Zhen (ed.), *The Urban Generation: Chinese Cinema and Society at the Turn of the Twenty-first Century* (Durham, NC and London: Duke University Press).
Ma, Jean (2010), *Melancholy Drift: Marking Time in Chinese Cinema* (Hong Kong: Hong Kong University Press).
Massey, Dorren (2005), *For Space* (London: Sage).
Mello, Cecília (2006), 'Everyday Voices: The Demotic Impulse in English Post-war Film and Television', unpublished PhD Thesis, University of London.
Mello, Cecília (2014a), 'Jia Zhangke's Cinema and Chinese Garden Architecture', in Lúcia Nagib and Anne Jerslev (eds), *Impure Cinema: Intermedial and Intercultural Approaches to Film* (London: I. B. Tauris).
Mello, Cecília (2014b), 'Space and Intermediality in Jia Zhang-ke's *Still Life*', in *Aniki: Portuguese Journal of the Moving Image* [online] 1: 2.
Mello, Cecília (2014c), 'Interview with Jia Zhang-ke'. In *Aniki : Portuguese Journal of the Moving Image* [online] 1: 2.
Mulvey, Laura (2006), *Death 24x a second: stillness and the moving image* (London: Reaktion Books).
Nagib, Lúcia and Cecilia Mello (eds) (2009), *Realism and the Audiovisual Media* (Basingstoke: Palgrave Macmillan).

Portugal, Ricardo Primo and Tan, Xiao (2013), *Antologia da poesia clássica chinesa – Dinastia Tang* (São Paulo: Editora Unesp).

Rosen, Philip (2001), *Change Mummified: Cinema, Historicity, Theory* (Minneapolis, MN: University of Minnesota Press).

Russell, Bertrand (1924), *The Analysis of Mind* (London: George Allen and Unwin).

Santos, Milton (2004), *Pensando o espaço do homem* (São Paulo: Edusp).

Wollen, Peter ([1969] 1998), *Signs and Meaning in the Cinema* (London: BFI).

The Economist, 31 May 2014 (a), 'Wild at heart: How the country – and the people – are changing. Available at http://www.economist.com/news/books-and-arts/21602978-how-countryand-peopleare-changing-wild-heart [accessed 26 February 2015].

The Economist, 16 April 2014 (b), 'Building the Dream: Special Report China', available at http://www.economist.com/news/special-report/21600797-2030-chinese-cities-will-be-home-about-1-billion-people-getting-urban-china-work [accessed 26 February 2015].

PART III

SLOW CINEMA AND LABOUR

10. WASTRELS OF TIME: SLOW CINEMA'S LABOURING BODY, THE POLITICAL SPECTATOR AND THE QUEER

Karl Schoonover[1]

Across a sixty-year trajectory, many art films have stubbornly confronted viewers with slowness. From the perspective of classical Hollywood, these chunks of fallow film time 'overspend', upset, or even foreclose on the continuity system's prized narrative economy, replacing eventfulness with an unproductive episodic meandering. From Antonioni to Apichatpong, these art films also encourage us to consider how watching wasted screen time differs from wasting time in real life. In doing so, this slower kind of film proposes the possibility that cinema can capture excess as a temporality. Though not all art-house fare can be labelled slow, I speculate here that valorising slowness characterises one crucial sociopolitical parameter of art cinema's consumption. In the idea of a spectator who recognises the value of slowness, I believe we can discover something of the art film's historicity.[2] The slow art film anticipates a spectator not only eager to clarify the value of wasted time and uneconomical temporalities but also curious about the impact of broadening what counts as productive human labour. This fact makes any slow film pertinent to the question of queer representation, and it asks us to consider what it might mean to be productively queer.

In 2010, however, *Sight and Sound* editor, Nick James, took aim at the contemporary art-house trend toward 'slow cinema'.[3] In a short but scathing editorial, James interrogates what he sees as a critical bias undermining the rigour of film criticism and the very basis of film aesthetics. He offers a blistering set of accusations motivated by a fear that slow films hinder our ability to appreciate Hollywood narrative, dulling our capacity for attention and diminishing our mental acumen. Unlike the noble 'slow food' movement, in which aesthetic authenticity arises from patient and sustainable modes of preparation, slow film-making is a 'passive aggressive' crusade that lulls its viewers into complacency by asking them to dwell excessively in image and squandering 'great swathes of our precious time to achieve quite fleeting and slender aesthetic and political effects'. According to James, the indulgent wastefulness of films such as those by Pedro Costa or Tsai Ming-Liang makes for lazy viewers. He is making a dig here at many of the world's most visible and institutionally positioned film critics for whom slower is better, more profound, artier. He reflects, 'I have begun to wonder if maybe some of [today's slow films] now offer an easy life for critics and programmers. After all, the festivals themselves commission many of these productions, and such films are easy to remember and discuss in detail because details are few.' While these statements infuriated many scholars, critics, and film-makers, there is also a productive conceptual terrain mapped by this description. James imagines a mutually beneficial equation: a conspiracy between film-makers and critics, and a broader collaboration of the slow filmic image with its viewer. Like a counterpart to Linda Williams's 'body genre' (1991), the slow film's wallowing image invokes an indulgent temporality in this viewer.

Not only James but also slow cinema's other detractors invert the classic formulation of the art cinema criticism that began with neorealism and its most vocal supporter, André Bazin. For Bazin and many of his followers, the slower the shot and the greater the sense of unfettered, living duration, or *durée*, the greater the effort required of the spectator. This dilation of time encourages a more active and politically present viewing practice – an engagement commended for the intensity of its perception. Seeing becomes a form of labour. The critical campaign against current slow cinema denies the political potential of this Bazinian mode of spectating and calls into question whether watching slow films 'is worth it'. James's editorial thus ends with an admission that sounds like a call to arms: 'I'll be looking out for more active forms of rebellion'. For him, slow films are passive films that aggressively foreclose on any active resistance. They seem to cheat political agency and discipline, and they eschew hard work.

While James's surety about measuring the political effects of particular techniques is as questionable as it is noble, a more subtle presumption underwriting his and other similar arguments deserves our attention. I am ultimately most interested in how a familiar accusation of political inactivity gets counterpoised here to the notion of real rebellion, sidestepping or jumping over complicated questions about what kind of work constitutes political labour – much less rebellion. After all, a central lesson of Marx is that labour is something that has been mystified and whose value capitalism conceals from our view. How then are we to measure the expenditure and the quality of labour when we do not know what labour looks like? Is labour's true value recognisable to us? Is labour exactly figurable to us at this historical juncture? At the very least, it seems that, when we attempt to describe either the work of spectators or their laziness, we must take care to ask whether we might be enacting a particular late-capitalist ideological myopia that removes certain kinds of labour from view and refigures them as apolitical.

The film blogs exploded with replies to James's attack.[4] Many of these retorts regrettably invoked connoisseurship and stylistic innovation. These defences overvalued a staid economy of artistic merit (virtuosity, mastery) rather than opening up the conceptual and theoretical questions of labour, value and productivity at the core of much contemporary slow cinema – questions probed in films such as *Le quattro volte/The Four Times* (Michelangelo Frammartino, IT/DE/CH, 2010), *Unser täglich Brot/Our Daily Bread* (Nikolaus Geyrhalter, DE/AT, 2005), *Hei yan quan/I Don't Want to Sleep Alone* (Tsai, MY/ CN/TW/ FR/AT, 2006); and *Wendy and Lucy* (Kelly Reichardt, United States, 2008). In this slow cinema debate, in which critics are accused of not working hard enough and bloggers defend contemplative film consumption, part of what is at issue is who gets to describe the work of the spectator.[5] Who can speak for the viewer and transform him or her into an abstract agent? In other words, who is authorised to quantify, substantiate, or measure the labour of reception? Who can attest to the productive political capacities of film-watching? Would that be *Sight and Sound*, academic film theorists, bloggers, or the *New York Times*, with its recent pining for the slowness of *Jeanne Dielman, 23 Quai du Commerce, 1080 Bruxelle* (Chantal Akerman, BE/FR, 1975)?[6]

Though viewers could be asked to express their will and/or to describe the quality of their own labour, apprehending that data is not my pursuit here. I do not wish to make empirical claims about reception; rather, my intention is to supply a few observations about the contested critical terrain of substantiating the labour of viewing. I am taking this broader approach because I believe that these debates reveal a resurgent interest in deciding whether or not watching is a valuable form of labour, a valid or measurable means of expending effort. Debates over whether a film spectator is actively or passively engaged have characterised a century's worth of conversations about the cinema and film aesthetics. Today, however, these persistent debates get restaged around the opposition of time wasted versus time laboured. If time is the way that the art film makes the question of labour visible in the image, then exactly what does non-productivity look like? Where does it fester? Can it accrue value, and can this value be measured?

Of course, the slow cinema debates make visible a set of assumptions that lurk under the polarities of art film versus mainstream cinema – assumptions too pervasive and important to account for fully here. Instead, I offer some preliminary explorations of this recent debate's metacritical logic, probing not only how it reifies and organises film history but also how it reflects and refracts the history of ideas concerning the cinematic image. Instead of simply retrieving the political potentiality of slowness, inactivity, or 'passive aggression', my aim is to begin unpacking the politics of value that these debates have brought to the surface. From this perspective, I quickly reprise the constitution of art cinema as a category and consider how labour gets discussed in debates around the actors in, and spectators of, one crucial inspiration for today's slow cinema: neorealist film-making and particularly the work of Vittorio De Sica. When considered alongside this moment from its prehistory, the slow film is not, I argue, simply in a pointless headlock with Hollywood's temporal economy.[7] Rather, it speaks to a larger system of tethering value to time, labour to bodies, and productivity to particular modes and forms of cultural reproduction. This, too, is the register of the actively political.

Two Bodies of Slowness

For critics, the questionably productive, but nevertheless importantly alternative, temporality of slow cinema gets manifested in two bodies: the body on the art film's screen and the body of its spectator. Is there a co-ordination of these bodies as in Williams's 'body genres' where the affective eruptions of a particular genre's spectator parallel the on-screen affective excesses associated with that genre? Does the on-screen body ameliorate or exploit the off-screen body's uncertainties? As we begin to answer these two seemingly descriptive questions, we cannot help but confront the implicit political fault line of an aesthetic debate. This fault line can be posed as the question of whether the art film promotes a particular kind of viewing practice in order to sooth anxieties about the value of our own labour and that of others, or to aggravate those anxieties to generate a different account of the very idea of productivity. More simply put, is slow cinema politically decadent or politically subversive?

To begin answering the question of how critical discourses about cinema (past and present) have intertwined labour and temporality, let us turn to the first body, the on-screen body, and examine how the art film has been understood to use the body as a means of making slowness visible in the cinematic image. In doing so, we can expand Steve Neale's canonical assertion that 'art cinema has always been concerned with the inscription of representations of the body that differ from those predominating in Hollywood' (1989: 31). Deleuze finds just such a new kind of on-screen body – the art-house deviant – facilitating a new post-war mode of cinematic temporality. Describing the shift from the movement–image to the time–image, he writes, 'a new race of characters was stirring, a kind of mutant: they saw rather than acted, they were seers' (1989: xi). We might also characterise these stirring mutants which populate the aggressively slow art film as 'wastrels' – an odd label that designates people who waste too easily and those vagabonds whom society treats as waste and who, like refuse, are thrown to the side of road. The art film's attempt to make empty or non-productive time visible through the presence of these on-screen bodies reverberates with a late twentieth-century anxiety about how to quantify human labour and the more general concern about the value of human life in late modernity.[8] For Deleuze, early examples of these figures populate the films of Rossellini, Antonioni and Fellini. With them on-screen, the priorities of the image now shift: 'time, "a little time in the pure state" . . . rises up to the surface of the screen . . . The body is no longer exactly what moves; neither subject of movement or the instrument of action, it becomes rather the developer of time, it shows time through its tiredness and waitings' (1989: xi).

Both Neale and Deleuze invoke Italian neorealist films as they describe modern cinema and identify the body as a site of the art film's characteristic expectancy and influential temporal distension. Neorealism, however, is a famously slippery designator, describing a variety of film practices and styles. For the sake of argument, let us take a closer look at the consummate neorealist body – that particular physicality imaged by the canonical figures now burdened by history with describing what constitutes neorealism. For director Vittorio De Sica, his collaborator Cesare Zavattini and their most vocal supporter André Bazin, potency resides in using non-professionals in key roles. The merits of this approach appear particularly visible in those amateurs whose life experience weighs heavily on their bodies. The ideal neorealist body, then, is one that performs without performing. This figure exemplifies what we might call an 'unbelabored labour' to describe how comportment and physicality bespeak a character's history and his or her present actuality more than any acting technique. These amateurs were often chosen for a defining physical characteristic – an automatic quirk or ingrained bearing that was taken to index their personal histories, national pain and the after-effects of a global war on the human community.[9] Bazin describes the casting process of *Bicycle Thieves/Ladri di biciclette* (De Sica, IT, 1948) as a search for the 'purity of countenance and bearing that the common people have' (1971: 56). Explaining how neorealism accrues its value through the performances of amateur bodies, Bazin's rhetoric plays with the collapsing of several profilmic, diegetic, narrative, filmic, performing (labouring), and just existing bodies.

Bazin believed that the narrative of *Bicycle Thieves* found its form in the distinctive strides of its main actors: a particular gait, a certain wandering. He writes: 'Before choosing this particular child, De Sica did not ask him to perform, just to walk. He wanted to play off the striding gait of the man against the short trotting steps of the child, the harmony of this discord being for him of capital importance for the understanding of the film as a whole.' The dawdling of a boy's body serves to enliven the story but it is also exemplary and constitutive of the meandering of the narrative itself. Therefore, the dawdle characterises the shape of one of the twentieth century's most famous revisions to narrative structure (Bazin, 1971: 52).[10]

For Bazin, the purest moments of this film occur when its narration seems to free itself from the dictates of a script and the limits of artificial *mise en scène*. Those pure moments appear most readily in the 'natural' action of bodies which, in turn, lend the screen image its unique presence, its immediacy, and allow it to emanate a palpable sense of duration. The tics and other specificities of bodies in *Bicycle Thieves* appear to determine the shape of the narrative for Bazin, just as Chaplin's physical antics mould plot structure and not the reverse.

Walks are not the only exemplary physicalities given full reign by neorealism. The climax of Bazin's reading of *Umberto D.* (Vittorio De Sica, IT, 1952) centres on a small and otherwise inconsequential action of a secondary character going through her morning routine: a young woman sits grinding coffee with a hand crank and nudges the kitchen door closed with the tip of her foot. The importance of this film and its revision to the terms of narrative fiction emerge from the camera's heightened attention to a quotidian micro-event, asking us to '[concentrate] on her toes feeling the surface of the door' as much as on the story (Bazin, 1971: 82). In this, one of neorealism's most famous events of uneventfulness, the body functions on-screen to amplify and expand the aesthetic registers of a slower spectating, demanding a different kind of labour from the off-screen spectating body. For Bazin, realism's 'meticulous and perceptive . . . choice of authentic and significant detail' is one of the truest uses of cinema because it highlights the medium's capacity to seize time in chunks. When describing this foregrounding of cinema's access to duration, Bazin invokes (or is it realism's provocation?) a corollary perceptual acuity on the part of the spectator, a careful look that mirrors the camera's lingering. Filmic realism offers the spectator a different temporal relationship from perception, 'glimpsing the fleeting presence' of things and meanings missed by ordinary seeing (quoted in Andrew, 1978: 80).[11]

According to Bazin, this *durée* is visibly palpable with amateurs when compared to more professionalised and obviously narrative kinds of film bodies. Neorealism asks us to recognise certain bodies as evidence of the performer's status as an amateur. De Sica, Zavattini and Bazin assume that this distinction registers on the viewer. The non-professionalism of certain performances must be detectable, visibly obvious to the spectator through a comparison with other types of acting – often within the same film. We might say then that the question of labour haunts any contemplation of these films.[12]

If slowness enlists special bodies on-screen, it also demands a special kind of viewing, a wastrel of a different space. This is our second body: the body off-screen. Through the lens of a classicist, art films are for people who can afford to spend and overspend time. They often frustrate the categories of consumption that Hollywood recognises.[13] A more generous perspective might understand the art film as encouraging its spectator to acclimate him- or herself to slow time and remain open to its potentialities. The restlessness or contemplation induced by art cinema's characteristic fallow time draws attention to the activity of watching and ennobles a forbearing but unbedazzled spectatorship.

Art cinema exploits its spectator's boredom, becoming as much a cinema of expectancies as one of attractions. It turns boredom into a kind of special work, one in which empty on-screen time is repurposed, renovated, rehabilitated.[14] Borrowing again from Williams (1991), we might say that, as the art film increases its demand on the spectator's labour, it reduces the expectations for its performer's labour. The boringness of art films exposes that genre's insistent disarticulation of the body on-screen from the body off-screen: a belaboured spectator mirrors in reverse the non-belaboured body of the character on-screen. A complex set of dependencies proceed from this formula: screen time's open or indeterminate quality triggers a different mode of spectatorial labour that appears enabled by the very determinate quality of the 'unbelaboured labour' of non-professional actors.

SEEING LABOUR DIFFERENTLY

The morning routine of the young Maria Pia Casilio in *Umberto D.* is a very different type of labour than that of Lucy and Ethel wrapping sweets in the classic episode of *I Love Lucy* (CBS, United States, 1951–57) though both sequences appeared on screens in 1952.[15] Bazin's description of neorealist bodies as relative entities (always defined by their distinction from other bodies) also introduces the possibility that cinema might remake and rework the picture of labour given to us by earlier films. The history of the moving image might in this sense be recast as a series of recognitions of divergent types of labouring bodies in which the flatness of Julianne Moore's performance in *Safe* (Todd Haynes, United States/United Kingdom, 1995) makes impossible the self-improvement promised in Lifetime's made-for-television films of the 1980s/1990s. Also recognised by this new history might be how the refusals of Mbissine Thérèse Diop, who plays Diouana in *Le Noire de . . .* (Ousmane Sembene, FR/SN, 1966), revoke the orchestration of sentimental attachments supplied by Danielle Darrieux's performance as the Comtesse in *Madame de . . .* (Max Ophuls, FR/IT, 1953). Such comparisons identify a common register across a group of films that complicates the traditional historicist privileging of progress as a means of marking social change.

One contemporary slow film seems to make these comparisons within its diegesis, or more accurately, among its various diegetic registers: Jia Zhang Ke's *Er shi si cheng ji/24-City* (CN/HK/JP, 2008). This film suggests in its form how the eclipse of industrial production based on human labour might be made visible in the image itself. The film beautifully strains to document cinematically the problem of non-productivity. It lingers on the overwhelming scale of emptied factories, the distended barrenness of a crowded city after the departure of large-scale industry, and the dystopic nostalgia of retired workers. Testimony is appropriated as an element of *mise en scène*. In other words, Jia stages his testimony, blurring the lines between the use of the image as a means of narrating a fiction and as a means of culling documentary evidence. In the midst of this rich visual and aural accounting, Joan Chen appears in the film playing a woman, Xiao Hu, who is often mistaken for the film star Joan Chen. Though other actors in the film, such as Liping Lü, will be recognisable to many Chinese cinema-going audiences as film actors, Chen's performance manages to hover in the film's ambiguous generic terrain that mixes documentary, reenactment, and fiction.[16]

Viewers of Jia's films have come to expect diegetic instabilities to disrupt the narrative of his films at their midpoints. Just as we are settling into the conceits, temporalities, and semantic use–value of his film *Still Life* (CN/ HK, 2006), for example, a spaceship hovers on the horizon. The breaches in his films are often not just out of the ordinary. They echo the wildly overdetermined images in his films that sometimes irritate and interrupt an otherwise realist narration: these are those almost stagy and over-the-top images, such as the ancient planter walking in front of the postmodern cityscape at the beginning of *The World* (CN/JP/FR, 2004). In *24-City*, however, Chen's own remarkable performance, and its reworking of what it means to labour as an actor, elevates the stakes of the film's diegetic intrusions. The duplicitous authenticity of Chen's star body feels like an intrusion of extratextual hybridity into what has been a realist diegesis. Chen's performance relishes the tensions between persona, self, and look-alike.

When we look closely at this film's temporal engorgement, we find it unable to avoid the awkward problem that human labour presents for a culture aspiring to a post-industrial future. The question of the value of human life in a post-industrial future is found in the collapse of these various bodies into the image of Joan Chen. That is why this portion of the film is so crucial. It describes the film's discomfort with ordinary cinema's instrumentalisation of bodies. David Bordwell suggests that we feel an art film's deviant loosening of Hollywood's linear temporality through its drifting characters who lack clear motivation. This aimless drifting figure first finds shape in the neorealist bodies mentioned above. This drifter, however, goes on to shape the quintessential performers of art-house auteurs: Antonioni's Monica Vitti, Fassbinder's Hanna Shygulla, Pasolini's Franco Citti, and Tsia-Ming Liang's Kang-sheng Lee. These are figures whose affective vacancy exemplifies the odd temporal dilation of the art film. These figures are the opposite of how Jia collaborates with Chen in *24-City*.

At first, the star body of Chen infuses the image with a kind of movie-magic charge that the rest of the film – and its meditations on waste and refuse – has avoided. We are hit by a sudden rush of excitement: this is what mainstream cinema tells us films are supposed to feel like. This magic does not last long. No sooner do we cathect on to the star aura of Chen than we feel this body slipping back into the mundane register of post-industrial detritus. Chen does not appear to labour much at being the character who labours at being Joan Chen. As the mortal body of Xiao Hu reabsorbs the star body of Chen (paradoxically via Chen's masterful performance of ordinariness), the film returns to the brutal question of how to measure the consequences of human labour.

Wastrel Time and Queer Living

In considering the functionality of narratively inconsequential time in relationship to the specificity of art films, we are asking about the political potential of that slowness. Barthes found those films that encourage distended spectatorial temporality to be replete with political potential. He writes the following in his tribute to Antonioni: 'To look longer than expected ... disturbs established orders of every kind, to the extent that normally the time of the look is controlled by society; hence the scandalous nature of certain photographs and certain films, not the most indecent or the most combative, but just the most "posed"' (1997: 67–8). For Barthes, Antonioni's slowness was a dissident protraction of the gaze, undermining narrative's hegemony. Do slow cinema's scandalous disruptions constitute a politically subversive practice? Or are they evidence of a reactionary bourgeois culture taking hold and driving Bataille's potlatch underground? According to John Frow, Thorstein Veblen identifies the leisure class as a group invested in activities that take time but do not 'conduce directly to the furtherance of human life'. Frow paraphrases: 'At the core of aristocratic labor is a "non-productive consumption of time", and the deliberate and ostentatious wasting of time' (2002: 27).

This description immediately calls to mind Andy Warhol and, in a different way, John Waters, both of whose cinemas, even more directly than De Sica's, refuse to depict bodies as labouring productively. Their films are populated with obstinately unproductive counterproductive bodies. The body becomes a site to resist labour, refusing to appear belaboured, or spoofing the very notion of production and reproduction. But if such physicalities provide these films the means by which to distend time, do they actually trouble modernity's definition of labour as well-timed bodies? In dilating time, do these physicalities subvert or simply reify the inextricability of timed bodies and the value of labour?

In different ways, the films of Warhol and Waters refute any critical practice that tries to make the aesthetic accountable to 'more significant' meanings, content, or narrative truths. When we begin dickering over the use–value of the excessive image, these films seem to warn, we are suddenly taking a referendum on queerness, questioning the validity of queer lives. In the broadest sense, then, the debates over slow cinema may be about the question of queerness or what it means to live queerly. Queerness often looks a lot like wasted time, wasted lives, wasted productivity. Queers luxuriate while others work. Queers seem always to have time to waste. In fact, when an innocent soul finds himself with too much time on his hands, the threat of too much time often gets coded as a vulnerability to homosexuality (as is clear in the flea-market sequence of *Bicycle Thieves*). One can imagine a queer reading of the ur-text of slow cinema *Umberto D.* that argues not for the latent homosexuality of its characters but that exposes the film's project – finding an aesthetic means by which to account faithfully for the temporalities of less eventful living – as a queer venture.

If we now return to the current slow cinema debates, we find that each side enacts a masculinist reaction to aberrant temporality that we should not let go unquestioned. On the one hand, slow cinema's detractors display an irritable impatience with fallowed time which they equate with refuse, useless activity, unproductive labour, and the overly aesthetic.[17] On the other hand, its supporters deploy a compensatory rhetoric that attempts to rescue it from aesthetic decadence. As with the erudite connoisseur's encounter with the excesses of the feminine, they suggest slowness is an otherness to be recognised and mined for its profundity, beauty or meditative qualities. A key figure such as Bordwell embodies both these impulses: compellingly describing the systematicity of classical Hollywood narrative as economical, unified and coherent while, at the same time, embracing art films for their deviations from classicism as evidence of authorial or artistic expression.

Gendered and sexed binaries maintain a firm (if implicit) grip here, one that begs for a limp-wristed intervention. While my observations here are preliminary, my motivation for unpacking the discourses of slow cinema is to reveal a stultifying logic of utility in current debates around cinematic aesthetics that dangerously confines our sense of what and who can be represented and for how long. Queer theorist and literary scholar Lee Edelman argues that, at their very core, ordinary, everyday notions of temporality – including linear narrative, teleology, reproduction, progress, history and so forth – constrict what can be political. 'Queer' names anything that works against, or is left unrealised under, that temporal regime. He writes, 'the queer comes to figure the bar to every realization of futurity, the resistance, internal to the social, to every social structure or form' (2004: 4). Edelman uses 'reproductive futurism' to describe the logic that compels us

> to submit to the framing of political debate – and, indeed, of the political field – as defined by the terms of . . . reproductive futurism: terms that

impose an ideological limit on political discourse as such, preserving in the process the absolute privilege of heteronormativity by rendering unthinkable, by casting outside of the political domain, the possibility of a queer resistance to this organizing principle of communal relations. (2)

Through a close consideration of the discursive history of slow cinema, we may be able to address larger questions, exposing how notions of utility conspire against queer temporality, how 'reproductive futurism' demands that queer forms of exertion and labour go unseen, and how alternate forms of living may remain unfigurable in mainstream cinematic language.

To think we can answer the question of slow cinema's value without such a careful consideration is to decide prematurely that we know what labour looks like and to predetermine what counts as productive. Since the value of human being is at stake here, it might be crucial to delay such judgements until we develop a more rigorous – even queerer – materialism of slowness. In the interim, and like the imposing stench of a rubbish heap, wasted time betrays the truths of a well-measured world.

Notes

1. I am grateful for the readings of earlier drafts of this essay provided by the anonymous reader, Jennifer Fay, Lloyd Pratt, Rosalind Galt, and Elena Gorfinkel. This chapter is reproduced (with minor emendations) from 'Wastrels of Time: Slow Cinema's Laboring Body, the Political Spectator, and the Queer' by Karl Schoonover, in *Framework: The Journal of Cinema and Media*, vol. 53, no. 1 (spring 2012). Copyright © 2012 Wayne State University Press. Used with the permission of Wayne State University Press.
2. Matthew Flanagan provides an excellent account of the slow film's characteristics and suggests a series of effects that the slow image has on its spectator in 'Towards an Aesthetic of Slow in Contemporary Cinema,' 16: 9, no. 29 (November 2008), www.16-9.dk/2008-11/side11_inenglish.htm [accessed 22 October 2011]. Dudley Andrew offers a different but relevant take on the temporality of contemporary art films in his formulation of '*décalage*' in 'Time Zones and Jetlag: The Flows and Phases of World Cinema', in *World Cinemas, Transnational Perspectives*, edited by Natasa Durovicová and Kathleen Newman (New York: Routledge, 2010), 59–89. For a broader discussion of the art film's historicity, see 'The Impurity of Art Cinema', in *Global Art Cinema: New Theories and Histories*, edited by Rosalind Galt and Karl Schoonover (New York: Oxford University Press, 2010).
3. For examples of additional scepticism toward slow cinema, see Steven Shaviro, 'Slow Cinema vs. Fast Films', The Pinocchio Theory blog, posted 12 May 2010, www.shaviro.com/Blog/?p=891 [accessed 22 October 2011]; and Dan Kois, 'Eating Your Cultural Vegetables', *New York Times Magazine*, 29 April 2011, www.nytimes.com/2011/05/01/magazine/mag-01Riff-t.html?_r=1 [accessed 22 October 2011].
4. For a representative retort to James see Harry Tuttle, 'Slow Films, Easy Life (Sight and Sound)', Unspoken Cinema blog, posted 12 May 2010, http://unspokencinema. blogspot.com/2010/05/slow-films-easy-life-sight.html [accessed 22 October 2011]. For interesting summaries of the debates and additional commentary, see Dan Fox,

'Slow, Fast, and Inbetween', *Frieze* blog, posted 23 May 2010, http://blog.frieze. com/slow_fast_and_inbetween/ [accessed 22October 2011]; Andrew O'Hehir, 'In Praise of Boredom, at the Movies and in Life', *Salon.com*, 7 October 2011, www.salon.com/ent/movies/andrew_ohehir/2011 /06/07/in_praise_of_boredom [accessed 22 October 2011]; Danny Leigh, 'The View: Is It OK to Be a Film Philistine?', the *Guardian*'s Film Blog, posted 21 May 2010, www.guardian.co.uk/ film/filmblog/2010/may/21/film-philistine [accessed 22 October 2011); and Vadim Rizov, 'Slow Cinema Backlash', Independent Eye blog, posted 12 May 2010, www. ifc.com/blogs/indie-eye/2010/05/ slow-cinema-backlash.php [accessed 22 October 2011]. Adrian Martin provides a uniquely rich response to James in 'Slow Defence', *Filmkrant* 323 (July/August 2010), www.filmkrant.nl/world_wide_angle/7218 [accessed 22 October 2011].

5. Also lurking here is the tense uncertainty of film journalism's future: the institutionally ensconced voice (*Sight and Sound* is the official publication of the British Film Institute) versus the peripheral voice, the professional versus the amateur, the paid versus the unpaid.

6. See Manohla Dargis's contribution to the discussion in 'In Defense of the Slow and the Boring', *New York Times*, 2 June 2011, AR10; A. O. Scott's contribution to this discussion is less approving.

7. Though I am not arguing that all art cinema directly or unselfconsciously inherits neorealism's interests, I do want to suggest that the question of what counts as political film-making and viewing practices in our current moment derives from a long legacy of thinking about cinema as a political medium. This is a legacy that seems increasingly important to young film-makers of the late twentieth and early twenty-first centuries. For more on this issue, see *Global Art Cinema* and my *Brutal Vision: The Neorealist Body in Postwar Italian Cinema* (Minneapolis, MN: University of Minnesota Press, 2012).

8. In her influential account of mid-century French consumer culture, Kristin Ross demonstrates how comparative temporalities of wasteful versus efficient time reflect a larger sociopolitical landscape of accumulation, overproduction, and neo-colonialisation. Kristin Ross (1959), *Fast Cars, Clean Bodies: Decolonization and the Reordering of French Culture* (Cambridge, MA: MIT Press), particularly pp. 159 and 168.

9. Thus, the ideal neorealist body imagined by certain critics stands at the intersection of two temporalities of labour: (1) a present labor that requires no effort, demanding only that bodies go through the motions rather than commanding a performance that requires the display of intention, skill, and virtuosity; and (2) a past labour that has left indelible physical markers. (Therefore, in his film *Harvest 3000 Years* [ET, 1976], Haile Gerima borrows from neorealist approaches to bodies: a life of difficult farming is inscribed – historiographically even – in the scars of overworked feet, and perpetual famines can be read in gaunt legs.) For more on neorealism's body, see my *Brutal Vision*.

10. Of course, *Bicycle Thieves* thematises the question of labour in a variety of ways throughout the film. The collective efforts to recover the protagonist's bicycle meet with no success. Furthermore, the question of a unionised workforce seems fraught with implicit anxiety. The film's most substantial encounter with organised labour represents actual union activity as a kind of lame social club. In a basement, the union is rehearsing what seems to be an amateur variety show. Frustrations arise as the lead singer of a song and dance routine appears unable to sing the words 'the people' on the right key. He must repeat 'the people' over and over again, as the director tries to echo it back to him in the right key. With each repetition further dissonance ensues. This scene holds little narrative import except as a parable about

the ineffectiveness of labour and suggests that unions only further alienate people from work – union leaders cannot even get their members to articulate the most essential elements of labour.

11. Keathley, Mary Ann Doane, and Elena Gorfinkel recognise a similar kind of attention to the body in their descriptions of the cinephile. Hoberman and Sconce describe a corresponding tendency in audiences for 'bad' films invested in a certain realism emerging from the inadvertent details of the performer's body that pierces through the fictions of shoddy, low-budget, or subindustrial productions. Keathley, *Cinephilia and History*; Mary Ann Doane, 'The Object of Theory', in *Rites of Realism: Essays on Corporeal Cinema* (2003), edited by Ivone Margulies (Durham, NC: Duke University Press), 84; Elena Gorfinkel (2008), 'Cult Film or Cinephilia by Any Other Name', *Cineaste* 34, no. 1, 33–8; J. Hoberman, 'Bad Movies', in *American Movie Critics* (2006), edited by Phillip Lopate (New York: The Library of America), 517–28; Jeffrey Sconce, '"Trashing" the Academy: Taste, Excess, and an Emerging Politics of Cinematic Style', *Screen* 36, no. 4 (winter 1995), 371–93.

12. The spectrality of labour complicates the legacy of these films. In fact, the nature of the actual kinds of labour necessary for neorealist film-making has at times been something of a controversy. An 'approar [*sic*]' broke out in a 1961 symposium on film labour politics, organised by the magazine *Film Culture*, when several panelists argued that Rossellini's films could not have been made without 'scab labour'. Rossellini officially respected the union policies but, according to comments made by Jonas Mekas, his films could be made only because the unions had a less powerful hold over productions at the time. Their lenient stance towards non-union workers meant that they often sanctioned productions with as few as four union members working on the film. James Degangi (former president of Local 161) then accused Rossellini of actively encouraging non-union labour and sees his cinema as one dependent upon scabs. 'Film Unions and the Low-Budget Independent Film Production – An Exploratory Discussion, with Gideon Bachmann, Shirley Clarke, James Degangi, Adolfas Mekas, Jonas Mekas, Lew Clyde Stoumen, Willard Van Dyke', *Film Culture*, 22–3 (summer 1961), 139. More recently, Toby Miller describes how 'runaway productions' often get out of using unionised labour and his work exposes the need for more research to be done on the shifting status of labour in various modes of production. 'Runaway productions' and co-productions are modes of production central to the formation of the category of art cinema and would be extremely interesting places to begin such a study. Toby Miller (2001), *Global Hollywood* (London: British Film Institute).

13. Increasing art-house audiences are understood by historians as an odd mixture of different affinities, conflicting class identifications, and divergent tastes. Adam Lowenstein (2005), *Shocking Representation: Historical Trauma, National Cinema, and the Modern Horror Film* (New York: Columbia University Press); Joan Hawkins (2000), *Cutting Edge: Art Horror and the Horrific Avant-Garde* (Minneapolis, MN: University of Minnesota Press); and Mark Betz (2003), 'Art, Exploitation, Underground', in *Defining Cult Movies: The Cultural Politics of Oppositional Taste*, edited by Mark Jancovich et al. (Manchester: University of Manchester Press), 202–22.

14. For more on boredom as a critical practice, see Siegfried Kracauer's (1995) essays 'Cult of Distraction' and 'Boredom', in *The Mass Ornament: Weimar Essays* (Cambridge, MA: Harvard University Press), 323–8, 331–4. See also Patrice Petro's (2002) essay on the importance of boredom to the Frankfurt School's notion of aesthetics, 'After Shock: Between Boredom and History', in *Aftershocks of the New: Feminism and Film History* (New Brunswick, NJ: Rutgers University Press). Chris

Fujiwara (2007) offers a rich and careful consideration of the issues of boredom and the exploitation of the film spectator in 'Boredom, Spasmo, and the Italian System', in *Sleaze Artists: Cinema at the Margins of Taste, Style, and Politics*, edited by Jeffrey Sconce (Durham, NC: Duke University Press), 240–58.

15. The *I Love Lucy* episode containing this famous sequence puts forward a parable of how males and females live life differently and, in doing so, explores the relationship of these two genders to work, time and consumption. As Fred explains to Ricky at the start of the episode: 'There are two kinds of people, earners and spenders. Or as they are more popularly known, husbands and wives.' Later in the episode, the harshness of the chocolate factory's production supervisor is represented by her gender trouble: a butchness that is underscored for the viewer by Lucy mistakenly using the wrong pronoun when referring to the supervisor. 'Job Switching' (Episode 39), *I Love Lucy*, CBS, first aired on 15 September 1952.

16. Kevin B. Lee's description of the film's Chinese reception demonstrates the centrality of performance labour to the question of the film's realism: 'For all of Jia's playful provocations with representation, some Chinese audiences found the blending of documentary and fiction distracting from the film's impact. As one blogger wrote: "The documentary style requires the stars to perform with a mask. Truth is concealed rather than revealed. The professional actors can never escape from being recognized, and their stardom becomes a vital disadvantage in performing their roles." On the other hand, another blogger maintained that foreign audiences, unable to discern the actors from the real subjects, would be better able to appreciate the fundamental truth of the film's characters' (Lee, 44). The legibility of the body as a labouring star or performing labourer seems to make the bloggers uneasy and anxious about the larger stakes of the film.

17. Kois admits his boredom with slow films and questions the sincerity of their audiences' appreciation. He prefers narratively fast films over art films whose slowness he likens to 'eating your cultural vegetables'. His tone throughout the essay carries a kind of folksy, common-sense attitude that equates to something like 'real men don't eat broccoli'.

BIBLIOGRAPHY

Andrew, Dudley (1978), *André Bazin* (New York: Oxford University Press).
Andrew, Dudley (2010), 'Time Zones and Jetlag: The Flows and Phases of World Cinema', in *World Cinemas, Transnational Perspectives*, edited by Natasa Durovicová and Kathleen Newman (New York: Routledge), pp. 59–89.
Bazin, André (1971), *What Is Cinema?*, vol. 2, edited and translated by Hugh Gray (Berkeley, CA: University of California Press).
Barthes, Roland (1997), 'Dear Antonioni . . .', reprinted in Geoffrey Nowell-Smith, *L'avventura*, BFI Film Classics (London: British Film Institute), pp. 63–8.
Betz, Mark (2003), 'Art, Exploitation, Underground', in *Defining Cult Movies: The Cultural Politics of Oppositional Taste*, edited by Mark Jancovich et al. (Manchester: University of Manchester Press), pp. 202–22.
Dargis, Manohla (2011), 'In Defense of the Slow and the Boring', *New York Times*, 2 June, AR10.
Deleuze, Gilles (1989), *Cinema 2: The Time–Image*, translated by Hugh Tomlinson and Robert Galeta (Minneapolis, MN: University of Minnesota Press).
Doane, Mary Ann (2003), 'The Object of Theory', in *Rites of Realism: Essays on Corporeal Cinema*, edited by Ivone Margulies (Durham, NC: Duke University Press), pp. 80–91.

Edelman, Lee (2004), *No Future: Queer Theory and the Death Drive* (Durham, NC: Duke University Press).

Flanagan, Matthew (2008), 'Towards an Aesthetic of Slow in Contemporary Cinema', 16: 9, no. 29 (November), www.16-9.dk/2008-11/side11_inenglish.htm [accessed 22 October 2011].

Fox, Dan (2010), 'Slow, Fast, and Inbetween', *Frieze blog*, posted 23 May 2010, http://blog.frieze.com/slow_fast_and_inbetween/ [accessed 22 October 2011].

Frow, John (2002), 'Invidious Distinction: Waste, Difference, and Classy Stuff', in *Culture and Waste: The Creation and Destruction of Value*, edited by Gay Hawkins and Stephen Muecke (Lanham, MD: Rowman and Littlefield).

Fujiwara, Chris (2007), 'Boredom, Spasmo, and the Italian System', in *Sleaze Artists: Cinema at the Margins of Taste, Style, and Politics*, edited by Jeffrey Sconce (Durham, NC: Duke University Press), pp. 240–58.

Galt, Rosalind and Karl Schoonover (2010), 'The Impurity of Art Cinema', in *Global Art Cinema: New Theories and Histories*, edited by Rosalind Galt and Karl Schoonover (New York: Oxford University Press), pp. 3–27.

Gorfinkel, Elena (2008), 'Cult Film or Cinephilia by Any Other Name', *Cineaste* 34, no. 1, 33–8.

Hawkins, Joan (2000), *Cutting Edge: Art Horror and the Horrific Avant-Garde* (Minneapolis, MN: University of Minnesota Press).

Hoberman, J. (2006), 'Bad Movies', in *American Movie Critics*, edited by Phillip Lopate (New York: The Library of America), pp. 517–28.

James, Nick (2010) 'Passive Aggressive', *Sight and Sound* 2, no. 4, April.

Keathley, Christian (2006), *Cinephilia and History, or the Wind in the Trees* (Bloomington, IN: Indiana University Press).

Kois, Dan (2011), 'Eating Your Cultural Vegetables', *New York Times Magazine*, 29 April, www.nytimes.com/2011/05/01/magazine/mag-01Riff-t.html?_r=1 [accessed 22 October 2011].

Kracauer, Siegfried (1995), 'Cult of Distraction' and 'Boredom', in *The Mass Ornament: Weimar Essays* (Cambridge, MA: Harvard University Press, 1995), pp. 323–8, 331–4.

Lee, Kevin B. (2009), '24 City', *Cineaste* 34, no. 4, autumn, 44.

Leigh, Danny (2010) 'The View: Is It OK to Be a Film Philistine?', *Guardian Film Blog*, posted 21 May, www.guardian.co.uk/film/filmblog/2010/may/21/film-philistine [accessed 22 October 2011].

Lowenstein, Adam (2005), *Shocking Representation: Historical Trauma, National Cinema, and the Modern Horror Film* (New York: Columbia University Press).

Martin, Adrian (2010) provides a uniquely rich response to James in 'Slow Defence', *Filmkrant* 323 (July/August), www.filmkrant.nl/world_wide_angle/7218 [accessed 22 October 2011].

Miller, Toby (2001), *Global Hollywood* [London: British Film Institute].

Neale, Steve (1981), 'Art Cinema as Institution', *Screen* 22, no. 1, 11–39.

O'Hehir, Andrew (2011), 'In Praise of Boredom, at the Movies and in Life', *Salon.com* (7 October), www.salon.com/ent/movies/andrew_ohehir/2011 /06/07/in_praise_of_boredom [accessed 22 October 2011].

Petro, Patrice (2002), 'After Shock: Between Boredom and History', in *Aftershocks of the New: Feminism and Film History* (New Brunswick, NJ: Rutgers University Press).

Rizov, Vadim (2010), 'Slow Cinema Backlash', *Independent Eye blog*, posted 12 May, www.ifc.com/blogs/indie-eye/2010/05/ slow-cinema-backlash.php [accessed 22 October 2011].

Schoonover, Karl (2012), *Brutal Vision: The Neorealist Body in Postwar Italian Cinema* (Minneapolis, MN: University of Minnesota Press).

Sconce, Jeffrey (1995), '"Trashing" the Academy: Taste, Excess, and an Emerging Politics of Cinematic Style', *Screen* 36, no. 4 (winter): 371–93.

Shaviro, Steven (2010), 'Slow Cinema vs. Fast Films', *The Pinocchio Theory blog*, posted 12 May 12, www.shaviro.com/Blog/?p=891 [accessed 22 October 2011].

Tuttle, Harry (2010), 'Slow Films, Easy Life (*Sight and Sound*)', Unspoken Cinema blog, posted 12 May, http://unspokencinema. blogspot.com/2010/05/slow-films-easy-life-sight.html [accessed 22 October 2011].

Williams, Linda (1991), 'Film Bodies: Gender, Genre and Excess', *Film Quarterly* 44, no. 4, Summer 1991: 2–13.

11. LIVING DAILY, WORKING SLOWLY: PEDRO COSTA'S *IN VANDA'S ROOM*

Nuno Barradas Jorge

Discussions of slowness in contemporary art cinema have been mostly centred on textual properties and aspects of visual and narrative style, as observed in a considerable number of works directed by the several and distinct global film-makers explored in this book. While aesthetic deceleration is the most predominant criterion in grouping many film-makers commonly subsumed under the term slow cinema, other aspects, related to technology and cinematic modes of production, can also be productively examined through the prism of slowness. While not proposing that all forms of aesthetic slowness in contemporary art cinema spring from a specific relation between production and recording processes, this chapter argues that, in the case of the Portuguese film-maker Pedro Costa, slowness should be understood as both an aesthetic proposition and as a particular mode of film-making resulting from a specific and patient work method.

Despite their respective differences, Costa's three first feature films – *O Sangue* (*Blood*, 1989), *Casa de Lava* (1994) and *Ossos* (*Bones*, 1997) – were made under modes of production and conditions broadly in tune with the late 1980s and early 1990s industrial art cinema. As Cyril Neyrat notes in relation to the shooting process of *Bones*, Costa's earlier films are 'traditional' productions, 'shot in 35mm, with tracks, floodlights, and assistants . . . The shoot proceeded with everyone doing his [*sic*] job, following the routine of the European art film' (Neyrat, 2010: 11). The film-maker's growing dissatisfaction with cumbersome filming and lighting equipment, frantic schedules and the traditional logistics identified with conventional film-making processes, however, made him abandon the last soon after the completion of *Bones*. Subsequently, in the late 1990s, Costa started shooting *In Vanda's Room* (*No Quarto da Vanda*, 2000) using an affordable middle-range digital video camera and enjoying the freedom and flexibility enabled by this support. More specifically, as Costa himself has noted on several occasions, digital technology allowed him to have the 'luxury of time' in a production process characterised by unscheduled and improvised location shooting, and accordingly freed from any economic and technological constraints in terms of the amount of recorded material, because the digital camera, unlike film equipment, would record for much lengthier periods of time without interruption (see Paradelo and Arias, 2012; Corless, 2008:12).

Within Costa's filmography, *In Vanda's Room* thus became exemplary of a radical approach in terms of a production mode detached from the traditional restrictions observed in industrial modes of film-making. The film testifies instead to a film-making process in which modes of production and address were affected in similar measure by the utilisation of digital technology, which enabled a slow shooting style as well as a slow cinematic style. As Neyrat goes on to note, Costa's 'slowness'

> is both the condition and the consequence of ethical standards he shares with precious few directors of his generation. This is no longer the old question of the relationship between subject and form but one of a daily work ethic endowing each decision regarding the frame and the lighting, and searching every face or word, with the same emotional gravity, the same seriousness, so that the film's rhythm is perfectly attuned to the rhythm of life. (Neyrat, 2010: 10)

Neyrat's observations thus shed light on a mode of film production in which filmic style is meticulously crafted through a protracted work routine adjusted to everyday rhythms, and the implicit freedom brought about by the digital equipment. This chapter further contextualises and gives nuance to this particular production process through a close analysis of *In Vanda's Room* while situating it in the context of Costa's *oeuvre*.

A DIGITAL AESTHETIC OF SLOW

In Vanda's Room is the second instalment of a group of feature films centred on the lives of the inhabitants of Lisbon's shanty town of Fontaínhas. Starting with *Bones* and followed by *Juventude em Marcha* (*Colossal Youth*, 2006), which documented their relocation to the housing project of Casal da Boba, this series of films has recently gained a new chapter with the release of Costa's latest, *Cavalo Dinheiro* (*Horse Money*, 2014).[1] A multicultural community situated in the periphery of the city, Fontaínhas has attracted successive waves of migrants coming to Lisbon in search of work opportunities, housing many immigrants originating from the former Portuguese colonies, mostly Cape Verde (see Jorge, 2014: 49). Largely made up of unemployed and low-income temporary workers, Fontaínhas has also gained a negative reputation in the Portuguese news media owing to its drug-related activities. Costa's connection with this community goes back to the shooting of *Bones* which was partially filmed in the neighbourhood and starred some of its residents. It was *In Vanda's Room*, however, that enabled the film-maker to strengthen his affective and professional ties with the community, which was, at the time, undergoing dramatic physical changes because of demolition.

As Jonathan Romney points out, the film is 'an engrossing but gruellingly unadorned semi-documentary study' of the Fontaínhas (2008: 46). It depicts the everyday life of a group of disenfranchised characters, most of them young adults with considerable drug-addiction problems, living in this degraded and maze-like neighbourhood, with its narrow streets and dark alleys, in the process of being demolished. More specifically, the film is centred on Vanda Duarte, who had previously appeared in *Bones*, together with her close family and friends. The film's minimal narrative, acted exclusively by non-professional actors primarily shows Vanda's repetitive daily routines. These are, in turn, punctuated by activities involving drug consumption (alone or accompanied by her sister, Zita Duarte) and by interactions with several local residents who pass and/or stop by at Vanda's precarious residence and the small room that she shares with her sisters, which functions as the film's visual and thematic epicentre. Parallel to Vanda's routines, other scenes present the life of other community dwellers, mostly male and also with drug-dependence issues, living in a squat nearby. These two groups of scenes mark the division between the universe of the 'girls' and the 'boys' that is significant in terms of the film's structural composition (as noted in Costa, Neyrat and Rector, 2012: 52–7). Complementing these two groups of scenes mostly filmed in interior locations, *In Vanda's Room* finally documents the surrounding streets of the area, bringing into full view the neighbourhood's daily routines: the preparation of the communal spaces and the street fires used to cook, the drug-addicts' incessant goings-on, children playing in the streets, Vanda's wanderings through the neighbourhood selling vegetables – all of which take place against the visual and audible background of the demolition.

In many ways, *In Vanda's Room* thus consolidates a slow and pared-down aesthetic, which, in the context of Costa's *oeuvre*, can be traced back to *Bones* or perhaps even to *Casa de Lava*. We can further locate in *In Vanda's Room* many of the stylistic characteristics that Matthew Flanagan identifies as belonging to an 'aesthetic of slow', such as 'the employment of (often extremely) long takes, de-centred and understated modes of storytelling, and a pronounced emphasis on quietude and the everyday' (2008). While the term slow cinema is, in fact, even contested by Costa,[2] it is fair to say that the film transmits a riveting sense of minimalism that is achieved by the sustained depiction of the inhabitants' quotidian routines and a rigorous style characterised by static camerawork and long takes.[3] However, while the slowness of this and subsequent Costa's films can surely be understood as an aesthetic mode that dialogues with, and is inserted within, a broader stylistic current, *In Vanda's Room* also begs for an analysis that examines its slowness not only as an aesthetic strategy but also as a characteristic resulting from its distinctively slow mode of production, in turn derived from the specific technological support utilised in its making.

As we know, the emergence of digital technology has elicited several discourses on artistic freedom, as the digital entails cheaper production processes and enables more flexible shooting and editing practices. In this sense, digital video has renewed the possibilities of directing and producing cinema independently of (or in conjunction with) established film industries. In other words, a characteristic of the use of digital technology is arguably a 'new, democratised form of filmmaking' which allows film-makers to become unrestrained from both industrial processes and standardised narrative formulas (Willis, 2005: 1). The work by numerous film practitioners who have resorted to digital equipment because of its low-budget properties clearly attests to this relation between aesthetics and independence. One needs only to remember the work of film-makers initially associated with the manifesto-driven *Dogme 95* (Thomas Vinterberg, Lars Von Trier), for example, or, indeed, the work of several East and South-east Asian film-makers who have developed a body of work characterised by production and aesthetic practices often at odds with those of their own national cinema industries (Apichatpong Weerasethakul and Jia Zhangke to name just two of the ones represented in this volume).

More relevant to this chapter's focus, the digital has allowed many film-makers to engage with forms of realistic representation that rely on real time, cinematic deceleration and duration. Indeed, digital technology has made possible (even if hypothetically) a 'one-to-one correspondence between real time and represented time', allowing the recording of much lengthier amounts of time (when compared with the length of film reels) while avoiding the cost of photochemical film stock (Rombes, 2009: 25; see also similar considerations in Flanagan, 2012: 201–5). Engaging with these possibilities, different practitioners have forged and sustained film-making practices that reflect an aesthetic preoccupation in shooting longer, slower and extended (and distended) narratives, thereby producing sensory forms of documentation such as the ones observed in the works of, for example, Wang Bing and Lav Diaz (see chapters by Smith and Brown in this volume).

Elaborating specifically on Costa's work, Àngel Quintana proposes that the Fontaínhas films convey a 'stylised' and 'static' depiction of the real, to which 'the digital [. . .] bestow a new plasticity' (2009: 24–5) – qualities that contribute to what Quintana understands as a possible 'aesthetic of poverty', defined by an undramatic and unflinching style that attests to the film-maker's 'clear personal involvement' (24). Likewise, Volker Pantenburg argues that Costa's use of digital video comes to challenge (and perhaps replace) aesthetic assumptions concerning the inherent indexical nature of cinema 'by an attempt to locate different forms of realism at different points of the production and reception of movies' (Pantenburg, 2010). With these considerations in mind, it can be argued that *In Vanda's Room* attests to a film-making practice that is bound to the particular visual quality of low-budget digital video as well as to its constraints and freedoms.

Looking firstly at the visual aesthetic that resulted from the use of digital video, the camera used by Costa, a Panasonic DX 100 (at the time a new middle-range but still affordable camera) inevitably conferred specific visual qualities on the footage related to depth of field, image density, and colour brightness and saturation. According to Costa, the 'green and blurred' colour processing of this camera (which contrasts with the 'blue' and sharper images produced by other digital cameras available on the market) visually matches the 'tatty' colours of the Fontaínhas (Costa, 2012). These visual characteristics significantly mark the cinematography of the film (also credited to Costa) which was further achieved through the use of key light sourced from small windows or small lamps and helped by improvised reflectors made of polystyrene sheets or domestic mirrors. Similarly, the camerawork deployed by Costa reflected a preoccupation with the constraints of the digital equipment. As he stated during an interview to the magazine *Sight & Sound* in 2009, he shot with 'exactly the same gentleness and care and precision' as when filming in 35 mm, keeping the camera still, even if struggling with the greater mobility of the digital camera (Corless, 2009: 30).

This shooting process is translated into a sense of aesthetic stillness whereby the actions of the Fontaínhas residents are patiently observed and in which Costa resourcefully explored the constricted possibilities of shooting in cramped spaces with no camera movement – the most perceptible example being the confined room inhabited by Vanda. As the film-maker explains, the movement in these scenes is solely confined to the reality being depicted within the frame, a formal strategy that Costa avowedly appreciates in the work of Yasujiro Ozu (Costa, Neyrat and Rector, 2010: 83–4). These prolonged and stationary shots may have contributed to alleviate the limitations of digital video such as pixellation. Yet the minimal and slow compositions of *In Vanda's Room*, while recalling the tonality of a painted still life (as noted by many commentators), are 'animated' by the aura-like light around the actors'

Figure 11.1   The digital texture of *In Vanda's Room* (2000).

presence and the unstable pixels reflected in Vanda's room walls, thus reveal-ing the unmistakably digital texture of this film.

RECORDING THE SLOWNESS OF THE EVERYDAY

These considerations tying aesthetic and technology in *In Vanda's Room* can be further extended to the ways in which Costa opted to shoot the film which, as previously mentioned, dispensed with the traditional logistics and techni-cal paraphernalia normally associated with recording processes in industrial cinema. At first, the film-maker did not rely on a script or shooting schedule, nor did he resort to other professionals or technical equipment, a self-sufficient and inexpensive shooting style that could have only been achieved thanks to the digital support. Nevertheless, it must be noted that *In Vanda's Room*, as all Costa's subsequent films, still attests to a mode of film-making that Thomas Elsaesser calls 'European post-Fordism' which he describes as sustained by 'small-scale production units, cooperating with television as well as commer-cial partners, and made up of creative teams around a producer and a director' (Elsaesser, 2005: 69).

Indeed, produced by Francisco Villa-Lobos (Contracosta Produções) with a meagre budget of the equivalent of approximately £320.000 (according to Villa-Lobos, quoted in Martins, 2001: 9), the film had the financial support of state-funded Portuguese schemes as well as of public and private partners across Europe, such as ZDF (Germany), RSI (Switzerland), Pandora Filmproduktion (Germany) and Ventura Films (Switzerland). Furthermore, as the film's editor Patrícia Saramago explains, the post-production process of Costa's digital films has always been done under the 'best conditions available', which alludes to the aesthetic rigour of his work (Saramago, 2013). Thus, while the shooting process of the film was particularly inexpensive, a significant amount of the budget was devoted to post-production processes, both in terms of the film's editing (by Saramago and Dominique Auvray) and digital operations to minimise the deficiencies of image and sound, not to mention the production of a 35 mm copy for distribution that would allow the premiere of the film at the Locarno Film Festival in 2000. Similarly, Villa-Lobos argues that, while Costa's discourse of self-sufficiency and personal agency should surely be taken into consideration, *In Vanda's Room* also depended on 'paid professionals' and relied on normative film-making processes that, ultimately, could not have been sustained by personal relations alone (Villa-Lobos, 2013). The film-maker came to rely later intermittently on a small number of professionals, such as sound technician Philippe Morel and assistant Cláudia Tomaz,[4] as well as Leonardo Simões and film producer Francisco Villa-Lobos who also occasionally assisted Costa on location (Tomaz, 2013; Villa-Lobos, 2013).

That said, as far as the film's recording goes, its initial shooting process was largely based on an organic, repetitive and laborious daily routine, and equally dependent on a fairly reduced filming support. Owing to his decision to use a digital camera, Costa was able to shoot a considerable amount of material mostly by himself, for an estimated period of almost two years, without relying on any other substantial technical equipment (Peranson, 2010: 140; Costa, 2012).[5] By the same token, Costa was able to maintain and gradually strengthen a prolonged and close relationship with his cast of non-professional actors, while enjoying considerable mobility in the space-restrictive locations within Fontaínhas, thanks to the portability of the digital camera. In particular, the slow, spontaneous and extensive shooting process of *In Vanda's Room* stands in stark contrast with the conditions under which Costa first filmed in the community while shooting *Bones* for the period of approximately six weeks – a comparatively limited period which did not allow him to forge any substantial and/or personal links with the local residents. It was only after a stretched, continuous stay at Fontaínhas that Costa was able to find the real ethos of a community that, in his words, became his 'extended family' (2012).

Establishing a work method which negotiates and reformulates the standardisation observed in normative processes of film-making, the shooting of

In Vanda's Room was thus directly conditioned by the everyday routines of the non-professional actors who appear in the film. As Costa points out, the location was marked by 'drug [routines], idleness', a neighbourhood 'which is a place where people are attracted to and [stay] without doing anything, [while something] is always happening [in the background]' (2012). Similarly, Tomaz recalls that Costa would spend most of the time inside Vanda's room or household and, 'depending on what was happening in people's lives or in the neighbourhood' elsewhere, other activities would be incorporated into this daily shooting routine, such as 'a demolition, men playing cards, someone making lunch or someone waiting for an ambulance . . .' (Tomaz, 2013). While these events testify, to an extent, to actions normally categorised under the rubric of the everyday, these routines were nevertheless situated within the context of harsh lifestyles because of the issue of drug dependency faced by many of the non-professional actors. As Tomaz notes,

> The conditions were physically and humanly difficult, it was cold, people lived in extreme poverty, some people were becoming homeless and displaced, there was the drugs routine . . . We had to keep up with it all and try to film it on a daily basis the best we could, sometimes it was challenging to be just an observer/filmmaker. (2013)

Early in the shooting process, Costa adapted to these everyday rhythms while steadily maintaining his own (professional) routine. As the film-maker explains: 'I would take the 58 bus everyday [to Fontaínhas], and for 45 minutes I would read the newspaper, or listen to the cleaning ladies conversations [. . .] I did stick rigidly to that routine and realised that I could keep a [professional] disciple only by myself . . .' (2012). From this gradual and organic rapport between the neighbourhood's own rhythms and Costa's shooting routine emerged two distinct approaches in the filming of scenes, both of which have remained in the final cut of the film. The first one concerns the purely observational images shot outside, in the actual streets of Fontaínhas, and which mostly register, in documentary mode, the inhabitant's street routines or the area's gradual demolition. The other type of images shows the lived and intimate daily realities of the film's participants, predominantly shot in interiors and punctuated by daily life occurrences: family meals, extensive conversations, house-cleaning chores; Zita preparing a desert, the sisters unravelling a hank of wool, and so on. In particular, interspersed with these events are long scenes showing the local residents engaged in drug consumption as well as under its effects, the latter thus being accordingly granted the same everyday status within the film's structure. [6]

Significantly, however, many of the latter scenes were not simply 'observed' by a camera which simply happened to be there. Instead, they were acted out by the participants as they recreated certain stories that they had previously told Costa. These were shot in successive and repeated takes without interruption, allowing the actors continually to improvise while being filmed without the need to stop the camera, which would remain rolling continuously (Costa, 2012; Costa, Neyrat and Rector, 2012: 61). From this last group of scenes emerge some of the most evocative moments of the film, such as the scene dealing with the childhood memories of Vanda and Zita (a bittersweet recalling of the environment before drug-trafficking activities overtook Fontaínhas); the long dialogue scene acted at the 'boys'' house, as they compare their respective wounds provoked by the use of heroin; the scene where both Zita and Vanda recall the period in which the latter was admitted to a hospital; reminiscences of deceased ones (such as the event of Geny's death, recalled by Vanda and Pedro Lanban).

These two filming approaches, and particularly the method of recalling fragmented memories from the film's participants, allowed Costa to reconstitute and bring back to life realities lying dormant in the non-professional actors' minds. This process of shooting assisted to what the film-maker calls a 'redefinition of the present', a reality of a community constantly mutating owing to successive absences and its gradual demolition – realities and memories that, inevitably, would become also part of the life of the film-maker (Costa, Neyrat and Rector, 2012: 69).

Conclusion

In Vanda's Room demonstrates that filmic slowness can be understood as an implicit intention concerning an aesthetic proposition as well as the result of specific interactions between particular modes of production and the corresponding technology available. The depiction of the Fontaínhas and its inhabitants was achieved through a laborious production and recording process through which and in which Costa was able to embrace and appropriate the aesthetic possibilities and particularities offered by the digital support. As Costa notes, this process was more than a 'normal' shoot, becoming ultimately a form of 'job routine' in which professional and personal commitments became ambiguously and complexly entangled (Costa, 2012; see also Burdeau, 1999: 61). *In Vanda's Room* thus intervenes in discursive and theoretical constructions such as slow cinema, which can be viewed as not just an aesthetic or critical formulation, but also as a film-making practice related to particular economic, technological and practical imperatives, and accordingly defined by the long time put into its making. From this slow and continuous process of documenting the younger residents at Fontaínhas emerged a less demanding, but equally effective, production framework. While still defined by constraints, Pedro Costa's short and feature films, released after *In Vanda's Room*, came to rely on less extreme shooting conditions, enabled by a fixed yet small shooting unit and having more options in terms of filming equipment. Yet the same slow film-making processes came to define the relation between Costa and the numerous participants of these follow-up films, such as *Colossal Youth*, creating a dialogue between protracted forms of film-making and the lived realities of the disenfranchised members of a socially marginalised community.

While the realities portrayed in *In Vanda's Room* may have a thematic link with the depiction of reality so markedly present in sensationally driven mainstream media, the slowness enabled by digital technology allowed for a specific representation of the everyday that is not dependent on immediacy but which, instead, came into being through observation, dedication and recreation. As such, *In Vanda's Room* not only testifies to a contemplative attention to the everyday as it also highlights cinema's constantly mutating nature both as an artistic expression and as a medium. Mediating between personal affection and professionalism, between reality and realism, Costa's shooting methods thus allowed the slowness of everyday at Fontaínhas, past and present, to emerge and re-emerge, crafted through a patient cinematic approach that stands on the frontier of spontaneity and artificiality.

ACKNOWLEDGEMENTS

I should like to thank Pedro Costa and Francisco Villa-Lobos for the extensive interviews conducted in July 2012 and February 2013, respectively, and Cláudia Tomaz and Patrícia Saramago for their detailed accounts of *In Vanda's Room*'s shooting and post-production processes.

NOTES

1. As well as these feature films, Costa also directed numerous short films at the Fontaínhas and Casal da Boba, such as *Tarrafal* and *Caça ao Coelho com Pau* (*The Rabbit Hunters*, both 2007), *O Nosso Homem* (2010), and *Sweet Exorcism* (2012).
2. Costa has avowedly distanced himself from the term slow cinema, in an interview conducted by myself in 2013, in which he maintained that a slow aesthetic approach does not encapsulate any of his formal preoccupations. Similarly, and surprisingly, Costa criticises the use of long stationary shots in contemporary art cinema in the documentary *Finding the Criminal* (director Craig Keller, 2010, included in the 2011 British DVD edition of *Colossal Youth* by Eureka!/Masters of Cinema).
3. Looking at the average shot length (ASL) of the three films shot at Fontaínhas, a deceleration is clearly noticeable: *Bones* has an approximate ASL of thirty seconds, *In Vanda's Room* of fifty seconds and *Colossal Youth* of ninety seconds (this analysis is based on the 2010 Criterion DVD boxset *Letters from Fontainhas*).
4. Cláudia Tomaz at the time was also experimenting with digital video, a process from which would originate her first feature film *Noites* (*Nights*, 2000). Tomaz's film also portrays realities related to drug addiction and was partially shot at an equally problematic neighbourhood, Casal Ventoso, at the time considered Lisbon's major (and most visible) drug-trafficking area.
5. Several sources indicate a different number of hours shot. Newspaper articles, at

the time of the film's release, commonly mentioned between 120 and 130 hours; in Mark Peranson (2010: 140) Costa mentions 140 hours of material; in a personal communication with the film's editor, Patricia Saramago, she informed me that the material available to be edited was approximately 200 hours (Saramago, 2013).
6. This relation between external and internal spaces was explored further in some of Costa's video installations, such as *Minino macho, minino fêmea* (*Little Boy Male, Little Girl Female*, 2005), presented in the exhibition *Fora!/Out!* (held at the *Fundação de Serralves* in Porto between 21 October 2005 and 15 January 2006).

BIBLIOGRAPHY

Burdeau, Emmanuel (1999), 'Seul le cinéma – Pedro Costa tourney *Dans la chambre de Vanda*', in *Cahiers du Cinéma*, no. 536 (June), 60–2.
Corless, Kieron (2009), 'Crossing the Threshold: Interview with Pedro Costa', *Sight & Sound*, 19: 10 (October), 28–31.
Costa, Pedro (2012), Personal Interview (Lisbon, 2 July).
Costa, Pedro, Cyril Neyrat and Andy Rector (2012), *Um Melro Dourado, um Ramo de Flores, uma Colher de Prata. Conversa com Pedro Costa* (Lisbon: Midas Filmes/ Orfeu Negro).
Flanagan, Matthew (2008), 'Towards an Aesthetic of Slow in Contemporary Cinema'. In *16–9*, no. 29 (November), http://www.16-9.dk/2008-11/side11_inenglish.htm [accessed 13 February 2014].
Flanagan, Matthew (2012), *'Slow Cinema': Temporality and Style in Contemporary Art and Experimental Film*, unpublished PhD dissertation, University of Exeter.
Jorge, Nuno Barradas (2014), 'Thinking of Portugal, Looking at Cape Verde: Notes on Representation of Immigrants in the Films of Pedro Costa', in Rêgo, Cacilda and Marcus Brasileiro (eds), *Migration in Lusophone Cinema* (New York: Palgrave Macmillan), pp. 41–57.
Martins, Susana (2001). 'No Palco da Vida', in *JL: Jornal de Letras e Ideias* (7 March), 9.
Neyrat, Cyril (2010), 'Rooms for the Living and the Dead', in *Letters from Fontainhas* (DVD booklet) (New York: The Criterion Collection), pp. 10–17.
Pantenburg, Volker (2010), 'Realism, not Reality: Pedro Costa's Digital Testimonies', in *Afterall*, no. 24 (summer) http://www.afterall.org/journal/issue.24/realism-not-reality-pedro-costa-s-digital-testimonies [accessed 21 January 2014].
Paradelo, Martin and Xiana Arias (2012) '"Eu acho que há cineastas que não têm a coragem de não fazer filmes"', in *Cineclube de Compostela*, 6 December, http://cineclubedecompostela.blogaliza.org/files/2012/12/entrevista-Costa.pdf. [accessed 13 January 2015].
Peranson, Mark (2010), 'Pedro Costa: An introduction', in *The Cinema of Pedro Costa* (Jeonju: Jeonju International Film Festival), pp. 125–46.
Quintana, Ángel (2009), 'Hacia un hiperrealismo de la imagen digital', in *Cahiers du Cinéma España*, special edition, no. 6 (May), 24–5.
Rombes, Nicholas (2009), *Cinema in the Digital Age* (London and New York: Wallflower Press).
Romney, Jonathan (2008), 'Exile and the kingdom', in *Sight & Sound*, 17: 6 (June), 46–7.
Saramago, Patrícia (2013), email communication (23 July).
Tomaz, Cláudia (2013), email communication (20 May).
Villa-Lobos, Francisco (2013). Personal interview (Cascais, 11 February).
Willis, Holly (2005), *New Digital Cinema – Reinventing the Moving Image* (London and New York: Wallflower Press).

12. WORKING/SLOW: CINEMATIC STYLE AS LABOUR IN WANG BING'S *TIE XI QU: WEST OF THE TRACKS*

Patrick Brian Smith

> If you want to make a film, you have to work on it . . . For me, my job is to get things done . . . It was mainly the actual work, practical matters on a daily basis.
> Wang Bing (2013: 123)

> The world is labour.
> Michael Hardt and Antonio Negri (1994: 11)

The 156 investment projects of Soviet aid were chief among several post-World War II relief programmes that helped to restabilise China's industrial economy. Shenyang's Tiexi district, located conveniently close to Russia, became one of the central torchbearers for socialist-planned economic and industrial growth. The reform era's shift from a planned to a market economy, however, caused significant problems within the north-east. Still dependent on centralised planning, the industrial hub – and Tiexi more specifically – could not compete with the relative economic flexibility of southern and central districts. By the end of the 1990s many of Tiexi's factories had closed, causing both a sharp rise in unemployment and a general level of social decline within local communities reliant upon the industrial economy (Hu, 2012; Lu, 2010).

Wang Bing, a young film graduate from the Beijing Film Academy, arrived into this social milieu in 1999. With no definitive film project in mind, as well as few contacts within the district, Wang hired a small, portable digital video

(DV) camera and, integrating with the local community, began to document the area's decline. Released in 2003, *Tie Xi Qu: West of the Tracks* is composed of three chapters: *Rust*, *Remnants* and *Rails*. *Rust* chiefly centres upon the collapsing industrial factories of Tiexi, tracking the precarious day-to-day living of several skeleton work crews. *Remnants* documents the mass evictions from a state-owned housing sector, initially focusing on a small group of unemployed teenagers before broadening its scope to examine the sector's destruction. *Rails* focuses on the faltering goods train infrastructure that supplies the industrial centre, picking out several workers to explore the effects of industrial collapse on family life (Lu, 2010).

West of the Tracks remains a crucial document of the area's industrial decline and concomitant societal restructuring, and has accordingly received critical and academic attention over the last ten years, with two trends being particularly discernible. On the one hand, Wang's film is often subsumed under the banner of slow cinema. While such a categorisation is readily justified, given Wang's predilection for extended shots, a protracted focus on quotidian activities and other staples normally associated with a cinema of slowness, it is often the case that the formal components of *West of the Tracks* are privileged at the expense of an engagement with the film's social and cultural specificity (see, in this respect, Tuttle, 2012; Lewis, 2010; Elliot, 2014). On the other hand, in-depth sociological critiques of the film occasionally fail to provide fine-grained stylistic readings.[1] This chapter aims to strike a balance between these two approaches, offering a localised and contextual reading of *West of the Tracks* while also demonstrating how specific formal elements of Wang's cinema of slowness aim to highlight the day-to-day precariousness of life within this industrial district. In particular, my aim here is to suggest that Wang's film-making might offer us an opportunity to forge a more nuanced understanding of cinematic style, one that is more conscious of a work's physical, environmental and technological specificity.

Significantly, both Karl Schoonover and Matthew Flanagan have touched upon the need to examine the depiction of labour practices within the slow cinema corpus. Flanagan suggests that many slow films 'depict the performance of (waged or unwaged) agricultural and manufacturing work that is increasingly obscured by the macro volatility of finance-capital's huge speculative flows' (2012: 118). For his part, Schoonover laments that the critical defence of slow cinema 'overvalued a staid economy of artistic merit (virtuosity, mastery) rather than opening up the conceptual and theoretical questions of labour, value, and productivity at the core of much contemporary slow cinema' (2012: 67). In many ways, this chapter aims to redress the imbalance that Schoonover and Flanagan perceive through a sociological, as well as a formal, analysis of *West of the Tracks*. By placing an examination of labour practices at the centre of slow cinema, we can begin to appreciate how the 'stylistic innovation' of these films often functions to frame human work processes (Schoonover, 2012: 67).

In his article 'Belaboured: Style as Work', John David Rhodes advances what he considers to be the current predominant approach to stylistic and aesthetic analysis: whenever 'we tend to think of style as something "belonging" to an individual or to a group of individuals, the fact of its "belonging to" remains the same. Style is something a person or a group has' (2012: 48). Rhodes argues that the notion of style is perhaps too often simplistically used as a way to demarcate groups or individuals working in new or different aesthetic ways, and proposes: 'what if, instead of thinking about style as something that an artist or artwork has, we thought of it as something the artist or artwork does? That is, what if we thought of style not as property, but as labour?' (2012: 48). Following on from this, this chapter will argue that Rhodes's concept of a 'belaboured style' provides a useful theoretical springboard upon which to grasp Wang's own cinematic style. As we shall see, Wang's proclivity for protracted handheld walking shots, alongside his emphasis on extended duration, self-reflexively foregrounds the labour-intensive nature of his film-making. Crucial to this physical, labour-intensive style is Wang's use of the DV camera.

This chapter will be divided into two parts. Firstly, it will argue that the particular stylistic and aesthetic choices adopted by Wang – enabled or enhanced by the capabilities of the digital – can be read as manifestations of his labour-intensive film-making, bringing into view the process of filmic construction itself. It will then move on to examine how this self-reflexive, laboured style, particularly evident in the use of protracted walking shots, might open out to reflect the transient status of the sidelined industrial labourer at the turn of the millennium, critiquing the previous instability of high rural surplus labour migration within China through the 1970s and 1980s.

DV HUMANISM AND THE 'PARTICIPANT CAMERA'

To begin with, it is important to flesh out more fully my own approach in relation to Rhodes's 'belaboured style' and its applicability to Wang's digital film-making. It is arguable that Rhodes's concept, highlighting as it does 'the labour of [a film's] making through its style, the particular way in which it has been made', can be productively understood through the theoretical framework of cinematic realism (2012: 48, 55). Of course, the digital turn and its implications for cinematic realism have a fraught and complex relationship that requires some unpacking. The digital's alleged break of film's indexicality – originally conceived by Peter Wollen's semiological approach, by way of Bazin's ontology, as the existential bond between sign and object – signalled for many the loss of cinema's bond to Bazinian realism (see Wollen, 1972: Chapter 3). And yet, those who expounded such a view turned predominantly to Hollywood cinema's use of digital effects to justify it (see, for instance, Prince, 1996). By limiting their analysis to one particular sector of cinematic production, their argumentation was relatively watertight, yet simultaneously geographically and culturally circumscribed.

Over the last decade, however, important rectifying analyses on the uses of the digital in relation to realism have taken place. By shifting objects of study to other cinematic practices across the globe, a markedly different picture emerges when confronting concepts of realism in a contemporary digital context. As Nagib and Mello suggest:

> What seems to be the real novelty about the current world cinema trend is its obstinate adherence to realism when all odds would point to its succumbing to the virtual lures of the digital. Instead, digital technology has been more often than not resorted to as a facilitator of the recording of real locations and characters . . . the digital can be applied to resist, as much as to elicit simulation. (2011: xv)

In the particular case of contemporary Chinese cinema, as noted by Chris Berry and Lisa Rofel, the steady rise in the use of portable DV cameras was central to the New Chinese Documentary Movement which included the films by Wang Bing. The proliferation of a 'jishi zhuyi' aesthetic, or 'on-the-spot realism', within the context of Chinese film-making is understood by Berry and Rofel as the combined result of two key events: the 1989 rise and suppression of the Tiananmen Democracy Movement, and Premier Deng Xiaoping's 1992 call for an 'increased development of the market economy'. The combination of these events shaped 'the cultural and artistic practices that have developed outside the new state–corporate hegemonic culture of China', giving rise to this particular digital 'style' (2010: 5–6).

Rhodes suggests that 'when we "see" style, we see the mark of human labour, a density, an opacity in the image/work/text . . . works of art get to be what they are because some labour has been expended in producing them, but what if we place the emphasis exactly here – on the work of the work, and on the making visible of that work as style?' (2012: 48). Through an analysis of Wang's film-making, operating within turbulent and transitional political and environmental conditions, I aim to suggest that this self-reflexive 'style as labour' is significantly enhanced by digital realism, working in tandem to highlight the hardships of existing and working within such a faltering post-industrial climate.

Let us have a closer look at the film's first part, *Rust*. During its first sequence, composed of five shots lasting roughly fifty seconds each, Wang presents his journey on board a goods train towards the Shenyang smelting factory. As the handheld camera is buffeted by wind and snow, Wang endeavours to maintain a uniform image composition: the railway lines and horizon roughly splitting the image on the vertical and horizontal axes respectively. Over the course of these five shots a visible conflict arises between Wang's desire to maintain compositional continuity and the environmental conditions that might undermine this pictorial strategy. In this respect, two pertinent theoretical examinations of human–camera interactions might illuminate Wang's compositional battle here.

Nagib, for example, formulating the concept of the 'participant camera', suggests that this shooting style behaves 'with an agency and assertiveness comparable to that of the characters . . . mostly handheld . . . it shakes when climbing steps or confronting action' (2011: 61–2).[2] Though discussing pre-digital cinema, Nagib's concept bears interesting correlations to Nicholas Rombes's exploration of the intersection between early low-grade DV film-making practices and their self-reflexive realism. Rombes suggests that

> the rough edges, the wavering cameras, the pixilated images . . . reveal and flaunt the seams that bind together reality and the representation of that reality; they assert a human presence in the face of smooth, invisible digital data. They offer a countermeasure – in the form of a human signature. (2009: 27)

The notion of a 'human signature', particular to the aesthetic qualities of DV film-making, aligns closely with Nagib's 'participant camera' while both concepts are suggestive of a particular self-reflexive referencing back to the process of filmic construction itself.

Rhodes, Rombes and Nagib thus seem to hit upon markedly similar points, highlighting the presence of textural or stylistic markings that give a palpable sense of the human agent behind the camera. Rombes goes on to suggest how 'such traces of humanness, in the era of digital cinema, are preserved in the imperfections – deliberate and accidental – that reveal themselves in the rough, spontaneous aesthetics of DV cinema' (2009: 27). Beyond battling the environmental conditions of Tiexi, Wang's physical traversing of the factory spaces manifests itself as deliberate or accidental 'human signatures' within the final image, once again frequently undermining his desire to maintain compositional control.

Throughout *West of the Tracks* there are multiple instances of such interplay between geographical/architectural topography and the manifestation of Wang's physical presence behind the camera. Another case in point, still within *Rust*, comes as Wang follows a set of workers from inside a copper plating plant restroom out on to the floor of the smelting factory. Wang endeavours to keep the workers framed centrally within the image, the small path they traverse providing a focal vanishing point. The uneven concrete floor of the narrow path, however, seems to distract Wang occasionally; small dips of the camera seem to suggest Wang is searching for a steady footing. Within this sequence, the DV camera's relatively unstable body is central to the manifestation of a belaboured involvement within the profilmic; the camera's lightweight and unbalanced construction seems to capture more minutely Wang's bodily reactions and movements around the factory spaces. Jie Li, commenting on the film's opening section, notes how Wang's physical interaction with the factory space is made manifest through such 'human signatures': 'the camera does not just objectively record what stands in front of its lens, but it also traces the imprint of its own experience, synonymous with that of the director' (2008).

It is perhaps chiefly through Wang's editorial decision to retain these apparent 'imperfections' that the film is potentially readable as highlighting his own physical labour. As Wang himself mentions, 'a film establishes its connection to its audience through the camera ... what matters is the manner in which the filmmaker works' (2014). The extremely long takes offered by Wang seem indicative of this desire to underscore his physically laborious shooting style. The extended duration and unique physicality of Wang's film-making, enabled by the DV camera, fuse a distinct bond between the body of the film-maker and the profilmic moment, accentuating the hardships of existence within China's faltering industrial climate at the turn of the millennium.

Indeed, if the interrelation between *West of the Tracks*'s cinematography and the environmental/geographical conditions of the district exposes a laborious style, it is also important to examine how Wang's presentation of the workers themselves fits into the equation. The film's opening segment is predominantly constructed around periodic visits to three factories: a copper smelting factory; an electric cable factory and a sheet metal factory, where production at each location is still being carried out by skeleton crews. It can be suggested that *West of the Tracks* not only registers the energy expended by the film-maker, it concomitantly gives the viewer a more palpable sense of the workers' physical trials in these extreme social and environmental circumstances.

A good example of this focus on the workers' labour occurs at around thirty minutes into *Rust*. The sequence opens with a slight zoom-in from a handheld long shot, focusing on a worker who is chipping at ice formed on the foundry floor. The striking thing about this shot is that, initially, the image is fairly steady, with the zoom-in appearing relatively smooth. Once the digital zoom is complete, however, Wang holds the shot for several more seconds. It is here that the camera seems to begin to tremor slightly. The tremor can, in part, be accounted for through the utilisation of the digital zoom, in combination with the handheld shooting style. The image also registers Wang's physical reaction to the cold, however, underscored by the following shot. It firstly focuses on the worker's face, his breath condensing in the cold, before it pans down to the ice at which he chips away, with the shot once more shuddering and shaking.

These seemingly irrelevant physical details – the tremor of the image, the breath of the foundry worker and the thick ice on the floor – all contribute to a self-reflexive presentation and interplay between the director and the protagonists' bodily reactions to the physical environment of Tiexi. As Jie Li points out, Wang's camera 'goes through the same trials by cold, heat, and dust as do the director and the subjects he films' (2008). As such, Wang's physically strenuous style not only serves to highlight his own efforts behind the camera but also assists in providing a more palpable sense of the profilmic action: the worker's physical exertion within the space of the factory. Throughout *Rust*, and *West of the Tracks* more generally, there is thus a constant emphasis on the difficulty of labour, both artistic and industrial.

A noticeable shift in thematic, stylistic and geographic preoccupations occurs across *West of the Tracks*'s second part, *Remnants*. Where *Rust* places the death throes of industrial labour centre stage, *Remnants* focuses predominantly on the resulting sociological impact outside the factory space, shifting to examine the local industrial communities. In the following, I shall thus look at how Wang's use of protracted walking shots throughout *Remnants* comments upon the industrial community's fear of a return to rural poverty, post-industrial collapse.

RURAL POVERTY AND THE WALKING SHOT

China's shift from planned to market economy throughout the 1980s, led chiefly by reformists within the Communist Party, brought about a relaxation of the *Hukou* system, a long-term government policy controlling internal migration. Alongside such policy relaxation, there was also an 'increased demand for cheap labour in China's new manufacturing sector, and booming development that encroached on rural lands pushed a large amount of rural surplus labour to the cities' (Hu, 2012). From 2000 onwards, China's Gini coefficient – measuring wealth distribution within a society – had steadily increased from 0.35 to above 0.4: the generally accepted level of dangerous inequality. Such a level of Gini coefficient is also indicative of a significant rural–urban wealth divide. Indeed, the disparity between urban and rural income has significantly increased over the last thirty years, with an estimated thirty million in rural areas living below the poverty line as of 2000 (Tobin, 2011). As *Remnants* demonstrates, however, the industrial decline of the Tiexi district around the turn of the millennium and into 2001 made urban life untenable for many migrant labourers and the return to rural poverty a real threat.

Remnants principally focuses on a 1930s-built, state-run housing sector, nicknamed 'Rainbow Row'. As the area is prepared for demolition, making way for privatised business, Wang tracks the paths of several local residents forced into rehousing. *Remnants*'s opening hour offers Wang's closest engagement with a defined group of characters and, additionally, the clearest sense of a stable, narrative thread. Shooting predominantly in close-ups, Wang intimately follows a young teenage group, led by seventeen-year-old Bobo, as they discuss their unemployment, love lives and familial disputes. Into the second hour, as information outlining the timescale for the planned demolition spreads, Wang's scope widens – both sociologically and pictorially – to encompass a wider slice of the sector's population. Accompanying the dissemination of the information about the demolition within the community is an explicit fear as to whether relocation properties will match the size of current holdings, and an implicit fear of potentially having to leave the urban environment altogether. Into *Remnants*'s third hour, Wang withdraws from close character engagement almost completely. As the demolition begins, his concerns shift to a thorough documentation of the sector's topographical and geographical reconfiguration. Therefore, while *Remnants* constructs most of its formal structure through tracking characters experiencing societal upheaval in the first two hours, Wang's engagement with Tiexi's rapidly transforming landscape into the section's third hour leads to a significant increase in the application of long takes and long shots.

Walking shot lengths markedly stretch as Wang focuses on, and sketches out the topography of, the demolished and collapsing urban environment. An example of this wider focus occurs around two hours and ten minutes into *Remnants*. Circumnavigating several buildings in a single unbroken shot, Wang pauses briefly to frame these partially demolished structures. Continuing to walk, Wang's footsteps and breath are audible, while the uneven, snow-covered topography causes the camera to jerk and jolt. Compositional control and environmental conditions are once more in conflict.

Martin Lefebvre suggests that 'landscape [in narrative cinema], as an autonomous entity, is clearly undesirable. One danger . . . might be for landscape to interrupt the forward drive and flow of narrative with "distracting" imagery, thus replacing narrativized setting with visual attractions and unwanted moments of pictorial contemplation' (2011: 64). Though discussing the role of landscape within narrative cinema, Lefebvre's analysis can be drawn into the documentary inclinations of Wang's *West of the Tracks*. The increase of such visual instances of pure 'pictorial contemplation' across *Remnants*'s third hour are presented in marked contrast to the previously intimate examination of the sector's population where close-ups and short-distance shots prevailed. More remarkably, such a thematic shift, from the personal to the geographical, serves to impress upon the viewer the true ramifications of the rehousing procedure. The marked increase of protracted walking shots – tracking sidelined industrial labourers as they attempt to eke out a living from the debris left after the demolition – once more provides a palpable sense of the protagonists' physical exertion, this time within the deconstructed, desolate space outside the factory. Whereas Wang's shooting strategies serve to emphasise viscerally the workforces' exertion within the hermetic factory spaces in *Rust*, these walking shots foreground an exertion of a different order, no longer within the structured confines of industry but rather exposed to the deconstructed landscape, 'labouriously' searching for a means to survive. In this sense we can connect the sidelined communities and workers within *Remnants*'s latter half to what Schoonover defines as the cinematic wastrel: 'those vagabonds who society treats as waste and who, like refuse, are thrown to the side of road' (2012: 68). It could be argued that wastrels of varying degrees are present across the entirety of *West of the Tracks*, such as the gradually decreasing skeleton factory workforces labouring day to day without security. The wastrel figure perhaps reaches its logical extreme within *Remnants*, however: forced out of both work and home, surviving on the land.

The deconstructed topography, which becomes Wang's central focus in *Remnants*, appears almost pre-industrial, pre-modern and *rural*. In this sense, Wang arguably appropriates this transitional landscape as a way to underscore further the feared return to widespread rural poverty among Tiexi's urban population. His traversing and contemplation of this collapsing area sit in marked contrast to the (albeit faltering) mechanised space of the factory: the deconstructed urban environment seems almost rural here. In a sequence that helps to explicate this juxtaposition, we see a former factory labourer collecting scrap wood within a sector of Rainbow Row (see Figure 12.1). In the distant background we can pick out the ghostly silhouettes of several industrial buildings.

Interestingly, this sequence visually resonates with one from Antonioni's early documentary *Sette Canne, Un Vestito* (*Seven Reeds, One Suit*, 1949) which focuses on Italy's rayon industry. Rhodes describes the sequence as follows:

> [A] slatted wooden cart full of reeds are hauled across the frame in a medium shot, and as the last cart disappears off frame left, we discover a modern factory gleaming in the background . . . the humbleness of the carts laden with reeds is clearly juxtaposed with the striking modernity of the factory . . . The intrigue of this image is its mediation of foreground and background as two planes of developmental, working landscape . . . we are frequently invited to notice the contradictions of Italy's uneven modernity. (2011: 279)

Through Wang's extensive inspection of landscape and his sustained focus on the work of the labourers, a similar point could be inferred from the aforementioned sequence in relation to China's 'uneven modernity', as it highlights the

Figure 12.1 Juxtaposition in a transitional landscape in *Remnants* chapter of *West of the Tracks* (2003).

potential instability resulting from mass rural–urban migration throughout the 1980s and 1990s. The work carried out by the scrap wood collector within the deconstructed foreground seems to speak of a prior pre-industrial labour outside the factory, and one that may, indeed, return again. Wang's extreme shot duration has its most potent effect across this sequence, opening up a site for the viewer to reflect on the juxtaposition between foreground and background, that is to say, between deconstructed landscape and developmental infrastructure.

CONCLUSION

As I hope I have demonstrated, the examination of film style as a form or mode of labour not only opens a space to explore the often sidelined practical matters of filmic style, production and construction, it also provides a counterpoint to the tendency to cover aesthetically vast numbers of geographically disparate and sociologically specific filmic texts. As suggested in the opening to this chapter, analysis of film style and construction can be used as a tool to delve into, not only cut across, individual films' cultural and sociological specificity. As Elena Gorfinkel and Rhodes suggest, 'the place and spaces of film production . . . are . . . vital to any understanding of its aesthetic, political, or cultural agency' (2011: 10). Wang's film-making, like the community he presents, is indissolubly attached to the environmental and geographical conditions of China. His belaboured style gives not only a palpable sense of the built and deconstructed environment of Tiexi but also provides a deeper understanding of the industrial community's transient status within this milieu. His is a film style that not only excavates the place of artistic labour post-2000 but also wider issues of where work exists in a post-industrial climate. Localised readings can only be of benefit to the study of contemporary slow cinema, 'opening up the conceptual and theoretical questions of labour, value, and productivity at [their] core' (Schoonover, 2012: 67) while simultaneously situating individual texts within their specific social and aesthetic contexts.

NOTES

1. Such politically and socially conscious analyses of *West of the Tracks* have a tendency to offer broad sociological critiques without thoroughly engaging in formal analysis. For example, Ling Zhang suggests that 'the tiny and flexible digital camera moves spontaneously; sometimes the usually unpremeditated shots even appear to be out of focus, lending the documentary an amateurish quality' (2009: 24). While this is also true, formal rigour is certainly present in *West of the Tracks*.
2. Nagib formulates this concept in relation to Glauber Rocha's 1964 film *Black God, White Devil* (*Deus e o diabo na terra do sol*) which, though primarily working within a narrative mode, frequently calls to attention its constructed fiction through direct address and Brechtian performance styles.

BIBLIOGRAPHY

Berry, Chris and Lisa Rofel (2010), 'Introduction', in *The New Chinese Documentary Film Movement: For the Public Record*, edited by C. Berry and L. Rofel (Hong Kong: Hong Kong University Press), pp. 3–13.
Elliot, Paul (2014), 'Tie Xi Qui – Slow Documentary and the Time-image', *Film-Philosophy*, 1 February, http://www.film-philosophy.com/conference/index.php/conf/F-P2014/rt/metadata/700/0 [accessed 6 November 2014].
Flanagan, Matthew (2012), *'Slow Cinema': Temporality and Style in Contemporary Art and Experimental Film*, unpublished PhD dissertation, University of Exeter.
Gorfinkel, Elena and John David Rhodes (2011), 'Introduction: The Matter of Places', in *Taking Place: Location and the Moving Image*, edited by E. Gorfinkel and J. D. Rhodes (Minneapolis, MN: University of Minnesota Press), pp. vii–xxiv.
Hardt, Michael and Antonio Negri (1994), *The Labor of Dionysus: A Critique of the State Form* (Minneapolis, MN: University of Minnesota Press).
Hu, Xiaochu (2012), 'China's Young Rural-to-Urban Migrants: In Search of Fortune, Happiness, and Independence', *Migration Information Source*, 4 January, http://www.migrationpolicy.org/article/chinas-young-rural-urban-migrants-search-fortune-happiness-and-independence [accessed 6 November 2014].
Jie, Li (2008), '*West of the Tracks* – salvaging the rubble of utopia', *Jump Cut* 50, http://www.ejumpcut.org/archive/jc50.2008/WestofTracks/index.html [accessed 6 November 2014].

Lefebvre, Martin (2011), 'On Landscape in Narrative Cinema', *Canadian Journal of Film Studies* 20 (spring), 61–78.

Lewis, Zach (2013), 'Without Theatres: "The Chronicle of Anna Magdalena Bach" may be critical to the "slow cinema" debate', *Sound on Sight*, 22 November, http://www.soundonsight.org/the-chronicle-of-anna-magdalena-bach-review/ [accessed 6 November 2014].

Ling, Zhang (2009), 'Collecting the Ashes of Time: The Temporality and Materiality of Industrial Ruins in Wang Bing's *West of the Tracks*', *Asian Cinema* 20 (spring): 16–33.

Lu, Xinyu (2010), '*West of the Tracks*: History and Class Consciousness', in *The New Chinese Documentary Film Movement: For the Public Record*, edited by C. Berry and L. Rofel (Hong Kong: Hong Kong University Press), pp. 57–76.

Nagib, Lúcia (2011), *World Cinema and the Ethics of Realism* (New York and London: Continuum).

Nagib, Lúcia and Cecília Mello (2011), 'Introduction', in *Realism and the Audiovisual Media*, edited by L. Nagib and C. Mello (New York and London: Continuum), pp. xiv–xxiv.

Prince, Stephen (1996), 'True Lies: Perceptual Realism, Digital Images, and Film Theory', *Film Quarterly* 49 (spring): 27–37.

Rhodes, John David (2011), 'Antonioni and the Development of Style', in *Antonioni: Centenary Essays*, edited by L. Rascaroli and J. D. Rhodes (London: Palgrave), pp. 276–300.

Rhodes, John David (2012), 'Belabored: Style as Work', *Framework* 53 (spring): 47–64.

Rombes, Nicholas (2009), *Cinema in the Digital Age* (London: Wallflower Press).

Schoonover, Karl (2012), 'Wastrels of Time: Slow Cinema's Laboring Body, the Political Spectator, and the Queer', *Framework* 53 (spring): 65–78.

Tobin, Damian (2011), 'Inequality in China: Rural poverty persists as urban wealth balloons',' BBC News, 29 June, http://www.bbc.com/news/business-13945072 [accessed 6 November 2014].

Tuttle, Harry (2012), 'My CCC Top 10 Canon', *Unspoken Cinema*, 21 August, http://unspokencinema.blogspot.co.uk/2012/08/my-ccc-top10-canon.html [accessed 6 November 2014].

Wang, Bing (2013), 'Filming a land in flux: Interview', *New Left Review* 82 (July–August): 115–34.

Wollen, Peter (1972), *Signs and Meaning in the Cinema* (Indiana, IN: Indiana University Press).

13. 'SLOW SOUNDS': DURATION, AUDITION AND LABOUR IN LIU JIAYIN'S *OXHIDE* AND *OXHIDE II*

Philippa Lovatt

In discussions of slow cinema, it is often claimed that the use of extended takes provides spectators with space and time to contemplate the image but, in this essay, I shall argue that, for these films, sound is also an important part of the experience of cinematic duration. In slow cinema, soundscapes composed of location sound recording, field recordings and an absence (or minimal use) of musical score, foreground the material and sensory nature of matter on-screen thus enabling a sense of 'connectedness' between the acoustic space of reception and that of the diegesis.

Films by 'slow' directors, such as Apichatpong Weerasethakul, Jia Zhangke, and Lisandro Alonso, for example, capture the mundanity of the everyday while creating an immersive experience for the spectator through long takes and a sound design that produces a dense auditory field. Shifts in pitch and timbre draw in the spectator more deeply, submerging us into the diegetic world of the film that is at times populated by the heavy drone of insect life, the violent sway of leaves in the trees or the reverberation of traffic noise. At other times, however, the films grant a sense of intimacy (sometimes uncomfortably so) through very localised sounds that appear too near or strangely audible considering their point of origin within the visual field. Often recalling the use of sound in structural/materialist film, in slow cinema ambient sound can become noise; detached from signification, the auditory dimension loses 'meaning' and becomes 'feeling', experienced on and through the body of the spectator, at the same time as it is experienced by characters on-screen (Suárez, 2008: 86; Lovatt, 2013: 65).[1]

Unlike those of the film-makers mentioned above, the films of Beijing director Liu Jiayin do not feature expansive rural landscapes or urban cityscapes in which the sounds of the natural or industrial worlds permeate and help shape the characters' day-to-day existence. Instead, Liu's stories take place within a confined interior and yet her use of diegetic sound and extended duration to communicate her characters' subjective experience of space and time in contemporary Beijing have a similar effect to that described above. Drawing from the fields of acoustic ecology and phenomenology, this chapter will discuss sound, duration and labour in *Oxhide* (*Niupi*, 2005) and *Oxhide II* (*Niupi er*, 2009), addressing their significance in the context of contemporary independent Chinese cinema, and, more broadly, it will attempt to open up some questions about what kinds of knowledge or understanding this embodied experience of sound in slow cinema might produce.

Oxhide was made in 2005 when Liu was twenty-three and still a student at the Beijing Film Academy. It takes place in her family home, a small apartment near Guangqumen in the Dongcheng District of Beijing, and she plays a fictional version of herself, named 'Beibei', while her father Liu Zaiping and mother Jia Huifen play themselves. The film tells the story of her father's failing leather-work business and the family's reaction to it over the course of 110 minutes in twenty-three static, carefully composed shots. *Oxhide II* concentrates the action on just one room within the apartment and takes place solely around the table on which Liu Zaiping handles the leather, and later, the family prepares dumplings together as part of their New Year rituals. This film ventures further into minimalism, as over 133 minutes, the camera moves 360 degrees around the table in just nine shots at 45 degree increments filming from above, across and below the table to reduce time and space. Within this framework, we are witness to the anxieties, disappointments and affections that bind the family together.

Like other examples of slow Chinese films discussed in this book, such as Wang Bing's *West of the Tracks* (*Tie Xi Qu*, 2003) and Jia Zhangke's *24 City* (*Er shi si cheng ji*, 2008), *Oxhide I* and *II* present a profoundly humanist perspective on the impact of capitalism on ordinary people's lives in the People's Republic of China, and seem to offer a particular kind of resistance to the accelerating velocity of the country's market-driven reforms. Set against the backdrop of Beijing's rapid development in the mid to late 2000s, when many of the older parts of the city were being demolished to make way for new skyscrapers and commercial properties, Liu's films are a record of cultural memory and heritage that persist despite the threat of obsolescence.[2] This chapter contends that the acoustic dimension of the films plays a particularly important role in capturing the poignancy of this historical moment because of the material nature of sound itself. As Walter Ong writes, 'Sound exists only when it is going out of existence. It is not simply perishable but essentially evanescent, and it is sensed as evanescent . . . If I stop the movement of sound, I have nothing – only silence, no sound at all' (Ong, 2002: 32). Ong's words describe the durative temporality of sound, at the same time as evoking its fragility, thus echoing and underscoring the films' treatment of the disappearance not only of space and time but also of cultural practices and shared heritage.

First-person Film-making and China's New Documentary Movement

Luke Robinson describes the recent shift in China's New Documentary Movement away from films recorded in public spaces, that focus on 'public topics' (*gonggong huati*) such as the nation, history, ethnicity, or the state, towards 'what is increasingly described as the siren, the "private" documentary' (Robinson, 2010: 177). While *Oxhide* and *Oxhide II* are fictional dramas based on real events, the connection between Liu's work and the documentary movement that focuses on 'individual, sometimes even autobiographical, emotional experiences; the familial; and internal domestic spaces' is important (177). In her essay 'First-Person Documentary in Twenty-first Century China', Tianqi Yu takes this point further and explains that the development of first-person film-making by women at the beginning of the twenty-first century corresponds with China's move towards de-collectivisation and individualisation. Yu explains that films such as *Oxhide I* and *II*, Wang Fen's *They Are Not the Only Unhappy Couple* (*Bu kuaile de buzhi yige*, 2000), Yang Lina's *Home Video* (*Jiating luxiang*, 2001), and Song Fang's *Memories Look at Me* (*Ji yi wang zhe wo*, 2012), differ from the documentaries made by male film-makers because they 'highlight a personal vision, by bringing their own intimate familial spaces to wider audiences and reflexively turning themselves into key characters in the films' (Yu, 2014: 23).

I have discussed elsewhere how sound design can communicate the atmosphere of the era in which a film is set at the same time as expressing characters' subjective experiences of it (Lovatt, 2012: 419). The formal aspects of Liu's films and, specifically, her use of synchronised sound and the long take, foreground her protagonists' anxieties around the commodification of time in postsocialist China. As in *24 City*, this anxiety presents itself sonically through the recurrent motif of a ticking clock which occurs at the very beginning of *Oxhide* and is heard intermittently throughout both films. Like the vibration of the nearby train that we hear (and sense) each time it rumbles past bringing commuters into the economic centre of Beijing, the sound seems to embody China's metanarrative of progress and development that conceptualises temporality as linear and forward moving, encoded historically by the rhythmic sounds of industry and production (Lovatt, 2012: 435). This understanding of time is, as Bliss Cua Lim describes: 'a means of exercising social, political, and economic control over periods of work and leisure [that] obscures the ceaselessly changing plurality of our existence in time' (Lim, 2009:11). This tension is evident in the extended prologue before the title sequence of the second film when Beibei's mother, Jia Huifen, returns from the marketplace and obliquely criticises her husband, suspecting him of being idle while she was away. Their dialogue reveals in particular the subjective experience of duration as well as an internalised pressure not to 'waste' time by being unproductive. Off-screen, we hear the bang of the door outside the apartment and again as Huifen opens and closes the inner door to their home.

> LIU ZAIPING. That was quick.
> JIA HUIFEN. Quick? It took me over an hour.
> LIU ZAIPING. [pause] I'm the slow one then . . .
> JIA HUIFEN. [pause] Is the G3 bag template ready yet? [pause]. Oh, you're still threading the needle. Didn't I thread the needles for you before I went out?

They then decide to move the table slightly to create more space to work before the title, *Oxhide II*, appears on the screen after just over twenty leisurely minutes of running time.

THE LABOUR OF PRODUCTION

As with *West of the Tracks* and Jia Zhangke's *Still Life* (*Sanxia haoren*, 2006), both *Oxhide I* and *II* not only foreground labour through the depiction of the production of goods and food but also the labour involved in making the film itself (see Jorge and Smith's chapters in this volume). In this respect, Liu's work is very different from the spontaneous, 'on-the-spot' (*xianchang*) realism of the New Documentary Movement and the *vérité* feature films of the 'Sixth' or 'Urban Generation' which are characterised by visual and aural instability, and the contingent (Zhang, 2007; Berry et al., 2010). By contrast, despite similarly using non-professional actors and location setting, *Oxhide* and, even more so, *Oxhide II* are highly controlled works. Though they are 'home movies' of sorts, recorded in real time and re-enacting events that had happened to the family, the films were fully scripted and rehearsed over many months before shooting took place. Yet, within this formal rigour, the films maintain some of the intimacy of the 'home movie' through the family's performance of quotidian routines, their sometimes banal conversations, their silences and, perhaps most importantly, *their recording of themselves* in the setting of their real living space. The family's performance also enacts the transference of embodied memories – the 'passing on' of the skills of wonton cookery from parent to child – as the location sound recording captures 'the micro-epistemologies and everyday terrains of auditory experience' (LaBelle, 2010: xxv).

Liu's attention to the intimate settings of everyday life and the dynamics of family relationships can be compared to that of Yasujiro Ozu, and her work shares some of the 'playfulness' of his techniques (such as shooting in 360-degree space) that David Bordwell argues makes 'spatial and temporal relations ambiguous' (Bordwell, 1988: 118). Liu's visual aesthetic flattens the perspective, producing a narrow depth of field, and, like Ozu, often uses a very low camera angle. However, while Ozu uses architectural framing to 'maintain a sense of harmony and balance in the face of narrative events that threaten the stability of home and family', Liu's tight framing and extended takes express the opposite: an intense and prolonged claustrophobia (Russell, 2003: 97). In this way, the spatial dynamics of the domestic setting seem both to embody and to reinforce the family's anxieties over the pressures of everyday life in China's new market economy.

Liu created a makeshift widescreen frame by taping up the lens of a cheap digital camera. The use of widescreen 2.35:1 aspect ratio is usually associated with films that depict wide-open spaces or stage performances, yet here, Liu deploys this technique to 'show less' in a manner reminiscent of the minimalist techniques of Robert Bresson (even though Bresson, of course, never utilised the widescreen format).[3] By placing the camera close to the protagonists' bodies, the vertical space is reduced, cropping parts of the body in order to concentrate our attention on the family's hands at work: sewing oxhide, kneading dough, chopping vegetables or stuffing dumplings (Bordwell, 2009).

While the darkness of the image and the highly 'reduced' framing could have a distancing effect because of the way it denies the spectator full access to the dramatic action (or what Metz described as 'mastery' over the image [Metz, 1982]), the auditory dimension serves to expand the diegesis, creating an immersive experience that allows the spectator a degree of intimacy with the characters and with the domestic setting as the narrative unfolds in real time.

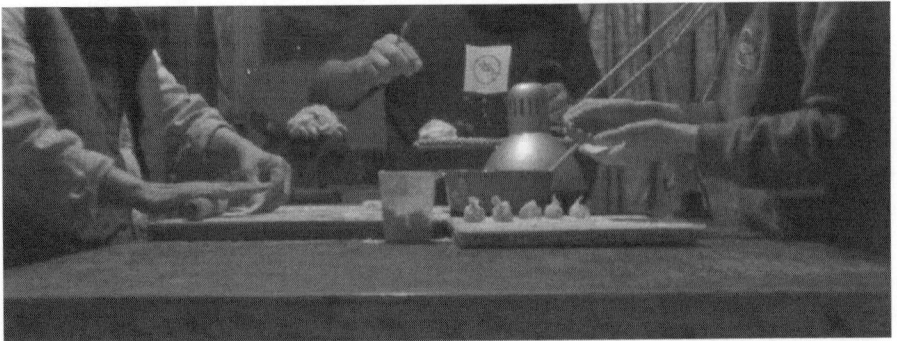

Figure 13.1 The family's hands preparing dumplings, *Oxhide II* (2009).

'CONCRETE' SOUNDS AND ACOUSTIC SPACE

Though sparse, sound in Liu's films is spatial and dynamic. In sound design, spatial depth is usually achieved through the inclusion of ambient or environmental sounds. What Michel Chion terms 'materializing sound indices' are noises ('concrete sounds') that 'flesh out' the scene by providing acoustic depth and texture, endowing it with the 'feeling' of the real (Chion, 1994: 114).[4] Because the framing of the image is so restricted, and the setting only partially lit, shifting the focus from the visual to the auditory as a primary mode of engagement at certain points in *Oxhide I* and *II* serves to provide clarity, helping the spectator understand the dynamics of the space by sonically describing the objects and surfaces within it. The sound design draws attention to the acoustic properties of the apartment, thereby capturing what Brandon LaBelle calls 'an auditory geography [that] exists . . . within the very meeting or interweaving of noise and silence' (2010: 47).

The absence of an external shot of the building or the neighbourhood to help situate the viewer and locate the narrative geographically means that we are held within the cramped interior of the apartment for the duration of both films. The only slight relief offered is through a small window in the room where Liu Zaiping works that allows in some natural light but, rather than illuminating the scene, the light casts his body into silhouette, restricting further an emotional engagement with the character via the image. At another point in *Oxhide*, when the family searches for their missing cat, we are allowed a glimpse of the outside world through another small, curtained window. Even this brief moment of relief is denied to us in the second film, however, where the camera does not leave its position at the edge of the table. The sense of claustrophobia is heightened further by the soundtrack: within the apartment itself, there is a surprising absence of mediated sound technologies – in particular, no radio or ambient television – nor are there any audible broadcasts from the street outside or from neighbouring apartments. This means that no other voices or perspectives (official or otherwise) can be heard other than those of the family, and our aural attention remains focused on the protagonists and the noises produced by their exertions and their immediate environment.[5]

Moreover Liu's films use neither diegetic nor non-diegetic music to provide emotional cues, and yet, the absence of music does not mean that the two films do not have their own 'musical' rhythms. For example, the percussive 'concrete' sounds of the mother, father and daughter chopping, stirring and rolling dough on the table juxtaposed against the many protracted instances of room tone, when the protagonists choose not to speak, provide rhythm, timbre and phrasing that affect the mood and pacing of the scenes that, in more conventional narrative cinema, may well be achieved through a musical score or through editing. As well as providing cinematic rhythm, however, they also provide insights into the micro-rhythms of the family's everyday life and their patterns of work and leisure. The idiosyncratic squeaks of the apartment's doors as people come and go, the rumble of the train that vibrates the whole apartment every half hour or so, and the metronomic ticking of the clock, as well as their own 'bodily' sounds (their slurps, sighs, sniffs and speech) provide the soundtrack with a pulse; these are what Don Ihde refers to as the 'flux and flow' of such 'daily sounds' that embody the 'rhythmic temporal movements of sound' (Ihde, 2007: 87).

Edmund Carpenter and Marshall McLuhan note that acoustic space is not temporally or spatially bound but is constantly evolving:

> auditory space has no point of favored focus. It's a sphere without fixed boundaries, space made by the thing itself, not space containing a thing. It is not a pictorial space boxed in, but dynamic, always in flux, creating its own dimensions moment by moment. (Carpenter and McLuhan, 1960: 67)

As mentioned above, in both *Oxhide I* and *II*, the location sound recording maps out the acoustic dynamics of the apartment as the soundtrack foregrounds the materiality of sounds within, and from just beyond, the space. While the visual framing of Liu's films contains the narrative within the apartment walls, it could be argued that the soundscape, by contrast, communicates a sense of space–time that is 'in flux', and thus potentially resistant to that sense of containment or control. In this way, the musicality and dynamism of the films' 'slow sounds' suggest a formal politics that counters the regulation of time and space in post-socialist and capitalist discourse.

On a functional level, we understand how the rooms connect to each other and to the outside world primarily through our sense of hearing. To do this, Liu makes extensive use of off-screen space and uses sound to communicate information about that which is just beyond the visual frame and the protagonists' movement through it. András Bálint Kovács suggests that in Bresson's films, this use of off-screen space is 'metonymic' in that 'narrative information is provided, especially by sound effects, from off-screen space that extends just beyond what is . . . visible onscreen. In other words, much of the plot is taking place in spaces not seen but contiguously attached to onscreen space' (Kovács, 2008: 142). Kovács goes on to explain that, in cinema, off-screen space is frequently used in this way for two purposes. Firstly, to 'enhance dramatic tension, to raise the viewer's curiosity, which . . . is then satisfied later by showing what was unseen before'. And secondly, 'to reduce information redundancy: part of the information is conveyed only by two channels, not by three: either by time and sight (we see what is happening) or by time and sound (we hear what is happening)' (142). Kovács's discussion of 'minimalist use of off-screen space' is useful for thinking about how Liu's sound design similarly allows us to hear events that we do not see: acousmatic sounds originating in off-screen space are never 'de-acousmatised', to use Chion's term, in order to satisfy the spectator's curiosity (Chion, 1994).

In Liu's films the only sound from the outside world, aside from some muffled conversations from the corridor or street outside, to penetrate the walls of the apartment is the deep resonance of the train mentioned briefly above. It is heard at several points in both films, and its presence, though fleeting, is dramatic, causing the fabric of the building to vibrate, shaking the table and the objects on its surface. The irony is that, although for the spectator, the intrusion of this external body is disruptive and disturbing, the characters themselves barely register its presence: the father alone seems to be bothered by it. Tellingly, within the overall aural environment (what Ihde calls the 'enduring gestalt'), it is the more personal sounds connected to character, embodiment, memory and ritual that capture their attention as, at times, the sounds themselves seem to become almost extensions of the characters (or at least of how they see one another and themselves).[6] In *Oxhide II*, for example, Beibei's parents try to teach her their skills, and a train rushes past:

> BEIBEI. Listen to that. Quiet for a moment. Listen.
> LIU ZAIPING [to Beibei]. All I can hear is the sound of the train.
> JIA HUIFEN. When mum does it there's a sound. Did you hear it? She's better than you at it.
> LIU ZAIPING [audibly pulling apart some of the dough. Beibei leans forward and puts her ear to her father's hands]. Your poor skills have rubbed off on me now.
> BEIBEI. That's not the right sound. You made it on purpose.
> JIA HUIFEN. [a quick snap as she pulls apart the dough]. Let me finish them off.
> BEIBEI [to her father]. Listen to that. There's a sound as she pulls it off.

While the train is a recurrent motif in Asian cinema, which often signifies hopes and anxieties around modernity, industrialisation, and mobility, here its presence *within* the acoustic ambience of the home seems to act as a reminder of what Jean Ma calls the 'discontinuities of time as well as space; rhythms of crisis, rupture, and repetition' in the 'globalized world of late modernity' (Ma, 2010: 10).[7] That is to say that, while the train may symbolise 'progress', embodying a sense of temporality that is linear and regimented, within the lived space–time of the family's Beijing apartment it appears in stark contrast to the extended duration of the rituals of traditional wonton cookery and the length of time and skill required to produce their leather goods (to which Liu Zaiping makes an oblique reference when lamenting his customers' attitudes towards his products). Li Zhang argues that: 'As socialist ethics, morality, and values are fading away, market forces and mass consumerism are taking a tight grip on everyday life in Chinese society' (Zhang, 2010: 127). For the family in *Oxhide* and *Oxhide II*, it is these anxieties around the loss of the 'value' of time following post-socialist China's neo-liberal turn, and the loss of dignity that goes with that, that form the centre of their own personal crisis.[8]

Sound, Duration and the 'Living Present'

Sound theorist Steven Connor notes that: 'the nature of sound is to occupy a passage rather than instant of time, duration, rather than a moment. In order to hear a sound, one must have already heard it start to decay' (Connor, 2000). The material properties of sound and the experience of listening have therefore a very specific relationship to temporality, and our sense of hearing can influence how the passing of time is perceived in lived space. Similarly, Chion contends that in audiovisual media sound 'temporalizes images', arguing that it 'vectorizes or dramatizes shots, orientating them toward a future, a goal, and creation of a feeling of imminence and expectation' (Chion, 1994: 12). Unlike more commercial sound design which uses overdubs to create complex, multilayered soundtracks, in *Oxhide* each diegetic sound, such as the snapping of the dough heard in the scene above, is given 'space' around it, which has the effect of drawing out cinematic time as the spectator is able to contemplate or 'experience' phenomenologically the auditory realm in which the narrative is unfolding (in much the same way one might perceive the 'decay' of a sound in lived space, to use Connor's terms).[9]

As I suggested earlier, location sound recording can communicate something about the dimensions of the rooms in which the narrative is set as well as the materiality of the surfaces and objects within them, information that is not always readily given over by the image. Yet this is more than paying attention to the individual sounds of 'things', as Don Ihde notes, from a phenomenological perspective, it is important to be aware of how these sounds relate to 'the larger gestalts of auditory temporality' (Idhe, 2007: 87). In his essay 'Timeful Sound', Ihde explains that what he calls a 'phenomenology of experienced temporality' is connected to the '*temporal span* or duration of sounding that is experienced as listening'. As he writes:

> I do not hear one instant followed by another; I hear an enduring gestalt within which the modulations of the melody, the speech, the noises present themselves. The instant as an atom of time is an abstraction . . . In

terms of a perceptual field . . . a thing always occurs as situated within a larger unity of a field; so temporally the use of *instant* here is perceived to occur only within the larger duration of a temporal span, a living present. (Ihde, 2007: 89, emphasis in original)

The connection between duration and the sonic here is important for understanding sound's relationship to both cinematic and 'lived' space, particularly, as I have argued in this chapter, in the context of slow cinema. Thus, with all their 'modulations' of 'melody', 'speech' and 'noise', the ambient soundscapes of Liu Jiayin's masterful *Oxhide* and *Oxhide II* present a perceptual field within which the characters' 'living present' – the intimacy of the everyday – can be felt and experienced by the spectator at the same time as it is by the characters on-screen. In this chapter, I have suggested how this embodied experience of 'slow sounds' might lead to a deeper understanding of the phenomenological experience of space–time in post-socialist China, and the tensions and anxieties that surround its accelerating velocity.

Furthermore, I have suggested that, through their depiction of labour, both within the narrative, and through the construction of the films themselves, *Oxhide* and *Oxhide II* offer a formal politics that reasserts compassion, care and dignity into the grand narrative of neoliberalism.

NOTES

1. See Suárez's excellent essay 'Structural Film: Noise' (2008) where he makes a convincing connection between the 'long takes and defamiliarized sound' of Chantal Akerman, Gus Van Sant, Jim Jarmusch, Hou Hsiao-hsien and Tsai Ming-liang's films, their treatment of the 'enigmatic everyday', and the use of noise in structural film (p. 86).
2. The threat of obsolescence is a recurrent trope in recent Chinese cinema: for example, Ou Ning's documentary *Meishi Street* (*Mei Shi Jie*, 2006) shows the effect of the widespread demolition of housing before the 2008 Beijing Olympics. Similarly, in the section entitled 'Remnants' in *West of the Tracks*, a neighbourhood which housed former factory workers is demolished to create space for commercial businesses. See Xinyu (2010: 69).
3. See Schrader (1972).
4. See de Luca (2014: 130) for a similar discussion of the sensual sonic qualities of the films of Tsai Ming-liang.
5. This 'private' soundscape provides an interesting contrast with the 'public' nature of the soundscapes in the films of Jia Zhangke (particularly his early films, such as *Xiao Wu* [1997] and *Platform* [*Zhantai*, 2000]) in which 'official' voices in the form of state propaganda and 'revolutionary' music are frequently heard across domestic and across public spaces.
6. John Belton also makes this claim of the sound design of *A Man Escaped* (Belton, 2008: 27).
7. For example, see Yasujiro Ozu's *Tokyo Story* (*Tôkyô monogatari*, 1953); Hou Hsiao-hsien's *Café Lumiere* (*Kôhî jikô*, 2003) and Jia Zhangke's *Platform* and *The World* (*Shijie*, 2004) as well, of course, as *West of the Tracks*.

8. The pathos of the family's situation is highlighted in one scene in *Oxhide* where they touch a deep scar on the leather where the cow had been branded, and empathise with the animal's suffering. Liu makes the connection explicit when she says later that 'the whole procedure of shooting was like uncovering a scar' (see https://www.berlinale.de/external/de/filmarchiv/doku_pdf/20050028.pdf) [accessed 11 December 2013].
9. An interesting comparison can be made here to the use of sound in Akerman's *Jeanne Dielman, 23 Quai du Commerce, 1080 Bruxelles* (1975), a film that similarly takes place within the home but which is also a place of work.

BIBLIOGRAPHY

Beckman, Karen and Jean Ma (eds) (2008), *Still Moving: Between Cinema and Photography* (Durham, NC and London: Duke University Press).
Belton, John (2008), 'The Phenomenology of Film Sound: Robert Bresson's *A Man Escaped*', in Jay Beck and Tony Grajeda (eds), *Lowering the Boom: Critical Studies in Film Sound* (Urbana, IL: University of Illinois), pp. 23–35.
Berry, Chris, Lu Xinyu, Lisa Rofel (eds) (2010), *The New Chinese Documentary Film Movement: For the Public Record* (Hong Kong: Hong Kong University Press).
Bordwell, David (1988), *Ozu and the Poetics of Cinema* (London and Princeton, NJ: BFI and Princeton University Press).
Bordwell, David (2009), '"Wantons and Wontons"', Observations on Film Art, 12 October, http://www.davidbordwell.net/blog/2009/10/12/wantons-and-wontons/ [accessed 25 May 2014].
Carpenter, Edmund, and Marshall McLuhan (1960) 'Acoustic Space', in Edmund Carpenter and Marshall McLuhan (eds), *Explorations in Communication* (Boston, MA: Beacon Press), pp. 65–70.
Chion, Michel (1994), *Audio-Vision: Sound on Screen*, translated by Claudia Gorbman (New York: Columbia University Press).
Connor, Steven (2000), 'Sounding Out Film' (an extended version of a paper given at the conference on Film, Literature, and Modernity, the Institute of English Studies, London, 13–15 January), http://www.bbk.ac.uk/english/skc/soundingout/ [accessed 1 May 2014].
de Luca, Tiago (2014), *Realism of the Senses in World Cinema: The Experience of Physical Reality* (New York and London: I. B. Tauris).
Ihde, Don (2007), *Listening and Voice: Phenomenologies of Sound*, 2nd ed. (Albany, NY: State University of New York Press).
Kovacs, Andras Balint (2008), *Screening Modernism: European Art Cinema, 1950–80* (Chicago, IL: University of Chicago).
Krause, Linda and Patrice Petro (eds) (2003), *Global Cities: Cinema, Architecture, Urbanism in a Digital Age* (New Brunswick, NJ and London: Rutgers University Press).
LaBelle, Brandon (2010), *Acoustic Territories: Sound Culture and Everyday Life* (New York and London: Continuum).
Lim, Song Hwee (2013), *Tsai Ming-liang and a Cinema of Slowness* (Honolulu, HI: University of Hawai'i Press).
Lim, Bliss Cua (2009), *Translating Time: Cinema, the Fantastic, and Temporal Critique* (Durham, NC: Duke University Press).
Lovatt, Philippa (2012), 'The Spectral Soundscapes of Postsocialist China in the Films of Jia Zhangke', *Screen*, 53. 4: 434–5.
Lovatt, Philippa (2013), '"Every drop of my blood sings our song. There, can you hear it?": Haptic Sound and Embodied Memory in the films of Apichatpong Weerasethakul', *The New Soundtrack*, 3. 1: 61–79

Lovatt, Philippa (2016), 'Sound, Music and Memory in Jia Zhangke's Hometown Trilogy', in Liz Greene and Danijela Kulezic-Wilson (eds), *Palgrave Handbook of Sound Design and Music in Screen Media* (Basingstoke and New York: Palgrave Macmillan).

Ma, Jean (2010), *Melancholy Drift: Marking Time in Chinese Cinema* (Hong Kong: Hong Kong University Press).

Metz, Christian (1982), *Psychoanalysis and Cinema: The Imaginary Signifier* (London: Macmillan).

Ong, Walter J. (2002), *Orality and Literacy: The Technologizing of the Word* (London and New York: Routledge).

Reynaud, Bérénice (2010) 'Men Won't Cry – Traces of a Repressive Past: The 28th Vancouver International Film Festival', *Senses of Cinema*, April, http://sensesofcinema.com/2010/festival-reports/men-won%E2%80%99t-cry-%E2%80%93-traces-of-a-repressive-past-the-28th-vancouver-international-film-festival/#b27 [accessed 1 June 2014].

Robinson, Luke (2010), 'From "Public" to "Private": Chinese Documentary and the Logic of Xianchang', in Chris Berry, Lu Xinyu, Lisa Rofel (eds), *The New Chinese Documentary Film Movement: For the Public Record* (Hong Kong: Hong Kong University Press), pp. 177–94.

Russell, Catherine (2003), 'Too Close to Home: Naruse Mikio and Japanese Cinema of the 1950s', in Linda Krause and Patrice Petro (eds), *Global Cities: Cinema, Architecture, Urbanism in a Digital Age* (New Brunswick, NJ and London: Rutgers University Press), pp. 87–113.

Schoonover, Karl (2012), 'Wastrels of Time: Slow Cinema's Laboring Body, the Political Spectator, and the Queer', *Framework: The Journal of Cinema and Media*, 53.1, spring: 65–78.

Schrader, Paul (1972), *Transcendental Style in Film: Ozu, Bresson, Dreyer* (New York: Da Capo Press).

Suárez, Juan A. (2008), 'Structural Film: Noise', in Karen Beckman and Jean Ma (eds), *Still Moving: Between Cinema and Photography* (Durham, NC and London: Duke University Press), pp. 62–89.

Xinyu, Lu (2010), '*West of the Tracks*: History and Class Consciousness', in Chris Berry, Lu Xinyu, Lisa Rofel (eds), *The New Chinese Documentary Film Movement: For the Public Record* (Hong Kong: Hong Kong University Press), pp. 57–76.

Yu, Tianqi (2014), 'First-Person Documentary in Twenty-first Century China', in Matthew D. Johnson et al. (eds), *China's iGeneration: Cinema and Moving Image Culture for the Twenty-First Century* (New York and London: Bloomsbury. Ebook).

Zhang, Li (2010), 'Postsocialist Urban Dystopia?', in Gyan Prakash (ed.), *Noir Urbanisms: Dystopic Images of the Modern City* (Princeton, NJ and Oxford: Princeton University Press), pp. 127–49.

Zhang, Zhen (2007), *The Urban Generation: Chinese Cinema and Society at the Turn of the Twenty-First Century* (Durham, NC: Duke University Press).

PART IV

SLOW CINEMA AND THE NON-HUMAN

14. IT'S ABOUT TIME: SLOW AESTHETICS IN EXPERIMENTAL ECOCINEMA AND NATURE CAM VIDEOS

Stephanie Lam

One of the challenges of environmental thought and environmental advocacy, in particular, is the ability to communicate and represent timescales that are outside human perception. Cultural habituation and the real physical limits of the human body's visual apparatus prevent us from seeing, and hence experiencing, certain environmental processes, both natural and human-made. The unfurling of a leaf, the eroding of a cliff face, the decomposition of a plastic bottle – these are processes that occur along timescales which are not immediately observable to the human eye; they are quite simply too slow to see. This chapter introduces what could be called a slow eco-aesthetics shared between a tradition of avant-garde film and nature cam videos that have the environment as a central subject. It explores how time-based media, such as film and video, can open up cinematic and virtual spaces for the observation of nature. I bring together two different phenomena: a tradition of slow ecocinema in the work of James Benning and Bill Viola, and a popular form of slow ecomedia in on-line live-streaming nature cams. No doubt these examples come out of different production and exhibition contexts and speak to dissimilar audiences but what they do share is a visual strategy that encourages an attentive mode of observation and the development of an ecologically oriented gaze.

A Slow Ecocinema

Curiously, two emerging areas of scholarship in recent years, 'slow cinema' and 'ecocinema', seem to draw near but never meet. While there has been stimulating work in each of these fields, they have for the most part evolved along separate trajectories. Both are areas of enquiry that converge in productive ways, however, and often share sets of questions concerning the experience of cinematic time and the experience of environmental change. Within the last decade or so, much has been written about slow cinema, frequently within the context of art-cinema and world-cinema traditions. Slow cinema has at once been exalted for providing a breathing space in an oversaturated and overstimulated media environment, and also dismissed as upholding certain pretensions about what an artful, 'good for you' cinema should look like. Certainly one can become mired in debates about slow cinema as a taste culture but that is to limit the conversation to disciplinary-specific concerns with genre, film style and national film histories.

Ecocinema is less defined by attention to a particular genre or tradition but is a rather flexible category that considers all moving-image media as appropriate subjects for environmental criticism. Despite diverse approaches and methodologies, what scholars working in this area share is a commitment to understanding how moving images, as part of a larger audiovisual culture, are actively involved in shaping and producing knowledge about the material world and the human place within it. Critical work in the field, so far, has tended to focus on narrative cinema or more obvious examples of environmental-issue documentaries (see Ingram, 2000). While mainstream narrative films and consciousness-raising documentaries can directly (and eliptically) speak to environmental issues, turning an eye towards media produced and exhibited through alternative networks can open up analysis of many more formal strategies, institutional histories, motivations and effects.

To this end, David Ingram asks one to look beyond the obvious environmental-activist film and towards a wider range of styles, genres and taste cultures that may promote ecological awareness (2013: 43). He reasons that films work along a number of different strategies and arguments, mixing cognitive and affective appeals to generate audience investment. Analysing the norms and aesthetic strategies of several different genres, including the 'slow eco-aesthetics' of the art film *sleep furiously* (2008), the 'moralist eco-aesthetics' of the popular *Sunshine State* (2002), and the 'eco-aesthetics and kitsch' of *Southland Tales* (2008), Ingram maps out a range of effects and relations that audiences may potentially have with the material. Idealising one strategy or genre over another may not be the most productive exercise for eco-film critics but does illustrate that the ecological film is, indeed, varied in construction and appeal. In the case of art or experimental cinema which emphasises slow and careful viewing, Ingram suggests that this structure may encourage an environmentally sensitive gaze, though he is careful to note that positive reception and impact depend on prior spectator training and disposition.

Scott MacDonald has written extensively on experimental 'films about place' that encourage a mindful form of spectatorship through the use of extended duration. In 'The Ecocinema Experience', he proposes that the goal of eco-cinema is to provide 'alternative film experiences that may help nurture an environmentally progressive mindset' (2013: 20). By 'alternative', MacDonald has in mind an aesthetic that directly challenges the classic, industrially pro-duced, action-centred, narrative-driven style of Hollywood cinema. Strategies include minimal camera movement, the favouring of direct sound over scored music, the decentring of human action and narrative, and, commonly, the use of extended takes and minimal editing. With reference to the specifically eco-centred films MacDonald cites, aesthetic estrangement also takes the form of temporal estrangement. Attentiveness to nature on-screen, he argues, can be a step towards retraining perception such that viewers may carry these experi-ences with them outwards into the world as more conscientious environmental stewards. Films falling within this tradition of experimental ecocinema include Larry Gottheim's *Fog Line* (1970), Peter Hutton's *Time and Tide* (2000), James Benning's *13 Lakes* (2004), and Sharon Lockhart's *Double Tide* (2009), among others.

Such films about place enable a form of cinematic dwelling by carving out a space and allowing a length of time wherein spectators may observe nature's rhythms and patterns as they occur on screen. Adrian Ivakhiv notes that cin-ematic time can be a way of exploring ecological time. Ecology, he argues, 'is about the enfoldment of objects or processes within other processes, all of which unfold according to their own durations' (Ivakhiv, 2013: 305). To this end, time is an essential variable by which film can communicate processes that typically escape human attention. He writes:

> to the extent that moving-image media can generate viscerally felt images of the *times of things* – things in production and in decay, in differen-tiation and synthesis, things making up the unfolding materiality of the world, of identity and of relationality (in all their narratively spun forms), and the swift, dark flow of their vanishing – to that extent cinema is a powerful tool for ecophilosophy. (2013: 307, original emphasis)

The ecophilosophy Ivakhiv constructs is partially indebted to a tradition of thought on film's indexical relationship to the material world. As Siegfried Kracauer eagerly pointed out, in his early formulation of a 'material aesthetic', significantly it is the medium's ability to capture change in time that produces forms of knowledge difficult to access (1997: 41).[1] To this end, the slow and the ecological can, and should, be thought together, especially given the emergence of new genres of film-making that emphasise deliberate, direct and sensuous engagements with nature on screen.[2] As more 'eco'-themed imagery is consumed via different platforms and within an array of environments and institutions, it becomes necessary to understand how moving images gain their power not only as symbols but also as mediums of affect and experience. Here the 'affective turn' in film theory can contribute much to the understanding of how moving images generate conceptual (and perceptual) knowledge of the environment.[3]

James Benning's *13 Lakes*

Playing with the tension between stillness and motion, James Benning's *13 Lakes* is a carefully crafted film that encourages a practice of simple looking. A landscape, for Benning, is 'always changing in very subtle ways and sometimes in very dramatic ways . . . it has to be *experienced*' (MacDonald, 2005: 5, original emphasis). For the film-maker, the long take is one way to mediate such an experience and to highlight the subtle changes that a given site undergoes. *13 Lakes* unfolds entirely through a series of still frames, each lasting ten minutes. There is a symmetry and minimalism in composition that allows spectators to notice the smallest changes. Each shot is framed such that the horizon falls more or less in the same position, producing a clear blocking between water and sky. The repetition in compositional arrangement provides the standard by which the spectator measures the minutest of changes: a bird flying through the frame, a cloud floating across the sky, its shadow doubled on the glass-like surface of water, the occasional ripple. On the audio track, there is also little happening: a few bird chirps, a chorus of frogs, the singular and distinct sound of a motorboat. Like animated postcards, the film cycles through each location: Jackson Lake, Wyoming; Moosehead Lake, Maine; the Salton Sea in southern California; Lake Superior in Wisconsin; and so on, producing a repeated series of views that invite comparison. Without narration or elaboration through text, Benning simply presents each scene for observation. If the changes occurring within a given frame seem more noticeable because of the lack of action, the cut that separates one frame from the next appears dramatic and unexpectedly exciting. One experiences an adjustment in expectation, perhaps impatience or boredom but also an amplified interest in noticing details.

For MacDonald, reading the film against what he identifies as a 'culture of distraction', *13 Lakes* serves as a kind of palate cleanser for the mind. The film, he argues,

> can function as a form of therapy, as a way of helping us learn to make space for careful perception and for sustained contemplation: that is as a form of resistance to the relentless distraction around us, distraction that in modern culture is emblemised by the movies and television (2007: 231).

In this sense, MacDonald adamantly celebrates a film like *13 Lakes* as a counter-cinema of sorts, evidence of how a technology so central in producing a visual culture of distraction and quick consumption can be 're-directed in the interest of the environmental, psychic and spiritual health of modern societies' (2007: 231). Beyond functioning as an alternative to entertainment media which reflects a culture of speed and immediate gratification, the film provides an opportunity to dwell with an image of nature in an immediate, prolonged and sensuous way.

Bill Viola's *Chott-el Djerid (A Portrait in Light and Heat)*

Reaching further back into the history of experimental film and video, one also sees the beginnings of a preoccupation with time and environmental consciousness in the work of Bill Viola. Before his commitment to large-scale installation pieces, the artist worked specifically with lo-definition video. Where others saw the medium as a cheap, consumer-grade technology, Viola was particularly interested in video's unique image quality as well as its ability to record much lengthier expanses of time relative to the 8 and 16 mm formats in film. Out of his prolific body of work, an early video piece, *Chott-el Djerid (A Portrait in Light and Heat)* (1979), stands out for its treatment of physical landscapes. Lasting nearly half an hour and composed of mostly long takes with minimal camera movement, the video allows ample time for the viewer to observe processes of slow environmental change as they occur across a series of landscapes. *Chott-el Djerid* is as much about place as it is about weather. The piece captures atmospheric shifts in locations ranging from the Sahara desert in Tunisia to the prairie expanses of Illinois and Saskatchewan. Mirages and snowstorms obstruct and abstract the image so that viewers become both estranged from what they are seeing while remaining highly attuned to alterations in light, atmosphere and the passing of time. The audio component is equally distorted, the synced sound capturing only blowing wind and white noise. Viola's later works, which employ extensive use of slow-motion cinematography shot on high-end digital video, deal more explicitly with human faces, physiognomies, art historical references and interior states of mind. *Chott-el Djerid*, in contrast, stands apart because of its intense focus on the material world as subject matter, the nature out there in all its physicality. Rarely do humans appear in any of the scenes and, when they do, they are merely travelling through the landscape as just another element. Along with the relative absence of camera movement and the exploitation of real-time recording capabilities, the piece is meant to produce a highly charged and emotive experience of landscape.

In line with the work of Marshall McLuhan (1994) and Gene Youngblood (1970) who, writing in the mid 1960s and early 1970s, saw media as an extension of the body's perceptual capabilities, Viola likewise pondered video's

Figure 14.1   Atmosphere and landscape in *Chott-el Djerid (A Portrait in Light and Heat)* (1979).

relation to the human sensorium.[4] Reflecting on the rationale behind his own work, he proposes that spectatorship is a distinctly embodied and psychically charged practice. 'Perception is the input channel to the mind', Viola writes, 'and with new technologies, the call is first to the body, then the mind will follow' (1995: 253). Significantly, for the artist, video's distinction from the other arts lay in its special relationship to time:

> It is not the monitor, or the camera, or the tape, that is the basic material of video, but time itself. Once you begin to work with time as an elemental material, then you have entered the domain of conceptual space . . . Awareness of time brings you into a world of process, into moving images that embody the movement of human consciousness itself. If light is the basic material of the painter or photographer, then duration is the material prima [*sic*] of the time-based arts of cinema and video. (1995: 173)

Similar to the way in which Benning uses the 'material prima' of duration to build a slow, patient and sensuous viewing experience, Viola makes the temporal and haptic dimension of video integral to the work. *Chott-el Djerid* is as much an audiovisual study of landscape as it is an invitation to reflect on the experience of perception itself. The grainy image and the equally 'grainy' soundtrack make it difficult to forget the mechanics of the apparatus. While the sheer beauty of desert scenes and snow-covered fields would seem to invite an immersive form of engagement, the humble production context and mode of exhibition – via the television monitor for the historic viewer or probably the computer screen for the contemporary viewer – effectively gets in the way of an easy viewing. The resolution is 'poor' but this lack of image quality is integral to the experience of, and appreciation for, processual changes in the environment and the materiality of video itself. Technological and weather-based interruptions prevent clarity of image and sound, radically altering the expectations and habits of the viewer.

Both Benning's and Viola's work, as represented in *13 Lakes* and *Chott-el Djerid*, invite a framing of screened nature as therapeutic experience set at a remove from the ebbs and flows of mainstream television, film and most of today's on-line environments. One might critique these pieces as reproducing a romanticised perception of nature as reprieve from culture, as eternal or timeless, or as impervious to human influence. Yet the pieces are more than time-based forms of nature worship. The imagery is hardly spectacular and is, in fact, quite ordinary: stationary views of urban water in the case of Benning, semi-rural landscapes and deserts in the case of Viola. Rather, in both cases, it is the element of time that frames these sites as significant, as scenes worth looking at and attending to. The dialectic between attentive and distracted modes of media consumption, which MacDonald reads into Benning's work and which Viola has articulated in his own writing, also appears in discussions of slow cinema. Similarly, attentiveness and distraction are also the terms by which proponents of various slow social movements couch their critiques and hopes for alternative relationships to consumption, work and the environment. 'Good' and 'bad' temporalities become a measure by which to diagnose critically a culture according to ideal standards of personal, societal and environmental health. Unspoken within these diagnoses is some understanding of what the proper relationship between human and nature ought to be, and to what extent and how technologies, including audiovisual ones, can or should be used to mediate between the two. A slow ecocinema built around long duration offers an invitation to reconnect with a practice of ordinary looking.

NATURE CAMS AS SLOW ECO-MEDIA

Crossing over into the realm of popular moving-image media, one notes the curious explosion and appeal of nature cam videos that have a surprisingly similar look and feel to certain examples of a slow experimental ecocinema, including the works described above. Many of these nature cam videos are hosted by conservation organisations that frame them as opportunities for virtual contact with a disappearing nature. Sir David Attenborough, in his endorsement for World Land Trust, an international conservation charity which protects biologically threatened habitats, articulates this position succinctly on the group's website:

> As human beings we are more urbanised than ever before, and we are out of touch with the natural world. Yet we are 100% dependent on its resources. World Land Trust's rainforest webcam is an extraordinary lifeline and communication with the natural world. (Attenborough, World Land Trust)

Famous for high-end BBC nature programmes, such as *The Life of Mammals* (2002–03) and *Planet Earth* (2006), the British naturalist and film-maker lends his support to the humble webcam as a technology that provides a transparent and direct link to the natural world. World Land Trust is just one of many conservation organisations that have incorporated webcam technologies as part of their visual lexicon. Viewers and supporters can log on to the organisation's website and see direct, live-streaming images of remote nature. Locations include the Buenaventura Cloud Forest in Ecuador and the Ornithos Atlantic Rainforest in Brazil. In a similar fashion, the United States's National Park Service provides a 24/7 live feed of the Old Faithful Geyser in Yellowstone National Park. Countless other web cameras have been mounted in relatively remote landscapes, ranging from Mount Washington in New Hampshire to Kruger National Park in South Africa. In these instances, this relatively low-tech device allows visitors access to virtual views of national parks and nature reserves at all hours of the day.

As slow-moving versions of nature photography, nature cam videos fulfil a cultural desire for contact with wild and remote spaces. They are a twenty-first-century visual strategy by which conservation groups reach out to a broad public to encourage an aesthetic appreciation of nature. With the interesting added dimension of time, it is also possible to regard them as an eclectic form of slow eco-media. Unlike slow cinema, which is often discussed and valued within the domain of art cinema, national cinema, or experimental cinema, nature cam videos exist within entirely different networks of production and circulation and are not granted much aesthetic value. There are productive ways, though, to put the two in conversation. Most obviously, such as *13 Lakes* or *Chott-el Djerid*, nature cams build time-intensive connections between remote viewers and specific natural sites. They encourage a form of attentive viewing and place attachment, with the aim of inciting feelings of intimacy with, and sensuous knowledge of, a given locale. Without overlooking the more insidious histories of webcam technologies and the unequal distribution of power that their visuality produces, one might also see how they can promote a viewing practice based less on a desire to dominate than a desire to care for.[5]

Notably, though, live feeds of remote nature are quite dissimilar end products relative to the images produced by Benning and Viola. First, nature cam views are significantly more ephemeral in that they are meant to be accessed and circulated in a very flexible manner; they exist on a web interface and are directed towards a user or viewer who may be logging on via laptop or handheld device. Image quality can also vary widely, and feeds frequently experience signal interruptions. Second, they are produced and distributed by organisations with a variety of agendas, funding schemes and audiences. Many of them are conservation groups, such as the World Land Trust, but also television networks, such as the Discovery Channel. Their modes of production, intentions, platforms, viewing environments, and imagined audiences, then, put them at quite a remove from the culture of experimental ecocinema.

Yet the intersection between nature cams and a slow experimental ecocinema is too fascinating to overlook. Through the use of minimal movement, together with the absence of editing and usually sound, the nature cam presents radically de-dramatised views of nature in real time. When camera movements occur, they appear obviously mechanical and resemble the work of a structural film.[6] The format also takes long duration to its most radical extreme. Views are ideally available at all hours, and at all times of the day, uninterrupted unless by some technical failure or seasonal constraint. Ike Kamphof suggests that nature cams can incite feelings of care and interest on the part of spectators specifically because they demand patient viewing. While her analysis is primarily geared towards cams that focus on animal subjects, one can extend her broader argument towards cams whose sole purpose is to transmit live streaming views of nature reserves. As she suggests, they do more than show events in another physical location. Rather, they ground the viewer in the place depicted, and provide a point of contact between the virtual and the real (Kamphof, 2010: 261). Or in Attenborough's words, they provide a 'lifeline and communication' with the natural world.

In using this technology, conservation websites are trying to encourage viewers to bond with the specific sites that appear on-screen. The real-time connection sensitises users to environmental changes as they unfold, connecting them on the same temporal plane. Visitors are encouraged to dwell on the image for as long as they please, and to share their experiences with other users on the site. Many viewers post comments in adjacent forums describing experiences of wonder and appreciation, and, if an animal happens to wander by, gratitude at having been patient and present at the right moment. Like the bird that flies across the frame in Benning's 13 Lakes, contingency and chance encounters serve as the dramatic fulcrum that hooks and rewards a viewer in an otherwise uneventful scene.

While nature cams no doubt rely on a complex network of cameras, satellites, servers and microchips to deliver nature instantly and 'on demand', once the image reaches the screen, it opens up the possibility of durational viewing that even the longest film cannot produce. Liveness, as well as slowness, are built into the experience of watching. Thomas Campenalla suggests that webcams are a form of tele-present media and, as such, they allow for remote, yet no less real, connections to distant places. Rather than seeing the entirety of cyberspace as a seduction away from the physical world, he suggests that one might also recognise how webcams 'open digital windows onto real scenes within the far-flung geography of the internet' (2000: 27). In this sense webcams serve as 'agents of geography and place' by bringing remote real environments into intimate virtual proximity. Displayed on the user's screen, the specificity of these views counters feelings of the Internet as a placeless entity (2000: 42). To this assessment, I would add that, in these instances, it is actually the temporality of nature cam videos – that is, the slowness in addition to the liveness – that allows for intimacy with, and knowledge of, these remote spaces.

That said, on the side of reception, it is difficult to determine exactly how users may be interacting with these views. There is no guarantee that people engage with nature cams in the same focused and deliberate way that spectators do when watching a Benning film as a discrete screening. Perhaps users may have a nature cam video (or multiple videos) streaming while attending to a variety of tasks both offline and online. In this instance, valorising nature cams as uncomplicated 'good', slow formats would not make much sense. The larger point, though, is that this kind of slow eco-media does exist online and, counter to the bits and bytes one typically finds on the Internet, they afford an alternative kind of temporality. If a user so chooses, he or she can, in fact, reproduce the kind of viewing situation and activate the kind of attention demanded of films such as *13 Lakes* or *Chott-el Djerid*. In contrast to the highly composed and structured encounter with nature on screen which one finds in the experimental tradition of slow ecocinema, nature cams produce a parallel kind of possibility. One has the freedom to determine whether or not to treat these views as ambient background or to attend to them as worthwhile in their own right. There is nothing inherently radical in either an experimental ecocinema or nature cam videos but, when viewed in the light of broader slow cultural movements, one can see how this kind of eco-aesthetic might at least inspire an alternative set of values. It is interesting to imagine how people may be using nature cam videos to redirect their attention, to actively retrain, in a sense, their own perception of what it means to be online and to rediscover, however mediated, some connection to nature out there. Further, if one regards nature cams as a slow format, one that exists as an antithesis to something like Vine or GIF, one would also need to acknowledge that there are layered temporalities that people navigate in their media usage.[7] This would help bring nuance to an easy binary between good-as-slow and bad-as-fast forms of media, as many advocates of conventional slow cinema do.

CONCLUSION

In many ways, experimental slow ecocinema and nature cam videos share little in common, especially in the light of the different ways in which they are produced, circulated, and consumed. Situated within a tradition of American experimental film and video, the works by Benning and Viola speak to a relatively small, self-selecting audience and, more commonly than not, can be seen only within the institutional setting of a university film programme, gallery or cinematheque. They are also formally self-aware experiments by individual authors. Nature cam videos, by contrast, are ubiquitous, authorless, and belong to another set of histories and cultures. One might situate them, for instance, with reference to conservation movements and their visual culture. An intriguing account could also be written of how such media fit within an emerging field of environmental surveillance technologies and programmes. Putting these two phenomena side by side, though, allows one to see how a slow eco-aesthetics might respond to, and fulfil, a desire for more immediate and extended visual contact with nature. With an eye to anxieties around environmental crisis, speed, modernisation, and digitisation, one might see how this kind of visual strategy provides opportunities to observe the material world along different temporal scales and to recover, however mediated, a utopian relationship to time. A slow aesthetic is ecological but, more than that, it is ethical. Without the ability to experience environmental change as a temporal condition, and to recognise nature as concrete, present, and all around us, it will be difficult to find ways or reasons to step out of habitual modes of seeing the world at a remove.

NOTES

1. See, for instance, Kracauer's chapter, 'The Establishment of Physical Reality', in Kracauer, 1997.
2. See, for example, projects coming out of Harvard's Sensory Ethnography Laboratory. Notable films include Lucien Castaing-Taylor and Véréna Paravel's *Leviathan* (2012) and Stephanie Spray and Pacho Velez's *Manakamana* (2013).
3. The 'affective turn' in film theory, while varied in approach, is primarily concerned with understanding the pre-personal- and precognitive-level effects of film and other moving-image media. More specifically, for ecocinema, see Weik von Mossner, 2004.
4. See, for instance, McLuhan, 1994 and Youngblood, 1970.
5. Concerns about civil liberties come into effect when states, businesses, and employers use webcams to monitor and control targeted populations.
6. Michael Snow's *Wavelength* (1967), for instance, constructs a whole cinematic experience around an apparent zoom-in to a photograph of ocean waves. Nature cam

videos, which are authorless and whose movements are dictated by remote operation, similarly create the experience of a mechanical eye.

7. Vine is a short-form mobile video-sharing service owned by the microblogging site
Twitter. It allows users to record and edit looping video clips that last six seconds or
less. The GIF, short for Graphics Interchange Format, is a popular single-file bitmat
image format that appears as a small, looping animated image.

Bibliography

Attenborough, David: World Land Trust, 'Wildlife Webcams: Rainforest Life Online',
http://www.worldlandtrust.org/about/patrons/david-attenborough/webcams-rainfor
est-life-online [accessed 25 March 2014].

Campanella, Thomas (2000), 'Eden by Wire: Webcameras and the Telepresent
Landscape', in Ken Goldberg (ed.), *The Robot in the Garden: Telerobotics and
Telepistemology in the Age of the Internet* (Cambridge, MA: MIT Press), pp. 23–46.

Ingram, David (2000), *Green Screen: Environmentalism and Hollywood Cinema*
(Exeter: University of Exeter Press).

Ingram, David (2013), 'The Aesthetics and Ethics of Eco-Film Criticism', in Stephen
Rust, Salma Monani and Sean Cubitt (eds), *Ecocinema Theory and Practice* (New
York and London: Routledge), pp. 43–61.

Ivakhiv, Adrian (2013), *Ecologies of the Moving Image: Cinema, Affect, Nature*
(Waterloo, ON: Wilfrid Laurier University Press).

Kamphof, Ike (2011), 'Webcams to Save Nature: Online Space as Affective and Ethical
Space', in *Foundations of Science* 16: 2–3: 259–74.

Kracauer, Siegfried (1997), *Theory of Film; the Redemption of Physical Reality*
(Princeton, NJ: Princeton University Press).

MacDonald, Scott (2005), 'Exploring the New West: An Interview with James Benning',
Film Quarterly 58: 3: 2–15.

Macdonald, Scott (2007), 'James Benning's *13 Lakes* and *TEN SKIES*, and the Culture
of Distraction', in Barbara Pichler and Claudia Slanar (eds), *James Benning* (Vienna:
Österreichisches Filmmuseum :SYNEMA–Gesellschaft für Film und Medien, vol. 6,
pp. 218–31.

Macdonald, Scott (2013), 'The Ecocinema Experience', in Stephen Rust, Salma Monani
and Sean Cubitt (eds), *Ecocinema Theory and Practice* (New York and London:
Routledge), pp. 17–42.

McLuhan, Marshall (1994), *Understanding Media: The Extensions of Man* (Cambridge,
MA: MIT Press).

Viola, Bill (1995), *Reasons for Knocking at an Empty House* (Cambridge, MA: MIT
Press).

Weik von Mossner, Alexa (ed.) (2014), *Moving Environments: Affect, Emotion,
Ecology, and Film* (Waterloo, ON: Wilfred Laurier University Press).

Youngblood, Gene (1970), *Expanded Cinema* (New York: Dutton).

15. NATURAL VIEWS: ANIMALS, CONTINGENCY AND DEATH IN CARLOS REYGADAS'S *JAPÓN* AND LISANDRO ALONSO'S *LOS MUERTOS*

Tiago de Luca

Whereas it would be fair to say that the films commonly subsumed under the term 'slow cinema' do not by necessity adhere to, or even engage with, environmental activism, the cinematic trend parallels ecocriticism's recent rise to prominence and ecologically minded movements such as 'slow living', 'slow food' and 'slow travel'. Through realist modes of production based on duration and observation, contemporary slow films arguably postulate a new-found awareness of the natural world and testify to a renewed fascination with rural lifestyles and untouched environments, such as villages, jungles and forests. This is exemplified by the films by directors as diverse as Carlos Reygadas, Lav Diaz, Apichatpong Weerasethakul, Béla Tarr, Lisandro Alonso and Michelangelo Frammartino among others, all of which place emphasis on remote spaces whose cyclical, seasonal and artisanal temporalities seem to impose themselves upon the film's own pace, thus opening it up to the vagaries of nature and animal life.

As I shall explore in this chapter, this environmental emphasis is, in principle, divorced from the anthropomorphic impetus that often animates conventional nature documentaries, being instead exemplary of a commitment to recording the natural world in its fortuitous and serendipitous quality. Thus, as exemplified by films as disparate as *Blissfully Yours* (*Sud sanaeha*, 2002), *Silent Light* (*Stellet Licth*, 2007) and *The Turin Horse* (*A Torinói ló*, 2011), one cannot fail to take notice that landscapes, vegetation, sunlight, water, the weather, the wind in the trees, in short, the sheer contingency of the natural world, are as much an integral part of the slow film's aesthetic as are its solitary and sparse human protagonists. If, as Derek Bousé notes, 'the slow unfolding of time' and 'stillness and silence have almost no place' in the wildlife film – reliant as they are on editing tricks, didactic voice-overs and a pronounced emphasis on dramatic, rather than ordinary, occurrences (Bousé, 2000: 4) – slow cinema would, instead, be closer to what Scott Macdonald has theorised as 'ecocinema', which he defines as durational films that provide 'visual/auditory training in appreciating the experience of an immersion within natural processes' (2013: 19; see also Lam's chapter in this volume).

One of the direct consequences of this sustained focus on natural processes is the conspicuous presence of non-human living creatures in the growing corpus identified with slow cinema. One could cite, for example, recent documentaries, such as *Sweetgrass* (Lucien Castaing-Taylor and Ilisa Barbash, 2009) and *Bovines* (Emmanuel Grais, 2011), which register, in contemplative mode, the worlds of shepherding and cattle respectively. Within the domain of fiction films, fantastic tropes of bestiality and human–animal metamorphoses, often derived from local traditions, also make regular appearances. An obvious case in point is Apichatpong's films, in which humans turn into non-human animals, an animistic trope which, as May Adadol Ingawanji notes, alludes to a 'disparate range of local forms and references' (2013: 93) pervading the multilayered work of the Thai director. Frammartino's *Le Quattro Volte* (2010), in its turn, follows the cosmological journey of a goatherd who dies, and his subsequent transmutations into a goat, a tree and a batch of charcoal.

The relationship between humans and other animals is also a dominant theme running through the films by Reygadas and Alonso. In fact, as I shall argue in this chapter, their *Japón* (2002) and *Los muertos* (2004) provide fertile ground on which to reflect on slow cinema's relationship with nature, contingency and animals, not least because their take on human–animal relations within remote environments involves the depiction of animal death. Before moving on to examine these two films and their theoretical implications, let me first provide a brief survey of the place of the animal both in film theory and practice so as to delineate the ways in which non-human creatures – and in a more radical form, their death – have come to embody one of the strongest markers of contingency in the filmic image.

CREATURELY SPONTANEITY

Within the discipline of film studies, a recent surge of engagement with animal studies coincides with the centrality of animals in contemporary film practices, and resonates with the attendant concerns of ecocriticism and animal rights in academic and cultural discourses at large. A relatively underexplored area of study until recently, a number of publications over the last decade have attempted to reposition the cinematic animal within frameworks that aim to displace anthropocentric and humanist models in film studies (see, for example, Burt, 2002; Pick, 2011; Pick and Narraway, 2013). Though the scope of this chapter prevents me from providing a full-range survey of these studies, it is striking, if unsurprising, that many of them return to the realist theory of André Bazin in their quest to expand the epistemological and representational borders of a 'cinema beyond the human'. This, incidentally, is the subheading title of the collection *Screening Nature* (2013), which includes chapters on slow films and in which the editors, Anat Pick and Guinevere Narraway, summarise this rehabilitation of Bazinian realism as follows: 'Bazin situated cinema at the juncture of filmmaker, camera and the world. The complex relationship between these three points is, for Bazin, revelatory and affirms – empirically and morally – the reality of the world and the realism of the medium' (2013: 2).

As with many questions presently animating film studies, Bazin is, indeed, an obligatory starting point for meditations on the cinematic animal and film's relationship with the non-human world more generally. Because of their unawareness of recording, animals consistently reappear in his writings as the dynamic and embodied evidence of an intractable reality surplus within the filmic image, often working against, and in spite of, its carefully planned structure and design. When used as fictional characters, notes Bazin, the unpredictable corporeal movement of animals presents crucial problems for any film-maker attempting to narrativise their biomechanical gestures, requiring a deft and laborious application of editing tricks. As Seung-hoon Jeong summarises, in film's attempt 'to anthropomorphize animals, Bazin notices the most muscular use of montage effects', which elicits 'the illusion of animals' humanized actions' at the expense of spatio-temporal integrity (2011: 179). By the same token, for Bazin, the diegetic presence of certain animals is a flagrant, exciting testimony to contingency, risk and danger: we see Chaplin, in a long shot, inside a lion's cage; in one particular shot of the British film *Where No Vultures Fly* (1951), a girl is framed next to a lioness within the same shot. Here, Bazin will similarly stipulate that montage should be ruled out so that both non-human animal and human beings appear in their shared spatial contiguity, thus preserving the sense of urgency experienced in reality by cast and crew during the shoot (Bazin, 2005: 49, 52).

If Bazin's writings, however, often revolved around risk and death, ultimate signifiers of a film-making process which is shaped through adventurous, unplanned encounters between film-maker and reality, the critic also set clear representational limits for the film medium in relation to the cinematic animal and profilmic contingency. In his essay on the French documentary *The Bullfight* (*La course de taureax*, 1951), Bazin postulates what, in his view, constitutes an 'ontological obscenity', namely death and sex on-screen: events whose resolutely contingent and experiential quality 'cannot be represented . . .

without violating its nature' (2003: 30). Yet on-screen death would seem to fascinate film-makers precisely because of this violation, offering a 'temporal and existential singularity' in its purest form (Lippit, 2002: 13). As the contingent is understood as that which escapes structuring, 'death functions as kind of cinematic Ur-event because it appears as the zero degree of meaning', that is to say 'pure event, pure contingency, what ought to be inaccessible to representation' (Doane, 2002: 163–4).

Indeed, if we are to follow the Japanese film-maker Nagisa Oshima, in his claim that a film-maker's deepest desire is 'to shoot the dying' (cited in Nagib, 2012: 177), animal killing would appear as shorthand for human death owing to the legislated ethical implications identified with the latter and comparative lack thereof surrounding the former.[1] Throughout film history, animal death emerges as an illustrious cinematic trope. It appears as early as 1903 in films such as Edison's *Electrocuting an Elephant* and early genres, such as execution and hunting films, and goes on to feature in world cinema's classics such as Luis Buñuel's *Un chien andalou* (1929), Eisenstein's *Strike* (*Stachka*, 1925), Tarkovsky's *Andrei Rublev* (1966), Godard's *Weekend* (1967), to cite but a very few. More recently, as Catherine Wheatley observes, the dying or suffering animal has also surfaced as a prolific visual trope in films pertaining to the 'new extremism', including those by Ulrich Seidl, Gaspar Noé and Michael Haneke (2012: 97).

If the cinematic animal cannot but puncture the realm of representation with its uncontainable and unpredictable life, then its on-screen death stretches this rupture to its limits, shifting the contractual terms of spectatorial engagement to the arena of ethics. As Vivian Sobchack remarks, in relation to the famous killing of a rabbit in Jean Renoir's *Rules of the Game* (*La Règle du Jeu*, 1939), such an event 'ruptures the autonomous and homogenous space of the fiction'; the rabbit's 'quivering death' immediately transforms 'fictional into documentary space, symbolic into indexical representation', with the consequence that 'aesthetic values are suddenly diminished and ethical ones are greatly heightened' (2004: 269; 271; see also Lippit, 2002).

It must be noted, however, that implications of an ethical order will be contingent upon a variable host of culturally specific assumptions, in turn informed by geographically and historically situated discourses. In the industrialised West, more sentimental attitudes towards (certain) animals seem to prevail, as does the complete dissociation of animal death from food consumption, since killings are carried out away from the public domain. This, in turn, would partly explain why countries such as Britain and the United States have been at the forefront of regulations against animal cruelty on film since the late 1930s, with the British Cinematograph Films (Animals) Act coming into effect in 1937 and the American Humane Association (AHA), known for its trademark disclaimer 'No animal was harmed in the making of this film', supervising the treatment of animals on set in American films since 1940 (Burt, 2002: 137,153).[2]

As Jonathan Burt points out, however, the 'creation of regulations for animal film imagery brings into play a whole series of codes, which make cruelty dependent upon the framework in which it is presented' (2002: 141). Thus, it would appear that it is one thing to record a death which was going to happen regardless, as in scenes filmed in real slaughterhouses. Conversely, the harming of an animal specifically for the purposes of a film would seem to fall into an entirely different ethical category which is equally dependent on the particular animal species and/or class harmed. Finally, culturally specific and class-based perceptions would also seem to entail distinct attitudes towards animals and, accordingly, legitimise different sets of practices and modes of interactions (pet ownership, for instance).

All of the above leads us to conclude that the presence of animals on-screen appears as the nodal point at which human actions and decisions, both behind and in front of the camera, coalesce in aesthetically complex and ethically charged ways. Thanks to its dynamic corporeality, which enhances the evidentiary qualities of the medium, the cinematic animal becomes a useful cinematic parameter against which human control over the film-making process is efficiently measured, and on the basis of which a film can define its own ethical stance as well as its commitment to contingency, which in its most radical form can lead to death.

As a means to explore these elements further, I shall now turn to *Japón* and *Los muertos* to investigate the complex relations between animals, contingency and death interwoven by both films. Though a select sample of their kind, they offer themselves as fertile case studies whose comparative analysis will, I hope, shed some light on slow cinema's pervasive aesthetic tendencies in relation to wider cultural debates on human–animal relations and the non-human.

The Dead: *Japón* and *Los muertos*

With a gap of only two years separating their respective releases, *Japón* and *Los muertos* arrive at remarkably similar aesthetic and narrative strategies. Both are centred on middle-aged men returning to crude natural settings: a remote Mexican village situated in arid Canyon landscapes in *Japón*, and an Argentinean jungle in *Los muertos*. The two films devote themselves to showing the wordless drift of these solitary protagonists as they are confronted with their own sense of animality and mortality and find themselves reduced to primal instincts. Their episodic narratives similarly proceed by registering the mundane activities of peasant rural life, being attuned to the quiet and slow rhythms of nature and leaving room for the incorporation of chance events as encountered in the film-making process. Finally, *Japón* and *Los muertos* are unsentimental in their depiction of human–animal relations, being punctuated by acts of animal killing. However, while recognising the ethically debatable nature of these killings from an animal rights perspective, moral judgements will not inform the following analysis, which is an attempt to understand and interpret these acts within the larger theoretical framework of cinematic contingency and through the aesthetic categories of anthropocentrism and non-anthropocentrism.

Let us start with *Japón*, which focuses on the perambulations of an unnamed man, played by an inexpressive amateur actor (Alejandro Ferretis), as he considers suicide for unexplained reasons. Presumably an artist, the laconic man leaves Mexico City to end his life in the remote village of Ayacatzintla where he eventually meets Ascen (Magdalena Flores), a septuagenarian Indian widow who agrees to shelter him in her ramshackle house and with whom he eventually has a sexual encounter. *Japón* puts forward an eminently physical world in which the traditionally separated categories of humanity and animal-ity often collapse into each other.[3] Throughout the film, shots highlighting the corporeality of animals continually crystallise the man's sexual impulses, an example being the three-minute-long scene in which two horses copulating in the middle of a field are observed by him.

By the same token, episodes showing or intimating animal death highlight their status as food sources within the remote region while conveying the man's suicidal thoughts and underlining the film's central themes: life, death and rebirth. We hear, for example, the agonising off-screen groans of a pig being slaughtered (presumably in a local abattoir). We also see the man inside a butcher's as the camera hovers over the raw meat on display; his encounter with a horse's carcass atop a hill; a beetle, in close-up, struggling to survive in the face of raindrops; and so on. In particular, the tension between the move-ment of life and the stillness of death is epitomised in the scene in which the man arrives at the village and helps a young boy tear off the head of a bird. The first attempt, unsuccessful, results in the strangled bird stumbling around injured on the ground, images that were excised in the DVD version released in the United Kingdom. This is followed by the second, successful attempt, in which the bird's decapitated head, magnified in close-up, is kept in full view while it gulps involuntarily for breath and then ceases to twitch, the viewer made witness to the transformation of the animal from physical being to non-being, that is, from animate to inanimate matter.

In addition to cruelty to animals and death, the contingencies of natural (and animal) life also take centre stage in *Japón*, recorded as they often are through long takes that invite the unintended element into the image. This is especially achieved through the film's mobile and independent camerawork, which con-sistently goes on autonomous itineraries and carries out 360-degree pans away from the human protagonist. As Dimitris Eleftheriotis observes, these pans render the man's 'presence in and control of the field of vision as a hindrance' insofar as '[f]rame mobility seems to be motivated by a desire to free itself from [the man's] agency, to roam at will in a visual exploration of the village and its stunning surroundings' (2012: 110). Implicit in Eleftheriotis's observations is a certain non-anthropocentric impetus that mobilises *Japón*'s camerawork in its decentring and denial of human presence and agency as the only purveyor of meaning and focus of attention within the frame. As the camera scans and surveys the natural environment, it allows for the integration of chance events and other living beings to enter its field of vision. At the film's beginning, for example, a 360-degree pan takes in the landscape after the man's arrival and fortuitously registers a herd of goats on the horizon. In another shot, the camera turns away from the man in Ascen's house and captures, as it moves forward, donkeys and chickens pottering about. Cinematic non-anthropocentrism is thus equated here with a quest to include the accidental, which is enabled by the movement of the camera and embodied by that of animals.

As Mary Ann Doane has shown in her historicising account of the cinematic pan and its representational ties with the panorama, its first uses in early cinema already indicate an indelible attraction to 'the unpredictability of the random movement of figures within the frame [which] consolidated the impression of the real. The cinematic pan, like the panorama, constituted a denial of the frame as boundary and hence promised access to a seemingly limitless vision' (Doane, 2002: 154). In *Japón* this desire for the limitless real, tinged with the unexpected, is further corroborated by its widescreen format which Doane has elsewhere similarly defined for its 'even greater plenitude of the visible and a denial of the frame as limit' (Doane, 2009: 74). Both combined, the recurring 360-degree pans and the widescreen format continually yield visual compositions that reinforce the film's non-anthropocentric ethos, on the one hand, and allow the fortuitous into the structure of the image, on the other. Screen mobility and horizontality are thus appropriated in *Japón* for their ability to relativise and diminish human presence in relation to the non-human world – whether we think of establishing shots in which human beings are nowhere to be seen, or when the protagonist appears as a mere dot within the rectangular frame.

This quest for a boundless vision culminates in the film's closure, an unbroken six-minute shot in which the camera, mounted on a dolly on rail tracks, continually moves forward while simultaneously carrying out 360-degree pans that gradually uncover the debris of an accident. These are the vestiges of a crash between a train and a tractor that carried Ascen and other village dwellers. The camera's concurrently forward and circular movement is brought to an abrupt halt when it finally chances upon Ascen's dead body on the railway lines, with the image suddenly turning into a freeze-frame before fading into black. The polarity between movement and stillness formulated by this scene resonates with the tension between life and death which reverberates throughout *Japón*, as crystallised in the aforementioned transition of the bird from animate to inanimate matter. The deadly stillness of Ascen's corpse suddenly forces the camera to stall its convoluted mobility and the moving image to become a freeze-frame, thus putting an end to the film and its desire for superabundant contingency.

Released only two years after *Japón*, Lisandro Alonso's second feature *Los muertos*, shot on his native soil Argentina, offers an interesting parallel in thematic and aesthetic terms, being equally concerned with nature, contingency and death. Like *Japón*, *Los muertos* tells the story of a middle-aged man, Argentino Vargas (his real name), returning to a jungle after twenty years of incarceration. Its slow narrative is similarly interspersed by major events involving real sex and animal death, namely Vargas's encounter with a prostitute and his killing of a goat towards the end of the film. The prospect of death takes on a different dimension here, however, since, unlike *Japón*'s protagonist, Vargas is not suicidal but presumably a murderer whose crime supposedly involved the killing of his two brothers. This is alluded to (but never confirmed) by the dream-like opening sequence which boldly announces to the viewer the film's quest for immersion in the accidental fabric of nature through a non-anthropomorphic gaze. As Jens Andermann succinctly describes,

> the swirling, meandering pans of the camera seem to mimic the very rhythms and movements of the forest, like an insect's or a reptile's gaze, before stumbling upon the bloodied corpses of children in the undergrowth (to which this strangely inhuman gaze pays no more attention than to the accidents of soil and vegetation). (2014: 68)

In the immediate following scenes, the viewer is then confronted with images of Vargas preparing for his release from prison, with the ensuing journey taking up the remainder of the film.

True to Alonso's auteur trademarks, and in line with in his previous *La libertad* (2001) and follow-up *Liverpool* (2008), *Los muertos* is a film quietly centred on the patient observation of nature, with a storyline so thin and opaque, and a protagonist so laconic and expressionless, that narrative engagement on the part of the spectator is often impossible. As the film follows Vargas's solitary journey deeper into the forest, primarily in long takes and long shots, the surrounding scenery calls attention to itself, occasionally, like *Japón*, to the detriment of human presence, as in the scene in which Vargas rides a canoe on a river cutting across the jungle. Initially the shot's central focus, the protagonist gradually leaves the field of vision as the camera pans to the left and pauses to focus contemplatively on the running waters and the wind on the trees. Similarly, *Los muertos* is populated with the spontaneous presence of animals, such as chickens, dogs and pigs, while also depicting rural forms of economic subsistence, an example being the scene in which Vargas meets a boatman dutifully cleaning some fish for sale.

As far as Vargas is concerned, his relationship with animals also attends sustenance needs. At one point in the film, he successfully smokes out a hive to remove a honeycomb from inside a nest of bees, which he subsequently uses for food consumption. Filmed in a single take, the scene reveals the dexterity of the amateur actor in accomplishing the task in the midst of a swarm of bees, thereby intimating the real danger that Bazin often cherished when examining human–animal relationships on-screen. It is, however, Vargas's killing of a goat stranded on the riverbank that impresses in the film through its realism and extended duration. Carried out with calculated precision and astonishing efficiency by Vargas, which attests that this is familiar territory for the non-professional, the killing is presented in two unbroken shots lasting approximately two and three minutes respectively. The first shot shows Vargas slitting the goat's throat while blood gushes on to the floor of the canoe. In the second the viewer is confronted with the image of the non-professional removing the goat's insides and scrubbing down the emptied carcass, hinting that the animal might be consumed as food, though this is never shown thereafter.

It is striking that this scene resonates with that of the bird being strangled in *Japón*, at least in that both take their time to depict solitary men who assert their human agency and power through real acts of killing perpetrated against animals. Similarly, the killing that interrupts the lives of these animals discloses the human agency, that is, the directors behind the films, both of which, conversely, welcome animals and natural accidents to interfere serendipitously in the film-making process as material signs of abdication of human control on the part of these same directors. In *Japón*, as we have seen, this abdication is largely achieved through screen mobility and horizontality. In *Los muertos* it is epitomised in the film's final shot which follows the encounter of Vargas with whom the viewer assumes to be his grandson and granddaughter. As the grandson takes the granddaughter (a toddler) into the hut and out of frame, the camera accordingly pans to the right and stops on Vargas, who fiddles with a small plastic toy – a miniature replica of a footballer in the Argentinian national strip – to then drop it on to the ground before walking into the hut. Subsequently, rather than following the human protagonist, the camera remains in place and, during one minute and twenty seconds, tilts unhurriedly down, revealing the human miniature lying next to a small wheel on the floor until both toys are framed centrally and circled by the shadows of trees moving with the wind. With the shot now static, the toys remain the camera's sole focus for twenty-five seconds until a small chicken swiftly walks into the frame only to be followed by another which stays in the visual field, pottering about for twenty seconds, before the screen fades into black and the credits start rolling.

Figure 15.1   The unplanned corporeality of animal life in *Los muertos* (2004).

In view of Alonso's spontaneous and organic film-making method, it seems fair to assume that the chickens in reality 'hijacked' this final shot which, as such, encapsulates in its visual fabric the film's welcoming of contingency as embodied in the corporeal locomotion of animal creatures.[4] Yet, even in the unlikely event that Alonso deliberately planted the chickens to enter the frame, one cannot fail to note that they still tint its planned visual design with the unplanned corporeality of animal life. The central focus of the shot ceases to be the inanimate and diminutive human replica, overshadowed as it is by the chickens pacing up and down the frame. Offering a stark counterpoint to the static and anthropomorphic miniature, the moving animals thus smuggle something of the unprogrammed into the image which, as a result, comes to visualise this film's oscillation between the human and the non-human, control and contingency, stillness and movement, and life and death.

Conclusion

As the Animal Studies Group notes, '[t]he killing of animals is a structural feature of all human–animal relations. It reflects human power over animals at its most extreme and yet also at its most commonplace' (2006: 4). In many ways *Japón* and *Los muertos* reiterate this complex duality of animal killing within their fictional universes. On the one hand, the killings of the bird and the goat visualise the human protagonists' assertion of superiority over these animals, a power relation that takes on added symbolic meaning in both films owing to their mobilisation of non-anthropocentric tenets and existential tropes. On the other hand, however, animal death is also portrayed as a constitutive, matter-of-fact aspect of rural lifestyles and forms of subsistence that entail more unsentimental attitudes towards animals than those found in industrialised Western societies. The visibility of animal killing, in both films, is thus also a result of their adherence to the peoples and areas they strive to depict through a realist approach which is not only open to physical nature and animal life but which is also eager, with all its ethical implications, to show and inflict death. As such, both films aesthetically rehearse the ambivalent attitude towards animals that has historically characterised cinema's fascination with the movement of animal life and the sudden stillness of its death as the harbingers par excellence of the real.

NOTES

1. As we shall shortly see, however, the exceptions here are Britain and the United States.
2. The British Cinematograph Films (Animals) Act prohibits 'any film depicting or purporting to depict combats with or between animals, or the suffering, terror or rage of animals', and remains in force today (Burt, 2002: 137).
3. I have elsewhere explored at length Reygadas's physical, and metaphysical, realism (de Luca, 2014: Chapter 1).
4. The visual trope of animals drifting into the frame in slow cinema is something that has also been picked up by Song Hwee Lim who observes how 'Tsai [Ming-liang's] static long takes allow living organisms to drift contingently into the frame' (Lim 2014: 110).

BIBLIOGRAPHY

Animal Studies Group, the (2006), 'Introduction' in the Animal Studies Group (eds) *Killing Animals* (Urbana and Chicago, IL: University of Illinois Press), pp. 1–9.
Andermann, Jens (2014), 'Exhausted Landscapes: Reframing the Rural in Recent Argentine and Brazilian Films', in *Cinema Journal* 53: 2, 50–70.
Bazin, André (2003), 'Death Every Afternoon', in Ivone Margulies (ed.), *Rites of Realism: Essays on Corporeal Cinema* (Durham, NC and London: Duke University Press), pp. 27–31.
Bazin, André (2005), *What is Cinema?*, vol. 1, essays selected and translated by Hugh Gray (London and Berkeley, CA: University of California Press).
Bousé, Derek (2000), *Wildlife Films* (Philadelphia, PA: University of Pennsylvania Press).
Burt, Jonathan (2002), *Animals in Film* (London: Reaktion).
de Luca, Tiago (2014), *Realism of the Senses in World Cinema: The Experience of Physical Reality* (London and New York: I. B. Tauris).
Doane, Mary Ann (2002) *The Emergence of Cinematic Time: Modernity, Contingency, The Archive.* Cambridge, MA and London: Harvard University Press.
Doane, Mary Ann (2009), 'Scale and the Negotiation of "Real" and "Unreal" Space in the Cinema', in Lúcia Nagib and Cecília Mello (eds), *Realism and the Audiovisual Media* (Basingstoke: Palgrave Macmillan), pp. 63–81.
Eleftheriotis, Dimitris (2012), *Cinematic Journeys: Film and Movement* (Edinburgh: Edinburgh University Press).

Ingawanji, May Adadol (2013), 'Animism and the Performative Realist Cinema of Apichatpong Weerasethakul', in Anat Pick and Guinevere Narraway (eds), *Screening Nature: Cinema beyond the Human* (New York and Oxford: Berghahn), pp. 91–109.

Jeong, Seung-hoon (2011), 'Animals: an Adventure in Bazin's Ontology', in Dudley Andrew (ed.), *Opening Bazin: Postwar Film Theory & Its Afterlife* (New York: Oxford University Press).

Lim, Song Hwee (2014), *Tsai Ming-liang and a Cinema of Slowness* (Honolulu, HI: University of Hawai'i Press).

Lippit, Akira Mizuta (2002), 'The Death of an Animal', in *Film Quarterly* 56: 1, 9–22.

Macdonald, Scott (2013), 'The Ecocinema Experience', in Stephen Rust, Salma Monani and Sean Cubbit (eds), *Ecocinema Theory and Practice* (New York: Routledge), pp. 17–42.

Nagib, Lúcia (2011), *World Cinema and the Ethics of Realism* (New York: Continuum).

Pick, Anat (2011), *Creaturely Poetics: Animality and Vulnerability in Literature and Film* (New York: Columbia University Press).

Pick, Anat and Guinevere Narraway (2013), 'Introduction: Intersecting Ecology and Film', in Anat Pick and Guinevere Narraway (eds), *Screening Nature: Cinema beyond the Human* (New York and Oxford: Berghahn), pp. 1–18.

Sobchack, Vivian (2004), *Carnal Thoughts: Embodiment and Moving Image Culture* (Berkeley, CA and London: University of California Press).

Wheatley, Catherine (2011), 'Naked Women, Slaughtered Animals: Ulrich Seild and the Limits of the Real', in Tina Kendall and Tanya Horeck (eds), *The New Extremism in Cinema: From France to Europe* (Edinburgh: Edinburgh University Press), pp. 93–104.

16. THE SLEEPING SPECTATOR: NON-HUMAN AESTHETICS IN ABBAS KIAROSTAMI'S *FIVE: DEDICATED TO OZU*

Justin Remes

I.

In 2006, the actress Tilda Swinton delivered a 'State of Cinema' address at the Kabuki Theatre during the San Francisco International Film Festival. Early in the address, Swinton remembered a conversation with her father: 'Dadda was telling me that his falling asleep in the cinema is a particular honour to the film in question. He was telling me this as a compliment, his having snored through three of the four films released last year in which I appeared' (2006: 111).

How should we understand these remarks? It is tempting to view them as a father's desperate attempt to placate his offended daughter, to spin a series of faux pas into gestures of approval. After all, I can imagine the sceptical look that would appear on my face if one of my students were to say, 'No, no. You don't understand. I was sleeping in class only because you are such a good lecturer!'

On the other hand, even if the comments were ultimately little more than damage control, what if they contain a kernel of truth? Can sleep be an appropriate – or even desirable – response to certain films? Films set out to evoke a diversity of responses: laughter, tears, shock, excitement, sexual arousal. Why not sleep?

The answer might seem obvious. When I laugh or cry or become aroused during a film, I am still engaging with that film. I continue to watch it. But sleep implies that my bond with the film has been severed. I might just as well get up and leave the theatre. This argument has a certain pull for me, particularly because I have long been adamant that, if I am going to watch a film, I am going to view it from beginning to end without interruption. (As much as it annoys some of my friends and relatives, this means that, unless there is a dire emergency, I refuse to leave the theatre until the credits are over.) In this respect, I am not unlike Alvy Singer, Woody Allen's character in *Annie Hall* (1977), who discovers that a screening of Ingmar Bergman's *Face* (1958) started two minutes earlier and so refuses to buy tickets to see it: 'I can't go in in the middle'. The titular character, played by Diane Keaton, tries to reason with him: 'We'll only miss the titles. They're in Swedish'! But Alvy is unmoved by her pleas: 'I've got to see a picture exactly from the start to the finish, 'cause . . . 'cause I'm anal.'

I have always sympathised with Alvy. A part of me feels that, if I miss just the opening credits of a film (Swedish or otherwise), I have not *really* seen the film. Perhaps this feeling betrays a deep-seated neurosis on my part but it is difficult to overcome. I imagine someone asking me, 'Have you seen Bergman's *Face*?' and having to respond sheepishly, 'No. I only saw part of it. I missed the opening titles in Swedish. How were they?'

2.

This pedantic approach to cinematic spectatorship has been challenged by several avant-garde film-makers. Andy Warhol, for example, asserted that his early films were not *meant* to be seen in their entirety. He claimed that those who wanted to view *Sleep* (1963) (which consists of five-and-a-half hours of his lover, John Giorno, sleeping; see Walsh's chapter in this volume) need not come at the start of the screening; rather, they could turn up at 'any time' (Hirschman, 2004: 41). Furthermore, spectators were not required to sit silently throughout the screening; Warhol encouraged them to 'walk around and dance and sing' (Hirschman, 2004: 41). And Warhol advocated similarly unorthodox modes of reception vis-à-vis his film *Empire* (1964), an eight-hour-and-five-minute static shot of the Empire State building. As I have argued in my book, *Motion(less) Pictures: The Cinema of Stasis*, *Sleep* and *Empire* are 'furniture films', 'works that invite a partial, momentary, and distracted glance' (Remes, 2015: 43). Audiences of these films generally attended only part of a screening and casually noticed the film intermittently while eating, drinking, and conversing with fellow spectators. But, to my knowledge, Warhol never explicitly encouraged sleeping during his films. In other words, spectators' eyes may not have been glued to the screen but they generally remained open.[1]

In some ways, Tony Conrad brings us closer to spectatorial slumber with his film *The Flicker* (1965). This thirty-minute, minimalist masterpiece is made up of clear and black frames placed in precise patterns on the filmstrip to engender stroboscopic and hallucinatory effects, and these are paired with a mesmerising and sinister electronic score. In spite of the apparent poverty of visual information, I regularly see shapes, colours and faces during screenings of *The Flicker*, and this response to the film is quite common: other viewers have reported seeing Catherine wheels, buckyballs, demons, cockroaches, eyes, and 'a lady and boy in garb of old frontier, standing by a stream, apart from a wagon train' (Richmond, 2012; Joseph, 2008: 341). But what interests me most about *The Flicker* here is the fact that Conrad encouraged certain spectators to 'view' this film with their eyes closed (Joseph, 2008: 302).

In fact, I recently screened *The Flicker* in a class in American experimental film, and one of my students claimed that the experience seemed to be a kind of visual assault. She decided to seek respite from the film's relentless flickering light by closing her eyes, only to discover that the film became even more intense with eyes closed. A number of other students had a similar experience, and several chose to watch the film in its entirety with their eyes closed precisely *because* of the overwhelming experience it provided. (For the uninitiated, when one's eyes are closed during *The Flicker*, the flashing lights continue to assault one's eyelids, and the stroboscopic patterns become intensely visceral and destabilising. The experience is comparable to encountering an unbearably loud noise, plugging one's ears, and paradoxically finding that this makes the noise louder.)

Warhol's viewers often look away from the screen (after all, there is little danger of missing something important in *Empire*), and Conrad's viewers often close their eyes during screenings of *The Flicker*. But we have not encountered the elusive sleeping spectator. (While I occasionally enjoy closing my eyes during *The Flicker*, it would be exceedingly difficult for me to fall asleep during the film and, if I did, I shudder to imagine what Kafkaesque nightmares might greet me.)

3.

I have discovered only one film-maker who has directly encouraged spectatorial sleep: Abbas Kiarostami. The eminent Iranian auteur is best known for thoughtful and contemplative works of slow cinema, such as *Close-Up* (*Nema-ye Nazdik*, 1990) and *Taste of Cherry* (*Ta'm e guilass*, 1997) (the latter film was awarded the *Palme d'Or* at the 1997 Cannes Film Festival). Like the films of other creators of slow cinema – such as Yasujiro Ozu, Chantal Akerman and Béla Tarr – Kiarostami's films often feature simple *mise en scène*, long takes with minimal movement, and little or no emotional expressivity (Jaffe, 2014: 3, 138–42). I would argue that this subdued aesthetic reaches its zenith in Kiarostami's experimental documentary *Five: Dedicated to Ozu* (2003; hereafter *Five*). Abandoning the narrative thrust of most of his earlier work, *Five* consists primarily of lengthy static shots of natural environments. As the title implies, the film is broken up into five segments, all of which were shot on the shores of the Caspian Sea. It will be useful to begin by providing a brief description of each of these segments. (The segments' titles come from Kiarostami himself.)

Part I: Wood
A piece of driftwood is tossed back and forth by the waves until it finally splits in half.
Part II: Promenade
People walk along a promenade in front of the Caspian, occasionally conversing with one another, before eventually exiting the frame.
Part III: Dogs
Tiny specks (barely recognisable as dogs) are seen moving about on the beach.
Part IV: Ducks
A flock of ducks runs across the frame from left to right. One duck rushes back in the opposite direction and is quickly followed by the others.
Part V: Moon and Swamp
For several minutes, the *mise en scène* is bathed in black. Eventually, the full moon is glimpsed, reflected in a pond (see Figure 16.1). Throughout this segment, the audience is enveloped in a rich and textured soundscape of croaking frogs, singing birds, and rainfall.

As the subtitle of the film suggests, the Japanese film-maker, Yasujiro Ozu, was an important source of inspiration for Kiarostami. A number of elements of Ozu's aesthetic can be glimpsed in *Five*, including the contemplative mood,

Figure 16.1   A pond reflects the full moon in Abbas Kiarostami's *Five: Dedicated to Ozu* (2003).

the still camera and the use of music when transitioning from one scene to another. Perhaps the most significant parallel, however, relates to Ozu's use of the 'pillow shot' in which narrative events are punctuated by static shots of objects or landscapes that seem to have no clear narrative significance. The most famous example of this technique appears in Ozu's *Late Spring* (*Banshun*, 1949) in which a shot of a woman lost in thought at an inn is replaced by a lengthy shot of a vase surrounded by shadows. One could argue that Kiarostami is simply removing these pillow shots from their narrative contexts so they become the heart of the film rather than its connective tissue.[2]

A number of scholars and critics have commented on the power and complexity of *Five*. It has been called 'extraordinary' (Andrew, 2005: 73), 'calming' (Jaffe, 2014: 68) and 'profound' (Brown, 2014: 135). What has received less attention, however, are the unorthodox modes of reception that are prompted by the film. Kiarostami has claimed that he would be pleased to see a spectator of *Five* enjoying 'a pleasant nap'. He adds,

> I am not joking. You know how annoyed some directors get on finding out that someone has fallen asleep while watching their film. I will not be annoyed at all. I can confidently say that you would not miss anything if you had a short nap. The important thing for me is how you feel once the film is finished, the relaxing feeling that you carry with you after the film ends. That is important. I do not believe in nailing the audience down at all. In certain films, you cannot miss a moment, but when the film is finished, you will have lost the whole film, your nerves, and your time. I declare that you can nap during this film.[3]

4.

I find these comments utterly fascinating. How can a film-maker encourage a viewer to lose touch with a film, to surrender to what Matthew Flanagan has called 'narcoleptic spectatorship' (2012: 177)? How can Kiarostami confidently assert that 'you would not miss anything if you had a short nap'? *Of course* you would miss something! In fact, you might miss an entire segment of the film, inadvertently changing the title to *Four*. You might miss the quasi-dramatic catharsis of the piece of wood finally breaking in two, or the whimsical humour of the peripatetic ducks waddling back and forth. Nevertheless, I want to defend Kiarostami's counter-intuitive claim. In a sense, the spectator who falls asleep during *Five* has absorbed the spirit of the film. She or he has given herself/himself over to the work's soothing quiescence, its uneventful tranquillity. Perhaps it is the spectator who struggles mightily to stay awake for the entire film who is missing something. I would argue that *Five*, like *Sleep* and *Empire* before it, is a furniture film. Neither Kiarostami nor Warhol has any desire to nail us down. We are free to watch as much or as little of the film as we want. We can drift in and out of attentiveness – or consciousness, for that matter – without worrying about what we are missing. When I watch *Five*, I am reminded of a comment by Warhol: 'I always felt that a very slow film could be just as interesting as a porch-sit if you thought about it the same way' (Warhol and Hackett, 1990: 260).

There is something sneakily philosophical about Kiarostami's fondness for cinematic sleep. Does a film exist only in relation to a spectator, a subject who objectifies the film and processes its sensory information? Or does a film exist independently, regardless of whether it is seen or heard? It is almost as if Kiarostami is asserting that *Five* exists and performs its function even (or perhaps especially) if the spectator cannot see or hear it. Or, to put it another way, if *Five* were projected in a forest with no one around to experience it, it would still make a sound. All of this moves us towards a radically non-anthropocentric cinema. *Five* eschews anthropocentrism not only because humans are only marginally present in the film itself – eclipsed as they are by waves, celestial bodies, and quacking ducks – but also because the film is quite content to run without a single conscious observer. In fact, there is a sense in which even the film-maker has disappeared. In a discussion of Part II of *Five* ('Dogs'), Kiarostami states,

> My duty as the director of *Five*, especially this episode, ends precisely when I start the camera. Normally, the director's role should start when shooting begins . . . How can I explain this role of having no role? . . . I switched the camera on and then I went to sleep . . . When I realized that the director, who was me, could do nothing, I slept.

So not only is the audience encouraged to sleep during *Five* but the director himself slept during the film's creation. Ira Jaffe's (2014) response to this authorial absence is perceptive: 'By going to sleep after setting up the camera, [Kiarostami] not only absented himself from both the shooting and what he terms "the obligation of narration", but also rehearsed his own death as *auteur*' (142).

This provisional death results in a film that is much more complex than it initially seems. Kiarostami has called *Five* 'an open film', or a 'half-made film', one that is co-constructed by the audience. Because of this open-ended and participatory structure, William Brown (2014) has argued that *Five* is actually more complex than a film such as Christopher Nolan's *Inception* (2010), in spite of the latter's sophisticated *trompe l'œil* shots, labyrinthine plot, and intricate *mise en abyme* structure of dreams within dreams within dreams. What makes *Five* more complex, according to Brown, is the sheer number of ways in which spectators can engage with the film's minimalist content. For

Brown, '[a] visually complex film like *Inception* leads to a simple/poor variety of responses, while a visually simple film like *Five* leads to a complex variety of responses' (2014: 136). Geoff Andrew makes a similar argument about Kiarostami's cinema:

> For Kiarostami close observation is not about inspecting every little twist in the plot, as some do with mind-bending puzzle films like *The Usual Suspects*, *Memento*, or *Mulholland Dr*. . . . it's a more interactive relationship that he has in mind. It's about venturing into a film's open or empty spaces, and bringing your own imagination, personality, and experience into play with whatever you find there. Thus, simplicity makes for complexity, omission for plenitude. (2005: 78)

Of course, Kiarostami's viewers have no obligation to fill in these empty spaces, just as viewers of *Late Spring* have no obligation to fill up Ozu's vase. As Jaffe puts it, Kiarostami gives a viewer 'the opportunity to build his or her own film' but also 'the freedom *not* to build or attend, freedom simply to drift within stillness and silence' (2014: 142).

But *Five's* complexity is not limited to the multifarious ways in which we might engage (or not engage) with its content; it is also far more complex in its construction than it initially seems. While each of the film's five segments appears to have the 'authorless' quality of Part II ('Dogs'), in which Kiarostami presses 'Record' and goes to sleep, the reality is more complex. For example, in Part I ('Wood'), it looks as if the driftwood breaking in two is an aleatory natural phenomenon captured by Kiarostami's camera. Kiarostami, however, actually covertly placed a small explosive inside the wood to achieve the effect (Sani, 2013: 16). Additionally, Part V ('Moon and Swamp') looks like a single long take of a pond reflecting the moon. But, in fact, as Selmin Kara (2013) points out in her essay, 'The Sonic Summons', 'The 28-minute pond sequence is constructed from around twenty takes filmed over several months and superimposed onto each other with invisible cuts. Similarly, the soundtrack of the sequence is also carefully crafted, juxtaposing amplified diegetic sounds from different takes during a four-month mixing process' (586–87). It is no wonder, then, that Kiarostami has asserted, '[*Five*] was the most difficult film I ever made, but it doesn't show on the surface' (Jeffries, 2005).[4]

While Kiarostami's active role in shaping the film's content might seem to undermine its non-anthropocentric nature, Kara suggests the opposite is true:

> Kiarostami's sound and image editing in *Five* sets duration as a relative, matter- or object-oriented (instead of subject-oriented) term, deflating assumptions about continuity. His long-take night is a rhythmic assemblage, one that takes into account the temporal patterns,

superimpositions, and cadences that might be observable among various nights on the Caspian shore, without privileging the linear logic of human perception. (2013: 590)

The film's indifference to human perception becomes especially salient when one considers its '"highly structured" soundtrack – composed of dense, layered, and amplified sounds' (Kara, 2013: 583). In Part V ('Moon and Swamp'), in particular, 'the rhythmic ebb and flow of water, howling wind, crickets, frogs, rain, and thunderstorm, conjures up the vision of a self-contained nature, inassimilable by human medi(t)ation' (Kara, 2013: 583).[5] Kiarostami's aesthetic critique of anthropocentrism is strikingly similar to the one put forth by La Monte Young in *Composition 1960 #5* (1960) in which a performer 'turn[s] a butterfly (or any number of butterflies) loose in the performance area'. When someone named Diane objected to calling this piece music, since 'one ought to be able to hear the sounds', Young responded by saying, 'I said that this was the usual attitude of human beings that everything in the world should exist for them and that I disagreed. I said it didn't seem to me at all necessary that anyone or anything should have to hear sounds and that it is enough that they exist for themselves' (1965: 75).

If the sounds of La Monte Young's butterflies 'exist for themselves', indifferent to the absence or presence of a hearing audience, perhaps *Five* also exists for itself. The film does not need you. A spectator is welcome to become absorbed in the film's evocative visual and sonic textures but he or she is also free to retreat, to lose contact with the film, to drift and fade as landscapes become dreamscapes. Kiarostami creates an intricate dialectic between consciousness and unconsciousness; in his words, *Five* represents 'an interaction of both observation and non-observation, presence and absence' (2005). Once again, the parallels between Kiarostami and Warhol are striking. As Vivienne Dick (1989) writes, regarding Warhol's cinema, 'We can let ourselves be absorbed into a meditative state or we can withdraw. The film will go on nevertheless in its own sweet time' (156).

5.

In 1951 Man Ray (2000) wrote, 'The worst films I've ever seen, the ones that send me to sleep, contain ten or fifteen marvelous minutes. The best films I've ever seen only contain ten or fifteen valid ones' (133). Discussions of this quotation tend to focus on Man Ray's thought-provoking claim that even bad films contain 'marvelous' moments – an insight that helps to explain the behaviour of his fellow surrealists vis-à-vis cinema. Think, for example, of the way in which André Breton used to watch only a few minutes of any given film before moving on to another one – or the way Joseph Cornell borrowed less than twenty minutes of footage from the forgettable Hollywood film *East of Borneo* (George Melford, 1931) for his own found-footage film *Rose Hobart* (1936). I am interested in examining a different dimension of this quotation, however: the way that Man Ray identifies the 'worst films' he has ever seen with those that put him to sleep. Notice how strange this sentence sounds if the reference to sleep is replaced with alternate spectatorial responses: 'The worst films I've ever seen, the ones that shock me, contain ten or fifteen marvelous minutes'. 'The worst films I've ever seen, the ones that turn me on, contain ten or fifteen marvelous minutes.' Yet it is not entirely clear why Man Ray's formulation should sound any less bizarre. Why should one assume that soporific films are bad films? It seems ironic that a surrealist who valorises dreams would see sleep as such an undesirable response to cinema.

Contrast this response with remarks made by Kiarostami shortly before the 1997 release of *Taste of Cherry*:

> I absolutely don't like the films in which the filmmakers take their viewers hostage and provoke them. I prefer the films that put their audience to sleep in the theater. I think those films are kind enough to allow you a nice nap and not leave you disturbed when you leave the theater. Some films have made me doze off in the theater, but the same films have made me stay up at night, wake up thinking about them in the morning, and keep on thinking about them for weeks. Those are the kinds of films I like.[6]

Notice the way in which Kiarostami's aesthetic becomes the antithesis of the one embraced by most early avant-garde film-makers. The Dadaists and the surrealists were often interested precisely in taking hostages, in disturbing spectators with provocative and shocking cinematic images. Think of *Le Retour à la Raison* (*Return to Reason*, 1923), for example, in which Man Ray assaults the audience with a hyperkinetic and dizzying series of images: drawing pins, nails, puffs of smoke, naked breasts. Or think of the scandalous content of the films of Luis Buñuel and Salvador Dalí, such as an eyeball being sliced open by a razor in *Un Chien Andalou* (*An Andalusian Dog*, 1929), or the depiction of Christ as a violent rapist in *L'Age d'Or* (*The Golden Age*, 1930).[7] In this context, the reason for the chasm between Man Ray and Kiarostami becomes clear. After all, if a spectator falls asleep during the eyeball-slicing sequence of *Un Chien Andalou*, something has gone terribly wrong. Buñuel and Dalí are taking hostages and, when one is in the middle of a hostage crisis, one must remain alert. *Five*, on the other hand, is a 'kind' film. It is soothing, delicate, beautiful. What better opportunity could there be to heed the advice of John Cage who, in his 1949 Lecture on Nothing, repeatedly intoned, 'If anyone is sleepy let him go to sleep' (1973: ix)?

While Man Ray's unfavourable stance towards cinematic slumber is widespread, there are a handful of figures who have challenged this view. In addition to Kiarostami (and Tilda Swinton's father), the film scholar William Brown offers a sympathetic assessment of spectatorial sleep in a 2011 blog posting in which he attempts to catalogue his own somnolent responses at cinemas: 'During the period from 1 September 2007 to 1 September 2008, I went to the cinema roughly 150 times. I fell asleep during roughly one third of the films that I saw at the cinema.' Brown discovers that the films which put him to sleep (usually art-house films) are often compelling and aesthetically satisfying:

> That I do not sleep during blockbusters leads me to believe that I prob-
> ably do not trust blockbusters; their fast movement may be arousing in
> terms of being attention-grabbing, but they also enervate me, making me
> alert and worried that something is about to happen. The art house film,
> meanwhile, is a friend, or a lover, with whom I feel safe, and in a space
> that feels safe to me. Since it exposes to me those things that are more
> intimate and meaningful than does the blockbuster, then I expose to it
> that which is most private in my life, my sleeping self. (2011)

I must confess that the idea of falling asleep during fifty films in a year is quite alien to me, probably due to my aforementioned neurosis. In over thirty years of film spectatorship, as far as I can recall, I have fallen asleep during only two films: one that I enjoyed (Peter Jackson's *The Lord of the Rings: The Fellowship of the Ring* [2001]), and one that I disliked (Michael Bay's *Armageddon* [1998]).[8] While this is clearly not a statistically significant sample size, the fact that I fell asleep during an enjoyable film is noteworthy. It suggests that Brown and Kiarostami are right: sleeping during a film need not be an indication of the film's poor quality. In some circumstances, sleep may, in fact, be a compliment.

What are the implications of Kiarostami's fondness of cinematic sleep? At the very least, his comments should prompt film theorists to take sleep more seriously. As Brown (2011) has noted, 'In an age when film studies wishes to map almost every aspect of the film experience – from ideological influence to affective response, from audience feedback to galvanic skin responses, sleeping in the cinema remains an overlooked aspect of spectatorship.' A detailed investigation of sleep in cinema may yield important insights about cinematic spectatorship, aesthetics and phenomenology. Beyond this, Kiarostami's comments raise interesting questions about pedagogy. In my experience, most film studies classes implicitly encourage a single kind of reception: students are expected to watch a film in silence from beginning to end with an alert eye (often while periodically taking notes). But might it not be valuable and informative to encourage a broader range of receptions? During screenings of Andy Warhol's furniture films – such as *Kiss* (1963), *Blow Job* (1964), and *Empire* – I have told my students to feel free to converse, text and play games with their mobile phones. (A number of students, who were initially sceptical of Warhol's cinema, told me that this approach enabled them to enjoy his films.) During screenings of *The Flicker*, I have encouraged students to close their eyes, look away from the screen, and move to different parts of the room throughout the screening to get a sense of how this alters the film's hallucinatory effects. I am currently preparing to screen *Five* in a world cinema class. Perhaps the time has come for me to encourage my students to fall asleep.

NOTES

1. Perhaps one day I shall arrange a midnight screening of *Sleep*, one in which spectators are asked to sleep through the film, thus creating a delicious symmetry between subject and object. (But object of what? The gaze? The gaze has disappeared, hasn't it?)
2. For an exemplary analysis of Ozu's aesthetic, see Nornes, 2007.
3. These quotations come from Kiarostami's *Around Five* (2005), a documentary on the making of *Five* that is included as a special feature in the Kino DVD of *Five*. Unless otherwise indicated, all quotations from Kiarostami in this chapter are taken from *Around Five*.
4. In its deceptive simplicity, *Five* has deep affinities with another experimental film by Kiarostami entitled *Seagull Eggs* (date unknown). This obscure, yet compelling, short film displays three eggs on jagged rocks at the beach. The waves attempt to steal the eggs, one by one, until, by the end of the film, all the eggs have been captured by the sea. While *Seagull Eggs* looks like a single seventeen-minute shot of nature, the superficial simplicity masks a deeper complexity. Kiarostami actually bought goose eggs, painted them, placed them on the rocks, and recorded hours of footage. The 'long take' of the film is, in fact, composed of almost thirty shots blended together seamlessly. (And the soundtrack of the film was also carefully constructed: Kiarostami added the sound effect of a gull crying out each time an egg was taken by the sea.) See Sani, 2015: 10–15.
5. Kara further argues that *Five*'s aesthetic provides an alternative to 'human-centered vision', and she intriguingly links this 'new media ecology' with the recent 'nonhuman turn' in the humanities and social sciences (2013: 583). For more on the nonhuman turn, see Grusin, 2015.
6. These comments are taken from an interview with Jamsheed Akrami which is included on Criterion's DVD release of *Taste of Cherry*. (The interview was initially recorded for Akrami's 2000 documentary, *Friendly Persuasion: Iranian Cinema After the 1979 Revolution*.)
7. In addition to calling *Un Chien Andalou* 'a passionate call for murder' (Williams, 1996: 200), Buñuel also claims to have put stones in his pockets when the film premiered, just in case he needed to fend off an angry, riotous mob (1983: 106).
8. My mother has informed that the first film I ever saw was Steven Spielberg's *E.T. The Extra-Terrestrial* (1982), which I saw shortly after my birth on 5 June 1982. I cannot recall whether or not I stayed awake for this film.

BIBLIOGRAPHY

Andrew, Geoff (2005), *10* (London: British Film Institute).
Brown, William (2011), 'Sleeping in the Cinema', blog posting, retrieved from

http://wjrcbrown.wordpress.com/2011/06/21/sleeping-in-the-cinema/ [accessed 23 February 2015]

Brown, William (2014), 'Complexity and Simplicity in *Inception* and *Five Dedicated to Ozu*', in W. Buckland (ed.), *Hollywood Puzzle Films* (New York: Routledge), pp. 125–39.

Buñuel, Luis (1983), *My Last Sigh*, trans. A. Israel, Minneapolis: University of Minnesota Press.

Cage, John (1973), *Silence: Lectures and Writings by John Cage* (Middleton, CT: Wesleyan University Press).

Dick, Vivienne (1989), 'Warhol: Won't Wrinkle Ever: A Film-Maker's View', in M. O'Pray (ed.), *Andy Warhol: Film Factory* (London: British Film Institute), pp. 154–9.

Flanagan, Matthew (2012), *'Slow Cinema': Temporality and Style in Contemporary Art and Experimental Film*, unpublished PhD dissertation, University of Exeter.

Grusin, Richard (ed.) (2015), *The Nonhuman Turn* (Minneapolis, MN: University of Minnesota Press).

Hirschman, Ruth (2004), 'Pop Goes the Artist', in Kenneth Goldsmith (ed.), *I'll Be Your Mirror: The Selected Andy Warhol Interviews* (New York: Carroll and Graf), pp. 27–46.

Jaffe, Ira (2014), *Slow Movies: Countering the Cinema of Action* (New York: Columbia University Press).

Jeffries, Stuart (2005), 'Landscapes of the Mind', *The Guardian* online, 16 April, retrieved from http://www.theguardian.com/film/2005/apr/16/art [accessed 23 February 2015].

Joseph, B. W. (2008), *Beyond the Dream Syndicate: Tony Conrad and the Arts After Cage* (New York: Zone).

Kara, Selmin (2013), 'The Sonic Summons: Meditations on Nature and Anempathetic Sound in Digital Documentaries', in C. Vernalis, A. Herzog, and J. Richardson (eds), *The Oxford Handbook of Sound and Image in Digital Media* (Oxford: Oxford University Press), pp. 582–97.

Man Ray (2000), 'Cinemage', in P. Hammond (trans. and ed.), *The Shadow and Its Shadow: Surrealist Writings on the Cinema*, 3rd ed. (San Francisco, CA: City Lights Books), pp. 133–4.

Nornes, Abé Mark (2007), 'The Riddle of the Vase: Ozu Yasujirō's *Late Spring* (1949)', in A. Phillips and J. Stringer (eds), *Japanese Cinema: Texts and Contexts* (London: Routledge), pp. 78–101.

Remes, Justin (2015), *Motion(less) Pictures: The Cinema of Stasis* (New York: Columbia University Press).

Richmond, Scott (2016, forthcoming), *Proprioceptive Aesthetics* (Minneapolis, MN: University of Minnesota Press).

Sani, Mahmoud Reza (2013), *Men at Work: Cinematic Lessons from Abbas Kiarostami* (Los Angeles, CA: Mhughes Press).

Swinton, Tilda (2006), 'State of Cinema Address: 49th San Francisco International Film Festival, 29 April 2006', *Critical Quarterly* 48, no. 3, 110–20.

Warhol, Andy, and Pat Hackett (1990), *Popism: The Warhol Sixties* (San Diego, CA: Harvest/HBJ).

Williams, Linda (1996), 'The Critical Grasp: Buñuelian Cinema and Its Critics', in R. E. Kuenzli (ed.), *Dada and Surrealist Film* (Cambridge, MA: MIT Press), pp. 199–206.

Young, La Monte (1965), 'Lecture 1960', *Tulane Drama Review* 10, no. 2, 73–83.

PART V

THE ETHICS AND POLITICS OF SLOWNESS

17. BÉLA TARR: THE POETICS AND THE POLITICS OF FICTION

Jacques Rancière

I must make a preliminary remark about my title: we have been used to opposing the invention of fictions to the reality of things. Fiction, however, is not the invention of non-existing beings. It is a structure of rationality. It is, firstly, a practice of presentation that makes things, situations, characters and events perceptible. Next, it is a practice of linkage which constructs forms of coexistence, succession and causality between events so as to make sense of those connections. In this respect, there is fiction wherever and whenever a sense of the real and of its intelligibility must be constructed. Politics and social science construct fictions as well as literature. Conversely, the forms of avowed fiction can both reveal and question the modes of presentation of things and connection of events at work in politics and social science or in the discourse of the media.

In this respect the case of cinema is a privileged one because it is an art that creates fictions through the assemblage of fragments of time. And Béla Tarr's cinema is a still more privileged case for two reasons: he is one of the filmmakers most committed to making time the very stuff of cinematic fiction. Moreover this commitment to the materiality of time is implemented in the construction of fictions dealing with an explicitly political context which is itself a matter of time. He started making films in Communist Hungary. At that moment, he pitted the official rhythm of the construction of socialism against the everyday ways of life, problems and aspirations of ordinary people. Then, his major films witnessed the decline and fall of Communism and, after its fall, the advent of a world apparently devoid of any orientation and any faith in the future. In short, his films deal with the end of the faith in the historical advent of a new world of freedom and equality and with the disenchantment regarding the capitalist promise following the collapse of the socialist one. It must be added that he made his films in collaboration with a novelist, László Krasznahorkai, who provided him with gloomy stories wherein mean and grotesque characters are manipulated by swindlers who falsely promise them either personal profit or collective paradises.

Béla Tarr's films thus deal with this overdetermined plot of the 'end' – end of utopias if not end of history or end of politics – that became so pervasive in the 1990s. This is why it is interesting to see how he – slightly – transformed this nihilistic plot and how he used for this the specific resources of cinema. I would like to show that the main aspect of his poetics consists in a move from the scenario of the end of illusions to the very matrix of production of so-called illusions. This move allows him to make time no more the empty medium in which a plot of illusion unfolds but the material fabric from which the expectations that produce illusions are engendered. Consequently, he can reconstruct the characters belonging to the plot of the end out of their material experience of lived time and give them the capacity of changing the plot of manipulation from the inside. Such are the shift and the twist that I would like to explore by examining a few sequences of three films.

I will start from *Damnation* (*Kárhozat*, 1998) which certainly is the most nihilistic among Tarr's films. It is the story of a sordid scheme imagined by a café owner who wants to hire somebody to go to seek out for him unspecified compromising wares. He proposes the deal to the hero of the story, Karrer, who declines the proposition but proposes someone else, namely the husband of the woman – a singer – with whom he has a love affair. From this point on, each of the four accomplices will betray the others. At the end, Karrer denounces the other three to the police and ends up barking with the dogs in a puddle. It is, therefore, a damnation without any salvation except the artistic salvation that displaces the interest from the story to the sensible duration from which it emerges. This is what I want to show by examining two shots that take place in the first part of the film. The first one shows us a street in the rain in front of the nightclub where the woman sings (Figure 17.1). In a way, this shot is a narrative articulation in the story. Karrer is expecting the arrival of the husband to whom he wants to propose the deal. But the way the scene is constructed clearly overturns the logic of the story: the street in the rain is not the place where the action of the characters takes place. Instead, the space is there before them and it is the milieu that shapes them. The real action is the affect that this milieu produces on them. This 'milieu' firstly is a historical landscape: the small industrial town which had probably been part of the big industrial and socialist project before being abandoned. We are among the wrecks of the socialist voyage into the future, and this feeling of wreckage is

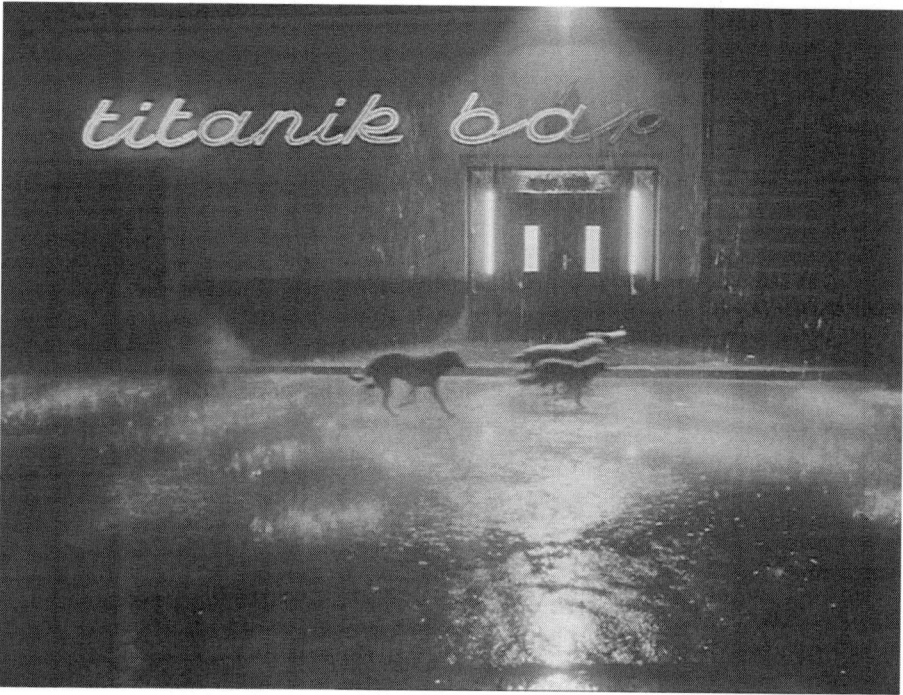

Figure 17.1   Still from *Damnation* (1998).

echoed by the neon letters displaying the name of the nightclub, *Titanik*. At the same time, it is a mythological landscape which is emphasised by a horde of dogs. The threat of animality, the threat of the non-human and possibly the inhuman is present almost everywhere in Tarr's films, running alongside these stories of swindle and betrayal. Now the mythological and the historical merge into the same element, the rain. The rain is, at the same time, an entirely material element and the condensation of a whole situation. In a way, it is the zero degree of history; it is that which falls, only falls, always falls and ceaselessly penetrates the bodies and the souls.

This penetration implies a determinate status of the bodies in the space and time of the fiction. In the same shot, a movement of the camera has shown us the back of Karrer waiting on the other side of the street (Figure 17.2). We see a body who is looking but we don't see his look. Nor do we see what he sees. This would require a shot plus a reverse shot. This is the most usual device in filmic narration: we see a fragment of space in a fragment of time, playing the role of the cause. Then another fragment of space in another fragment of time plays the role of the effect. Such a division of time and space makes a link between the mastery of the character with that of the film-maker and

Figure 17.2   Still from *Damnation* (1998).

also with that of the spectator. In the traditional logic of storytelling, seeing means having, both before one's eyes and in one's mind, the elements of a situation. This is what connects the logic of the stories with the 'normal' ways of constructing reality, notably in the media: you perceive at once the thing and its meaning which also means that you know what can happen out of them. But there is nothing as such in Béla Tarr's films. Space and time are not the frame within which events happen. They are material realities. The characters and what they see are included in the same space. That's why the right form of articulation between the visual structure of the shot and the narrative structure of the whole is the sequence shot. Béla Tarr's sequence shots, however, have two main characteristics which specify his films. Firstly they take 'too much' time. Their length always exceeds what is required to select the visual elements which make the story intelligible, and this is why his films are often categorised under the rubric of 'slow cinema', as per the title of this collection. This is most obvious in the long scenes of walking. In a 'normal' film, when somebody needs to go somewhere, we see him or her leaving the first place, then arriving at the second one. In a film by Béla Tarr, we see them walking until they get to their destination. This is so because walking is a material activity instead of being a mere narrative transition. But, if the sequence shot takes too much time, it also embraces too little space. It introduces the viewers into a space that cannot be embraced from a privileged point of view. The view is obstructed by the content of the space. In this shot, our perception is obstructed by Karrer's body and by the iron railing. But it is a general feature in Tarr's films: there are always bodies obstructing the view. Consequently, either one does not see or one must go round to see what was unseen. And it is an operation that takes time. The situation is never encompassed as a whole. It is grasped through the production of a global affect that requires time to be produced. This is what is obvious in the sequence which comes just after this one in *Damnation* when we are inside the *Titanik* and the camera slowly goes around the room, the customers, the singer and the musicians in a six-minute shot.

In this sequence, the rain has been internalised in the form of an art of time, namely music. Music here shifts from its usual status of 'illustration' to a structural function. On a first level, the desperate song of the singer, telling the end of love, the end of illusions and so on, epitomises the desolation of the environment. But those desperate words were already anticipated by the six notes that are obsessively repeated and even accompanied by a metronome which reduces them to a mere tick-tock: the noise of the rain inside, of the rain in the bodies and the souls. But that's not all. Music is not only an art among others. It is also an idea of art. Since Schopenhauer, it has embodied the idea of the anti-representative art which expresses a power of affection exceeding the forms of identification of situations and emotions provided by the representative arts. It has become the art of the unnameable. The unnameable is not the monstrous or the horrible. It is just the global affect that penetrates the bodies without being identifiable and nameable. This is how the milieu, the rain, the law of repetition are condensed in a common-sensory fabric. Music then has a structural role instead of being an illustration of the story. But there is something more: cinema itself takes on the power of music, the power of condensing the global affect that exceeds the identification of feelings and emotions in the traditional narrative logic. But this condensation, itself, can be perceived only by way of a distension of time. It requires the time taken by the camera to move from a partial point of condensation to another one; here, for instance, from the columns and the moulding of the ceiling to the glasses on the tables, the characters – some of them immobile as if they were sticking to their seats, some others discussing at the bar, without us knowing what they say, the eyes of the singer, her hands, the arpeggios of the keyboard and so on and so forth (Figures 17.3 and 17.4). In another shot, in the café, the camera will circulate between the characters seated around a table, the shock of billiard balls, characters standing at the bar, the sound of an accordion, a smile, a knife knocking a glass or scratching a plate, and so on. There are always in a shot things which appear and disappear and things which are heard without

Figure 17.3   Still from *Damnation* (1998).

Figure 17.4   Still from *Damnation* (1998).

being seen. But, in the same way that there is no reverse shot, there is no off-screen. Everything is in the shot, everything takes part in the production of the global affect. We could say that Tarr practises a form of haptic montage by touching one thing after another. I am referring here to the notion elaborated by Gilles Deleuze in *Cinema 2: The Time Image*. Deleuze illustrates this notion with an image that is not very convincing because it is a perfectly functional action: the wallet passing from hand to hand in *Pickpocket* (1959). Instead, Béla Tarr practises an authentic haptic montage as it makes the viewers experience a sensible continuum that can be presented only by way of the obstructed movement which goes from a point of condensation to another one. This means that his films are made of blocks of time but those blocks of time are not crystal images as Deleuze defines them: images emancipated from movement and emerging from the void so as to connect the actual and the virtual, the past and the present, the real and the imaginary. Instead, they construct time as the lived experience of the possibility or impossibility of movement. They do so by focusing on a particular form of experience of time: the experience of expectation. Expectation is this form of condensation and distension of time that opens up to either the repetition of the same or the apparition of the new, either the inertia that internalises the rain or a deviation, a bifurcation, the production of a new movement. It this deviation, or correction of the movement, that I should like to examine out of two sequences, borrowed from *Satantango* (*Sátántangó*, 1994) and *Werckmeister Harmonies* (*Werckmeister Harmóniák*, 2000). Both of them are stories of manipulation. Béla Tarr, however, takes hold of the characters of the victims of the manipulation, the *idiots*, so as to superimpose on the plot of manipulation a visual plot that diverges from it, a plot of deviation of the movement. The idiots then witness the capacity of the most destitute persons to split up the time of repetition and to break the round-and-round movement which it engenders in order to draw straight lines or harmonious circles.

This is the case in *Satantango*. The film tells the story of a big swindle that takes place in a small village after the liquidation of a collective farm. The survivors are about to share out the money from the cattle that they have sold, and to seek their fortunes elsewhere, when the eloquent swindler, Irimias, comes and persuades them to give him the money to create a new collective farm. To persuade them he takes advantage of the guilt which they feel about the suicide of the most destitute member of the community, a young girl, Estike, who had been cheated by her own brother. He had taught her the wisdom of the new age: being a winner. That's why she had gone with him and buried her money so that it would grow into a bush of gold coins; after that she has tortured and poisoned her cat, the only living being over which she could win. In the meantime, of course, the brother has stolen the money and, when she perceives the swindle, Estike starts walking, with the dead cat under her arms, up to a ruined castle where she kills herself with the same rat poison. Her suicide is the event that allows the big swindle to work: the peasants are convinced by Irimias's rhetoric that they must change their lives: they give him the money and abandon everything to get to the future collective farm which is, in fact, a devastated manor, where Irimias will tell them that their project is postponed and that, in the meantime, they must disperse throughout the region.

Such is the plot provided by the novelist. But, at the very articulation between the little swindle and the big one, the film-maker imposes its own scenario, a visual scenario that subverts the plot by subverting the figure of the idiot. This subversion can be seen in three shots. In the first one, Estike is looking, from the outside, through the window of the inn where the drunk villagers turn round in a grotesque and obscene dance. Such is the circling movement of internalisation of the 'rain' (Figure 17.5). Then come two long sequence shots of walk, the first one taking place at night and the second in the morning light. In those two sequence shots the straight line of the walk gives to the film-maker the opportunity to reconstruct the figure of the idiot. He does it by way of three main procedures, three main dissociations.

The first one, most perceptible in the first shot, is a dissociation between the visual and the sound. We hear Estike's steps but we don't see them. Nor do we see the muddy land. We see only her face and her shoulders in the darkness. We perceive the resolution on that face that seems to project itself towards the final destination. Estike's resolution has become entirely material and we 'hear' it in the rhythmed pace of the steps. It must be noted that the dissociation

Figure 17.5   Still from *Satantango* (1994).

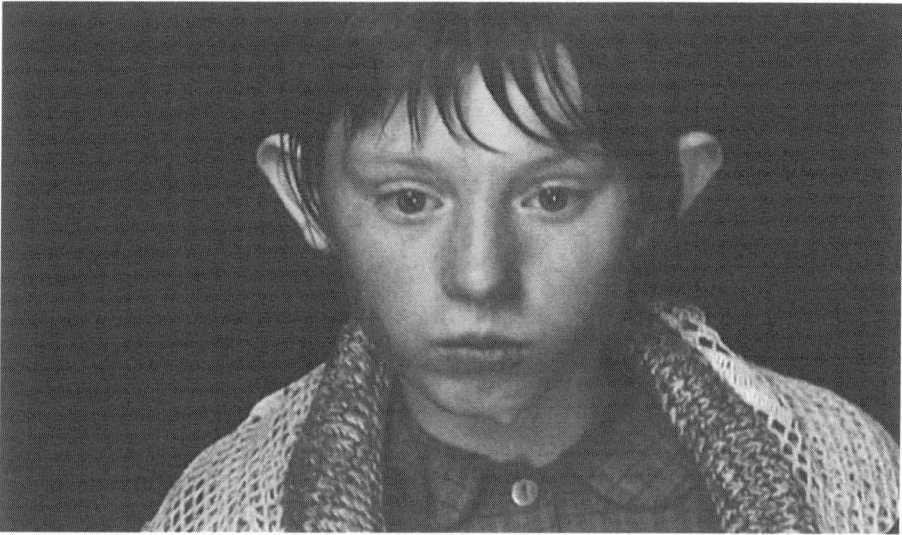

Figure 17.6 Still from *Satantango* (1994).

between the visual and the sound does not work here as it is often described, as a form of fragmentation or critical disorientation. On the contrary, it works here as an addition that emphasises the movement straight away, far from the circles of repetition (Figure 17.6).

Then comes a dissociation inside the visual itself. This is most perceptible in the second shot. It is a medium shot in the grey light of the morning that makes perceptible, along with the desolated environment, the fatigue of her body. She seems to wear on her shoulders not only the weight of the long walk but also a whole universe of rain, mud and misery. This is visible in the piling up of all the clothes which are packed over one another and, notably, the cardigan which is too big for her and the lace curtain that she has fashioned into a shawl. Moreover she wears her crime – the dead cat – under her left arm. Her protruding eyes do not seem to see any more. She walks like an automat. But precisely this very automatism becomes a positive force. It means the transformation of inertia into movement. Her walk becomes the sole manifestation of the inner force that sets all this weight into movement and continuously resets a body on the verge of its collapse. The idiocy is thus reconstructed as the combination of two capacities: the capacity of absorbing and incorporating the rule of the outside, the empire of the rain, and the capacity of putting that misery in motion, of betting against it out of the very 'virtue' of the idiots, their way of taking everything literally (Figure 17.7).

This virtue itself works by way of a third dissociation, a dissociation between the visual and the words. In the novel, Estike's walk is accompanied

Figure 17.7   Still from *Satantango* (1994).

by her 'idiot' reflections. Estike tells herself that everything makes sense, every-thing is fine. She understands the meaning of her story. She believes that the angels will come and take her. In such a way, she adds to the empirical idiocy, which consists in believing any incredible tale, the transcendental idiocy, which consists in thinking that life and death make sense. Béla Tarr dissociates those reflections from her walk and puts them off to the end of the episode: they are told by a voice-over when Estike has reached the term of her travel, when she is no longer here.

Idiocy is thus visually reconstructed in the time of the sequence shot as a form of correction of movement, a form of reappropriation of one's destiny. Estike commits suicide but she makes *hers* the way that leads to that suicide. From this point onwards, the visual and plastic power of those two shots will be transmitted to the whole story and produce an inner splitting of the plot. The peasants will be cheated and stolen from because of Estike's death. But, because of Estike's walk, the manipulation will be split from the inside. It will become a positive mobilisation of their bodies; they will tear themselves away from the circle of repetition and spinelessness and draw the straight line making them face the unknown. This gives their strength to the extraordinary sequences showing their arrival in the devastated manor which is supposed to be the place of their new community. Firstly, we follow a peasant woman holding a lantern and we discover with her the dilapidation of the walls (Figure 17.8). Then, suddenly, a slow movement of the camera, accompanied by a strange musical phrase, pans across the faces of each member of the

Figure 17.8   Still from *Satantango* (1994).

community – one after another – their heads isolated in the dark and their eyes fixing the same point above them. This shot, which looks like the unfolding of a reel, also creates an affect which has no name. It is neither disappointment nor anger. It is the pure encounter with the unknown. The villagers have lost their habits and their bearings, their usual way of looking at the same repetitive spectacle. It seems that they are trying to take the full measure of the unknown which falls upon them and to see how they can lift up themselves to its level (Figures 17.9 and 17.10). This encounter splits up the plot of manipulation. It allows them to draw their own line up to the place of their final dispersion, a straight line that diverges from the circle of the plot which goes back to its point of departure.

Werckmeister Harmonies presents us with another case of bifurcation of time and of correction of movement, wherein the performance of the 'idiot' and the performance of the film-maker are reflected on to each other. It appears in the ten-minute shot which opens the film. It takes place in a café at the moment when the café owner starts to throw the regulars out before closing. Something happens then: one of the customers asks the postman, Valuszka, to give his performance: the representation of the movement of the planets. In the novel, it was a grotesque scene: the drunkards only exploited the hobby of the 'idiot', fond of the celestial harmony, to delay the closing time. They laughed at him, gesticulated stupidly and eventually staggered and fell upon one another. Nothing like that happens here. It all starts with the ceremonious gesture of the customer who asks Valuszka to give his performance and

Figure 17.9   Still from *Satantango* (1994).

Figure 17.10   Still from *Satantango* (1994).

the others to clear the room (Figures 17.11 and 17.12). What happens then is the demonstration of another way of turning round that we can exactly pit against the disordered and obscene scene that Estike saw through the window in *Satantango*. Not coincidentally, it is the same actor who played the clown in

Figure 17.11   Still from *Werckmeister Harmonies* (2000).

Figure 17.12   Still from *Werckmeister Harmonies* (2000).

that scene who plays the master of ceremonies and the sun here. The regulars take the proposal to represent the spectacle of immortality seriously and they progressively get into the circle (Figures 17.13 and 17.14). They break the rule of rain, mud and repetition. They exchange it for another sort of repetition: the

Figure 17.13   Still from *Werckmeister Harmonies* (2000).

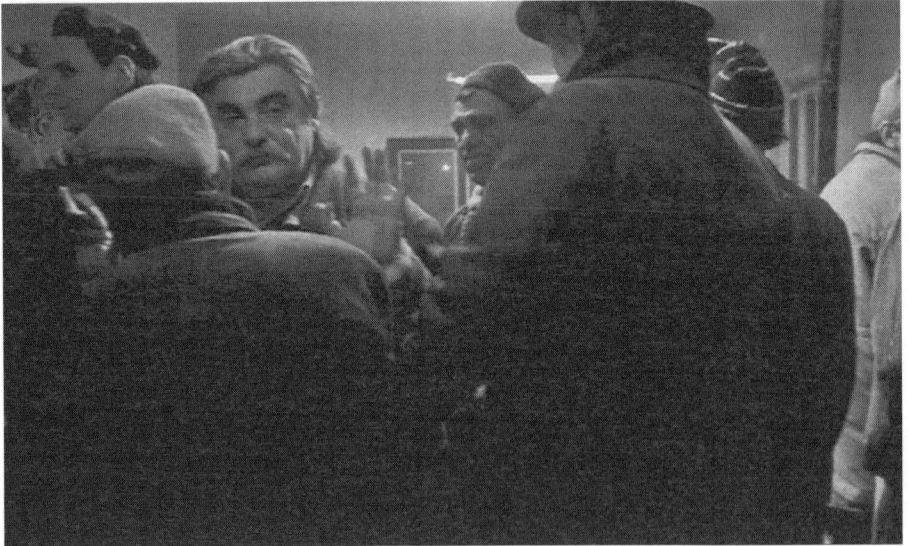

Figure 17.14   Still from *Werckmeister Harmonies* (2000).

eternal repetition of the ordered movement of the planets which also has some dramatic episodes (the eclipse of the sun and the glaciation that suspend life for a moment before the restoration of the order). They carry out an experiment: a rectification of movement, a kind of spiritual redemption which is, at the same time, entirely material. They discover a capacity to be an actor in the celestial harmony which belongs to everyone.

In his prose poem, *Conflict*, Mallarmé staged the relationship between the poet who looks at the magnificence of the sunset and the drunk workers who obstruct his horizon as they are lying on the grass, sleeping off the Sunday binges. He says he would like to fix a few points of light on this 'blind herd' in spite of those 'sealed eyes' that don't perceive them. Here, Valuszka fixes such points of light, and he fixes them on eyes that perceive them. But this is also what Béla Tarr does himself: he takes characters abandoned by history, living in an aftertime of mean and grotesque stories, and he gives them back their capacity and their dignity by a certain way of making them turn and of turning with them. In fact, each of the movements and episodes which make up Valuszka's performance can also characterise Béla Tarr's performance. The eclipse of the sun echoes the obstacle course of the camera blocked by the movement of the bodies and those black bands that so often invade the screen because of that obstruction. In the same way the invasion of coldness, narrated by Valuszka, evokes the 'austerity' of Tarr's *mise en scène*, its slow pace and apparent impassiveness which are required for creating the global affect that also is the milieu of a possible conversion. The performance of the *mise en scène* and the performance of the character exactly echo each other. There is a correspondence between a materialist poetics and a political attempt to wrest the characters from the nihilistic scenario of the 'post-history' and create the positive dynamism of a 'time after'. This attempt implies a tension between the scenario and the *mise en scène*. In the plot provided by the novel, the celestial harmony is destroyed by the schemes of the manipulators. The story revolves around the disquieting arrival in a small provincial town of a long truck containing two attractions: a gigantic stuffed whale and a mysterious 'prince'. As a threatening crowd gathers around the truck and occupies the square, a group of schemers tries to capitalise on the unrest and the fear and expects the unleashing of the mob to take over the power in the name of the defence of the honest citizens. As it turns out, the 'prince' calls the mob to destroy everything. The celestial dreamer, Valuszka, is then carried by the mob and he witnesses the mob ransacking the hospital and beating up the sick. After that he escapes the justice of the 'honest citizens' only by being sent to an asylum when we see him sitting absolutely silent and motionless.

Such is the justice of the plot. But it is overturned by the 'poetic justice' of the *mise en scène*. The unfolding of the intrigue leads to the victory of the schemers. But their power as schemers is strictly counterbalanced by their cinematographic insignificance. They weigh almost nothing in the cinematographic density of the film. Those who are given presence and density are the 'victims': Valuszka, with his performance of celestial harmony, and his patron and friend, the musician Ezter, who wants to go back to the 'natural harmonies' dismissed by the modern harmonic system initiated by Andreas Werckmeister. Both are crushed as characters in the story. But they are given in exchange the sensory presence and density that make the film what it is. It is particularly the case with Valuszka. He is not only a dreamer, he is, throughout the film, the character who dares take the measure of the extraordinary, be it the harmony of the planets, the eye of the dead whale or the unleashing of the mob. He is the character who tries to rise to the level of their common intensity. In such a way, what we see is not just the deviation of the straight line straying from the circle of repetition. It is the opposition of two sensible worlds. The poetics and the politics of Tarr's films, then, are connected by way of two principles. Firstly, they break the monotonous narration of the 'post', thought of as a homogeneous time in which everything turns at the same rhythm in the same circle. Instead they construct a dissensus, an opposition of two sensible worlds, which reopens time as the site of the possible. Secondly, they identify this disruption of the dominant narrative with the affirmation of the capacity of anyone at all. It is not a grandiose political action but it is a consistent one.

18. ETHICS OF THE LANDSCAPE SHOT: *AKA SERIAL KILLER* AND JAMES BENNING'S PORTRAITS OF CRIMINALS

Julian Ross

Between 11 October and 5 November 1968, teenager Nagayama Norio murdered four people in a killing spree across Japan with a handgun stolen from a United States army base.[1] In November 1957 at Plainfield, Wisconsin, Ed Gein was arrested for the murder of Bernice Worden and, confessing to the killing of another person, he was later convicted for a series of now infamous crimes. In June 1984, sixteen-year-old cheerleader Bernadette Protti stabbed her classmate to death in Orinda, California. Between 1978 and 1995, mathematician Ted Kaczynski, nicknamed the Unabomber, planted and posted handmade bombs in a nationwide attack in the United States, killing three people and injuring another twenty-three.

Spanning a spectrum of motivations from personal to political, what the four cases have in common are not only that their actions ended the lives of others but also that they became subjects of films which abided by an ethics of representation that portrayed them as fellow people. Disconcerted with the ways in which the news media illustrated these criminals, the makers of the films sought alternatives to the lures of narrative to which such outlets succumbed, and resorted to a film-making strategy that accommodates many of the tropes which have been described in this volume as slow cinema. The first, Nagayama Norio, was depicted in the film *Ryakushō renzoku shasatsuma* (*AKA Serial Killer*, 1969) shot by a collective of young Japanese film-makers who sought an alternative mode of address to what was offered by the media in the illustration of their subject's life. For the film-makers, the rejection of drama, the implementation of long takes and stationary shots provided them with a method in which they were able to avoid imposing a narrative on to their subject and encourage the audience to arrive at their own understanding of events. They gave their method the name *fūkeiron* (landscape theory) in reference to the landscapes that the shots depicted, and debated the relevance of the approach in ensuing years. Some decades later, American film-maker James Benning faced a similar set of ethical issues when he sought to illustrate the lives of criminals in a series of films in the 1980s and, once again, in the 2010s. Seemingly unaware of the Japanese film-makers, Benning arrived at a similar solution by applying his signature long takes and static shots which have since been categorised as features of slow cinema.

This chapter aims to bring together the two unrelated activities by the Japanese film-makers and by James Benning that show remarkable resonance with one another. It proposes that their approach to filming the lives of the criminals are rooted in a shared desire to establish an ethical relationship with their subjects and the audience of their films. Developing in chronological order, the chapter will first introduce the documentary project *AKA Serial Killer* and the subsequent outcome of the project articulated in writing as theory of landscape (*fūkeiron*). The film will be presented here as a precursor to the contemporary trend in world cinema described as slow cinema, with which it shares many characteristics. Secondly, the chapter will proceed to discuss James Benning's *Landscape Suicide* (1987) as a comparative cross-Pacific counterpart to *AKA Serial Killer* in its ethical stance towards film-making. The chapter will conclude by exploring the persistence of the methodology in Benning's most recent *Two Cabins Project* (2007–continuing). Through the analysis of the three projects, the chapter will propose an objective behind the stylistic features of slow cinema to be the production of an ethical cinema where slowness is employed not only as a methodology against studio and conventional film-making but also against approaches to representation in general. In the three projects in which the film-makers follow the footsteps of their subjects, the chapter will suggest, the slowness which is implemented in their journeys not only positions the directors with their documentary subjects but also creates an opportunity for sharing a durational experience with their audience.

AKA Serial Killer

Nagayama Norio, the first in the list of criminals mentioned in the introduction, became the documentary subject of *AKA Serial Killer*, collectively directed by film-maker Adachi Masao, scriptwriter Sasaki Mamoru, film critic Matsuda Masao, Iwabuchi Susumu, Nonomura Masayuki and Yamazaki Yutaka. Made in a climate of social unrest running up to the re-signing of the Anpo United States–Japan Security Treaty, the film-makers bore witness to the ways in which protestors and their actions were filtered in the news media through a politics of sensation, codified representations and a magnetic attraction to images of violence. Upon being apprehended on 7 April 1969, Nagayama similarly became a target of media furore and his background and personal history a subject of interrogation by reporters seeking an intelligible explanation for his actions. According to the story proposed for general readership, Nagayama's criminality derived from a deprived upbringing, being brought up in a poor and dysfunctional family. After completing junior high school, Nagayama took part in a group employment programme where school leavers were recruited from rural towns to Tokyo factories to support the burgeoning economy, which was surmised by the papers to have worsened his feelings of isolation and anonymity. The causal and digestible narrative was implemented, for example, in Shindō Kaneto's *Hadaka no jyūkyūsai* (*Live Today, Die Tomorrow!*, 1970) a fiction film, based on Nagayama's case, where a teenage killer's action is suggested to have been a consequence of urban alienation. In fact, Nagayama had restlessly decamped from one place to another, up and down the islands of Japan, complicating the dichotomy between rural and urban space which is explicitly addressed by Matsuda as redundant in the contemporary age where Tokyo and rural villages now look

Figure 18.1   Still from *AKA Serial Killer* (1969). Copyright Adachi Masao Screening Committee.

the same (2013: 26). Frustrated by the anecdotal reports from the media, which categorically imposed a way to comprehend his story, the collective of film-makers decided to trace Nagayama's footsteps, with awareness that their questions would probably remain unanswered. [2]

In their travels chasing the shadow of Nagayama Norio, the collective of film-makers arrived at a distinctive method of shooting that was consistent with their ethical stance concerning the portrayal of others. The resulting film, described by Adachi Masao as a 'process' and 'scenario hunting', was primarily composed of long takes of landscapes Nagayama may or may not have seen in his journey across the archipelago of Japan.[3] Providing a counterpoint to the strategies of news media, the mostly static shots deflate all sense of sensation or drama in their composition by avoiding assigning centrality or points of focus. A recurring shot of the film is a 360-degree pan that embodies the process of searching initiated by the film-makers. The little action in play, both on- and off-screen avoids the codes of storytelling to propel the film forward while, with its lack of sequential emphasis, the editing encapsulates the sense of aimless wander of the film crew and their subject. With complete absence of dialogue, the film sparsely distributes a voice-over read out by Adachi Masao. He narrates Nagayama's life with a resolutely de-dramatised delivery based upon a series of facts, suspicious of the capacity for language to foist interpretation. Though not all shots in the film share the stylistic characteristics of slow cinema, the film's cumulative effect certainly resonates with its tenets, described by Matthew Flanagan as 'a certain undramatic sensibility or nascent durational style' (2012: 6). What the film-makers hoped to achieve, through the accumulation of these stylistic strategies, was an opportunity for contemplation as an alternative to representations in news media.

In their critical writing that followed the production of the film, Matsuda Masao, Adachi Masao and Iwabuchi Susumu articulated their ethics of film-making as fūkeiron (theory of landscape), and their debates concerning the method ensued on the pages of Eiga Hihyō (Film Criticism), an activist film journal Matsuda relaunched as chief editor in 1970, among other journal publications. During this period, AKA Serial Killer struggled to be released and it was not seen until six years after its completion in 1975 when it received a cinema release. Thus, though the process of making the film was what had informed the theoretical writing of fūkeiron, the audience of the film would have been familiar with the concept first and, in some cases, even films subsequently made based on fūkeiron.[4] One realisation at which they arrived during the process of film-making was the homogeneity of landscape in the age of modern industry which is suggested by the film-makers to have been a contributing factor in driving Nagayama's antisocial behaviour. Matsuda Masao, who described himself as the spokesperson of fūkeiron, suggested that the homogenisation of landscape was carried out by state authority and was spreading at accelerated speed (2013: 286). Describing the landscape to be the same wherever he went across the islands of Japan, Matsuda went on to propose that 'the only way Nagayama Norio could tear through this landscape was to pull the trigger' (2013: 133). In the film, the uniformity of landscape is made visible with the banners of advertisements and logos that are present throughout the shots of cities and rural villages. For example, after the voice-over which describes Nagayama's arrival in Osaka, the montages of streets in the city show scenes of activity with banners in the background advertising the upcoming 1970 World Exposition, a clear marker by state and industry to celebrate Japan's rising status in the world economy. Though these convictions voiced by the film-makers in writing may be sensed in the shots, it is never explicated, as their ethical stance goes against the imposition of interpretation on their viewers. The long takes, stationary camera positions and the de-dramatised sense of motion in these images allow space for contemplation by the audience to reach their own conclusions regarding to what extent the landscapes which Nagayama inhabited were responsible for driving the teenager into criminal acts.

Recent writing, looking back at the political value of *fūkeiron*, has focused primarily on what the film-makers discovered in the process of shooting the landscapes in *AKA Serial Killer*. Hirasawa Go notes that the landscapes in *AKA Serial Killer* depict not only the omnipresence of state authority but also the capitalist economy that contributed to the homogenisation of the nation (2013: 329). In the most comprehensive account of *fūkeiron* in the English language so far, Yuriko Furuhata suggests the invisibility and seamless integration of sovereign control, with such systems of organisation as traffic control, infrastructure development and urban planning, are conveyed in the landscapes of *AKA Serial Killer* (2013: 142–3). Indeed, it was the discovery by the film-makers that the landscapes across the Japanese islands were indistinguishable from one another that had set the foundations for the critical debates on *fūkeiron*. Nevertheless, I should like to propose that the lasting value of *fūkeiron* lies not in the results of their film-making journey but in the approach they took to embark on it. As Furuhata notes, the stylistic techniques implemented in *AKA Serial Killer* were meant to counteract strategies of news media and other contemporary activist documentaries by the likes of Tsuchimoto Noriaki and Ogawa Shunsuke, both of whom show many scenes of protest and direct action (2013: 171). Upon visiting the 5 square metre flat in Nakano, Tokyo, where Nagayama lived for a period, Matsuda described feeling a shiver looking out of the small window realising the familiarity of the landscape he saw as something he also sees daily (2013: 132). As much as the stylistic strategies were a counteraction, it was also the desires of Matsuda and his colleagues to share their subject's point of view with their audience that resulted in a film-making method that accommodated slowness and contemplation.

AKA The Butcher of Plainfield

Some fourteen years after the completion of *AKA Serial Killer*, American film-maker James Benning began shooting a series of experimental documentaries based on the life of murderers in the United States. In response to the death of a friend, which was channelled directly in *Him and Me* (1981), Benning found himself attracted to the topic of murder for a loosely connected series of film projects, and explained that 'it was the ultimate way to understand about death' (quoted in Pichler, 2011: 84).[5] The first film, *American Dreams (lost and found)* (1984), is based on the murder case of Arthur Bremmer, who shot and paralysed Governor Wallace in 1972. The film is an intertextual play between word, image and sound, and juxtaposes the diary by Bremmer, faithfully rewritten and optically printed on to the film by Benning, together with pop music from the period and baseball cards that span the career of Hank Aaron, who became the hitter of the most home runs in the history of the game. The second, *Landscape Suicide* (1986), is a film about the serial killer Ed Gein and the cheerleader Bernadette Protti who ended the life of her classmate in 1984. The third, *Used Innocence* (1988), is a portrait of Lawrencia Bembenek, based in Benning's local Wisconsin, and the murder of her husband's ex-wife which she claims she had not committed. Despite being seemingly unaware of his Japanese counterparts and their methodology, Benning arrives at remarkably similar film-making techniques to the group of film-makers, who shot *AKA Serial Killer*, to render the lives of his subjects. Focusing on *Landscape Suicide*, this section will articulate the ways in which he echoes the Japanese film-makers in his stylistic strategies to propose that, unknown to him, Benning is an artist whose methodology has strong resonance with landscape theory (*fūkeiron*) as articulated in 1960s Japan.

Landscape Suicide is composed of two halves, which structurally mirror each other, with the first devoted to Bernadette Protti and the second to Ed Gein. Each half is further divided into two halves, one involving re-enactments of individual subjects undergoing police interrogation and the other with landscapes which surrounded their lives and the particular events. The staged re-enactments are both shot from a static position with the actors shot against a blank white wall in medium close-up. With the conversation based on the transcripts of the actual interviews, the actors deliver their responses to the questions posed by the off-screen interviewers in monotone delivery, limited gestures and absent facial expressions, rejecting an interpretation of their character into patterns of behaviour. Shot in the home towns of the murderers in Wisconsin and Orinda, California, the landscape shots in the film are captured in static long takes with compositions that disallow centrality within the frame, a formal strategy Benning employs in his rejection of didactic film-making. In describing *Landscape Suicide*, Barbara Pichler suggests, '[h]is images pose a question as to what can be read in the topography of the landscape, without directly providing an answer' (2011:85). Presented in the film as landscape shots, it is left uncertain for the audience whether it was the banality of the landscape that brought about the violence or the acts of murder and their aftermath that saturated the place with such coldness.

Images of landscapes are signature shots for James Benning whose work throughout his career has been imbued with a sense of space and place. Now established as a film-maker strongly associated with slow cinema, Benning has shot extreme long takes with landscapes as their central visual theme since his early short *9-1-75* (1975) up to his recent *BSNF* (2013). Benning's turn to digital cinema in recent years has produced works, such as *Nightfall* (2011) and *BSNF*, that show renewed dedication to landscapes and the long take. Shot entirely from one point of view and for the same period of time depicted in the film, the two films mark single takes of ninety minutes and 283 minutes, respectively, which were previously unattainable on the 16 mm film format. Despite being a stylistic characteristic to which Benning continuously returns, the application of landscape shots in *Landscape Suicide* is markedly different from that of his other films for they are real-life settings of the lives of his criminal subjects. As critic Katherine Dieckman attests, '[t]he homicides allow Benning to deal in emotion that is external to him (yet deeply felt), while imbuing his trademark "still" images . . . with newly charged meaning' (Dieckman 2002).

Similarly to the Japanese film-makers who shot *AKA Serial Killer*, James Benning expressed dissatisfaction with the media coverage of the two cases. Though Benning, like most of us, encountered the cases through news reports, he felt a certain compulsion to investigate further as the information he received was not enough for him to formulate an understanding of death, violence and murder. Further similarities with *AKA Serial Killer* can be established through the perpetual use of long takes and static shots in both films. A key difference can be noted, however, in Benning's use of sound and voice-over in *Landscape Suicide*. Voiced by a woman, the reconstruction of the events encompasses reports by the police, fragments from news media and responses from the cases by the community which are laid over the static images that are, at times, in correspondence with the spoken content and, at other times, not. Rather than succumbing to the possibility of dogmatism in voice-over narration, Benning offers multiple accounts and perspectives of the events that fragment them even further and convey the irreducible complexities of the murder cases and the impossibility of fully comprehending the actions. An approach to the voice-over which corresponds with *AKA Serial Killer*, however, is the disembodiment of the source of the voices that deliver these accounts, a strategy implemented by both to ensure the restriction of empathy from the audience. The disembodied voice-over is a method Benning returns to in his portrait of another criminal, Ted Kaczynski, the subject of his most recent film and a surrounding series of works that will be explored in the next section.

AKA The Unabomber

Almost thirty years after the shooting of *Landscape Suicide*, James Benning recently revisited his treatise on criminality in a series of works – Two Cabins Project – that retains his ethical stance on the representation of criminals. Once again, Benning focuses on two subjects, the nineteenth-century political philosopher Henry David Thoreau and the serial bomber Ted Kaczynski who operated from the 1970s to the 1990s. What brings the unlikely pairing together is that they both built cabins; Thoreau lived inside a cabin he built at Walden Pond, where he lived for two years, and Kaczynski built a cabin in Montana where he made bombs. Benning's study of the subjects manifests itself as a diverse range of works that span different media and interconnect in their commentary on escapes into nature, a lifestyle he himself has endorsed with his move to the mountains in High Sierras where he lives in isolation in a self-built house.

The first of the series is an architectural project, on which Benning had embarked between 2007 and 2008, involving the constructions of replicas of the cabins built and inhabited by Thoreau and Kaczynski. Inside the cabins, Benning's replicas of paintings by other artists decorate the walls. The second is the essay 'Twelve People' which Benning wrote and published as part of Julie Ault's book, *Two Cabins by JB*, that documents the lives of the twelve people whose works he has reproduced (2011: 85–102). The film installation *Two Cabins* (2012), shown in a solo exhibition at Neugerriemschneider, Berlin, is the third of the series and involves a two-channel, high-definition video projection of two films shot from inside the cabins looking out through its windows into the wilderness. The installation also includes two pedestals, a typewriter, a wooden desk and pencils which are presented together with the projections. Finally, the feature film *Stemple Pass* (2013) is composed entirely of shots of his replica of Kaczynski's cabin. Despite spanning a range of artistic disciplines and a number of years, Benning's series of works is consistent with the ethics of representation that he developed early on in his career.

Similarly to the film-makers involved in *fūkeiron* in Japan, an impetus for Benning to embark on the cabin project stemmed from a frustration with the ways in which the news media depicted Ted Kaczynski as a convict. Despite entering Harvard University at an early age and working at the University of California, Berkeley, as an assistant professor teaching mathematics, news report coverage of Kaczysnki's arrest in 1996 portrayed him as mentally unstable. Foreseeing how the media would characterise him, Kaczynski articulated his political theory in numerous journal entries and in his manifesto

'Industrial Society and its Futures'. His efforts were not met with success, and his cabin, where he had lived since 1971, was brought into court as a testament of his insanity. Recounting his initial thoughts on the media responses on Kaczynski's character, James Benning said: '[o]nce he was arrested and was immediately painted as this weird fellow, I questioned who he really was. Whenever the media makes [sic] someone look so different than what they probably are, I get interested' (quoted in Ault, 2011: 104).[6] Kaczynski's cabin was, in fact, modelled after Thoreau's after he had read its description in the classic book *Walden: or, Life in the Woods* (1854), and Benning posed his critique of media representation through the juxtaposition of the two. On the one hand, Thoreau's cabin, built in 1845, has been celebrated as a result of an intellectual naturalist pursuing an intimate correspondence with nature; on the other hand, Kaczynski's cabin was portrayed as a creation of an individual who inhabited the dangerous peripheries of society (Ault, 2011: 105). Building the two cabins 40 metres apart, Benning poses the paradox in the architectural project of the two cabins that are positioned in visible proximity to each other. The juxtaposition is once again highlighted in the placement of the two screens on perpendicular walls in his installation, *Two Cabins*, where both images echo each other. The static shots from the window of the cabins looking out into the surrounding forest involve natural sounds, presumably recorded in situ.[7] The projections pose a contrast to the media coverage of Kaczynski's life, with its absence of interpretative registers, and a point of view that embodies his own, asking the audience to share his viewpoint rather than rejecting outright any association with him. While the typewriter, pencils and desk in the installation signify the writing processes of Thoreau and Kaczynski in their respective cabins, they also symbolically invite the visitors of the exhibition to arrive at their own interpretations of the subjects' lives.

As well as the viewing process to which the audience is subjected, the mode of production also remains integral for the film-makers abiding by the principles of *fūkeiron*. For the film-makers involved in *AKA Serial Killer*, the film was as much a documentary on Nagayama Norio as a document on their own process of attempting to understand him. The artisanal commitment of James Benning, in his replication of the cabins, similarly testifies to his devotion to the process and to the dedication of time that he felt is required to arrive at an understanding of his subjects. Benning attempted to construct the cabins as closely to the originals as possible, following the descriptions offered by Thoreau in *Walden* and the details depicted in the photographs by Richard Barnes of Kaczynski's cabin which he discovered in public records. By undergoing the same physical and durational processes as his subjects, Benning's architectural project echoes the physical journey that the team of film-makers behind *AKA Serial Killer* embarked on. For both Benning and the Japanese film-makers, it is not only the time for which they ask their audience to view the films but also the time which they took themselves to make it that underpin their ethical stance.

In his depiction of Ted Kaczynski in *Stemple Pass* (2013), James Benning once again utilises a disembodied voice-over on top of landscape shots as a method of delivering information. Entirely composed of four separate shots of the same cabin in the same landscape, the shots in *Stemple Pass* are roughly separated into two halves, the first involving Benning's own voice reading selected pages from Kaczynski's journals, and the second with only the sounds of the landscape. Gaining access to the forty volumes of journals bought by his friend, Benning's voice-over reads the journal entries in a de-dramatised fashion that refuses to offer channels of identification through conviction of delivery.[8] The content of the passages reveal Kaczynski's growing frustration with technology and industrialisation impeding nature and his own sense of autonomy in the modern world, a complaint that echoes the homogeneity of landscapes the film-makers behind *AKA Serial Killer* discover in the process of shooting their film. In particular, Kaczynski complained in his journal entries about the inescapability of modern industrialisation that can be heard through the sounds of engines and machines which infringed on his solitary existence. As if to tease out a similar sensation for the viewer, Benning includes the noise of an approaching helicopter in the soundtrack as one of the few sounds in the film that is out of sync with the image. With the insertion of the helicopter sound as an exception, Benning avoids interpretation, finding it more important for his audience to arrive at their own conclusions. In his written essay 'Twelve People', the lives of Kaczynski and the eleven others are depicted as a list of facts that sequentially illustrate their lives (Benning, 2011: 85–102). Distrusting the ability of written or spoken language to impose understanding, the biographic notes on Kaczynski provided by Benning stem from a similar ethical stance to that of the film-makers of *AKA Serial Killer*, who also provided only a list of facts as a voice-over in the illustration of Nagayama Norio's life.

ETHICS OF THE LANDSCAPE SHOT

In the separate portraits of Nagayama Norio, Bernadette Protti, Ed Gein and Ted Kaczynski, James Benning and the film-makers behind *AKA Serial Killer* resorted to a cinema of slowness for their depiction of murderers. The long takes, decentralised compositions and the disembodied voice-over allowed Benning and the team behind *AKA Serial Killer* to explore an ethical mode of address for the criminals which rejected the imposition of judgement or a sensationalisation of their stories. Despite the use of different mediums – film, high-definition video, written essay and architecture – and in spite of encompassing a series of unrelated murder cases in Japan and the United States – the film-makers arrived at remarkably similar methods for depicting murder cases. Providing the deceleration of film with an ethical objective, their approach stemmed from an attempt to build a relationship with their documentary subjects and the audiences of their films. A process-driven cinema was what they aimed for not only in the experience for their audience in the act of viewing but also for themselves as they followed the trajectories of their subjects in the act of film-making.

Nevertheless, their cinema derived from a viewpoint that acknowledged the impossibility to fully understand their subjects. Acknowledging their journey would not have been exactly the same as Nagayama Norio's (2013: 30), Matsuda Masao proposed that tracing the trajectory of his subject's journey would only create the same result as a world map which has different interpretations of details depending on the perspective (2013: 104–5). Looking back at the making of the section on Ed Gein in *Landscape Suicide*, James Benning admitted that 'I couldn't get a sense of the murder, but the feeling of collective guilt still lingers' (quoted in Mairs, 2005: 121). The complexities of the individuals and their criminal acts superseded any attempt to reduce them into a landscape shot, or even a feature-length film: 'Despite being everywhere, *fūkei* is hard to find' (Matsuda, 2013: 144). Given the opportunity to stare at the sustained shots of landscapes, we realise that each one of us would see the same landscape differently.

NOTES

1. The Japanese names in this chapter will be listed in the local way, surname first. In the case of Yuriko Furuhata, however, I have chosen to retain the English order as most of her publications are in the English language.
2. A certain nuance is lost in the English translation of the title of the film which is worth pointing out. The word 'ryakushō' used in the original Japanese title implies an omission or an abbreviation, used with a tinge of irony that accepts the impossibility to provide anything but a truncation of an individual's life in any retelling.
3. Adachi provides this description while he reflects on *AKA Serial Killer* as part of Eric Baudelaire's documentary film, *The Anabasis: Fusako and May Shigenobu, Masao Adachi and the 27 Years Without Images* (2012).
4. Other films which are said to have applied *fūkeiron* include Ōshima Nagisa's *Tokyo senso sengo hiwa* (*The Man Who Left His Will on Film*, 1970), Hara Masato's *Hatsukuni shirasumera Mikoto* (*The First Emperor*, 1973) and Takamine Gō's *Okinawan Dream Show* (1971–4), as well as Adachi's own *Sekigun-P.F.L.P: Sekai senso sengen* (*The Red Army/PFLP: The Declarations of World War*, 1971), codirected with Wakamatsu Kōji, that functions as a propaganda newsreel film for the Japanese Red Army's efforts in Palestine.
5. The statement was made during a series of interviews with him conducted by Barbara Pichler and Claudia Slanar between spring and autumn 2006.
6. The statement was made during a conversation with Julie Ault, 25 January 2011.
7. James Benning has mentioned the strong association between the two cabins project and his own film, *American Dreams (lost and found)* (1984). The film depicts two pursuits of the American dream: firstly, the ascent of Hank Aaron into

a record-breaking home-run scorer; and, secondly, the quest for Arthur Bremer to shoot President Nixon. These are inscribed into the film in forced juxtaposition, the former as image and the latter as handwritten text.

8. Just as the construction of the cabin demonstrates Benning attempting to establish a direct association with Kaczynski, the act of reciting passages from Kaczynski's journal similarly evokes this process. We are also reminded of Benning's handwritten rewriting of Arthur Bremer's journals which were optically printed on the film in *American Dreams (lost and found)*.

BIBLIOGRAPHY

Ault, Julie (2011), 'Freedom Club', in Julie Ault (ed.), *Two Cabins by JB* (New York: A. R. T Press), pp. 103–43.

Benning, James (2011a), 'Twelve People', in Julie Ault (ed.), *Two Cabins by JB* (New York: A. R. T Press), pp. 85–102.

Dieckman, Katherine (1986), '*Landscape Suicide*', in *40 Frames: Exhibition Program Archive*, winter/spring 2002, http://www.40frames.org/past_screenings/2002/winter_spring/ [accessed 21 September 2014]. Originally published in *Village Voice*.

Flanagan, Matthew (2012), '*Slow Cinema': Temporality and Style in Contemporary Art and Experimental Film*, unpublished PhD dissertation, University of Exeter.

Furuhata, Yuriko (2007), 'Returning to Actuality: *Fūkeiron* and the Landscape Film,' *Screen*, vol. 48, no. 3 (autumn): 345–62.

Furuhata, Yuriko (2013), *Cinema of Actuality: Japanese Avant-Garde Filmmaking in the Season of Image Politics* (Durham, NC: Duke University Press).

Hirasawa Go (2013), '*Fūkeiron no genzai*' ('The Theory of Landscape Now'), in Matsuda Masao (ed.), *Fūkei no shimetsu* (Tokyo: Kōshinsha), pp. 319–41.

Mairs, Gary (2005), 'Charged Symmetry: The Landscape Films of James Benning', in *argosfestival* catalogue (Brussels: *argosfestival*), pp. 118–29.

Matsuda Masao (2013). *Fūkei no shimestsu: zōhoshinban* ('The Extinction of Landscape', newly enlarged edition) (Tokyo: Kōshinsha). Originally published in 1971.

Pichler, Barbara (2011). 'American Dreams to American Nightmares, *Him and Me* (1981) to *Used Innocence* (1988)', translated by Eve Heller, in Barbara Pichler and Claudia Slanar (eds), *James Benning* (Vienna: Filmmuseum Synema Publikationen), pp. 75–84.

19. SLOW CINEMA AND THE ETHICS OF DURATION

Asbjørn Grønstad

It takes time to see things.[1]

The film begins with a five-minute shot of a woman brushing her hair and watching children asleep nearby. Its penultimate shot is a fifteen-minute long take showing two characters staring at an image on a wall. Sandwiched between these tableaux is a nominal narrative about a vagrant single father trying to care for his two kids while working as a sandwich-board man on the congested streets of a city that might be Taipei or Chung Cheng. The film in question is *Stray Dogs* (*Jiao you*, 2013), the tenth and supposedly final feature by the celebrated Malaysian-born, Taiwan-based director Tsai Ming-liang. The maker of several critically admired art-house films, such as *Rebels of the Neon God* (*Qing shao nian nuo zha*, 1992), *Vive l'Amour* (*Ai qing wan sui*, 1994), *What Time Is It There?* (*Ni na bian ji dian*, 2001), *Goodbye Dragon Inn* (*Bu san*, 2003) and *The Wayward Cloud* (*Tian bian yi duo yun*, 2005), Tsai – upon the film's launch in the autumn of 2013 – has been quoted as saying that he has to 'let things rest and be digested'. He is at a loss, he says, when 'faced with the speed modern life imposes on us'. Thus, 'being slow is a technique to find one's way in the confusion' (DeHart, 2013).[2] With *Stray Dogs*, this particular technique – which is also an approach, a stance, and a method – is honed to perfection. As one critic has remarked, the film with its 'glacial attitude towards shot-duration' could be regarded as 'the very last word in Slow

Cinema' (Young, 2013). In this chapter, I take *Stray Dogs*, Tsai's first extended foray into digital film-making, as my reference point for an examination of the ethical context(s) of slow cinema. In passing I shall first consider the historically vexed nexus of ethics and aesthetic styles more generally, before making the argument that slow cinema becomes an ethical practice when it enables the filmic production of duration as material form. While duration as a temporal mode and experiential frame might not necessarily be ethical in and of itself, it nevertheless provides a condition of possibility for intrinsically ethical acts, such as recognition, reflection, imagination and empathy.[3]

While richly present in major predecessors, such as Antonioni, Tarkovsky, and Angelopoulos, the concept of 'slow cinema' has, over the last decade particularly, emerged as a fully formed critical term. It straddles both art cinema and documentary film, and extends to directors such as Bruno Dumont, Carlos Reygadas, Andrey Zvyagintsev and Lucien Castaing-Taylor, to name but a few. That the notion of slow cinema is not just a casual term, connected by association to a motley crew of 'artistic' directors, but rather that it has become something which has congealed into a more official school of film-making is evidenced by, for instance, the AV Festival, *As Slow As Possible,* held in Newcastle and other British cities in March 2012. Featured on the programme was recent work by a roster of artists whose names have tended to come up when the phenomenon of slow cinema is mentioned: Lisandro Alonso, Fred Kelemen, Lav Diaz, Sharon Lockheart, Ben Rivers, James Benning and, of course, Béla Tarr. The aesthetics of slow has also crossed over into television, most notably exemplified in the Norwegian Broadcasting Corporation's transmission of a complete seven-hour train ride along the Bergen Line in November 2009 and its live coverage of the cruise ship *Hurtigruten*'s 134-hour voyage from Bergen to Kirkenes in June 2011, both programmes resulting in record ratings for the NRK 2 channel.[4]

Empirically, then, there appears to be an abundance of instances of an aesthetics of slow. But the phenomenon has also congealed into a critical discourse, with both champions and detractors, that is operative not only in academic publications (the current book being a prime example) but also in more mainstream media, such as the *New York Times*. Through some of its distinctive features – the long or super-long take, action unfolding in real time, framed tableau shots, hyperrealism, and de-dramatisation – slow cinema generates, across its very different films, a recognisable poetics that is observational, meditative and poetic. The films are often galvanised by a sense of persistent quietude and a compositional stillness. Mood usually trumps action, and graphic properties regularly supplant speech or dialogue. Particularly significant to my analysis here is Jonathan Romney's statement that slow cinema produces what he terms 'an intensified sense of temporality' (2010: 43). This is somewhat imprecise because the intensification in question involves the level of duration, in particular. Slow cinema, as I shall argue, spatialises duration and thus it makes something invisible visible. By evacuating all but the most infinitesimal action from the frame, by bracketing inaction, what the extreme long take visualises is the passing of time itself.

To some extent, slow cinema acquires its import relationally, as something of a negation of the terms of commercial film-making. It could be argued that the chasm between art cinema and the mainstream has widened over the last decade, and that this development is, in part, epitomised by the disparity between fast and slow, between a penchant for ever faster editing and an unwavering reliance on the long take. Thus, the two forms of cinema constitute both a stylistic and a conceptual macro-structure within which questions of aesthetic and ethical value might be framed. Insofar as the long take is a hallmark of much contemporary art cinema, and ultra-fast cutting defines current commercial transnational film-making, one could consider temporal/durational vectors to be of primary importance not only for identifying what could be seen as two major incarnations of group style but also for exploring the ethical ramifications that might be generated from these different aesthetic configurations. If tracking shots, as Jean-Luc Godard once famously proclaimed (paraphrasing Luc Moullet), are a matter of morality, so it would seem that all the other formal techniques, which film as a medium has at its disposal, could likewise be subjected to a kind of scrutiny informed by a range of ethical considerations. One of the critical benchmarks for this way of thinking ethics through cinematic form is the case in which Jacques Rivette and, later, Serge Daney ardently condemn the infamous tracking shot in Gillo Pontecorvo's somewhat forgotten film *Kapò* (1959).[5] The dilemma is this: on the one hand, it seems dubious, and perhaps even counter-intuitive, to claim that some aesthetic practices are inherently 'better' than others; on the other hand, it seems too easy, and also a little nonchalant, to maintain that all formal and compositional devices are equally 'good'. Several troubling implications arise from the second position, perhaps chief among them the question of what such a politics of aesthetic levelling will do to the criticism and the critical enterprise which, obviously to a large degree, hinge on the production of aesthetic judgements and on the ability to discriminate qualitatively between different artistic objects not only with respect to form but also with respect to ethics.

This seemingly irresolvable problem – that is, the tendency to evaluate particular aesthetic techniques in moral terms – constitutes the starting point for the argument I should like to make here. In what follows, I want merely to begin a mostly theoretical exploration of the optics of slow, focusing on the interconnection between temporality and ethics. I shall not so much answer, as flag up, a host of questions. For example: how are temporal forms and modes entwined, if at all, with ethical experience? How might moving images be construed as mediations of the imbrications of temporality and ethics? Is the formal apparatus of slow cinema – the long take, the *temps mort*, de-dramatised sequences – inherently more ethical than other kinds if cinema? If so, why? Does slow cinema herald a new ecology of seeing, one that may be linked to similar movements in other fields? What might be the political potential of slow cinema?[6]

The Long Take and the Politics of Slowness

Before delving into these issues, it is pertinent to situate the current wave of slow films within a longer history of art cinema. We might do well, or so I argue, to revisit André Bazin's epochal ruminations about the long take as a particular aesthetic. I also want to describe a couple of recent thematic readings of slow cinema, what it does and why it does it. Finally, I should like to offer some embryonic remarks about the possible benefits of bringing the work of thinkers such as Jean-Luc Nancy and Hans Gumbrecht to bear on the slow cinema phenomenon. While Romney cites Béla Tarr's *Sátántangó* (1994) and *Werckmeister Harmonies* (2000) – as well as Fred Kelemen's *Frost* (1997) and Aleksandr Sokurov's *Russian Ark* (2002) – as the founding texts of the contemporary slow cinema movement (if we may call it that) (2010: 43), the tradition clearly has its roots in a certain strand of 1950s modernist cinema. Here I am thinking not only of the material or formal components (such as the long take) but also of the concomitant gravitation towards a particular subject matter. As we all know, its discrete constituents have long since become clichéd tropes of the cerebral post-war art film: alienation, spiritual malaise, social isolation, aimlessness and drift, and failed communication. And, while not unique to the long-take aesthetic, the stylistic traits of this tradition persist in many of the current slow cinema works: the use of ellipsis, minimal exposition, episodic progression, diluted causality, contingency, ambiguity, open endings, improvisation, location shooting and use of natural light.[7] In the 1960s, slowness – which, in a sense, is a medium-specific property; only the moving image can have the quality of slowness – was increasingly associated with the avant-garde and entailed what could be considered a historical rupture with the fundamental nature of the medium of cinema as the offspring of urban modernity and part of the same cultural space as, for instance, the telegraph, photography, the motor car, the department store and jazz. Techniques such as montage and dissolves pushed film towards an aesthetics of spectacle shared by many other contemporaneous manifestations of the modern world. In this context, the emergence of slow cinema might be seen almost as a negation of the very essence of the cinematic.

If there is a quintessential film theorist for the slow cinema aesthetic, it must surely be André Bazin who, in two of his most well-known essays, emphasised the significance of duration. In 'The Evolution of the Language of Cinema', he talked about 'a respect for the continuity of dramatic space and, of course, its duration' (1967a: 34). Additionally, there is the famous passage in his foundational essay on the 'Ontology of the Photographic Image' in which he writes that, with the onset of cinema, 'the image of things is likewise the image of their duration' (1967b: 15). Matthew Flanagan, among others, has picked up on Bazin's remarks and tied them to the slow aesthetic which, as he notes, 'uncompresses time, distends it, renewing the ability of the shot to represent a sense of the phenomenological real' (2008). The italicising of temporality and form in slow cinema – where to an unusual degree form is temporalised and time is formalised – is, in the Bazinian framework, intimately linked to a politics of disclosure. The film image, the French critic states, is 'evaluated not according to what it adds to reality but what it reveals of it' (Bazin, 1967a: 28). It seems sensible enough to presume that the process of revelation, the dynamics of phenomenological emergence, require a certain sense of duration. 1.8 seconds, the average shot length of *The Bourne Supremacy* (Paul Greengrass, 2004) and *The Bourne Ultimatum* (Paul Greengrass, 2007), do not quite seem to cut it (no pun intended). The 35.1 seconds average shot length in Reygadas's *Silent Light* (*Stellet Licht*, 2007) not to mention the 229.2 seconds of Tarr's *The Turin Horse* (*A torinói ló*, 2011) appear more amenable to the kind of transcendental, revelatory experience the film image, according to Bazin and others, is capable of transmitting.

Slow cinema is the antithesis of a cinematic breakneck aesthetic and, in actively resisting its ultra-fast arsenal of formal devices, it represents a form of productive negativity, a form of negation.[8] In this, slow cinema obviously forms part of a much broader cultural project – 'slow living' – whose driving impetus is also an act of resistance, and that has spawned phenomena such as slow media, slow food, slow travel, slow fashion, slow science, slow money and so on.[9]

The concept of slow might thus be said to be inherently political, and the nature of slow films, one could argue, cannot be properly comprehended without reference to its opposite. Every long take then also simultaneously articulates an impatience with, and perhaps distaste for, the regime of ocular speed. This ethics of negation is what I propose to call *the external dimension* of slow cinema. If, furthermore, we ask *why* it is opportune to critique the dominant visual temporality of our time ('isn't faced-paced editing innocent enough?'), we will soon find ourselves in the vicinity of *the internal dimension* of slow cinema. Accused as slow cinema often is of purposeless drift, its objective is nonetheless clear enough; this is a form of film whose final destination is always presence. A condition of possibility, when it comes to presence, seems to be duration; it is at least very difficult to imagine a form of presence that does not rely on temporal unfolding, on duration. A 1.8 seconds shot has a material existence, undeniably, but, at the same time, it is evacuated of presence. Or is it more accurate to say that it *destroys* presence? In the following, I want briefly to sketch the contours of an intellectual framework which may help us get a firmer idea of the relation between slow cinema and presence.

THINKING PRESENCE: GUMBRECHT, NANCY AND SEEL

The most substantial argument in favour of presence as a critical concept may be Hans Ulrich Gumbrecht's judicious analysis of the hegemony of the hermeneutic tradition in his book, *The Production of Presence: What Meaning Cannot Convey* (2004). In this text, Gumbrecht points out that the information overload of the Internet age seems to have rekindled a longing for being, for presence:

> ... the more we approach the fulfillment of our dreams of omnipresence and the more definite the subsequent loss of our bodies and of the spatial dimension in our existence seems to be, the greater the possibility becomes of reigniting the desire that attracts us to the things of the world and wraps us into their space. (2004: 139)

While Gumbrecht does not directly oppose meaning and presence – he still allows a place for the former – his book does represent an intervention through which the regime of interpretation gets interrogated, the suspicion being that the incessant search for meaning, as well as the production of too much meaning, may be detrimental to the actual experience of presence. Writing around the same time, Martin Seel argues that both the principal traditions of the philosophy of aesthetic perception – which he refers to as, respectively, the 'aesthetics of being' (in which art can reveal hidden layers of reality) and the 'aesthetics of illusion' (in which there is a radical rift between reality and art) – neglect appropriately to take into account the reality of presence or the presence of the real. Aesthetic perception, Seel claims, 'is conceived as a flight from the phenomenal presence of human life' (2003: 19). Finally, I want to bring in Jean-Luc Nancy's work with Abbas Kiarostami in which the philosopher launches a new aesthetic theory of sorts, built around what he sees as the positive implications of the loss of meaning in modernity.[10] Drawing on Heidegger's phenomenology, Nancy argues that the loss of a world which makes sense is actually an improvement because a world without meaning, without signs, is exactly what it takes for the real to open itself up to us. For Nancy, cinema's function is not to present a preconceived world nor to represent the loss of a meaningful world (a job often attributed to modernist art, literature and film) but to *present* the world itself:

The evidence of cinema is that of the existence of a look through which a world can give back to itself its own real and the truth of its enigma (which is admittedly not its solution), a world moving of its own motion, without a heaven or a wrapping, without fixed moorings or suspension, a world shaken, trembling, as the winds blow through it. (2001: 44)

This line of thinking is not very far from that of Bazin in the 'Ontology' essay. Temporality – that is, duration – is what makes presence and its effects possible, and presence, again, is what makes the unfolding (and unlocking) of the world with all its enigmas possible. The *temps mort* of slow cinema, for instance, is thus something more than just empty time, empty shots; it is an attempted visualisation of that which cannot be visualised, presence. Film 'puts the empty moment to work', as Leo Charney writes (1998: 34). This mobilisation of presence in slow cinema might open up into the domains of both spirituality and ethics. The experience of boredom, exhaustion and sheer drudgery, which some claim accompanies slow cinema, is therefore not an impediment to an appreciation of the form, nor is it exactly its 'point,' as Erika Balsom has suggested (Carleton Film Society, 2012); rather, the process of making duration visible is a stylistic means by which to trigger an empathetic investment in the world depicted on screen.

TEMPORALITY AND ETHICS: *STRAY DOGS* AND THE EXTREME LONG SHOT

This is palpably the case in *Stray Dogs* in which the very form of the film accentuates its content – the condition of stasis and precarity that the main protagonist has to endure – the basic mode of which it then reproduces on a spectatorial level. The father in the film, played by Tsai regular Lee Kang-sheng, is a homeless alcoholic with seemingly few prospects. Spending his days in horrendous immobility, advertising housing complexes in the middle of noisy, unending traffic, then his nights squatting in derelict buildings, the protagonist is caught in a kind of existential inertia caused, we have reason to believe, by the country's struggling economy. Minimal living conditions translate into aesthetic minimalism, material austerity similarly into formal austerity. For some viewers, *Stray Dogs* may be draining and even excruciating to watch but, because it is a film fundamentally about patience and perseverance, the lapse into impatience on the part of the spectator seems a largely disingenuous response. While the film collected the Grand Jury Prize in Venice in 2013 and has consistently attracted favourable appraisals, there has also been a fair amount of discussion around the topic of its physically and mentally taxing pace. Possibly more than most films in the slow cinema vein, *Stray Dogs* has been routinely accused of 'abusing' the attention of its audience. As the following extract points out, however, the rhetoric of the long take as Tsai deploys ultimately promotes understanding and empathy:

> If the audience is becoming uncomfortable and bored with how long they're being asked to watch a static composition, what does that tell us about how the character must feel? It's somewhat sacrificial of the viewer's enjoyment, but is a necessary burden in order to achieve eventual moments of understanding. Each shot is left on screen longer than you expect it to, allowing time for eyes to wander the frame, learning more about the foreign culture and characters through context. Small movements catch the eye, and the scrutiny of a resting face begins to tell you more than an actively emoting one. This sort of filmmaking stretches and perverts neorealism – prompting a certain number of walkouts at every screening. Tsai is in absolutely no hurry to advance the plot, in fact this is anti-plot – the absence of a traditional narrative in the father's life is what makes it so distressingly sorrowful to watch. (Sinople, 2014)

Speaking of neorealism, the critic's account is reminiscent of Sam Rohdie's definition, in his book on Antonioni, of the *temps mort* as the 'place at which the narrative dies' in order to give precedence to 'another, non-narrative interest' (1990: 51). This interest could, of course, be graphic or pictorial in nature but it would be reductive to maintain that Tsai's cinema is principally about aesthetic meditation (his previous feature, *Visage*, could, in fact, be read as a critique of such a perspective).[11] Rather, the *temps mort* conveys a particular distribution of temporality which serves to concretise duration and presence in the non-narrative, non-teleological interest of ethical exposure. But, if we presume that what I have previously termed 'slow seeing' is the lesson some, but not all, cases of slow cinema teach us (2010: 313), what, more specifically, is at stake in this phenomenological mode? And, no less importantly, what might the content of these effects of duration and presence be? As far as *Stray Dogs* is concerned, I should like to propose, by way of conclusion, that the filmic articulation of duration comprises these three domains in particular: that of mundanity, that of labour, and that of art.

Many of the trademark tropes, motifs and techniques associated with Tsai's cinema reappear in *Stray Dogs*: the tableau compositions, the reliance on song as a form of escape, the distinctive rectilinear framing, the near absence of dialogue, the use of an established ensemble, the significance of water, the absurdist touches (see, for instance, the much discussed 'cabbage sequence'), and the slightly oneiric, enigmatic mood, to name a few. But the film arguably also pushes the slow cinema aesthetic as far as it can go, as *Stray Dogs* abandons continuity editing entirely in favour of a single-shot approach (with one significant exception) that nudges Tsai's style close to what Tony Rayns sees as an 'installation-art aesthetic' (2014: 68). No less crucially, *Stray Dogs* also contains notably longer shots than we are used to even within this particular *oeuvre*. This complex minimalism, non-narrative and opaque as it may be, exploits the inherent nature of largely static shots in order to spatialise duration. If, for some theorists, the possibility of a visual ethics arises from the faith in the superiority of the cut, the long take – slow cinema's defining property – seems an even better conduit for the kind of ethical experience particular to the film image.[12]

The first of Tsai's tableaux in *Stray Dogs* is the long shot of a woman brushing her hair to which I alluded at the very beginning of this chapter. Later in the film, there is a close-up sequence of similar length showing the father eating an entire meal. Images of domesticity and leisure also occur elsewhere in the film. The ostensibly disproportionate attention Tsai pays to routine, humdrum activities in *Stray Dogs* connects the film (as well as most of Tsai's *oeuvre*, of which this aspect is something of a specialty) with the 'corporeal cinema' of Chantal Akerman, in particular her *Jeanne Dielman* (1975) (Margulies, 1996). While a significant context for Akerman's film is 1970s feminism, a concern hardly at the forefront of Tsai's film, the aestheticisation of monotony and the emphasis on giving form to duration are salient preoccupations for both filmmakers. But the visualisation of duration is also tied to the domain of labour which appears to be a persistent characteristic across a range of slow films.[13]

Secondly, *Stray Dogs* produces an experience of temporality strenuous enough to approximate the excessive monotony of labour as endured by the main protagonist. Diligently holding up a sign advertising luxury apartments, the father in Tsai's film spends his days practically motionless, like a human statue, sometimes in heavy wind and rain. In one shot, which also makes up most of the official trailer for the film, we see him in close-up, teary eyed, singing a despondent song, the lyrics of which go 'In anger my hair stands on end/And as the rain stops/I launch a shrill cry at the heavens/My valiant heart loses hope/My exploits are naught but mud and dust/And my wanderings but a cloud under the moon/Regret may turn my still-young head grey/O vainglorious pain!' Labour in these shots is shot through with a mix of stoicism and despair.

Lastly, the struggle to give form to duration and presence in *Stray Dogs* also encompasses the sphere of art. Possibly influenced by *Visage* – the 2009 film shot inside the Louvre and deeply invested in the business of looking at art – the unusually long, penultimate shot finds the man and the woman captivated by a mural they see inside an empty, dilapidated building. Tsai himself came across this large landscape painting when scouting for locations for *Stray Dogs*. Taking up the entire wall of a deserted house, the picture is actually a repurposed and enlarged photograph taken by John Thomson in the Liugui Village in Kaohsiung City in 1871. The artist, Kao Jun-Honn, happened upon the photographs when doing research for a historical project on the remnants of the coal industry in the mountainous areas in southern Taiwan. It would seem that the film-maker and the artist share a fascination with ruins and uninhabited buildings. Using charcoal to refashion the photograph before enlarging it, thus transforming its texture, Kao Jun-Honn then transferred it to an abandoned site. The original photograph also contained two Taiwanese children positioned in the left-hand corner. They were excised from the altered image but, as Tsai is quick to point out, they re-emerge as the children in the film (Young, 2013). Kao Jun-Hoon apparently had no interest in exhibiting the images, preferring, instead, that viewers stumble upon them by accident, and it could perhaps be argued that Tsai was the ideal intruder in that regard. While other forms of temporality in *Stray Dogs* give prominence to the duration of a specific activity or a task, however tedious, the prolonged scene with Kao Jun-Honn's mural gives prominence to the duration of the look itself. This scene, then, becomes in a sense a literalisation, or an externalisation, of the durative poetics of slow cinema, a poetics perhaps uniquely equipped to capture temporal presence as spatial form.

NOTES

1. Peter Catapano (2013), 'Can We See Philosophy? A Dialogue With Ernie Gehr', *New York Times*, 3 October 2013, http://opinionator.blogs.nytimes.com/2013/10/03/can-we-see-philosophy-a-dialogwith-ernie-gehr/?_r=0 [accessed 31 October 2013].
2. For a comprehensive study of Tsai Ming-liang's work in relation to the concepts of slowness, stillness and silence in particular, see Song Hwee Lim's contribution to this volume as well as his *Tsai Ming-Liang and a Cinema of Slowness* (2014).
3. For more about the visualisation of duration, see my article 'Dead Time, Empty Spaces: Landscape as Sensibility and Performance' (Grønstad, 2010).
4. Sukhdev Sandhu interestingly points out that slowness is also 'an intrinsic element of contemporary visual culture', the evidence for which may be found in devices such as the screensaver, the gallery installation, surveillance footage, night-cam images of sleeping *Big Brother* participants, and so on.
5. Rivette's scathing review of Pontecorvo's film centred on what the French critic found to be a failure on the director's part to adjust his formal choices to the subject matter of the film. In Rivette's view, the decision to dolly in on the dead woman, who had committed suicide by throwing herself on to an electric fence, was exploitative and morally offensive. In a much later article, Serge Daney takes up and elaborates Rivette's position, arguing that the tracking shot was 'immoral for the simple reason that it was putting us – him filmmaker and me spectator – in a place where we did not belong' (Daney 2004).
6. The ways in which slow cinema, through its emphasis on sensory experience, also contains a political dimension are among the topics addressed by Tiago de Luca in *Realism of the Senses in World Cinema* (2014).
7. These are all characteristics of art-cinema narration identified by David Bordwell in his *Narration in the Fiction Film* (1985: 205–33).
8. I have previously considered slow cinema in terms of a rhetoric of negation in my book *Screening the Unwatchable*.

9. See, for example, the website *The Slow Media Manifesto*, http://en.slow-media.net/manifesto [accessed 23 May 2014].
10. The growing literature on the notion of presence evidently extends beyond these examples. Consider also Georges Didi-Huberman's critique of 'meaning' at the expense of experience (Didi-Huberman, 2005) and, furthermore, the anti-epistemological approach taken by Gilles Deleuze and Felix Guattari (1991) as well as Alain Badiou (2005). Slow cinema, in general, and *Stray Dogs*, in particular, could be seen as artistic materialisations of a broader cultural orientation towards a politics of presence long suppressed by post-structuralist positions.
11. See my article 'Enfolded by Cinema: The Transvisual Gaze in Tsai Ming-liang's *Visage*', forthcoming in *TRANS VISUALITY: The Cultural Dimension of Visuality* (Liverpool: Liverpool University Press, 2014).
12. See, for instance, Sarah Kember and Joanna Zylinska, *Life After New Media: Mediation as a Vital Process* (Cambridge, MA: MIT Press), 2012.
13. For a fuller discussion of the relation between slow cinema and labour, see Karl Schoonover's chapter in the current volume.

BIBLIOGRAPHY

Badiou, Alain (2005), *Handbook on Inaesthetics*, translated by Alberto Toscano (Stanford, CA: Stanford University Press).
Bazin, André (1967a), 'The Evolution of the Language of Cinema', *What is Cinema?*, vol. 1, translated by Hugh Gray (Berkeley, CA: University of California Press).
Bazin, André (1967b), 'The Ontology of the Photographic Image', *What is Cinema?*, vol. 1, translated by Hugh Gray (Berkeley, CA: University of California Press).
Bordwell, David (1985), *Narration in the Fiction Film* (Madison, WI: University of Wisconsin Press).
Bordwell, David (2002), 'Intensified Continuity: Visual Style in Contemporary American Film', *Film Quarterly*, 55. 3: 16–28.
Carleton Film Society, 'Erika Balsom and Slow Cinema', 1 October 2012, http://carletonfilmsociety.wordpress.com/2012/10/01/erika-balsom-and-slow-cinema/
Charney, Leo (1998), *Empty Moments: Cinema, Modernity, and Drift* (Durham, NC: Duke University Press).
Daney, Serge (2004), 'The Tracking Shot in *Kapo*' [*sic*], *Senses of Cinema*, 30, http://sensesofcinema.com/2004/feature-articles/kapo_daney/ [accessed 3 October 2014].
DeHart, Jonathan (2013), '*Stray Dogs*: Tsai Ming Liang's Last Film Urges Us to Slow Down', *The Diplomat*, 17 September 2013, http://thediplomat.com/2013/09/stray-dogs-tsai-ming-liangs-last-film-urges-us-to-slow-down/ [accessed 27 May 2014].
Deleuze, Gilles and Felix Guattari (1991), *What is Philosophy?*, translated by Hugh Tomlinson and Graham Burchell (New York: Columbia University Press).
de Luca, Tiago (2014), *Realism of the Senses in World Cinema: The Experience of Physical Reality* (London: I. B. Tauris).
Didi-Huberman, Georges (2005), *Confronting Images: Questioning the Ends of a Certain History of Art* [1990], translated by John Goodman (University Park, PA: Pennsylvania State University Press).
Flanagan, Matthew (2008), 'Towards an Aesthetic of Slow in Contemporary Cinema', *16:9*, 29, http://www.16-9.dk/2008-11/side11_inenglish.htm [accessed 23 May 2014].
Grønstad, Asbjørn (2010), 'Dead Time, Empty Spaces: Landscape as Sensibility and Performance', *Exploring Textual Action*, edited by Lars Sætre, Patrizia Lombardo and Anders M. Gullestad (Aarhus: Aarhus University Press), pp. 311–31.

Grønstad, Asbjørn (2011), *Screening the Unwatchable: Spaces of Negation in Post-Millennial Art Cinema* (Basingstoke: Palgrave Macmillan).

Gumbrecht, Hans Ulrich (2004), *The Production of Presence: What Meaning Cannot Convey* (Stanford, CA: Stanford University Press).

Kember, Sarah and Joanna Zylinska (2012), *Life After New Media: Mediation as a Vital Process* (Cambridge, MA: MIT Press).

Kuhn, Annette and Guy Westwell (2012), *A Dictionary of Film Studies* (Oxford: Oxford University Press).

Lim, Song Hwee (2014), *Tsai Ming-Liang and a Cinema of Slowness* (Honolulu, HI: University of Hawai'i Press).

Margulies, Ivone (1996), *Nothing Happens: Chantal Akerman's Hyperrealistic Everyday* (Durham, NC: Duke University Press).

Nancy, Jean-Luc and Abbas Kiarostami (2001), *The Evidence of Film*, translated by Christine Irizarry and Verena Andermatt Conley (Brussels: Yves Gevaert).

Rayns, Tony (2014), 'Stray Dogs', *Film Comment*, 50: 3, 68–9.

Rivette, Jacques (1961), 'De l'Abjection', *Cahiers du Cinéma*, 120, 54–5.

Rohdie, Sam (1990), *Antonioni* (London: BFI).

Romney, Jonathan (2010), 'In Search of Lost Time', *Sight and Sound*, 20.2, 43–4.

Sandhu, Sukhdev (2012), '"Slow cinema" fights back against Bourne's supremacy', *The Guardian*, 9 March, http://www.guardian.co.uk/film/2012/mar/09/slow-cinema-fights-bournes-supremacy [accessed 7 April 2014].

Seel, Martin (2003), 'The Aesthetics of Appearing', *Radical Philosophy*, 118: 18–24.

Sinople, Taylor (2014), 'Stray Dogs Review', *101 Room Magazine*, http://www.thefo cuspull.com/features/review-stray-dogs/ [accessed 26 May 2014].

Young, Neil (2013), 'Of Cabbages and Kings: Tsai Ming-Liang's Stray Dogs', *Neil Young's Film Lounge*, 20 November, http://www.jigsawlounge.co.uk/film/reviews/straydogs/ [accessed 26 May 2014].

PART VI

BEYOND 'SLOW CINEMA'

20. PERFORMING EVOLUTION: IMMERSION, UNFOLDING AND LUCILE HADŽIHALILOVIĆ'S *INNOCENCE*

Matilda Mroz

Towards the end of Lucile Hadžihalilović's *Innocence* (2004, Belgium/France), five girls on the cusp of puberty perform a dance in the underground theatre of their boarding school in which they have been confined since they were about six years old. Four of the girls wear butterfly wings and flitter across the stage while the fifth wields a white streamer that casts a symbolic web. The performance dramatises a section of the life cycle of butterflies which concludes with the insects twitching on the stage floor in death throes. For the girls, the dance is the culmination of years of ballet and gymnastic exercise, part of a strict programme imposed by the school to model the tiny, formless limbs of children into elegant movements and postures. Like the butterfly dance, the film as a whole can be seen as a performance of evolution, a tracing of the transformations of young girls as they mature, and as a play with evolutionary concepts, a creative mediation of natural history.

As Elizabeth Grosz has pointed out, the term 'evolution', derived from the Latin *e-volvere*, means 'to roll out', to 'unfold' (2004: 24). This chapter uses the concept of evolutionary performance as a base from which to leap into questions of temporal unfolding, particularly where such unfolding is slow and gradual. Despite not being associated with the slow cinema movement per se, *Innocence* employs many of the attributes of the more obvious exponents of this grouping. Within the relatively compact confines of 122 minutes of film, *Innocence* displays an attention to the leisurely pace and rhythms of the girls' everyday lives. The precise nature and purpose of their education and of the school in which it takes place are not immediately given to us; instead, viewers are treated to the gradual unfolding of (ambiguous) significance. The film slows down narrative exposition through an attention to the details of the environment: the rushing of a small waterfall, the crawling of insects, the gliding of molluscs and reptiles, and the stillness of uninhabited corridors.

This chapter draws on the philosophical writing of Henri Bergson and Elizabeth Grosz, among others, to suggest ways in which the idea of duration can help to navigate slowness in cinema. In relation to *Innocence*, specifically, the chapter identifies a dynamic oscillation between different visions of temporality: one that is imposed by the educational system, which sees change as the movement from one state of development to another, and the operation of duration as a ceaseless unfolding of multiple temporal rhythms which belies attempts to measure and control it. The chapter extends the notion of duration as infinitely graduated changes to the viewing process itself, arguing that the slow unfolding of scenes, moments and images in *Innocence* allows for a continual modulation between interpretative and sensory impulses.

PERFORMING EVOLUTION

'You're still just ugly little caterpillars. You'll have to work hard.' So Mademoiselle Eva (Marion Cotillard), the ballet mistress, benignly tells the youngest girls during their first dance lesson. In their natural history class, the children are shown a phylogenetic tree which branches out from the sea, as Mademoiselle Edith tells them that 'we all came from the same force that brought life'. The chart depicts various animals on an evolutionary line that ends on the figure of a young female, 'the most evolved species', the girls are told. In this same class, the girls look at small animals in aquariums and differently coloured cages which parallel the girls' own colour-coded hair ribbons and wardrobes: red for the youngest, violet for the eldest. The eldest girls, for their part, watch a butterfly emerge from a chrysalis while Madame Edith (Hélène de Fougerolles) remarks that 'you girls metamorphose too', suggesting that they are nearly ready to emerge from their own scholastic chrysalis into the outside world.

The hermetically enclosed school grounds can be seen as a kind of aquarium in which the girls play in water and on land, and which the camera at times observes via what Wilson has termed a 'surveillant mode', that 'view[s] little girls from above and afar, as an entomologist observes a colony of ants' (2007: 176). The girls are often shown pressing against window glass or framed against windows through which lush green vegetation is visible. Wilson further describes how the film presents the girls initially through their 'uniform skirts and socks', and thus 'shows them first not as individuals but as an identically clad social group' (2007: 177) or, one could add, a species. The first lesson for each new arrival involves learning how to swim, an activity which is, aptly, used by Bergson in *Creative Evolution* (2007: 124) to illustrate instinctual adaptation to an ecosystem.

Within this enclosed environment, the educational system imposes a particular programme of development. The film, however, interests itself in the imperfect outcomes of this programme; in a Darwinian spirit, it traces the variation among 'individuals of the same species inhabiting the same confined locality' (Darwin, 1996: 67). While the novel on which the film is loosely based, Frank Wedekind's *Mine-Haha, or, On the Bodily Education of Young Girls* (1903), focuses primarily on an individual, *Innocence* explores the heterogeneous experiences of several girls. Though the responses of Iris (Zoé Auclair), Alice (Lea Bridarolli) and Bianca (Bérangère Haubruge) to their environment occupy most of the screen time, the film also draws attention to the reactions of other individuals, such as Laura (Olga Peytavi-Müller), Iris's red-ribboned contemporary, Selma (Alisson Lalieux) who is loathe to give up her red ribbons, and Nadja (Ana Palomo Diaz) who is unwilling to take Bianca's place in the underground theatre. In tracing how the girls adapt, or fail to adapt, to their environment, the film explores the Darwinian suggestion that fitness to survive in a particular setting 'carries with it the notion of an openness to changing environments [. . .] fitness must be understood as an openness to the unknown, the capacity to withstand the unexpected as well as the predictable' (Grosz, 2004: 47). While Iris eventually adapts to the changes in her environment, Laura and Alice do not. Laura drowns in her attempt to escape while Alice breaks down when the headmistress unexpectedly rejects her.

The school's precise purpose, and the fates of its pupils, are left largely opaque in *Innocence*. Certain future possibilities are tentatively suggested: they

Figure 20.1   Still from *Innocence* (2004): the girls inspect an opening within the film's 'aquarium-forest'; their possible future trajectory is given spatial form by the elderly woman watching them.

can, for example, flaunt the school rules and remain as instructors, and perhaps end as the silent, elderly women who haunt the frame (Figure 20.1). Possible trajectories also find a spatial echo in the paths, corridors and tunnels that remain 'uncharted and unexplored' in the film (Wilson, 2007: 177). According to Grosz's reading of Darwin, however, 'it is impossible to predict what will follow, what will befall a particular trend or direction, let alone a particular individual' (Grosz, 2004: 8). As Grosz further argues, 'the individuals who never developed into maturing adults – the evolutionary residue, those that leave no trace, no progeny' should be regarded as 'the undeveloped, the latent, the recessive, a virtual forever unactualised' (2004: 50). Alice and Bianca, in particular, are left at crucial moments of development, their futures remaining unactualised narrative lines, existing only within viewer speculation.

Evolving Durations

Grosz is interested in a Bergsonian Darwinism; in moving towards a more explicit focus on temporality and slowness specifically, however, it seems appropriate briefly to register Bergson's critique of Darwinism. While Bergson appreciated the important contribution made by Darwin to a theory of evolution, he considered that, as Ansell Pearson has pointed out, 'a prevailing conception of evolution is one where duration and invention are lacking' (2002: 38). By the time he wrote *Creative Evolution*, as Ansell Pearson argues, Bergson had 'reached the view that duration is "immanent to the universe"', and aimed to show that 'duration is the key notion for thinking the idea of a creative (non-mechanical and non-finalist) evolution' (2002: 36). His vision of life refused the notion of change as states set beside one another like objects in space but rather figured the enfolding of multiple interpenetrating tendencies. Such a conception of life grew out of Bergson's conception of duration in general. Duration, wrote Bergson, is 'a continuity which is really lived, but artificially decomposed for the greater convenience of customary knowledge' (1962: 243). We habitually think of time through clocks and calendars that falsify duration by presenting time as measurable movements in space. Our conscious states, however, change continuously through duration. 'If we artificially arrest this indiscernible transition', writes Grosz, 'we can understand states as separate entities, linked by succession, but we lose whatever it is that flows in change, we lose duration itself' (2004: 158-9). Bergson compared duration to a 'myriad tinted spectrum', with insensible gradations leading from one shade to another. 'A current of feeling which passed along the spectrum, assuming in turn the tint of each of its shades, would experience a series of gradual changes, each of which would announce the one to follow and would sum up those which preceded it' (1999: 26). This is a vision of gradually evolving changes, of fusion and interpenetration.

While *Innocence* performs visions of evolution, it also stages different notions concerning the operation of time which can be seen to underpin the evolutionary concepts. Exemplifying the educational system's attempt to regulate change via clearly defined stages is the ritual by which the girls change the colour of their hair ribbons, signalling the movement from one 'stage' of growth to the next, inaugurated by the arrival at the school of younger girls. The school dictates what the girls can do at particular stages of development: for example, blue-ribboned girls can be selected to leave and navy-ribboned girls are able to join the eldest girls in the theatre. This colour coding recalls precisely the kind of spatialisation of time and falsification of duration that Bergson's 'myriad-tinted spectrum', with its emphasis on the subtle nuances between tints and shades, aimed to oppose. Instead, as Bergson writes, 'what is properly vital in growing old is the insensible, infinitely graduated, continuance of the change of form' (2007: 12). Against the slow, 'infinitely graduated' transformations of living creatures, the school imposes a strict hourly schedule to which the girls must adapt, and they even count as they play ('Can you tell time? It's very important here. Can you count?' Iris is asked early on).

The clock, symbol of spatialised time par excellence, is a recurring motif in *Innocence*. In our first vision of the school grounds, the film itself seems to tick like a clock, offering us a series of successive, static shots in a regular rhythm that mimics the mechanism of clockwork. To pass into the underground theatre, however, a large longcase clock must be stopped and a passageway opened within the clock itself. Here, then, the clock becomes a threshold, suggesting that to grasp the unfolding of evolution and change we must, literally and figurally, move 'beyond' the spatialised surface of the clock face. In his analysis of Henri Matisse's *The Red Studio*, Antliff describes the artist's depiction of a clock, 'the very symbol of the temporality the Bergsonian artist seeks to efface', as being opposed by 'the durational experience and rhythmic extensity that [gives] shape to the "plastic space" of his canvases' (1999: 192). *Innocence*, too, displays an attention to what Antliff calls the 'theme of contrasting approaches to temporality', highlighting the distinctions between what the clock may symbolise and the lived experience of passing time (1999: 192). The sound of the ticking clock, which can be heard during many of the scenes depicting the girls' everyday activities, can, in fact, serve to heighten our awareness of slowly passing time and of rhythms of duration other than, or outside, our own. Like the sound of dripping water heard in the underground spaces of the school, the ticking of the clock 'imposes a real and irreversible time on what we see [. . .] it presents a trajectory in time' (Chion, 1994: 19).

Grosz has written that 'duration is experienced most incontrovertibly in the phenomenon of waiting' (2004: 197). Waiting, she continues, 'is the subjective experience that perhaps best exemplifies the coexistence of a multiplicity of durations, durations both my own and outside of me' (2004: 197). In Bergson's famous delineation of the durational rhythm of melting sugar, I must wait for the sugar to melt, and the time of waiting is not a mathematical time, but coincides 'with a certain portion of my own duration, which I cannot protract or contract as I like. It is no longer something *thought*, it is something *lived*' (2007: 6, emphasis in original). As Mullarkey comments, this is always Bergson's fundamental temporal question, 'why aren't things instantaneous? [. . .] Why is the universe temporal? Why do we have to wait for the sugar to dissolve?' Such questions are, he continues, as true of film as they are of life, and 'are the first ones that come when there is *felt* time' (2010: 165, emphasis in original). Cinema allows encounters with other durational rhythms which may, to use Grosz's words, 'coalesce to form a "convenient" rhythm or coincidence, or may delay me and make me wait' (2004: 197). Moments of waiting in *Innocence* highlight precisely this sense of protracted, lived duration; even in our first glimpse of the girls, for example, the camera waits patiently for them to gather, one by one, around the newly delivered coffin, before revealing its contents.

The sequence presenting Iris's first night in the school is exemplary in its presentation of 'felt time'. Iris, disorientated by her new environment, lies in bed, waiting for Bianca to return from her mysterious nightly excursions. The scene proceeds through a series of cuts that show Iris looking while the reverse shot roughly approximates her point of view to show what she is looking at: Bianca's empty bed, the other girls, Bianca's empty bed again. Following this, there are five static shots of empty spaces in the school. Like the very first shots of the school, these frames have the regular rhythm of clockwork but their emptiness now specifically speaks to Iris's experience of waiting, despite the momentary shift from her literal point of view. These are, in other words, *spaces where Bianca is not*. After the film cuts back to Iris, we watch a spider crawling, slowly and erratically, across the ceiling. In this moment, the spider is an embodiment of slow-moving time which has a certain shapelessness and lack of direction impossible to measure faithfully in mathematical terms, a temporal expression of Bataille's identification of the spider with a formless universe (1985: 31).

Our experience of being in time can be formulated in terms of immersiveness. For Grosz,

> time is not merely the attribute of a subject, imposed by us on the world [. . .] it is what the universe imposes on us rather than we on it; it is what we find ourselves immersed in, given, as impinging and as enabling our spatiality. We will not be able to understand its experiential nature unless we link subjectivity and the body more directly to temporal immersion, to the coexistence of life with other forms of life. (2004: 4–5)

Grosz's way of describing temporal immersion resonates across many layers of *Innocence*; the girls are spatially immersed in an enclosed world they do not fully comprehend, and temporally immersed within the slow changes of pubescence. There are several points in which the film explicitly announces that it, and we, are becoming immersed in the subjective duration of another 'form of life'. When Alice is rejected by the headmistress and scolded by Mademoiselle Eva, for example, the static framings of previous shots give way to a frame that wobbles slightly as it is trained on Alice's devastated expression. The camera falls to the floor with Alice, briefly tracing a wild arc of blurred space. Just before she faints, we hear a low rumble which is muted as she falls, then returns as an inharmonic tone in a higher register; the sound's lack of stable foundation underlines Alice's own. The sound of the ticking clock is transformed by a granular delay, as though even measurable time is becoming slow and sticky. In the next shot, a canted frame shows a partial, side-on view of the bedroom which blurs into and out of focus, before revealing Alice lying on her side in bed, thus suggesting that the blurred frame has been her point of view. From this point on, Alice is catatonic, and the film's editing accentuates her fragmented experience of time. As she becomes more and less aware of her surroundings, there is a series of disjunctive episodes, each with several shots punctuated by images of the silent Alice: Madame Eva at her bedside, trees framed by the window, a woman washing Alice's legs. Fragments of music from her ballet recital drift in the bedroom. This music, particularly when set against an extreme close-up of Alice's sleeping face, seems to emanate from her dreams, signalling the 'return of grief and rage' (Wilson, 2012: 25), the past interweaving itself into the present. Finally, we see the wall of the school grounds, once closer, once further away. If the latter is what Alice 'sees' in her mind's eye, then it moves her to decisive action; she gathers her clothes and attempts her escape by climbing over the wall.

As significant as such moments of shared subjective duration are, it is interesting to note the points at which they are interrupted and intruded upon in the film. Extremely short or disjunctive shots frequently rupture the progress of an activity. In an early scene, for example, the children are seen in long and mid shots playing with a skipping rope, before there is a yelp and a sudden cut to a close-up of Selma's hand holding the rope, with which she seems to have whipped Iris. The next shot, of Iris flinging herself face down on to a bed, is similarly disjunctive. Similarly again, in Nadja's first dance, the film establishes a particular rhythm made by a series of still long and mid shots, which frames the girls as a group, until this pattern is suddenly broken, as the pattern of the dance itself is interrupted. Via a cut which isolates her sprawled body, we see that Nadja has fallen on to the stage floor. She runs for the wings but is forced back by Mademoiselle Eva and, when she falls again, the film suddenly cuts to Nadja sitting up in bed with a startled cry.[1] In both these scenes, a particular rhythm or pattern is disrupted by a diegetic event as well as a 'nick' in the film's form. These are examples of events that may, to use Grosz's words, 'disrupt our immersion in and provoke our conceptualisation of temporal continuity' (2004: 5). Like long takes that temporally exceed our expectations, such 'untimely' moments, ruptures and instances of dislocation, bring duration as a multiplicity to the forefront.

One does not need to be waiting for something definite (the sugar to melt, Bianca to return) to experience a sense of abeyance and deferment. As Wilson has pointed out, childhood in general is, in *Innocence*, perceived as 'a time of waiting and latency' (2012: 28). The film stages 'the very gradual process of gestation, the duration of waiting and entrapment' (2012: 28). To a large extent, this sense of latency is likely to be experienced by the viewer too, as narrative trajectories slowly unfold, tremulous, uncertain meanings accumulate, and full explication of significance is ever deferred. What we are encouraged to do, however, is to pay attention to the process of unfolding (the grain of the sugar as it dissolves, the rhythm of Iris's interior and exterior worlds). One of the important consequences of deploying slowness in unfolding cinematic images is that we are able, to use Schliesser's words, 'to ponder the stillness and mystery of what would ordinarily pass as mundane' (1998: 280), and to feel the textured and tactile resonance of the images before us.

IMMERSION AND MEANING

In *Cinema 1*, Deleuze, almost in passing, describes the space of Robert Bresson's *Lancelot du Lac* (France, 1974) as an 'aquarium-forest' (2005: 112) which vividly recalls the verdant greenness that pervades this film, and the awkward gait of the knights in their armour, almost as though they were walking through water. Deleuze does not dwell on the descriptive resonance of his metaphor. Instead, the 'aquarium-forest' signifies the containment of the film's world: 'the external world itself therefore seems to be a cell, like the aquarium-forest of *Lancelot du Lac*' (2005: 112). Deleuze's broader argument here relates to the way in which Bresson's films construct 'a space of tactile value', spaces that can be linked together in different ways depending on 'new conditions of speed and of movement, on rhythmic values which are opposed to all prior determinations' (2005: 112). Such spaces he will call 'any-spaces-whatever', a term that re-emerges powerfully in *Cinema 2* (2005: 112). What I want to take from this is rather more literal: *Innocence* encloses its developing life forms in an 'aquarium-forest' of its own, which has a powerful tactile resonance, and which opens up different ways in which to consider immersion. It strikes me, however, that, when we speak about the tactile in relation to the viewing experience, we are talking less about enclosure and more about a sense of permeability, or at least about a spectrum upon which such oppositions can be ranged.

Arguably, a sense of immersion is present from the opening moments of *Innocence*. After a long credit sequence, an image appears that depicts bubbling water which is not contained by the frame; its sensorial pulse seems to spill over the screen to immerse us in its depths. Julie Banks describes the 'immediate experience' of the 'mobile texture' of this image (2013), Wilson also writes of its 'haptic immediacy' (2007: 176), while Sobchack argues that these images 'immerse and dislocate us in turbulent water' (2005: 47). The wateriness which we experience during the film's opening will return to permeate the film itself; while the girls swim, the camera floats gently on the surface of the water; when Laura attempts to escape by boat, the film lowers itself into the depths, projecting images from beneath the lake's surface. When the older girls play in the fountain beyond the school grounds, jets of water propel themselves directly towards the camera, briefly becoming scratches on the surface of the film itself (Banks, 2013). These images, in particular, illustrate how, to use Trotter's words, the material elements of an image can be seen to be 'bristling or thrusting out at the viewer' (2007: 70). At its conclusion, the film returns to the material plenitude of watery depths, immersing itself for the last time within aerated teal-blue liquid. As Sobchack writes, 'immersion rather than interpretation – [. . .] this is how *Innocence* begins (and ends)' (2005: 47).

What I want to focus on here, however, is the dynamic relationship between immersion or hapticity and interpretation or meaning, and how this dynamic is explicitly bound up with the film's slow development in duration. In the duration of the viewing experience, our intimate, sensory responses are likely to be continually modulating into and out of interpretive trajectories; part of the pleasure of slowness in film is precisely that it allows for, indeed rewards, movements across a spectrum of responses. As Bergson wrote, 'there is no feeling, no idea, no volition, which is not undergoing change every moment' (2007: 1). Interpretation and intellectual endeavour should not be thought of as static: 'my mental state, as it advances on the road of time, is continually swelling with the duration it accumulates' (Bergson, 2007: 1). Both sense and meaning, that is, unfold and change, and *Innocence* allows them to do so slowly.

The film's opening sequence is, in fact, exemplary in this regard, once we reinsert the immersive liquid images back into their temporal context. Before the images of water, we see a section of what will turn out to be a wooden coffin, with a star-shaped grille inset, suggestive of a contained life form. Its gentle rocking and a sound reminiscent of a moving train imply that the coffin is journeying somewhere. A long credit sequence and the aquatic scenes follow, which can be seen as *both* haptic and symbolically resonant. The watery images may be sensory but they are also perplexing and invite comprehensive questioning. As Marks has argued, faced with an image that we do not understand, such as images that are defamiliarised through an intense close-up focus on their textural properties, we are 'forced to search our memories for other virtual images that might make sense of it' (2000: 47). The provocation to thought may be as powerful as the evocation of tactile response. Particularly on repeated viewings, once we have glimpsed the film's narrative and thematic developments, images of water may pass into and out of symbolic interpretations, becoming, for example, minnow, sperm (Sobchack, 2005: 47) or the primordial liquid within which evolution began. The static shots of the school grounds which follow culminate in revealing Iris inside the coffin. As Quinlivan has pointed out, the opening of the film suggests 'an abstract entering into Hadžihalilović's contained world' (2013: 39). The film is thus both thematising and enacting an immersion within a space, including our own immersion 'within' the film.

We can also approach this dynamic from the other end of the spectrum and consider how the operation of temporality in film can put meaning into flux, unsettling the theoretical frameworks that we may want to attach to particular images, scenes, or the film as a whole. As I described above, the film encourages us to make particular connections between the maturation of the girls and the life cycle of caterpillars as they transform into butterflies, and the moment in which a butterfly emerges from a chrysalis in the schoolroom can easily be 'read' in light of this. This connection may be made in an instant but the scene extends in time, and the material presence of the creatures in the frame is not, to use Trotter's words, 'used up in meaning' (2007: 66). Instead, across several cuts, we watch the fluttering of the newly emergent insect. It forms a dynamic green blur within a frame which barely contains it, alighting gently on Madame Edith's hand before taking off again. This image is a resonant example of how cinema can activate, in Marks's terms (2000, xi), memories of the senses, potentially transferring the soft trembling of powdered wings on to our own skin. Other encounters with the natural world refuse to fit neatly within interpretative frameworks. During a walk in the park, for example, Bianca and Iris come upon a deer grazing on a path. They watch it for a moment before it skips away into the undergrowth. The film here draws out a moment that resonates with an uncertain importance; it pulsates with a significance, suggested partly by the film's focus on Iris's intense gaze, which nevertheless remains ambiguous. This moment, like the one in which a snail crawls slowly along a rock, or a caterpillar is blown about on a leaf by a strong wind, instead draws attention to microscopic changes within slowed-down time, both in the film, and in our own responses to it.

Though the educational system in *Innocence* attempts to impose a homogeneous evolutionary programme on its developing life forms, envisioning temporal progress as embodied in clocks, schedules and colour-coded stages of development, the film affords us glimpses into a Bergsonian universe. In Bergsonian terms, 'evolution involves something quite different than the realization of a programme [. . .] the "gates of the future" are open' (Ansell Pearson, 2002: 79). Through *Innocence*, we can see the ways in which the ceaseless operation of duration, particularly in its multiplicity and in the inter-penetration of variegated rhythms, escapes measurement and containment. At particular moments, the film asks us to share the slow unfolding of 'felt' time alongside the characters, moments of waiting, latency and uncertainty that unfold gradually and tend towards an unknown future. Similarly, *Innocence* resists the neat imposition of a programmatic, interpretive framework, as temporality unfixes symbolism, and allows the development of a spectrum of response that may move freely between the sensory and the meaningful. It is the film's slow and gradual unfolding that allows us to pay attention to the modulation of the images through time, to linger on their aesthetic and compo-sitional transformations, as well as to attend to the evolution of our individual responses to the film's images which vary infinitely between each viewer and each screening.

NOTES

1. This sequence is reminiscent of a similar moment in Luis Buñuel's *The Discreet Charm of the Bourgeoisie* (*Le charme discret de la bourgeoisie*, 1972) when one of the lead characters finds himself on a stage participating in a theatrical perfor-mance; just at the point at which he realises he doesn't know his lines, the film cuts to him waking up. Like *Innocence*, though in its own distinct way, Buñuel's film also creates a rhythm of elongation and interruption, predicated on a surreal unex-pectedness.

BIBLIOGRAPHY

Ansell Pearson, Keith (2002), *Philosophy and the Adventure of the Virtual: Bergson and the Time of Life* (London and New York: Routledge).
Antliff, Mark (1999), 'The Rhythms of Duration: Bergson and the Art of Matisse', in J. Mullarkey (ed.), *The New Bergson* (Manchester and New York: Manchester University Press), pp. 184–208.
Banks, Julie (2013), 'Innocent When You Dream: Affect and Perception through Lucile Hadžihalilović's *Innocence*', *Screening the Past*, available at: http://www.screeningthe past.com/2013/09/innocent-when-you-dream-affect-and-perception-through-lucile-hadzihalilovic%E2%80%99s-innocence/ [accessed 9 November 2014].
Bataille, Georges (1985), *Visions of Excess: Selected Writings 1927–1939* (Minneapolis, MN: University of Minnesota Press).
Bergson, Henri [1896] (1962), *Matter and Memory* (London: George Allen and Unwin).
Bergson, Henri [1912] (1999), *An Introduction to Metaphysics* (Indianapolis, IN: Hackett Publishing Company).
Bergson, Henri [1911] (2007), *Creative Evolution* (Basingstoke and New York: Palgrave Macmillan).
Chion, Michel (1994), *Audio-Vision: Sound on Screen* (New York: Columbia University Press).
Darwin, Charles [1859] (1996), *On The Origin of Species* (Oxford: Oxford University Press).

Deleuze, Gilles [1986] (2005), *Cinema 1: The Movement–Image* (London and New York: Continuum).

Deleuze, Gilles [1989] (2005), *Cinema 2: The Time–Image* (London and New York: Continuum).

Grosz, Elizabeth (2004), *The Nick of Time: Politics, Evolution and the Untimely* (Durham, NC and London: Duke University Press).

Marks, Laura U. (2000), *The Skin of the Film* (Durham, NC: Duke University Press).

Mullarkey, John (2010), *Philosophy and the Moving Image: Refractions of Reality* (Basingstoke: Palgrave Macmillan).

Quinlivan, Davina (2013), 'The French Female Butterfly Collector: Hadžihalilović, Denis, de van and the cinema du corps', *Studies in European Cinema* 10: 1, 35–44.

Schliesser, John (1998), 'Antonioni's Heideggerian Swerve', *Literature Film Quarterly*, 26.4, 278–87.

Sobchack, Vivian (2005), 'Waking Life', *Film Comment* 41: 6, 46–9.

Trotter, David (2007), *Cinema and Modernism* (Malden, MA: Blackwell).

Wedekind, Frank [1903] (2010), *Mine-Haha, or, On the Bodily Education of Young Girls* (London: Hesperus Press).

Wilson, Emma (2007), 'Miniature Lives, Intrusion and Innocence: Women Filming Children', *French Cultural Studies* 18: 2, 169–83.

Wilson, Emma (2012), 'Beauvoir's Children: Girlhood in *Innocence*', in Jean-Pierre Boulé and Ursula Tidd (eds), *Existentialism in Contemporary Cinema: A Beauvoirian Perspective* (New York and Oxford: Berghahn), pp. 17–31.

21. THE SLOW ROAD TO EUROPE: THE POLITICS AND AESTHETICS OF STALLED MOBILITY IN *HERMAKONO* AND *MORGEN*

Michael Gott

This chapter will consider the intersection of slow cinema with road movies that narrate voyages to and through Europe. The two films under consideration here, *Heremakono* (Abderrahmane Sissako, France/Mauritania, 2002) and *Morgen* (Marian Crişan, Romania/France/Hungary, 2010), are concerned with slow voyages towards Western Europe with starting points in Africa and Eurasia. Despite the frequent association of the road movie with speed, slow cinema and road movies are a natural pairing in a contemporary European context where, for political and economic reasons, certain journey narratives are apt to become 'slow' – or paused – road movies. Travel by foot has traditionally been more prevalent in European road films which have tended to place less emphasis on auto-mobility and speed than in the American strain (Laderman, 2002: 258; Mazierska and Rascaroli, 2006: 8). At the same time, the 'single minded walk-in-the-wilderness' film is a staple of slow cinema (Romney, 2010: 43). *Heremakono* and *Morgen,* however, both take 'slow' a step beyond the simply plodding or meandering trek by focusing on pauses in the respective voyages rather than on the voyages themselves. Scholarly examinations of European road cinema have recently drawn attention to a number of films that depict stalled voyages and focus on 'socio-cultural tension that cannot find release in the transformative experience of the journey' (Rascaroli, 2013: 22).

In their 'articulation of motion in terms of confinement' (Laderman, 2013: 175), stopover films problematise the very concept of a 'road' movie. Ute Fendler, writing on francophone African contributions to the genre, defines a 'true' road movie as one in which 'all of the action unfolds on the road, between the point of departure and arrival' (Fendler, 2008: 79).[1] If we accept this criterion, films such as *Heremakono* and *Morgen,* which zero in on what happens during a pause in the voyage, could arguably be read as anti-road movies. Indeed, within contemporary Fortress Europe, speed is often equated with movement across spaces: in particular, the ease of border crossing, as in Wim Wenders's *Lisbon Story* (1994) and numerous other European films from the past twenty years.[2] In many examples of what, for Fendler, would qualify as 'true' road movies, however, Wenders's film included, mechanical malfunctions or other vicissitudes of the road leave travellers initially short of their intended destinations. Whether planned or unanticipated, pauses and stopovers are practically ubiquitous elements of the road-movie formula, and the waypoints of the voyage are a crucial extension of the road itself. While *Heremakono* and *Morgen* both open and close with travellers on the road between points A and B, it is their scrutiny of narrative pauses that truly marks both films aesthetically and politically as road movies of a 'slow' variety.

Slow cinema and road movies are categories that also go well together from a political perspective. Indeed, the road movie template has commonly provided a vehicle for cultural critique (Laderman, 2002: 1) and, as Cohan and Hark have argued, 'a road movie provides a ready space for exploration of the tensions and crises of the historical moment during which it is produced' (Cohan and Hark, 1997: 2). With this in mind, there is arguably no more salient example of the politics of slowness in contemporary European cinema than in the 'negative' category of road movies. While films that might be labelled 'positive' are more closely 'associated with open roads and by extension mobility, those on the negative side are primarily concerned with the implications of closed borders' (Gott and Schilt, 2013: 3). If mobility is increasingly the norm in Europe, as Mazierska and Rascaroli put it in the first study of the European road-movie genre (2006: 4), then those not empowered with the mobility bestowed by passports and bank accounts languish on slow, abortive treks encumbered by border patrols and cut short by unscrupulous smugglers or, as in the films discussed here, are left in persistent waiting mode. The intense, deliberate and thoughtful gaze levelled on both ponderous voyages and the general sense of indeterminacy in a growing number of negative road films invites us to align them with the 'austere' minimalism (Romney, 2010: 43) that is characteristic of slow cinema. Through my readings of *Morgen* and *Heremakono* I aim to explore the links between cinematic slowness and resistance to European immigration policy as well as the aesthetic connections between each film and the formal qualities normally associated with slow cinema.

Fortress Europe and the Politics of Slowness

The films under consideration here are a distinctive part of a growing canon of works narrating voyages to and through Fortress Europe. Essential to my reading of the relationship between these films and European border policy is the understanding of the 'fortress' element of that equation as not simply an impermeable exterior barrier but a constellation of efforts to limit access to Europe's external frontiers, as well as to police and detain migrants from outside the European Union already present within those borders (Thomas, 2012: 177). In Fortress Europe, borders and checkpoints are 'ubiquitous' within the territory (Balibar, 2009: 203). Moreover, the efforts to police and control migrants also extend far beyond the outer limits of the EU to spaces, such as the Sahara, which must be traversed by migrants en route to Europe (Mezzadro, 2004). We join the protagonist of each film just as their respective treks are reaching a stopping point that is short of the intended final destination. Waiting is the central focus of each narrative and, as I shall discuss later, a concept that permeates the formal qualities of each film. *Morgen* is about two characters in limbo whose paths cross. Nelu (András Hatházi) is a Romanian from the town of Salonta, near the Hungarian border, whose daily routine involves crossing that frontier for his job as a security guard in a supermarket and whose life is mired in a seemingly futureless transitional state between old and new economic systems. One day, while fishing in the border zone, he encounters Behran (Yilmaz Yalcin), a Turkish migrant attempting to cross the official frontier into Schengen Europe[3] to join his family in Germany. Berhan is waylaid in Romania when smugglers deposit him short of his intended destination.

In *Heremakono,* Abdallah (Mohamed Mahmoud Ould Mohamed) makes a planned pause on his south–north trek in the Mauritanian village where his mother resides in order to wait for a passport to be issued. While it is not yet European border policies which are directly holding him back, several oblique side narratives involving other waiting migrants more clearly demonstrate the dangers facing those attempting to reach Europe without the requisite documents. One waiting migrant announces his intention to call off his voyage to Spain and return home to Heremakono, the town that provides the film's title. The body of another traveller washes ashore near his point of departure soon after his friends speculate about the progress of his voyage.

The stopovers are necessitated by political and administrative formalities but, most importantly, are also related to fundamental structural factors inherent both to the road movie and to EU policies. Rather than representing anomalies in the traditional fabric of road movies, such pauses in forward progress are extenuated versions of what might be called the 'road event', a staple element in road cinema. As Timothy Corrigan explains, 'unlike other genres, such as the detective film where characters initiate events, in the road movie events act upon the characters' (Corrigan, 1991: 145). Yet, here, the intermittency of both travellers' trajectories towards Western Europe is not the product of individual misfortune or the twists of fate that punctuate road films and divert or stall forward progress. On the contrary, the slowness of roads to Europe is entirely consistent with the logic of European migration policy which simultaneously attracts and repels people from less economically developed regions. Some fifteen million migrants reach or cross the European Union annually (Verstraete, 2010: 5), and *Heremakono* and *Morgen* represent the two primary trajectories involved: from the east and from the south (Rascaroli, 2013: 23). Dominic Thomas points out that if 'migration has emerged as a key geometric coordinate of globalization today, then so too has the concern with *controlling* the planetary circulation of human beings (labour forces, asylum seekers, refuges), particularly when it comes to the African continent' (2012: 157, original emphasis). Thomas argues that, despite the effort to police the borders of Europe, migrants remain drawn to Europe by 'push' factors and 'pull' factors that motivate migration (Thomas, 2012: 163–5, 170). The latter point explains why, as Étienne Balibar contends, European policies have the dual functions of attracting and repelling migrants, ultimately 'installing them in a condition of permanent insecurity' (Balibar, 2009: 203). In a similar vein, while Sandro Mezzadra goes as far as to label European border policy as effectively an unconventional war, he also insists that Europe does not aim to seal 'hermetically' its exterior borders but has instituted a system of 'dams' that allow for the selective inclusion of migrant labour (Mezzadra, 2004). *Morgen*, in particular brings attention to this state of affairs.

A slow cinematic approach is well suited to capture the tangible, lived experience resulting from this push–pull ambivalence and chronic insecurity. Crişan's film continuously points out the contradictions of European law and the concomitant 'unevenness' (Verstraete, 2010: 5) of mobility to, and within, Europe as seen through the vantage point of the film's Romanian protagonist. The unexpected visit by Behran leads Nelu, who crosses the border between Hungary and Romania regularly, to become familiar with the political and practical components of European external border policy. Constant border-crossing complications elicit the resigned objection of the Romanian whose futile refrain, 'But we are all in the European Union?', ultimately goes unanswered by authorities. His encounter with the 'clandestine' Behran, however, will engender a deeper reaction to regulations that draw lines of demarcation not only between his spheres of everyday living (work, home and fishing) but also between a Turkish man and his family, culminating with an uncharacteristically fervid monologue on the fundamental unfairness of Europe's closed borders by the typically demure Romanian. Such outbursts are rare in both films in which understated emotions and the slow passage of time of paused

Figure 21.1 'But we are all in the European Union?': Nelu (András Hatházi) approaches the border crossing between Hungary and Romania in *Morgen* (2010).

migrations predominate. Rather than incitements to action, these films invite viewers to contemplate these travellers' political status and their tangible experiences of waiting.

If slowness seems singularly adapted to represent the waiting component of migration, it espouses an approach that is distinctly different from typical representations of migration issues in Europe, which remain under the surface – unseen or 'clandestine' – until they become a spectacular event. As Ursula Biemann observes, 'capsized boats and clandestine immigrants washing up on European shores: these are the dramatic images that put Europe's southern border in the news again and again' (Biemann, 2008: 3). Recent European cinema abounds with depictions of perilous border crossings that end in death or arrest.[4] By contrast *Heremakono* and *Morgen* stand out for their banal representations of migration. They are slow in part because they do not represent the drama involved in the confrontation with Europe's line of demarcation, be it a border post or the sea, but, instead, explore the tediousness, inevitable waiting and wasted motion involved in all treks by outsiders to and through Fortress Europe. The particular political significance of the slow road movie emerges from the framing of such stalled mobility and frustrated, if not entirely dashed, aspirations within the context of EU policy and discourse. I have already noted the push–pull factors which work at cross purposes by attracting and repelling migrants but it is worth considering another contradiction inherent in the elaboration of Fortress Europe. The escalated effort to police external frontiers and increased attention to border control have been accompanied by an opening of internal frontiers within European Union member states (Thomas, 2012: 71). In fact, the concept of mobility so critical to the project of European unification is fundamentally based on the principle of 'free movement of goods, people, services and capital' as well as the recognition that all citizens of the European Union have the right to reside wherever they desire within the limits of the union (Verstraete, 2010: 4). The waiting and the wasted motion by migrants, chronicled in great detail in *Heremakono* and *Morgen*, are rendered particularly poignant against such a backdrop of ostensible openness and increased (and idealised) mobility.

THE AESTHETICS OF WAITING

Having briefly outlined the social and political framing of slowness, I shall use the remainder of the chapter to draw attention to how *Heremakono* and *Morgen* adapt slow cinema aesthetics to represent the migrant experience. Let us briefly explore some of the characteristics of the slow approach that encourage viewers to consider the flip side of European mobility. In slow journey films in general, the logic of linear progression, as an essential narrative force, is typically undermined. As Tiago de Luca writes of Mexican director Carlos Reygadas's 2002 film *Japón*: 'the scenes of his solitary wanderings undermine narrative momentum, inviting the viewer to contemplate, in silent long takes, images of the landscape he traverses' (de Luca, 2012: 194). Matthew Flanagan cites 'the employment of (often extremely) long takes, de-centred and understated modes of storytelling, and a pronounced emphasis on quietude and the everyday' (Flanagan, 2008). For Ira Jaffe, slow movies 'restrict motion, action, dialogue and glitter', resulting in characters who 'do little but wait over long stretches of time' (Jaffe, 2014: 9, 12). Finally, the principle of restrained narrative movement extends to the slow cinema camera, which generally remains 'unusually still' and results in a preponderance of long takes, but also in a preference for long shots over close-ups (Jaffe, 2014: 3).

In the following I shall address specific examples with a focus on how, in each film, the juxtaposition of waiting with motion contributes to the representation of the political, economic and social realities highlighted above. Both films can be identified as slow in several key ways: most notably by a narrative focus on the pause in a voyage rather than its progression and through the cultivation of duration, both as enabled by the long take and by other means, which offers spectators some insight into the act of waiting. *Morgen* belongs, both thematically and aesthetically, to the current known as New Romanian cinema, which started making waves on the film-festival circuit in 2005 with Cristi Puiu's *Moartea Domnului Lăzărescu* (*The Death of Mr Lăzărescu*). Poverty is both a significant theme of this cinema and a widely cited source of inspiration for the particular New Romanian style which Nasta describes as a 'minimalist model' (2013: 155) characterised by

> recurrent use of long shots, lateral framing of tableau-like compositions, minute scrutiny of everyday, often non-spectacular details, a consistent refusal to use any score . . . plus a constant challenging of audience emotional participation, through the lack of ellipses and the use of everyday small talk close to documentary 'live shooting'. (Nasta, 2013: 157)

Morgen is marked by austere cinematography and Crişan's focus on the banality of waiting. The generally static (if, sometimes, ever-so-slightly unsteady) camera homes in on extraordinarily rudimentary details of Nelu's everyday existence: chopping wood, washing dishes, peeling potatoes, getting dressed, fishing, shopping for a fishing rod, and loafing or pacing to pass time at work. Much of this takes place as the stalled traveller Behran waits in the cramped, dim cellar of Nelu's dilapidated house. Waiting is the most common activity in the film. Behran is constantly entreated to sit down and wait, and the characters often wait together in situations which emphasise their precarious positions in Europe: at the office of Nelu's brother-in-law, where they are looking for temporary work for the Turk, and in the crowded waiting room of a medical clinic. In several scenes Behran takes part in Nelu's above-ground drudgery all of which involves some sort of waiting. These sequences often feature yet another trademark of contemporary slow cinema, the 'stubbornly stationary camera which refuses to follow a character that has left the screen' (de Luca, 2012: 192). In *Morgen* the camera itself appears to be waiting patiently for action, not bothering to follow the characters' generally futile movements which do not – as Rascaroli puts it in her conceptualisation of stalled road movies – offer any relief from states of strain and discomfort associated with waiting to travel (2013: 21). In other words, this type of slow, static scene composed of takes as long as ninety-six seconds is what results when the characters seek to be in motion but the narrative logic, imposed by political realities, does not allow for mobility.

In *Morgen* the camera generally remains static unless a character is 'on the road', in which case movement is registered by tracking shots that have a distinctly slow feel. The travel sequences, including the montage that closes the film with a successful border crossing, are good examples of what slow iterations of travel in road movies might look like. The sequences are filmed in long tracking shots that bear little resemblance to the spirit or speed of the archetypal road movie 'travelling shots' which David Laderman contrasts with 'conventional' tracking shots. Whereas tracking shots are generally slow, at walking or perhaps running speed, 'travelling shots' express 'a visceral sense of travelling at a hyper-human, modernized speed' (2002: 15). Travel in *Morgen* is captured by two distinct types of tracking shots. When Behran walks, a shaky, handheld camera follows him closely from behind. When Nelu travels by motorised vehicle, whether alone or with Behran, the camera is mounted on another vehicle either behind or, occasionally, in front of his.

Morgen opens with a deliberately paced tracking shot which, at just over four minutes, is the longest sequence shot in the film. The black credit screen disappears to reveal a motorcycle and sidecar slowly approaching the Hungarian border. In keeping with the Romanian minimalist style, the only sound is furnished by the puttering motorcycle. A 40-kilometre speed limit sign emerges on the right. The camera keeps its distance, framing the vehicle in a long tracking shot from behind that precludes any initial insight into the driver's demeanour or identity. As the machine coasts into the border crossing, the camera settles in a bit closer. The dim, dawn lighting makes it impossible to see more than silhouettes as border guards argue with Nelu over the fish he intends to bring across the border. This might be the European Union, explain the guards, but the fish requires a permit to cross the border. Ultimately defeated, Nelu resignedly dumps the fish next to the bike and sputters off. Rather than following him, the camera remains static and lingers on the border crossing as the fish flops desperately outside the border post. Thus, the opening montage of what could have been 'travelling shots', in the sense of the term suggested by Laderman, is transformed by border policy into a static shot. The profound political symbolism and implications for mobility represented by the dying creature will become evident in due course: Behran, like the fish, will be pulled from the water to ride in Nelu's sidecar and, lacking the requisite documentation for crossing the border, will ultimately be destined to repeat the same useless motion as the writhing aquatic creature.

In the service of smuggling Behran across the border into Hungary and setting him back on his way to Germany, the duo engages in a number of other futile attempts at mobility. Practically speaking, these circular forays offer no advantage over immobile waiting. In one case, they attempt to cross the border in a road-painting machine, marked with a 20-kilometre speed limit, that has ostensibly been commissioned to paint on both sides of the national frontier, certainly one of the slowest motorised modes of conveyance imaginable – jokingly referred to as 'Formula 1' – and followed with a suitably slow tracking shot (the speed limit sign reprises an image from the opening sequence, making it a recurring symbol of the slow road to Europe). At another point, they do successfully cross the border undetected aboard a bus full of football fans headed to a match with a cross-frontier rival, only to return to Romania after Behran is spooked by the police and a scrum between fans and players breaks out, sending them both to the hospital for treatment of minor injuries. Beyond representing a darkly comical addition to Behran's accumulated border-crossing difficulties, the scene also subtly mocks wider aspirations of cross-border European unity.

Despite its focus on narrative pause and ineffectual motion, *Morgen* does allow Behran some modest and precarious mobility and charts Nelu's transformation from passive waiting subject to active agent. After being arrested by the Romanian border police, Behran is eventually set free and, ultimately, yet again delivered to the other side by Nelu who stows the Turk in the sidecar of his motorcycle and opens a gate, marking an isolated border crossing, with the same axe featured in earlier wood-chopping scenes. Once delivered to the other side, Behran sets off again towards Germany, the camera following him into the borderland brush before stopping to allow him to walk out of the frame in the final shot.

Heremakono shares the rudimentary aesthetic and narrative of *Morgen*. Larry Daressa reads it as 'essentially plotless', noting that 'characters appear without explanation and vanish without closure' (2003: 72). These characteristics align *Heremakono* with other wander-through-the-landscape contributions to the slow cinema canon. *Heremakono* provides sparse detail on the motivations, destinations and points of origins of the characters; a narrative choice that clearly underscores the anonymity of the tens of thousands of the migrants who make paths for Europe each year. While the slow qualities of *Heremakono* serve a political point, I should like to suggest another way to understand this slowness. Beyond the association of travel-as-waiting with death and suffering, Sissako's film also endorses the slow movie gesture of promoting reflection. Abdallah's mother confides to an acquaintance that 'He just sits alone . . . He thinks all the time.' Such a contemplative impulse within the narrative should be situated within the context of Sissako's work. His 1998 film, *La vie sur terre/Life on Earth* (1998), depicts a world in Mali (Sokolo, his father's village) where 'time has no meaning' (Armes, 2006: 193). Harrow finds in that film's slow pace, exemplified by the 'old-fashioned technologies of the South', by contrast to the excess and consumption of the north, an evocation 'of the beauty of Sissako's humanism' (2012: 178). With this in mind, the pensive element of *Heremakono* should be seen as a necessary complement to the political and realist representation of slowness.

For Fendler, road movies lend themselves particularly well to the representation of the state of development and transition in African societies, a social project that finds visual expression in an 'abundance of sites of transit and suspended movement' (2008: 86). *Heremakono* is in this sense an archetypal African road movie in which, much like *Morgen*, waiting is featured as both a pastime and a metaphor. While he awaits the passport needed to continue his travels, Abdallah passes the time idly at his mother's home and waits at a medical clinic and at the home of a relative. Both films are concerned with the implications of closed borders and the experience of waiting and harness slow cinema elements in the service of promoting contemplation about social and political components of waiting. The directors, however, portray passing time differently. Whereas episodes of waiting in *Morgen* do not reflect deep reflection on the part of the characters, focusing instead on their futile and slow circular movements, Sissako fills the narrative pause with meditative silence. The stasis in *Heremakono* is imbued with a pensive feel first established by the opening scene. As we witness a desert devoid of human presence, the mechanical ambient noise of the motorcycle from *Morgen's* opening is replaced by the sound of wind-blown sand and softly crashing waves, signifiers of two ultimately inhospitable and uncrossable natural features. Desert vistas and seascapes devoid of human presence are regularly framed with deliberate camera movements, suggesting a very different concept of time (indeed, the question of time and of passing time is raised by several characters and evoked through imagery). And, in contrast to Nelu and Behran, whose constant fidgeting reflect a profound tension between motion and stasis, Abdallah is generally content to sit and contemplate in solitude.

My analysis will focus on two pensive moments: one during Abdallah's immobile wait, and the other after he packs his suitcase and ostensibly sets off. While he occasionally reads or practises Hassaniya, Abdallah spends the majority of his time sitting, standing in a doorway or lying in bed looking out through a knee-level window on to the street. One early waiting sequence exhibits a slow passage of time that is evoked without recourse to the long takes which predominate in *Morgen*. The scene opens with Abdallah on the courtyard steps of his mother's home, observing a neighbour as she braids a young girl's hair. The entire episode lasts a little less than five minutes, with the longest take lasting shortly more than twenty seconds. The monotonous passing of time is represented by the absence of any narrative thread beyond the act of waiting and by narrative and visual repetition. A shot-reverse-shot series cuts between Abdallah and the girl several times before being interrupted by a cut to a wandering salesman hawking veils. Another cut follows, this time to another young girl waiting, seated next to a sleeping woman under a tent in the same courtyard. The camera will return to them; as Abdallah continues to pass time the woman awakes off camera and when we next join them she is playing a kora (a West African harp) and giving the girl a signing lesson. This detail – an insignificant narrative fast-forward – suggests that the waiting montage is constructed by a series of hardly perceptible ellipses with little narrative purpose beyond the representation of Abdallah's wait: the musician, once sleeping, is now doing something else, whereas Abdallah is simply still waiting.

Later Abdallah walks inside and gazes out at the feet of passers-by through a very low window in a static shot lasting 22 seconds. As Harrow observes in relation to *Bamako* (2006), such 'cut-off images . . . of partially viewed people crossing the screen horizontally' are signatures of Sissako's cinema (2012: 185). He suggests that this technique, which contrasts with panning or tracking, creates the impression that the viewer remains fixed and motionless while the world passes by (Harrow, 2012: 301). The next cut returns us to a twenty-four-second Steadicam shot of the courtyard music lesson in which the camera slowly circles the singing girl. Before this waiting sequence ends, the camera cuts back to Abdallah, who is now standing in the doorway, close to where he sat as the scene began. Yet this sequence is about more than the ponderous passage of time. The longer takes are interspersed with regular, short close-ups of quotidian, yet symbolic, details – shoes, to cite one example – which suggest that waiting makes possible careful observation of the world.

The camera will revisit these spaces and images several more times, capturing more waiting, before Abdallah finally resumes his trek. The onward voyage is perhaps even more enigmatic than the often unexplained episodes in the earlier portion of the film. Abdallah departs but it is not entirely clear how far the voyage will progress or, indeed, if it will continue. The sequence begins when the camera cuts to a long shot of him framed by endless sand. In this shot, lasting twenty-eight seconds, suitcase in hand, Abdallah plods up a dune that fills much of the frame, only to turn back before reaching the summit. He retraces his steps to the bottom and sits in the sand to wait once again. A stranger will pass by and light a cigarette for him before continuing silently on his way, over and beyond the dune that halted Abdallah's progress. Left unclear is if, or why, the voyage was again paused and what precisely Abdallah is waiting for now. An equivalent of sorts to various futile movements in *Morgen*, Abdallah's short return voyage up and down the hill echoes in one pithy sequence the earlier narrative sidebars about circular voyages; one aborted and another that results in death at sea and return by tide to point of departure.

Conclusion

Morgen and *Heremakono* share visually similar endings. Each frames a protagonist grappling with the landscape as his trek ostensibly resumes. The narratives close with the voyagers doing the same thing we first glimpsed them doing: waiting in the desert in one case, plodding through marshy borderland terrain in the other. The settings evoke the two most typical routes towards Europe and, in the case of *Morgen*, offer a reminder that, in many ways, the road to Europe remains slow for those from the eastern margins of the European Union.

Though they close with their respective characters back on the road, neither film instils the idea that the voyages are entirely back on course or that the intended destinations are likely to be attained. The slow elements of these films invite the viewer to ponder the travails of those struggling to achieve true mobility which are inextricably linked to their political contexts.

If the narrative end points do not correspond to the ends of the voyages, it is not because the travellers are back on the road, as is common in road movies, but because their stopovers took over the narrative. Nor is the slowness of these films entirely explained by the slow cinema impulse towards, as theorised by Jaffe, a reaction to the 'ruthless pace of global consumerism' (2014: 7). Meandering is not a form of escape, the product of a choice to embrace slowness. In fact, the protagonists in question are desperately seeking to join the fast-paced consumerist world but are more probably destined to languish on the slow road instead.

If, as Verstraete argues, mobilities in Europe are 'differentially produced' (2010: 6), then the contours of these differences are highlighted by slow cinema approaches. Slow road movies represent the inevitable inversion of the 'fast' variety of European road film in which borders in the broadest sense are traversed and transgressed with ease. For every open internal frontier opened, an outside barrier is reinforced; for every border check, there is a 'pull' factor drawing a migrant to Europe; and for every segment of forward voyage, there is a stop. The intersection of slow cinema and the contemporary European road cinema is found at this narrative and political pause. *Heremakono* and *Morgen* create a unique commentary on the underside of the EU border and migration policy by extending this pause, making it the centre of the narrative itself. In doing so, these slow road movies therefore invite discussions of movement versus mobility, and of which aesthetic and generic approaches are best suited to represent the contemporary realities of migration to Fortress Europe.

NOTES

1. My translation from French.
2. Recent films which emphasise the ease of flows across national borders within Schengen Europe include *Im Juli/In Juli* (Fatih Akin, 2000, Germany), *Comme des voleurs (à l'est)* (*Stealth,* Lionel Baier, 2006, Switzerland), and *Rabat* (Victor Ponten and Jim Taihuttu, 2011, Netherlands). Many films produced in Central and Eastern Europe have been more likely to focus on the difficulty of cross-border travel towards Western Europe.
3. Hungary joined the European Union in 2004 and was admitted to the Schengen area in 2007. Romania became an EU member in 2007, three years before *Morgen* was released, but, as of 2014, has still not been admitted to the Schengen area.
4. *In this World* (Michael Winterbottom, 2002, Britain), *Spare Parts* (*Rezervni deli,* Damjan Kozole, 2003, Slovenia), *Harragas* (Merzak Allouache, 2009, Algeria/France) and *Welcome* (Philippe Lioret, 2009, France) are examples of films that narrate perilous border crossings by migrants.

BIBLIOGRAPHY

Armes, Roy (2006), *African Filmmaking: North and South of the Sahara* (Bloomington, IN: Indiana University Press).
Balibar, Étienne (2009), 'Europe as borderland', *Society and Space,* 27, 190–215.

Bieman, Ursula (2008), 'Writing Video – Writing the World: Videographies as Cognative Medium', *Transit*, 4: 1, 3, http://escholarship.org/uc/item/5542b0rw [accessed 2 June 2014].

Cohan, Steve and Ina Rae Hark (1997), 'Introduction', in Steve Cohan and Ina Rae Hark (eds), *The Road Movie Book* (London, New York: Routledge), pp. 271–86.

Corrigan, Timothy (1991), *A Cinema Without Walls: Movies and Culture After Vietnam* (New Brunswick, NJ: Rutgers University Press).

Daressa, Larry (2003), 'Heremakono', *Cineaste*, 28: 4, 72.

de Luca, Tiago (2012), 'Realism of the Senses: A Tendency in Contemporary World Cinema', in L. Nagib, C. Perriam and Rajinder Dudrah (eds), *Theorizing World Cinema* (London: I. B. Tauris), pp. 183–206.

Fendler, Ute (2008), 'Le road movie dans le contexte interculturel africain', *CiNéMAS* 18: 2/3, 68–88.

Flanagan, Matthew (2008), 'Towards an Aesthetic of Slow in Contemporary Cinema', 16: 9 in English, November, http://www.16-9.dk/2008-11/side11_inenglish.htm [accessed 18 March 2014].

Gott, Michael and Thibault Schilt (2013), 'Introduction', in Michael Gott and Thibault Schilt (eds), *Open Roads, Closed Borders: The Contemporary French-language Road Movie* (London: Intellect), pp. 1–17.

Harrow, Keneth W. (2012), *Trash: African Cinema from Below* (Bloomington, IN: Indiana University Press).

Jaffe, Ira (2014), *Slow Movies: Countering the Cinema of Action* (London: Wallflower).

Laderman, David (2002), *Driving Visions: Exploring the Road Movie* (Austin, TX: University of Texas Press).

Laderman, David (2013), 'Traffic in Souls: The Perils and Promises of Mobility in La Promesse', in M. Gott and T. Schilt (eds), *Open Roads and Closed Borders: The Contemporary French-language Road Movie* (Bristol: Intellect), pp. 173–86.

Mazierska, Ewa and Laura Rascaroli (2006), *Crossing New Europe: Postmodern Travel and the European Road Movie* (London: Wallflower Press).

Mezzadra, Sandro (2004), 'Citizenship in Motion', *MakeWorlds*, 22 February, http://makeworlds.org/node/83 [accessed 18 March 2014].

Nasta, Dominique (2013), *Contemporary Romanian Cinema: The History of an Unexpected Miracle* (London: Wallflower).

Rascaroli, Laura (2013), 'On the Eve of the Journey: Tangier, Tbilisi, Calais', in Michael Gott and T. Schilt (eds), *Open Roads, Closed Borders: The Contemporary French-Language Road Movie* (Bristol: Intellect), pp. 21–38.

Romney, Jonathan (2010), 'In Search of Lost Time', *Sight and Sound* 20: 2 (February), 43–4.

Thomas, Dominic (2012), *Africa and France: Postcolonial Cultures, Migration, and Racism* (Bloomington, IN: Indiana University Press).

Verstraete, Ginette (2010), *Tracking Europe: Mobility, Diaspora, and the Politics of Location* (Durham, NC: Duke University Press).

22. CRYSTALLISING THE PAST: SLOW HERITAGE CINEMA

Rob Stone and Paul Cooke

With the crystal-image, Gilles Deleuze describes the fusion of the past tense of what is filmed with the present tense of its viewing, resulting in an ongoing exchange between the virtual and the actual (2007: 66–94). The crystal-image therefore begs some affinity with the genre or subcorpus of the period film known as heritage cinema, which may promise to oppose that which Frederic Jameson describes as 'the disappearance of a sense of history [and] the way in which our entire contemporary social system has little by little begun to lose its capacity to retain its own past' (1982: 125). Because, however, the disappearance of history is the result of living 'in a perpetual present and in a perpetual change that obliterates traditions' (Jameson, 1982: 125), so heritage cinema at times, paradoxically, seems to contribute to this disappearance by rendering the past as spectacle for immediate consumption. Heritage films can resemble cinematic pageants that allow for what Svetlana Bohm (2002) has described as the display of two images at once: the past and the present conjoined in nostalgia. They also underpin a dominant trope in contemporary European cinema, that of a homecoming which requires difficult or impossible negotiations with heritage, that is seen so often in the 'Heimat Film' in Germany, for example, as well as in relation to a similar obsession with homeland in Basque cinema. In addition, the relationship of the contemporary audience to this spectacular past may be understood in terms of identifying the present as a palimpsest of such histories, presented in allegorical mode. Like the crystal-image, which is a philosophical construct, heritage cinema can become, in effect, a two-way mirror dividing and uniting past and present. Reading certain instances in historical dramas as a form of slow cinema via the optic of Deleuze's crystal-image allows us to contemplate the temporal complexity of the image. In so doing, the subversive potential of slowness becomes apparent in heritage cinema, where the suturing of nostalgia can, in fact, be severed and any glib simultaneity of past and present can be shattered. Resisting the auteurist approach which dominates the study of slow cinema, this chapter opts instead for a consideration of slowness in relation to a specific genre. It examines the occasion of slowness in heritage cinema, excavates possible crystal-images, and examines the meanings that such instances provoke.

Defining Heritage Cinema

On the face of it, those films which have been described as heritage cinema would appear to be very different from the other films explored in this volume. The term 'heritage cinema' emerged in the 1990s in Britain to describe a wave of costume dramas which began a decade earlier, when films such as *Chariots of Fire* (Hugh Hudson, 1981) and *A Room With A View* (James Ivory, 1985) were increasingly analysed as a new genre, characterised by slow-moving, episodic narratives organised around props and settings as much as they were around narrative and characters. These films were often read as part of a national project of nostalgic remembrance celebrating British (or rather English) heritage culture, just as the country was undergoing the seismic social shifts of the Thatcher years. Yet they also indicated a mode of film-making that could offer reactionary cinematic reimaginings of English heritage (Higson, 1993, 2003; Monk, 2011). In his defining discussion of this trend, Andrew Higson explored the manner in which heritage films present the past as a 'visually spectacular pastiche, inviting a nostalgic gaze that resists the ironies and social critiques so often suggested narratively by these films' (1993: 109). In so doing, he identified a key tension at the heart of this cycle of film-making which, on the one hand, offered the potential for alternative, and particularly queer, readings of history through their plots, while, through their *mise en scène*, on the other, presenting a conservative (with both a large and small 'c') image of Englishness, readily consumable by international audiences. Discussion of heritage cinema has since tended to focus on the genre's fetishisation of the materiality of the past, along with its representation of gender and sexuality, but Higson's original definition of the term, together with the parameters of the debates it engendered, has also been challenged, redefined and stretched almost to breaking point. Moreover, it has been increasingly noted that such films were not, and are not, unique to British cinema (Galt, 2002; Koepnick, 2002; Vincendeau, 2012). Such films are produced and consumed within very different and distinct social and political contexts, all of which inflect the specific concept of heritage they seek to communicate. For example, a country house draped in a swastika, such as we see in *Napola* (*Before the Fall*, Dennis Gansel, 2004), immediately creates a very different affective relationship with the spectator from a shot of a similar building in a British heritage drama such as *Maurice* (James Ivory, 1987), two films that, on the face of it, would appear to have much in common. The disparate modes of engagement with the past we see across European heritage films, such as *Zemsta* (*The Revenge*, Andrzej Wajda, 2002), *Obaba* (Montxo Armendáriz, 2005), *En kongelig affære* (*A Royal Affair*, Nikolaj Arcel, 2012) and *Tähtitaivas talon yllä* (*Stars Above*, Saara Cantell, 2012), explore a very wide array of historical moments. Yet what unites them is the fact that they are always invariably inflected by the preoccupations of the present, evoking conflicting emotions among those who make and consume such films, emotions driven variously by nostalgia, mourning, or more nationalist, even jingoistic strategies. By drawing on a broad selection of non-British heritage films with notable differences in terms of their production, representation and reception, including the UK–Luxembourg co-production, *The Girl with a Pearl Earring* (Peter Webber, 2003), and the French–German–British–Belgian–Romanian–Norwegian co-production *Joyeux Noël* (*Merry Christmas*, Christian Carion, 2005), Belén Vidal has recently presented the heritage film not as a rigid category but as 'a hybrid genre with porous borders, a genre that is becoming less consensual and more political through its own staunch preference for emotional histories' (2012: 4). The function of slowness in this 'less consensual' dimension of heritage cinema is what we shall investigate via discussion of the crystal-image.

DETERRITORIALISED OUTSIDERNESS

Before turning to a discussion of Deleuze, let us first consider the relationship of the contemporary audience to what such films invariably present as a spectacular past. This may be understood in terms of a structure of deterritorialised outsiderness, similar to that which pervades the art of exiles, which commonly focuses on the spatial relationships between the familiar and the unfamiliar but is defined here by temporal alienation. The audience may assume the temporalised tourist gaze on such representations of history as *Chariots of Fire*, *Indochine* (Régis Wargnier, 1992), *Emma* (Douglas McGrath, 1996) or even certain Hollywood historical-event films, such as *The Patriot* (Roland Emmerich, 2000), which would not normally be discussed in the same breath as these other films but with which they can have a good deal in common. Heritage films, such as these, tend to be punctuated and driven by dramatic scenes, yet long takes and minimal camera movements can also slow them down for the haptic encounter that allows the spectator to experience, even fetishise, the detail of the visual: the embossed wallpaper and paint-chipped walls that figure prominently in *The King's Speech* (Tom Hooper, 2010), the scars on bodies in *Django Unchained* (Quentin Tarantino, 2012), the food on Hitler's plate in *Der Untergang* (*Downfall*, Oliver Hirschbiegel, 2003) or the more sumptuous fare we are encouraged to consume visually in *Chocolat* (Lasse Hallström, 2000), to name just a few examples. The defining shots of these films, which momentarily freeze the tableaux, intensify the pleasure of the gaze of the time-tourist, offering textures that corroborate the veracity of the recreation and provide sensorial evidence of the experience which lodges in the audience's memory of the film and, indeed, creates, as Alison Landsberg suggests, a 'prosthetic' one of the time portrayed (2004). At the same time, such films can also upend chronology by rendering the past of the film as a palimpsest of the immediate present in a way that supports contemporary hegemony. *The King's Speech*, for example, invokes the British class system and monarchical privileges in a way that contextualises the shift to a Conservative government in contemporary Britain within a return to the kind of values which are also evident in the popular television series *Downton Abbey* (2010–), a drama that provides a template of a structured, hierarchical society which mirrors (and to some extent, therefore, justifies) the contemporary austerity measures of the British government. In a similar fashion, *Akelarre* (*Witches' Sabbath*, Pedro Olea, 1984) depicts the witch-hunts visited by Spanish inquisitors on Basque peasants in the seventeenth century as an allegorical precursor of the torture of members of ETA (Euskadi Ta Askatasuna) by the Spanish security forces at the time of the film's making. There is also the trend in Germany that seeks to re-establish the so-called 'German–Jewish symbiosis' in the now 'normalised' post-unification state (Taberner, 2005) in heritage films, such as *Comedian Harmonists* (*The Harmonists*, Joseph Vilsmaierm, 1997), *Aimée & Jaguar* (Max Färberböck, 1999) and *Rosenstraße* (Margarethe von Trotta, 2003), where the relationship between Jewish and non-Jewish culture is presented as having been central to the development of the German intellectual tradition of the nineteenth and early twentieth centuries. Such films seek to reclaim the importance of this relationship, which was destroyed by National Socialism, in order to deepen and complicate an understanding of Germany today. In a similar vein, *12 Years a Slave* (Steve McQueen, 2013) was positioned by its director as a challenge to contemporary society to remember that, even at a time when there is a black president in the White House, racial inequality and, indeed, slavery are still very much current issues, while also underlining our collective commitment to the eradication of this inequality. In all these ways of mirroring past and present, of contrasting the virtual with the real, of twisting chronology and folding non-linear time into itself in order to create new and evolving shapes for history, memory and identity, the heritage film is an ideal vehicle for the necessary slowing down of narrative momentum to get a better view of the complexity that is offered by the occasion of the crystal-image.

The Crystal-image

The crystal-image merges the subjective, remembered, virtual and essentially 'timeless' image of the past with the actual image that recalls it in a supposedly objective manner in the present. The past and the present coexist in the crystal-image, as if afflicting déjà vu. Its occurrence in heritage cinema therefore reveals visions of anterior states in conjunction with the present and finds them both in evolution. A crystal-image occurs in *Vertigo* (Alfred Hitchcock, 1958), when Scottie (James Stewart) calls forth the resurrected Madeleine (Kim Novak) from Judy (also Novak) in her hotel room, and their embrace and the surge in music provokes the circling camera to propel them into the past and future that reflect each other in their crystalline present of their magical relocation in the stables at the mission outside time and San Francisco. Deleuze claims that, beyond this classic scene, the potential of the actual crystal-image is mostly unrealised in the cinema, though its theoretical nature endures as an analytical or explanatory device. That said, one might also note that its illustration of the non-linear workings of time, its revelation of how the past is positioned on-screen and how this implicates the spectator, and its propensity for repeating, doubling or engendering of a *mise en abyme* of time offer a means of understanding how the past operates upon the present and vice versa in slow instances of heritage cinema. The crystal-image might therefore be found or referenced in shots or scenes that disengage from plot and the movement towards narrative resolution. They offer, instead, moments of reflection upon the self and nationhood in terms of prevailing versions of history that meet within the crystal-image, the experience and awareness of same in the present, and the consequences for the projection of individual and national identity into alternative, future possibilities. The crystal-image confuses memory (virtual: Madeleine in *Vertigo*) and the image (actual: Judy in *Vertigo*) via an aesthetic consideration of shots that lend themselves to consideration of the subjectivity of the spectator who becomes aware of temporalised exile from a reimagined past in the heritage film, the present version of the past in which consciousness resides, along with the as yet unrealised potential for self and nation in possible futures. The paradox is that the crystal-image clarifies by revealing this confusion in heritage films such as *Akelarre*, *The King's Speech* and *12 Years a Slave* where it exhibits how their virtual versions of history are confused with actual histories in order to realign the present and so affect the future. Indeed, as Deleuze explains, the crystal-image is a mutating form of the time–image that 'has two definite sides which are not to be confused. For the confusion of the real and the imaginary is a simple error of fact, and does not affect their discernibility: the confusion is produced solely "in someone's head"' (2007: 67).

This confusion is often celebrated in the spectacle of period detail and reanimated historical figures, such as Abraham Lincoln (Daniel Day Lewis) in

Lincoln (Steven Spielberg, 2012), King George VI (Colin Firth) in *The King's Speech* and Solomon Northup (Chiwetel Ejiofor) in *12 Years a Slave*, or the 'bringing-to-life' of their literary counterparts, such as Elizabeth Bennet (Keira Knightley) in *Pride & Prejudice* (Joe Wright, 2005) and Alatriste (Viggo Mortensen) in *Alatriste* (*Captain Alatriste: The Spanish Musketeer*, Agustín Díaz Yanes, 2006), because the extravagant spectacle of society balls or battle scenes, as well as award-baiting prosthetics, foreign accents along with 'realist' film techniques, tend to aid in the creation of an immersive experience which promotes confusion 'in our heads'. Nevertheless, it is in moments of slowness, where long takes stall the narrative and allow for contemplation and even reflection upon the nature of the spectacle and its essential duality, that the distinction between the real and the imaginary can trigger revelations about the purpose of the confusion. An example of this is *12 Years a Slave*, where moments of contemplative pause deliberately punctuate the narrative and even challenge our expectations of film as a medium. On the one hand, the camera might pause on a moment of disturbing emotional intensity, daring the spectator to watch while also forcing them to reflect, the slowness of the shot seeming to normalise its intensity, thereby refusing any sense of sensationalism or exploitation. On the other hand, a shot might be held at the instant *before* the image can be resolved into an emotional response, thereby maximising its affective *potential* and again foregrounding the need for spectatorial engage-ment. At times, such shots use the present to offer an intervention in the past in order to suggest the more enlightened sensibilities of present-day society. Thus, the long take of the semi-lynched Northup, trying to stay alive while on tiptoes in slippery mud as the rest of the plantation goes about its business, offers a moment of intense emotional reflection on Northup as the civilised 'other' caught up in a world defined by the 'Banality of Evil' long before Hannah Arendt coined the term to describe Nazi atrocities. The shot endures, as does the audience, which is prompted to fill the postponement of Northup's rescue with reflection upon the multifarious meanings of the image reached by associative links to other times, struggles and victims. The film, however, also uses slowness to suggest the continuity of the past into the present, to argue that the past is not another country, such as in the prolonged low-angle close-up of an old female slave's face caught in silent contemplation, a shot that radically extends the moment of affect, delaying emotional resolution in the spectator and forcing us to contemplate not only the historical representation of the slave but also the contemporary role of the actress and singer (Topsy Chapman) playing her. Both these shots foreground the profilmic event they capture as opposed to their narrative function, linking the 'present' of the instant it was filmed with the present of the viewing experience, while also holding these temporal levels in tension with the 'past' of the film's narra-tive. Slowing down heritage films with such shots allows for reorientation, the reterritorialisation of one's awareness and its remapping in relation to the immediate and wider context of a film's viewing. In such slowness, the image crystallises, budding geometric mirrors and planes that reflect the image from many temporal angles, forcing audiences to perceive complex, evolving meanings occurring between the virtual and the actual. As Deleuze contends, the relational aspect of such slowness can implicate time:

> What constitutes the crystal-image is the most fundamental operation of time: since the past is constituted not after the present that it was but at the same time, time has to split itself in two at each moment as present and past, which differ from each other in nature, or, at what amounts to the same thing, it has to split the present in two heterogenous [sic] directions, one of which is launched towards the future while the other falls into the past. [. . .] Time consists of this split, and it is this, it is time, that we *see in the crystal*. (2007: 79; emphasis in original)

Thus, there is a simultaneity of present and past in the crystal-image, and it is our contention that incidents of slowness in heritage films clarify the confusion in which audiences collaborate, in turn raising awareness of the ploy of heritage films which are often funded and fostered in order to push a particular version of history. Indeed, the ultimately successful Oscars campaign that accompanied the release of *12 Years a Slave* was built upon exactly this awareness, with press advertisements insisting 'It's time' designed to promulgate temporal links, evoke associative guilt and reward the corrective strategy of the present-day film-makers (Hammond, 2014).

Suggesting that slowness in heritage cinema can make a crystal-image visible goes far beyond merely allowing the spectator time to consider allegorical readings. Slowness contrasts so greatly with the generic conventions and narrative momentum of the heritage film that it allows a theoretically eternal

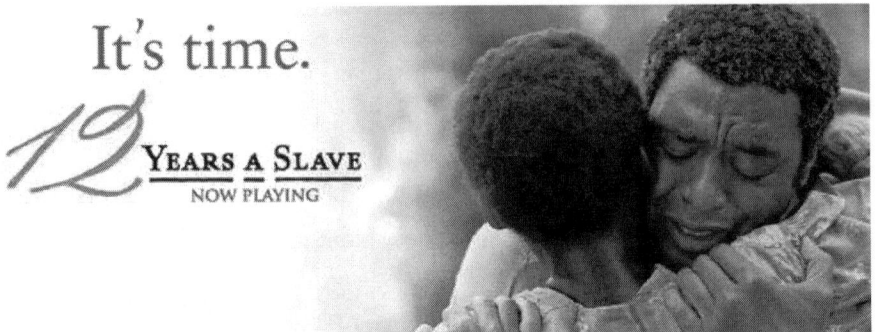

Figure 22.1   Promotional image for *12 Years a Slave* Oscars campaign.

comparison and contrast of relational times, both virtual and actual, that resembles an instance of modernism as described by Henri Lefebvre, who supposed in *Introduction to Modernity* that:

> The period which sees and calls itself entirely new is overcome by an obsession with the past: memory, history. History begins *hic et nunc*, with the here-and-now, with each passing minute. Historical becoming is immediately upon us, and immediately it becomes history, known and recognised historicity, historical consciousness, chained to a vaguely distant past according to which the present vainly attempts to situate itself. (1995: 224)

The tension between the past and the present, between the virtual and the actual, in a crystal-image offers 'life as spectacle, and yet in its spontaneity' (Deleuze, 2007: 87). The crystal-image depicts this tension without abstracting it, only using it to promote awareness of its endless multiplication of temporal planes which offer an accumulating depiction of non-linear time that sees the past and the present as simultaneous, with each point in the future continuing to crystallise, that is, splitting into a passing present and a preserved past. Following Henri Bergson, Deleuze explains that the constant production of this circuitry is how we move through time.

Versions of History

The particular version of history or 'how we move through time', presented by heritage films, might be nationalist or postcolonialist, neo-liberal or even subversive, revisionist in spectacle and detail, installing a 'corrective' history where other regimes or hegemonies may have fitted other films and histories. An example of this is the attempt in the early 1980s by the government of the newly autonomous Basque Country, which is made up of three provinces in the north of Spain, to aid the construction of a modern nation by supporting films that would entertain and educate domestic and foreign audiences about Basque heritage. The aforementioned *Akelarre* is an example that trades in pro-Basque allegory but *La conquista de Albania* (*The Conquest of Albania*, Alfonso Ungría, 1994) is doubly subversive. The film recounts a fourteenth-century expedition into Albania in which the sense of rousing a nation and building an empire (in the past and so in the present) is duly expressed in scenes of chivalry enacted by Basque knights who attend to noble causes supported by peasants, damsels and priests. As the knights cross the Mediterranean, however, Louis of Navarre (Xabier Elorriaga) is afflicted with crippling melancholy, and long takes of his troubled contemplation of the ocean undermine the narrative momentum and the mission. Interrupted and delayed journeys are, of course, a dominant trope in slow cinema, provoking contemplative and even existential periods of apprehension. Here, any expectation of a country worth conquering is frustrated on arrival in Albania by the endless dusty plains which the knights encounter. The narrative stalls as the knights wander inland, failing to construct a narrative of nationhood that will expand the Basque audience's perception of space in both the historical and the cultural sense, and the film stumbles into stasis: 'Where the hell is our enemy?' yells one frustrated knight. The film therefore employs slowness to rebel against its own commission as a Basque heritage film because its promise of a bellicose adventure yarn about nation-building is spoiled by a dreary trudge through a barren land that drains the film of energy and purpose. Its lengthy shots of aimless, puzzled knights signify a pointless and misguided crusade that prompts an allegorical reading which implicates the cultural and political strategies of the modern Basque government.

The occasion of slowness in a heritage film such as *La conquista de Albania* thus functions like a short circuit in the process of passive spectatorship. Slowness sets an audience adrift in the crystalline structure of time, drawing their attention to the folly of such endeavour in the past and linking the political strategies of the past and the present. More than merely allegory, however, the shots of aimless warriors peering into the distance may be identified as crystal-images because, in addition to expressing a *mise en abyme* of past and present, they also reveal the projection of Basque identity into the future as a similar mirage. The film's slowness brings on malignant homesickness and superstition which see the images crystallise further as the knights resort to their *own* nostalgia for an imagined past, exclaiming: 'Who made us forget our gods?'. Meanwhile, their leaders succumb to madness as their historic campaign and the present campaign of the Basque government fall into dream-like stagnancy. Simultaneity is evident because, as Deleuze describes, 'what we see through the pane or in the crystal is time, in its double movement of making presents pass, replacing one by the next while going towards the future, but also of preserving all the past, dropping it into an obscure depth' (Deleuze, 2007: 84). This obscure depth is even signalled by the film deploying an old, blind man as the unreliable narrator of events in which, it is revealed, he does not even participate until well into the 'adventure' which is then rendered in flashback, adding further planes to the crystal-image. *La conquista de Albania* recovers some momentum with the mutiny of the soldiers but it ends with an ignominious final shot of their return to Navarre which suggests how the consequences of this disastrous campaign were visited on the homeland, over which the ancient, blind narrator intones: 'I returned [. . .] trying to understand why sometimes the result of logical things leads to such absurd situations. But it seems to me that the people of this country are like that.' Much derided by Basque critics and audiences at the time of its release and in subsequent literature by Basque academics on Basque cinema, the subversive *La conquista de Albania* blends the epic delusionality of *Excalibur* (John Boorman, 1981) with the psychological implosion of *Aguirre, der Zorn Gottes* (*Aguirre, The Wrath of God*, Werner Herzog, 1972) which follows another Basque knight into madness. Most importantly, however, the film illustrates the crystallisation of numerous actual and virtual pasts and presents that creates a *mise en abyme* of the Basque Country building an ideal nation in just as ill-fated a manner as Scottie attempting to construct his perfect woman in *Vertigo*.

Slowness in heritage cinema can be subversive, as in *La conquista de Albania* whose crystalline structure reveals the switching of one heroic allegory for another far less noble. Slowness can also illustrate the othering of times that are assumed to be known, traditional and historical. In the German context, for example, where *Heimat* (homeland) only ever exists elsewhere, slowness in the heritage film can offer a moment of the uncanny where *Heimat* can be revealed but, in the process, its temporal otherness foregrounded. At the same time, the presentation of *Heimat* can also highlight the continuity of this past with the present and, in the process, crystallise moments of critical reflection on this present. The term *Heimat* suggests an idealised version of Germany which has always already gone, the *Heimat* film reaching its zenith of cinematic popularity in the 1950s when West German audiences enjoyed films which offered idealised German family values and celebrated a fully integrated German community that had overcome the trauma of the war (von Moltke, 2005). The link between *Heimat* and the recent wave of heritage films has often been asserted, generally as a means of dismissing the presumed intention of German heritage films of presenting the nation's 'difficult' past in such a way as to draw a line under it and thus reassert the 'normality' of the German national project. The critic Georg Seeßlen, for example, writes of a disturbing new 'supergenre of Heimat-historical-family-feel-good movies' (2008: 26) that often present a quintessential rendering of the past and present conjoined in nostalgia. In so doing, they can seem to concertina time, short-circuiting history to create a teleological narrative of resolution that is achieved almost before the trauma itself has been identified. *Das Wunder von Bern* (*The Miracle of Bern*, Sönke Wortmann, 2003), for example, reworks the story of West Germany's first football World Cup win as the story of the nation overcoming its Fascist past, pre-empting the generational unrest the country would, in actual fact, face over a decade later and providing a visual accompaniment to the widespread nostalgia for aspects of pre-unification consumer culture to be found in both the eastern and western parts of the country at the time. In the film's final long take we watch the train carry the victorious German team, along with the film's representatives of a now 'healed', 'normal' German family, off into the sunset, a shot that could have come from a 1950s *Heimat* film. That said, even here, in a film which might be defined as perfect example of 'consensual' heritage film-making, the length of this final shot offers a moment of slowness that allows other layers of Germany's history to emerge and to trouble the audience's feelings of nostalgia because the long take of the railway lines receding into the distance seems also to recall those images of more famous tracks in a German context, namely 'the arrival ramps at Auschwitz where the horrors of the "selection" took place' (Taberner, 2005: 371). Slowness allows competing versions of past and present to coexist, providing the spectator with a crystal-image that has the potential, however tentative, to provide a space for a more critical engagement with history than is often acknowledged.

That said, there are other films that offer a more explicit means of repositioning this kind of concertina affect as a crystal-image which can draw the layers of time together while also differentiating them and thus forcing the spectator to reflect upon them anew. *Barbara* (Christian Petzold, 2012), for example, tells the story of a young East German woman who is seeking to emigrate from the German Democratic Republic (East Germany) to be with her lover in the West, a wish that sees her subjected to the state's psychological and physical authoritarian control tactics. Set and shot in the provinces of the former East German state, the camera often simply presents what it sees as the past in long takes that offer no attempt to reconstruct it 'authentically'. The buildings and landscape of this part of Germany have changed little since unification. The presentation of the present *as* the past, however, highlights both a sense of timelessness *and* the fact of historical change. This is the reality of the German *Heimat*, which the shots seem to capture, yet fail to fix, while, at the same time, underlining the continued value of both *Heimat* and history as necessary points of national orientation within the crystalline imagery of German and, indeed, European heritage. The heritage film is usually intent upon turning time into something fixed, static, and ultimately conservative which may be consumed, like a Jane Austen theme park. The short circuit of slowness, however, and the often consequential occasion of the crystal-image upsets the narrative search for closure, discomfits nostalgia, deconstructs stereotypes and highlights contradictions in the ways that a given nation imagines itself (or is imagined by others) instead of eliding these tensions in a wash of readily consumable spectacle. The occasion of slowness in heritage cinema demands broader approaches to history, often inveigling haptic and affective responses. Instances of slowness in heritage films and, for that matter, slow heritage films in the genre of heritage cinema, resonate with a need for cultural preservation at the same time as they counter a loss of memory in the digital age. Yet they also warn against prosthetic memory by illustrating the dangers of preserving unreal cultures in the present or accepting any singular view of the past.

BIBLIOGRAPHY

Bohm, Svetlana (2002), *The Future of Nostalgia* (New York: Basic Books).

Deleuze, Gilles (2007), *Cinema 2*, translated by Hugh Tomlinson and Robert Galeta (London: Continuum).

Galt, Rosalind (2002), 'Italy's Landscapes of Loss: Historical Mourning and the Dialectical Image in *Cinema Paradiso*, *Mediterraneo* and *Il postino*', *Screen*, 43: 2, 158–73.

Hammond, Pete (2014), 'Oscars: '12 Years a Slave' Telling Voters "It's Time" – But How Will It Resonate?', *Deadline*, 19 February, online: http://www.deadline.com/2014/02/oscars-12-years-a-slave-telling-voters-its-time-but-how-will-it-resonate/

Higson, Andrew (1993), 'Re-Presenting the National Past: Nostalgia and Pastiche in the Heritage Film', in L. Friedman (ed.), *Fires Were Started: British Cinema and Thatcherism* (London: University College London Press), pp. 109–29.

Higson, Andrew (2003), *English Heritage, English Cinema: Costume Drama since 1980* (New York and London: Oxford University Press).

Jameson, Frederic (1982), *Signatures of the Visible* (New York and London: Routledge Classics).

Koepnick, Lutz (2002), 'Reframing the Past: Heritage Cinema and the Holocaust in the 1990s', *New German Critique*, 87, 47–82.

Landsberg, Alison (2004), *Prosthetic Memory: The Transformation of American Remembrance in the Age of Mass Culture* (New York: Columbia University Press).

Lefebvre, Henri (1995), *Introduction to Modernity* (London: Verso).

von Moltke, Johannes (2005), *No Place Like Home: Locations Of Heimat In German Cinema* (Berkeley, CA: University of California Press).

Monk, Claire (2011), *Heritage Film Audiences: Period Films and Contemporary Audiences in the UK* (Edinburgh: Edinburgh University Press).

Seeßlen, Georg (2008), 'Neue Heimat, alte Helden', *epd Film*, 22–27, 7, 26.

Taberner, Stuart (2005), 'Philo-Semitism in Recent German Film: Aimée und Jaguar, Rosenstraße and Das Wunder Von Bern', *German Life and Letters*, 58, 357–72.

Vidal, Belén (2012), *Heritage Film: Nation Genre Representation* (New York and Chichester: Wallflower).

Vincendeau, Ginette (2012), 'Exhibiting heritage films in the digital age: interview with Vincent Paul-Boncour', *The Network*, 7 September, online: http://www.europa-cinemas.org/en/News/The-Network/Exhibiting-heritage-films-in-the-digital-age-interview-with-Vincent-Paul-Boncour

INDEX

Page numbers in **bold** refer to illustrations